THE KNOSSOS TABLETS

FOURTH EDITION

THE
KNOSSOS
TABLETS

FOURTH EDITION

A Transliteration by
JOHN CHADWICK
J. T. KILLEN and J.-P. OLIVIER

CAMBRIDGE
AT THE UNIVERSITY PRESS
1971

481.7
K72a4

Published by the Syndics of the Cambridge University Press
Bentley House, 200 Euston Road, London NW1 2DB
American Branch: 32 East 57th Street, New York, N.Y. 10022

© Cambridge University Press 1971

Library of Congress Catalogue Card Number: 75-142242

ISBN: 0 521 08085 1

Previous editions published by
the Institute of Classical Studies, University of London
Printed in Great Britain by Lewis Reprints Ltd

CONTENTS

UNIVERSITY LIBRARIES
CARNEGIE-MELLON UNIVERSITY
PITTSBURGH, PENNSYLVANIA 15213

MAY 24 '82

PREFACE

The first edition of this book was itself a revision of an earlier transcription of the Knossos tablets, edited by R. Browning and published by the Institute of Classical Studies of the University of London in 1955. The need for this revision became evident as the result of the collation of the texts published in <u>Scripta Minoa</u> II (Oxford, 1952, referred to here as SM II) with the originals. It was executed by Michael Ventris, with the aid of material supplied by E.L. Bennett and J. Chadwick and published in 1956.

Three years later a second edition became necessary, and this was undertaken by J. Chadwick with the assistance of F.W. Householder. It was largely a reprint of the first edition with a few corrections and additions, especially a concordance based upon that published by M. Lejeune in <u>Mémoires de Philologie mycénienne</u> I, Paris, 1958.

A third edition in due course became necessary, and the study of these documents, first on the photographs now held in Cambridge, and subsequently on the originals, led to numerous improvements in the readings, many as the result of joining fragments. The earlier stages of this work, which owed a great deal to J.T. Killen, were incorporated in the third edition, published under names of J. Chadwick and J.T. Killen in 1964.

Progress after that date was even more rapid; Killen was joined by J.-P. Olivier, whose study of the scribal hands led also to the discovery of large numbers of joins. The resultant texts were so much changed that it became essential to make all the new information available in convenient form; and although stocks of the third edition had not been exhausted, the London Institute of Classical Studies generously agreed to allow the publication of a fourth edition and, owing to technical difficulties, to entrust this to the Cambridge University Press.

The editors of this edition do not imagine that their task is yet completed. There are doubtless more joins to be made, indeed some have been discovered since this edition went to press; but

every text has been carefully revised from the originals by both
Killen and Olivier with checks by Chadwick on difficult points, and
the latest reading is reported. Here too we are aware of the
difficulties of establishing the text of fragments; several have,
as the result of joins, been shown to read differently from the texts
proposed before they were joined. A total of 785 new joins are here
recorded; for lists of joins see J.-P. Olivier, Les Scribes de
Cnossos, Rome 1967 and L. Godart, J.T. Killen and J.-P. Olivier in
MINOS Vol. X (forthcoming).

The editors hope to proceed to the publication of a major
edition, to include both drawings and photographs, and they are
well aware of the imperfections necessarily imposed upon a transcription such as this. They would like to renew their appeal to
anyone who may know of the existence of unrecorded fragments from
Knossos to communicate with them.

NUMERATION

No fresh changes have been introduced into the system of
numeration since the third edition, except in so far as numbers
are now left vacant as the result of joins, or, in a few cases,
identification of missing fragments. The major changes made
earlier were: the elimination of 'bis' numbers, now mainly beginning
1801; the replacement of M 1 to M 138 by 2001 to 2138; the change
of 0401-0495 to 4401-4495. The Concordance has been brought up to
date and includes the new fragments. Numbers which have been
suppressed because the pieces have now been identified with texts
published under other numbers are shown there in parentheses ( ).

CLASSIFICATION

The original classification was devised by E.L. Bennett
previous to the decipherment, relying therefore almost entirely on
ideograms, though with some attributions on the basis of common
formulas. Some modifications were introduced into the third edition,
mainly as the result of work by J.T. Killen on the D- tablets. But
the systematic classification of scribal hands (see below, p.   )
by J.-P. Olivier entailed a drastic revision of the prefixes, which
was undertaken by J. Chadwick in consultation with the other editors,

and published in the Proceedings of the Fifth International
Colloquium on Mycenaean Studies held at Salamanca in 1970.

It now became possible for the first time to attribute tablets
to sets on the basis of hand, and to split earlier series into sets
on this same principle. Although there would have been great
advantages in scrapping the old system and devising an entirely
new one, it seemed preferable to modify the existing classification,
since it is already familiar and is still sound in outline. The
chief change introduced has been the insertion after the prefix in
appropriate cases of a number to indicate the set within the prefix
class to which each tablet can be assigned. For typographical
reasons this appears as (1), (2), etc., but could more elegantly be
shown as a superior numeral. This classification is of course
incomplete, since not all fragments can be assigned even tentatively
to a hand, and it has not been allowed to disturb the ordering of
tablets, which follows the numerical sequence inside each prefix
irrespective of set. In quotation this set-number can be ignored,
except in cases where the discussion demands it.

Many other changes have been introduced, mainly as the result
of the allocation of tablets to scribal hands. Thus where a scribe
is known to have written only tablets of one series, any fragment
in this hand may be assigned to this series. However, the attribution
to hand is often doubtful and in cases where serious doubt exists
about the placing of the tablet in a series the prefix is underlined to indicate this doubt.

SCRIBAL HANDS

The study of this subject by J.-P. Olivier, published as Les
Scribes de Cnossos, Rome 1967, has been the starting point for many
of the changes in this edition. The scribal hand to which each
tablet is assigned is shown in parentheses at the right margin
opposite the tablet number; the numerical system established by
Olivier has been followed, and where this edition disagrees with
Les Scribes, these modifications have been introduced by Olivier
himself.

list. Some of these seem to have been fragments which appeared in Evans' notes with a different reading.

Further batches of tablets have come to light since, both in Iraklion Museum and in the store-rooms at Knossos. The main addition, numbers 7000-8075, was transcribed by Ventris in 1955 and published in the first edition of this book. Other additions were published in <u>Annual of the British School at Athens</u> 52, pp. 147-181; 57, pp. 46-74; 58, pp. 68-88; 62, pp. 267-323. Among these many of the texts previously only known from copies have been identified, but in some cases doubts still persist. Special mention should be made of the work of J.-P. Olivier and E.L. Bennett in tracking down and identifying missing texts. The present volume contains the texts of all Linear B tablets from Knossos now known to us, together with those of tablets previously copied but now apparently missing.

TRANSLITERATION

This has been made to conform with the 'Wingspread Convention' adopted by the Third International Colloquium for Mycenaean Studies at Racine in 1961, and amended by the Fourth and Fifth Colloquia at Cambridge and Salamanca. A few divergences from the conventions have been forced upon us by the method of type-setting which has prevented us from making use of italic type (underlining being employed instead) or small capitals. We apologise for these inconveniences, which do not detract from the usefulness of the transcription.

Phonetic signs are transcribed in roman script except for *18, *19, *22, *34, *35, *47, *49, *56, *63, *64, *65, *79, *82-84, *86, *89. These signs are represented by numbers prefixed by an asterisk. A table of signs, showing only a typical specimen of each, is to be found at the end of the book. The signs making up a word are separated by hyphens. A change to a smaller size of script is indicated by /, to a larger size by // . The divider is transcribed by the comma (,).

Ideographic signs are transcribed by Latin words; where no Latin transcription has been agreed, the sign is transcribed by its number, preceded by an asterisk and underlined to avoid confusion with Mycenaean numerals. A list of those used will be found at the end of the book. Phonetic signs used as ideograms

are printed in underlined capitals; when used as adjuncts to
ideograms they are in lower case, underlined. Ligatures are
indicated by the sign +. Superscript numerals added to TELA,
*146 and *164 indicate the number of strokes in the lower fringe.

Weights and measures are transcribed in accordance with
the system of single capital letters:

Weights	L	M	N	P	Q
Dry measure	T	V	Z		
Liquid measure	S	V	Z		

LACUNAE

The point at which a tablet becomes illegible (ordinarily the
broken edge) is indicated by square brackets at left and right,
thus:

]to-so	No epigraphic evidence for the completeness of the word.
]-to-so	Epigraphic evidence for a sign immediately preceding to.
] to-so	The word appears to be complete.

These conventions extend to numerals:

]31	Number not less than 31 (possibly 61, 91, 131, etc.).
31[	Number not less than 31 (possibly 32, 33, etc.).
] 31 [	Number apparently complete.

If the upper or lower edge of the tablet is broken off and missing,
this is indicated by the words sup(ra) mut(ila) or inf(ra) mut(ila).
An uninscribed space is indicated, where necessary, by vacat(vac.).
Traces of unidentifiable signs are shown as vestigia (vest.). All
notes appearing in the text are in Latin.

Erasures are indicated by double square brackets [[ ]] .
Any signs enclosed within these brackets were deleted by the scribe
but remain legible. Where the text is written over an erasure,
this fact is recorded in the notes.

ARRANGEMENT

The tablets are arranged by alphabetical prefixes; two-letter prefixes precede single-letter ones, otherwise the order is alphabetical. The set numbers (see above under Classification) are ignored in the arrangement. Inside each class the tablets are arranged in serial order. Tablets composed of joined fragments are shown under the lowest serial number involved, and other numbers are added after the sign +. The order of these numbers does not therefore reflect the order in which the pieces are arranged in the composite text. The abbreviation fr. indicates that an unnumbered fragment has been joined to the tablet; more than one such fragment is indicated by frr., and if more than two the number of fragments is given in parentheses. The sign [+] indicates that the fragments concerned belong to the same tablet, but do not physically join.

Line numbering follows the division of the original tablet by guide lines. The line number .0 indicates the presence of a guide line preserved above the first line of writing. The obverse (recto) is not specially indicated; the reverse (verso) is shown by v., edges by lat(us) sup(erius), inf(erius), dex(trum).

Where the tablet begins as a single line and is then divided into two or more lines, these are shown as .A, .B, .C. Lines of writing not separated by guide-lines are shown as .a, .b, .c. The different faces of a sealing are listed as .α, .β, .γ. A small annotation above the line of writing is shown thus: 'do-e-ra', generally placed after the parallel entry at a lower level.

LOCATION

All tablets are in the Iraklion Museum, except where an abbreviation precedes the indication of scribal hand. Where two locations are quoted the fragments composing the text have not been physically reunited but the join has been checked by casts.

IR   The Archaeological Museum, Iraklion, Crete.

ASHM   The Ashmolean Museum, Oxford.

BM   The British Museum, London.

DES   Collection of V. Desborough, Esq., Oxford.

KAN   Kanellopoulos Collection, Athens.

UCL   Archaeology Department, University College, London.

NOTES

The brief notes included in the third edition have been expanded to provide a more detailed account of the epigraphic facts. No attempt has been made to provide a commentary or to list earlier readings which we now believe to be erroneous.

MISSING TABLETS

A number of texts known from SM II or occasionally from other sources are now missing. The numbers of these texts are shown in pointed brackets (e.g. Ak(2) <631>, and these texts must be treated with some caution. Fair progress has been made in identifying tablets previously thought to be missing among the fragments not published in SM II, and some of the numbers assigned to new fragments are now blank, since they have been identified with texts in SM II. The circumstances under which pieces have gone astray ought to be kept on record, and the following account is taken with slight changes from the Preface to the third edition (p. iii).

It is known that in 1901 certain tablets were stolen from the excavations and were subsequently recovered in Athens (A.J. Evans, Scripta Minoa I, p. 46). Another group appears to have been stolen after Evans had noted their readings and made drawings: their numbers lie between 288 and 398 but do not include all within these limits. Of these, fifteen and another damaged fragment were acquired by the Giamalakis collection as having been found at Phaistos, but there is little doubt that they are the tablets already noted by Evans at Knossos (Scripta Minoa II, p.109). There remain, however, 53 pieces which have not been recovered, and it must be feared that these have been destroyed.

When it became possible to compare the tablets recorded by Evans in his notebooks and published in Scripta Minoa II with the collection in Iraklion, other discrepancies came to light. On the one hand Evans had on occasion made two drawings of the same piece, both of which were numbered and published (e.g. 1221 is the same tablet as 1224 but with the addition of a fragment at the left); and this is especially liable to be the case where Evans' notes contained a transcript but no drawing (e.g. 1638 = 1061, SM II, p. 108). On the other hand E.L. Bennett in 1950 found more than a thousand fragments in Iraklion Museum which did not appear in Evans'

ACKNOWLEDGEMENTS

We should like to express our deep gratitude to the present Ephor of Antiquities in Iraklion and Director of the Museum, Dr. St. Alexiou, his predecessor, Prof. N. Platon, and his assistant Miss A. Lebessi, for the unfailing kindness and consideration they have shown us over a period of many years, in making the tablets available for study and photographing, as well as for much other encouragement and assistance.

We should also like to thank all others who have helped in the preparation of this book: Mrs. E.B. French, who took the photographs which form the basis of the Cambridge collection; the Keeper of the Ashmolean Museum; the Trustees of the British Museum; Professor E.L. Bennett, who has continued to share his unrivalled experience of Mycenaean epigraphy; Monsieur Louis Godart of the Instituto per gli Studi micenei of Rome; Prof. E.W. Handley, Director of the London University Institute of Classical Studies; the Syndics of the Cambridge University Press; and many others who have contributed directly or indirectly to the production of this edition or the preceding ones.

We owe a special debt of gratitude to Mrs. M. Clements who has typed the whole text for reproduction, a task the difficulty of which cannot be overstated; to Mrs. B. Black whose assistance in the preparation of the book has been invaluable; and to the Classical Faculty Board of the University of Cambridge and the Triopian Foundation of Chicago, who have helped our work with substantial grants.

JOHN CHADWICK
J.T. KILLEN
J.-P. OLIVIER

Cambridge and Brussels, December 1970.

Ag

Ag 87   ("124"a)
      ]wa   VIR 1   MUL 2   'ko-wa 1'   ko-wo 1

Ag 88 + 7033   ("124"a)
      pe-re-ko   VIR 1   MUL 1   ko-wa 2 , ko-wo 1

Ag 89   ("124"a)
      ]to-ro-wo   VIR 1
        Cut at right.

Ag 90   ("124"a)
      e-ri-*19   VIR 1   ko-wo 1
        Cut at right. <u>wo</u> of <u>ko-wo</u> over [[<u>wa</u>]] .

Ag 91   ("124"a)
      ke-re-u   VIR 1   MUL 1[

Ag 1654   ASHM ("124"a)
      qe-ri-jo   VIR 1   MUL 1   ko-wa[

Ag 7000   ("124"a)
      ]VIR 1   MUL 1   ko[

Ai

Ai(1) 63   ("124"b)
  .a   pe-se-ro-jo , e-e-si
  .b   MUL 1 ko-wa 1 ko-wo 1

Ai(1) 115   ("124"b)
      pa-ro , u-wa-si-jo , ko-wo [
        Perhaps nothing lost at right ?

Ai(1)   190   ("124"b)

    ]ko-wa 1   <u>di</u> ko-wa 1

      Faint trace after <u>di</u> might be divider, but is too small
      for 1.

Ai(1)   194   ("124"b)

    ]MUL   3   ko-wa   1   ko-wo   2[

<u>Ai(1)</u><321>   ("124"?)

    ]MUL 1   ko-wo 1[
    ...
      Missing ; text from SM II. ( ]<u>wo</u> 1   SM II.)

Ai   338   (-)

  .A   ]   ko-wa 6
  .B   ]ja   MUL   5̣   ko-wo 2

      .B Figure after MUL apparently 6 with last stroke
      deleted (intentionally or accidentally).

Ai   632   (-)

    ]ta-ra$_2$ MUL 1

Ai   739   (207?)

  .1   ra-su-to , 'a-ke-ti-ri-ja' MUL 2
  .2   ko-wa 1   ko-wo 1

Ai(2)   750   (102?)

    ]ko-wo 2   GRA 1 T 2[

Ai(2)   751   (102?)

    ko-]wạ 1   GRA   T 5
    Cut at right.

Ai(2)   752 + 753   (102?)

    ]re-ja MUL   3   ko-wa 1   ko-wo 1   GRA Ṭ[

2

Ai(2) 754   (-)
        ] MUL 3   ko-wa 2   ko-wo 2
        Trace at left, perhaps]n̤a̤ .

Ai(2) 762   (-)
        ]na , / e-ne-ra   MUL[

Ai(3) 824   (-)
   .1   a-pi-qo-i-ta / do-e-ra MUL 32 ko-wa , me-zo-e 5 ko-wa
                                                      me-wi-jo-e 15
   .2   ko-wo me-wi-jo-e 4

Ai(3) 825   (204)
   .1   ]ta-na-qo , a-mi-ni-si-ja ,   [
   .2   ]ra   MUL [
        MUL at full height of the tablet (over line erased at
        this place).

Ai(3) 966 + 7855 + 7856   (204)
   .a   te-o , do-e-ro [
   .b   a-ri-ke-u , / ka-pa-so ja-[
          .b ka-e̤-so not impossible. ja-[over erasure, and
             perhaps also the preceding word.

Ai(3) 982   (204)
   .1   ]-qo-ta , / o-du-ru-wi-ja   [
   .2   ]MUL 1   [

Ai(3) 1012   (204)
   .1   ]w̤e̤-re-ki-ja [
   .2   ]we-ka-ta   [

Ai(3) 1036   (204)
   .1   ]*56-so-jo , / a-mi-ni-so , // do-e-ra
   .2   ]   vacat

                              3

2

Ai(3) 1037   (204)

  .1 ?do-]e-ra   we-ka-sa[

  .2   ]   qi-ri-ja-to , [

Ai 1805   (= 84 bis)   ("124")

  .1 di-ka[

  .2 MUL 200[

  .3   inf. mut.

Ai(2) 5543   (-)

  .0   sup.mut.

  .1   ko-]wo 6 GRA 2 T 2[

  .2   ]2 ko-wo 8   GRA 2 T[

  .3 ko-]wa 8 ko-wo [ ] GRA 2 T 1[

      .3 Possibly a 10 in the gap after ko-wo.

Ai 5849   (-)

    ] MUL 10 [

    Traces to right.

Ai(3) 5976 + 8268 + frr.   (204)

  .1]ko , / si-ra-ko , // qi-ri-ja-to , [

  .2   ]   [[V1R 1]]

      .2 Very difficult to decide whether [[V1R 1]] or [[MUL 1]].

Ai(2) 7014   (-)

    ]1 ko-wo 1[

Ai(2) 7017   (-)

    ] MUL 12 ko-wa [

    Trace at left. Perhaps ko-wa 9[.

Ai(1) 7023 + 7605   ("124"a?)

    ] ko-wa 2 ko-wo 1

Ai(2)   7026 + 8662 + <u>fr</u>.   (205)

      ] MUL 6 ko-wa 6   ko-wo 4   GRA 1 T 7[
         Trace at left. At least T 6[, but possibly T 6 V[instead
         of T 7.

Ai(2)   7027   (205)

      ]3 ko-wo[

<u>Ai(1)</u>   7029   ("124"a?)

      ]ko-wa 2[

<u>Ai(3)</u>   7745   (204?)

  .1   ]ja-to , si-qa , [
  .2   ] <u>vacat</u>   [
         .1 <u>qi-ri-]ja-to</u> ?. Possibly <u>si-za</u>. Trace of two more
         signs at right (<u>pa-ro</u>[?).
         .2 Perhaps erasure at left.

<u>Ai(3)</u>   7867   (204?)

      <u>sup. mut.</u>
  .1   ]ra , pi-ja[
  .2   ] <u>vacat</u>   [

<u>Ai(2)</u>   7883   (205?)

      ]ko-wo 5[

<u>Ai(2)</u>   7890   (205)

      ]no   MUL [ ]   ko[
         Perhaps MUL 2 .

Ai(2)   7952   (205)

      ]MUL 11   ko[

Ai(2)   7962 + 7969   (205)

      <u>sup. mut.</u>
      ]te-ja-ne   MUL[
         Probably not]<u>te-ja</u> ne <u>MUL</u>[.

Ak

Ak(1) 610   (103)

.1]TA 1 'DA 1'   MUL 10 de MUL 1

.2] ko-wa / me-zo-e 3   de , ko-wa 1

.3] ko-wo / me[-zo] 1   ko-wo / me-wi-jo 2

Ak(1) 611   (103)

.1 to-te-ja , TA 2 'DA 1'   MUL 10[   ]de-di-ku-ja MUL 1[

.2 ko-wa , / me-zo-e 4   [   ] ko-wo , /me-wi-jo 1[

.3   vacat   [

Ak(1) 612   (103)

.A   TA 1 'DA 1'   MUL 9

.B   ko-wa ,/ me-zo 1   ko-wa / me-u-jo 1

.C da-te-we-ja /   ko-wo / me-zo 1   [[ko-wo me-   ]]

Ak(2) 613   (108)

.1 qa-mi-ja , / TA 1 'DA 1' MUL [

.2 ko-wa , / me-u-jo-e 9   ko-wo[

lat. sup.]7 T 1

        lat. sup. written after drying.

Ak(1) 614 + fr.   (103)

.A] TA 2   MUL 30 pa di 4[

.B] ko-wa / me-zo-e 5   ko-wa / me-u-jo[

.C] ko-wo , / me-zo 1   ko-wo / me-u-jo 2[

        .A There is room for DA 1 in the broken area above TA 2.
           di over erased sign, perhaps de.

        .C Trace at left, consistent with large ja.

Ak(2) 615   (108)

.1]a-no-qo-ta   MUL 30   [

.2] ko-wa , me-zo-e 6   ko-wa , me-u[

.3] ko-wo me-zo-e 3 ko-wo me-u-jo[

lat. inf.]a-pe-a-sa 24[

6

Text largely from SM II photograph ; the tablet has
suffered considerable damage since that was taken.

Ak(2) 616   (108)

.1   ]36   pe di MUL 2   di za MUL 2   [

.2   me-]u-jo-e 8

.3   ] me-u-jo-e 13

Ak(2) 617   (108)

.1   ]TA 2   MUL 73   au MUL 1̣[

.2   ]me-zo-e 13   ko-wa , / me-u-jo[

.3   ]ṃe-zo-e 12   ko-wo / me-u-jo[

Ak(1) 619 + 5633 + 5892 + 5963 + 6010 + 8258 + 8687 + fr.   (103)

.1   ]1̣   MỤL 22 pa di 3   [

.2   ]   ko-wa   me-zo-e · 4 [

.3   ko-]ẉạ[me-wi-]jo-e 5   ko-wo di 2   [

.4   ] ko-wo / me-zo-e 1[ ] ko-wo / me-wi-jo-e 2 [

Ak(1) 620 + 6028 (+ fr.)   (103)

.A   ]   TA 2 'ḌẠ [1]' MUL 14[

.B   ]   ko-wa di 1   ko-wa [

.C   ]ke-ja /   ko-wo , de 1 [

Ak(2) 621   (108)

.A   ]1̣   MUL 34   pe 'dị'[

.B   ]   ko-wa , me-zo-e 4   ko-ẉạ[

.C   ]jọ , / da-wo , / ko-wo , me-zo-e 6 [

lat. inf.] [[vestigia]]   [

Ak(2) 622   (108)

.1   we-we-si-jo-jo , [

.2   ko-wa , me-zo-e   [

.3   ko-wo[

        .1 Over erasure. Trace at right.

7

Ak(1)   624   (103)

.1   ri-jo-ni-ja ,   TA [ ] 'DA [ ]' [

.2   ne di 3   ko-wa , / me-zo-e [

.3   ko-wo , di 3 ko-wo , / me-zo-e 1[

Ak(1)   626   (103)

.1   ] pa di 2 'ko-no-so' pa di 2[

.2   ] me-wi-jo-e 7   [

.3   ]me-wi-jo-e 6   [

Ak(2)   627 + 7025   (108)

.1   da-*22-to , / a-no-zo-jo TA 1 'DA 1' MUL[ ]9 pe di 2

.2   ko-wa / me-zo-e 7   ko-wa / me-wi-jo-e 10

.3   ko-wo / [me-]zo-e 2 ko-wo , / me-wi-jo-e 10
        .2.3   10 over [[9]] .

Ak(1)   630   (103)

.1   tu-ni-ja[

.2   ne di 3 we-ko-we-ka-te[

.3   ko-]wo di 1[
        .2   3 we-ko-we-ka-te[over erasure.
        we-ko-we-ka-te written below 3.

Ak(2) <631>   (108?)

.1   ] pe 'di'   MUL 6

.2   ] ko-wo , me-u-jo-e 4

.3   ] vacat
        Missing: text from SM II.

Ak(1)   634 + 5767   (103)

.A   [ ]'DA 1'[   ]74[ ]   di 5   [

.B   se-to-i-ja / ko-wa , me-u[-jo-e] 10   ko-wo me 5[

lat. inf.   vacat   [   ] ru-si [
        .B me-u[-jo-e] : the two last signs are now completely
        missing but were apparently seen by Bennett in 1950.

        lat. inf. Perhaps erased.

8

Ak(2) 636   (108)

       <u>sup. mut.</u>

.1   ]<u>vest.</u>[

.2   ] ko-wa me-zo 1 [

.3   ] ko-wo me-u-jo-e 2[

        .3 Possibly <u>me-u-jo 1</u> changed into <u>me-u-jo-e 2</u> .

Ak(1) 638   (103)

.A   'e-ne-re-ja['

.B   ko-wa[

.C   a-mi-ni-so / ko-wo[

Ak 640   (-)

.0   <u>sup. mut.</u>

.1   ]sa-tu 1

.2   ] <u>vacat</u>

.3 ko-wa 8   ko-wo 2

.4   ] <u>vacat</u>

      Cut at bottom.

Ak(1) 643   (103)

.a   ] ko-no-so [

.b]ko-u-re-ja /   [

      Probable division into .A.B.C. or .A.B.C.D.

Ak(3) 780 + 7004 + 7045 + 7767   (102)

.1 da-wi-ja , ne-ki-ri-de   MUL 2   <u>pe</u> VIR 2

.2 ko-wa me-wi-jo[   ]1

.3 ko-wo me-wi[-jo-]e 3

      Whole tablet erased and rewritten; [[------ <u>wo</u> - ? - 4]]
      still visible at the end of .2, [[<u>ko-wo</u> - ? <u>- di</u> - ? -- 2]]
      at the end of .3 .

Ak(3) 781 + 8339   (102)

.1   ] MUL 17 [[di-da-ka-re]][
.2   ]1   ko-wa [   ]vest.[
.3   ] , di-da-ka-re , ne 1 // ko-wo [
        .1 Trace at left, possibly]ja.
        .2 Possibly]5.

Ak(3) 782   (102)

.1   ] MUL 3
.2   ]me-wi-jo-e 2
.3   ] vacat

Ak(3) 783 + 7011 + 7535   (102)

.1   ]   di-da-ka-re   pe MUL 2
.2   ]me-wi-jo-e 14
.3   ]e 9

Ak(3) 784   (102)

.1   ]we-ra-ti-ja   [
.2   ]me-zo-e , di-da-ka-re[
.3   ]me-zo-e , di-da-ka-re[
        .1 Over erasure. Trace of upright at right, perhaps DA[.

Ak(3) 828   (102)

.1   pa-i-ti-ja ,   DA 1 TA [
.2   ko-wa / me-zo-e , di-da-ka[
.3   ko-wo / me-zo-e , di-da[

Ak(3) 830   (102)

.1   ]du-wi-ja , po-si[
.2   ko-]wa / me-zo-e [
.3   ]me-zo-e 3[

Ak(2) <1807>   (= 509 bis)   (-)

.1   ]ko-wa[ ]me-zo [
.2   ko-]wa me-u-jo-e [
        Missing: text from SM II.

10

Ak(2)   2126   (108?)

 .1   sup. mut.

 .2a   ]   ko-wa me-wi-jo-e 1[

 .2b   me-]zo 1   ko-wa me-zo 1   [

 .3   ]   vacat   [

          .2b Trace at right, perhaps e[, or (less likely) MUL[.

Ak(1)   5009 + 6037 + 8588   (103)

 .A   ] ka-pa-ra₂ [

 .B   ]   ko-wa me[

 .C   a-ra-ka-te-ja ,/ ko[

          .A Perhaps DA[.

Ak(1)   5553   (103)

 .1   ko-ro-ka-[

 .2   ]ko-wa / me-zo 1[

          .2 Probably nothing lost at left.

Ak(1)   5604   (103?)

 .1   ]TA 2 'DA 1'   MUL[

 .2   ] vest.[

       inf. mut.

          .2 Perhaps ko-]wo / me[.

Ak(1)   5611   (103)

       sup. mut.

        ] ko-wo me[

       inf. mut.

          Perhaps trace of line at top.

Ak(1)   5648 + 5967 + 8606   (103)

 .A   ]   TA 2   [

 .B   ]ja / [ ]ko-wa [

       inf. mut.

          .A Perhaps TA 1 over [[2]] , but second stroke perhaps
              erased accidentally. Enough space above TA for DA
              on a lost fragment.

11

Ak(1)   5655   (103)

   .0   sup. mut.

   .1   ] di [

   .2   ]wo di [

Ak(1)   5741 + 5895   (103)

   .1   ]10   ko-wa / me-zo 1 [

   .2   ]   ko-wo / me-zo-e 2   ko-wo me 1

          .2 me-zo-e 2 probably corrected from me-zo 1.

Ak(1)   5876 + 5928 + 5971 + 6068 + frr.   (103)

   .1   ] ko-wo , di 4   qa-mi-ja ko-wa 'di' 3   ko-wo di 3[

   .2   ] 'di' 1   ri-jo-no   ko-wo di 2   [

   .3   ]   vacat   [

Ak(2)   5879   (108)

       sup. mut.

   .1   ]3[

   .2   ]1 ko-wo [

         .2 Traces at right.

Ak(1)   5884   (103)

   .1   ]   vacat

   .2   ko-]wa / me-u-jo 2

   .3   inf. mut.

Ak(1)   5893 + 8623   (103)

   .1 · ko-]wa me-zo-e[

   .2   ]wo[

       inf. mut.

         .2 Perhaps]wo me[.

Ak(1)   5896   (103)

       sup. mut.

   .1   ] vacat [

   .2   ]5   [

   .3   ]e 4 [

Ak(1) 5907   (103?)

.1   ] MUL 2   pa di 1

.2   ko-]wạ 'me-wi-jo-e' 5

.3   inf. mut.

      .1 Perhaps traces before MUL.

Ak(1) 5918   (103?)

.1   ]sị-jo-jo[

.2   ]mẹ-zo-e [

      .2 Traces of erasure.

Ak(1) 5926 + 5933 + 8219   (103)

.1   ] MUL [   ] ne 'dị' 1

.2   ]mẹ-zo-e 3

.3   ] ko-wo / me-wị̣[

Ak(1) 5940 + 8667   (103)

.1   ]8   ne di 1

.2   ]ko-wa / me-wi-jo 2

.3   inf. mut.

Ak(1) 5948   (103)

.1   ]de MUL 1   pa di[

.2   ]   vacat   [

Ak <6048>   (-)

.1   ]3̣ zo[

.2   ]ko-wo[

.3   ] vest.[

         Missing: text from Bennett's 1950 drawing.

Ak(3) 7001   (102)

.1   a-]kẹ-ti-ri-ja ,   MUL 1[

.2   me-]wị-jo-e 4   [[ko-wa]] [

.3   ]   vacat   [

      .2 [[ko-wa]] perhaps followed by erased numerals.

13

Ak(2)   7002   (108)

.1   ]26   ko[

.2   ] me-zo-e 9   ko-wo me[

.3   ] vac. [

      .1   26 perhaps changed from 28.

Ak(3)   7003   (102?)

.1   ]MUL 2

.2   ]e 9

.3   ]e 9

Ak(3)   7005   (102)

.1   ]84   di-da[-ka-re

.2   di-da-]ka-re , ne 5   ko-wa[

.3   di-da-ka-re] , ne 3   ko-wo[

      .1   Probably]MUL . 84 over [[87]] or [[88]] .
           di- perhaps over erasure.

      .3   Perhaps trace of -re.

Ak 7006   (-)

     ]   MUL 18[

      Trace at left, perhaps]ja.

Ak(3)   7007   (102?)

      sup. mut.

.1   ] vacat [

.2   ]   ko-wo[

Ak 7008   (-)

     ]3   ko-wo[

Ak(2)   7009   (108)

.1   ko-]wa , me-zo[

.2   ]me-u-jo-e 4[

14

Ak(2) 7010   (108)

  .1 me-]ẓọ-e 3[
  .2   ] me-u-jo-e[

Ak(2) 7012   (108?)

      sup. mut.
  .1]   4[
  .2]jọ-e 4 [
       .1 Perhaps]ẉọ at left.

Ak(2) 7013   (108?)

  .0 sup. mut.
  .1] ko-wa [
  .2] ko-wo [

Ak 7015   (-)

      sup. mut.
      ]ko-wa 1[

Ak 7016   (-)

      ]ko-wo 3
      inf. mut.

Ak 7018   (-)

  .1 ko-]wa 6   ko-wo 3
  .2   ] vacat

Ak 7019   (-)

  .1]4   ko-wa , 4[
  .2] vestigia [
      inf. mut.
       .2 Possibly] kọ-wọ 2[.

Ak(2)   7020   (108)

        <u>sup. mut.</u>

.1   ] <u>vacat</u> [

.2   ko-]w̦a me-u-j̣o[

.3   ]m̦e̦-u-jo[

Ak(2)   7021   (108?)

.1   ]   MUL [

.2   ]   ko-w̦a[

Ak(2)   7022   (108)

.1   [.]-ki '<u>DA</u> [ ]' <u>TA</u> 2   MUL [

.2   ko-wa me-zo-e̦[   ] ko-wa me[

.3   ko-wo me-w̦i̦-j̦o-e 12[

        Probably same tablet as Ak 7024.

.1 șa̦-ki or d̦o-ki possible.

.2 Perhaps m̦e̦-zo-e̦ 1̦0̦ or 2̦0̦ (no units).

Ak(2)   7024   (108?)

.1   ] 2[

.2   ]ko-w̦o̦ , me[

.3   ]d̦o-e-ra   MU̦L̦[

        Probably same tablet as Ak 7022.

Ak(2)   7028   (108?)

.0   <u>sup. mut.</u>

.1   ]e 5 [

.2   ]e 3   [

Ak(2)   7030   (108?)

      ] MUL 1[

      <u>inf. mut.</u>

Ak   7031   (-)

      ]MUL 1[

      <u>inf. mut.</u>

Ak 7858   (-)

        sup. mut.
        ]ko-wo , di[

Ak(1) 8218 + 8336   (103)
    .A   sup. mut.
    .B   ]   ko-wa[
    .C   ]   ko-[

Ak(1) 8334 + 8335   (103?)

                    sup. mut.
    .1   ]vest.[
    .2   ]ko-wa / [me-]u-jo-e 14   ko[
            Probably same tablet as Xe 8724.
            .1 Perhaps]MUL 20[.

Ak 8337   (-)

        sup. mut.
        ]ko-wo[

Ak(1) 8338   (103?)
    .1   ]1   ko[
    .2   ] vest.?[
        inf. mut.

Ak 8340   (-)

        sup. mut.
        ]di 12[
        inf. mut.
            Perhaps 13[.

Ak(1) 8341   (103)
        sup. mut.
        ]ne di[

Ak(1)   8444   (103)

.1   ]jạ   MUḶ[

.2   ]vest.[

inf. mut.

Am

Am(1)   568   (103)

.a   to-so [

.b   da-wi-jo /   VIR[

Am(1)   597   (103)

.a   ]i̱-ta$_2$ [

.b   ]   LUNA 1 VIR 4[

.c   ]1̱   [

Probably nothing lost at right.

Am(1)   600 + 665 + 8307   (103)

.a   to-so , e-te , e-so-to , a-mo-ra-ma

.b   ko-no-si-jo , /   VIR 25

Am(1)   601   (103)

.a   e-te , e-so-to , a-mo-ra-ma

.b   to-so , / a-mi-ni-si-jo ,   VIR 9

Am(2)   819   (-)

.A   ]   we-ke-i-ja   VIR 18   'ko-wo' 8

.B   ]qạ-ra /   si-to   LUNA 1 HORD 9 T 7 V 3

Am(2)   821 + fr.   (-)

.1   ]ra-jo ,/ e-qe-ta-e , e-ne-ka , ẹ-mi-to VIR 2 // ki-ta-ne-to,/
                    su-ri-mo , e-ne-ka 'o-pa' VIR 1̱

.2   ]dụ-we , ta-ṛa , / i-je[-re-]u , po-me , e-ne-ka , 'o-pa' X
                    VIR 1 // ko-pe-re-u , /e-qe-ta ,e-ki-'si-jo' VIR 1

.3   ] vacat

.1 Many traces of erasure; ka of e-ne-ka over [[ṾỊṚ]] .

18

Am(2)   826   (-)

.1   a-pa-ta-wa-jo , / te-re-ta   VIR 45[

.2   te-ko-to-ne   VIR 5   [

    .1 a-pa-ta- over erasure.

Am(2)   827 + 7032 + 7618   (-)

.1   si-mi-te-u VIR 1   a-wa-ti-ka-ra MUL 1 [

.2   ko-wo 1   [

Am(1)   2009   (103)

    ]jo   VIR 2[

      Possibly divider after]jo.

Am 5755   (103)

.1   ]8   VIR 4   se-to-i-ja[

.2   ]e 2   [

Am(1)   5882 + 5902   (103)

    ]-so / ka-ma-jo ,   VIR 16[

Ap

Ap 618 + 623 + 633 + 5533 + 5922   (103)

.1   a-pe-a-sa / i-ta-mo , 'do-ti-ja' , MUL 1   ki-nu-qa
                                       '*56-ko-we' MUL 1   [

.2   ti-wa-ti-ja / a-*79 'a-no-qo-ta' MUL 3   ko-ma-we-to MUL 2
                                       we-ra-te-ja MUL 2   [

Ap 628 + 5935   (103)

.1A   vac. [

.1B   ]-ja , / a-ke-wo   'do-e-ra' MUL 4   [[ko]][

.2   ]ro , / do-e-ra   [MUL] 1   di-qa-ra[

.3   ]ne-o , /   do-e-ra   MUL [

    .1 Sign before -ja either si or i.

    .2 Trace after -ra[.

Ap 629   (103)

.1   tu-ni-ja   'tu' MUL 4 ne 'di' 3   'ko 1' ri-jo-no 'tu'
                                                MUL 3 ko-wo 3[

.2   do-ti-ja   'tu' MUL 4 ne 'di' 6 [   ] vacat   [

.3   vacat   [

Ap 637   (103)

.1   [.]-ke-si-ja , ka[

.2   ko-so-jo , MUL 1 tu 2[

.3   da-[
          .1 ka[(and perhaps -si-ja) over erasure.

Ap 639   ASHM (103)

          sup. mut.

.1   [.]-me-no X MUL 1 tu-zo X MUL 1 ko-pi X MUL 1 [

.2   a-to-me-ja MUL 1 da-te-ne-ja MUL 1 X pa-ja-ni MUL 1 [

.3   wo-di-je-ja MUL 1 ko-wo 1   du-sa-ni X MUL 1
                                                        ma-ku[

.4   pa-i-ti-ja X MUL 1 pi-ra-ka-ra X MUL 1 *18-to-no,/tu MUL 2 X
                                                wi-so MUL 1 X

.5   e-ra-ja   MUL 7   ko-wa 1   ko-wo 1

.6   to-sa   MUL 45   ko-wa 5   ko-wo 4

.7   ke-ra-me-ja X MUL 1 ko-wo 1 tu-*49-mi X MUL 1 i-du X MUL[

.8   tu-ka-to X MUL 1   e-ti-wa-ja MUL 1   sa-ma-ti-ja X MUL 1
                                                        si-[

.9   ku-tu-qa-no X MUL 1 wi-da-ma-ta₂ X MUL 1 ka-na-to-po X MUL 1
                                                sa-ti-[.] MUL 1

.10   tu-ka-na X MUL 1 sa-*65 X MUL 1 u-jo-na X MUL 1 sa-mi MUL 1

.11   a-de-ra₂ X MUL 1 tu-ka-na X MUL 1 pu-wa MUL 1 X si-nu-ke X
                                                              MUL 1

.12   [a-]qi-ti-ta X MUL 1 si-ne-e-ja MUL 1 X u-pa-ra MUL 1 X
                                                ru-ta₂-no MUL[1

.13   du-tu-wa MUL 1 ko-wa 2 ke-pu MUL 1 ko-wa 2 wa-ra-ti MUL[1

.14   ]ta-si-ja MUL 4 a-nu-wa-to MUL 1[

          Some readings of damaged areas to the right are derived
          from SM II, pl. 63. All the check marks (very faint)
          after drying. Probably same tablet as Ap 5864.

          .1 Traces of another sign at right.

          .2 Traces of another sign at right.

          .8 Perhaps wi-[.

20

.9 MUL 1 partly on <u>lat. dex.</u>

.10 <u>u</u>- of <u>u-jo-na</u> over erasure.

.12 cf. <u>a-qi-ti-ta</u> MY Oe 103.3.

.13 Over erasure.

.14 4 visible on SM II, pl. 63.

Ap 694   (-)

.1]<u>j̣a</u> , / ko-u-re-ja MUL 1̣[

.2] ka-ra-we   MUL 1[

.3] a-ze-ti-ri-ja   MUL 1[

.4]   <u>vacat</u>   [

Ap 769   (-)

.1]i-ta-no   MUL 1   ka-*56-so-ta   MUL 1   a₃-du-wo-na   MUL 1

.2]wi-ja-na-tu   MUL 1   i-ta-ja   MUL 1

     .1 Perhaps divider after <u>a₃-du-wo-na</u>.

     .2]<u>wi-ja-na</u> <u>tu</u> MUL (Grumach) theoretically possible,
         but no spacing between <u>na</u> and <u>tu</u>.

Ap 5077 + <u>fr</u>.   ("124")

.1   ]e-ke

.2   ko-]ẉạ 1̣   ko-wo 1

.3 [[OLIṾ 1̣   ]]

.4 [[?   ]]

     Cut at bottom. Traces of a previous ruling.
     .2 Perhaps [[ko-]ẉạ 1̣]]
     .3 Perhaps <u>ẓọ</u> visible left of centre.

Ap 5547 + 8162   (-)

.1]ja-mi-nu   MUL 1 [

.2   ]   MUL 1̣ [

Ap 5748 + 5901 + 5923 + 8558   (103)

.1]si 1 <u>tu</u> 1 ki-zo 1   MUL 3[   ]a-ma-no[

.2]1   o-ri-mo MUL 3 TELA[1]+TE 1 pu-zo , ti-no , pi-ja-mu-nu
                                                          ṂỤḶ[

.3   ]ni-ta , o-sa-po-to MUL 3   TELA[1]+TE 1   [

.4   ]   <u>vacat</u>   [

     .1 Perhaps MUL 3̣ TẸḶẠ[1+TE]. Perhaps]<u>a-ma-no</u>-[.

21

                          sup.mut.

.1   ] X MUL 1

.2   ]-ra MUL 1 X

.3   ]na MUL 1[   ]ka-na MUL 1

.4   ]ma MUL 1   te-qa-ja MUL 1

.5   ]ja MUL 1[   ]ja-mu-ta MUL 1[

.6   ]ta₂-no[

                          inf. mut.

Probably same tablet as Ap 639.

.1 Perhaps erasure at the end.

.3 Perhaps]na X MUL 1[.

N.B. Check-marks made after drying.

.1   ]-ja /   to-sa   MUL 26 di[

.2   ]7 ko-wo 9   ka-ra-we   MUL 6   [

lat. inf.]   e-u-[

.1 Trace of 2 signs before ja (perhaps]-ra-ja).

.2 MUL 6 : probably MUL 9 originally; the 3 lower
    units were erased, intentionally or by accident.

    lat. inf. : Perhaps e-u-ke[, e-u-de[,e-u-me[or e-u-ne[.

As

                  sup. mut.

.1   o-[   ] , ko-no-so VIR[

.2   a-to , / da-*22-to   VIR 1

.3   zo-do-so , / da-*22-to   VIR 1

.4   a-sa-ro , / da-*22-to   VIR 1

.5   ko-so , / da-*22-to   VIR 1

.6   su-ke-re , / se-to-i-ja   VIR 1

.7.8   ]   vacant

.9   to-so   VIR   10

.10   ] vacat

.7-.9 Traces of erasure and of an erased previous ruling.
v.   Ruled (9 lines) but not inscribed.

                            22

As(1) 566   (103)

.1   ]di-ka-ta-ro   VIR[

.2   ]si̯-ja-qo   VIR[

.3   ]ke-we-da   VIR[

As(1) 602 + 650 + 1639 + <u>fr</u>.   (103)

.1   ]VIR 1   TELA¹ 1

.2   ]jo̯   VIR 1[   ] VIR 1   TELA¹ 1   [

.3   ] , qe-ro-a-ta-qe   VIR 2   TELA¹ 1   ka-nu-se-u , ta-to̯-qe
                                                     VIR 2 TELA⁺ 1[

.4   ]da̯-ro , a-ka-sa-no[-qe]VIR 2 TELA¹ 1 pe-re-*82-ta ,
                               qo-wa-ke-se-u[-qe VIR 2   TELA¹ 1

.5   ]to-so [   ]VIR   12 [TELA¹]1 [

        .2 Traces of at least 3 signs before the second VIR.

        .3 Trace at left.

As(1) 603 + 8157 + <u>fr</u>.   (103)

.1   ] VIR 1   no-si-ro   VIR 1[   ]a-ta-no   VIR 1

.2   VIR]1   ma-di   VIR 1   o-po-ro-u-si-jo[VIR 1

.3   VIR]1   pe-te-u   VIR 1   ku-ro₂ VIR[1

.4   ] <u>vacat</u>   [

As(1) 604 + 606 + 5863   (103)

.1   ] e-re-dwo-e̯ , ka-ta₂-ro̯ 'si-ra̯-so' VIR 1 e-ri-ta-qi-jo , /
                                                     ka-mo 'VIR 1'

.2   ]ra-su-to VIR 1   ta-de-so̯ ra̯-su-to[VIR] 1   au-ri-jo
                                                  'wi-na-to' VIR 1

.3   ]te-so 'wi-na-to' VIR 1   te-na̯-ja-so[VIR]1 qa-qa-ro
                                                    'pu-so' VIR 1

.4   ]to, / u-ta[-no   ] <u>vestigia</u> ?

        .1 Trace of sign or divider at left.

As(1) 605 + 5869 + 5911 + 5931 + <u>frr</u>.   (103)

.1   ]ni-jo VIR 2 TELA¹[   ]ra̯-wo-ke-ta , e[

.2   ] VIR 2 TELA¹ 1 qe-[. .]-no , pe-ro-qe VIR 2[TELA¹ 1

.3   ]VIR 2 TELA¹ 1 tu-ma-i-ta , qe-ta-se-u[VIR 2 TELA¹ 1

.4   ] <u>vacat</u>   [

.5   ]2   [

        .1.2 Traces of erasure.

23

.2 Traces consistent with qe-ro-me-no , but qe-to-ro-no
   is equally possible.

As(1)   607 + 5524 + 5996 + 8257 + frr. (3)   (103)

   .1   ]VIR 1   a-ra-ko VIR 1
   .2   ]1   ta-ta-ro VIR 1
   .3   ]VIR 1   si-mi-do VIR 1 *56-ni-sa-ta VIR 1
   .4   ]1   [   ]ro-ti-jo VIR 1
   .5a   ]   ke-re-to[
   .5b   ]1 i-ne-u ,ra-ja[
        .3 Perhaps X after first VIR 1.
        .5b ra-su[not impossible.

As(1) 608   (103)

   .1   sup. mut.
   .2   ]1 / [ ]pa-ta-u-na // a₃[
   .3   ] ta-so DA 1 / ke [
   .4   ]ko-me-no VIR 1[
lat. inf.   ]DA 1 a-ma[
        .3 ke looks more or less like a X, but cf. As 625.4.

As(1) 609 + 5866 + 8589 + fr.   (103)

   .1   ]vestigia[   ]re-po-so   [
   .2   ka-ri-se-u [VIR 1] wi-je-mo VIR 1   pi-ro-qa-wo[
   .3   qe-te-se-u   VIR [1] no-da-ro   VIR 1   a-ku-ri-jo[
   .4   vacat   [   ]to-so VIR 7
        .1 Possibly]-jo[.
        .2 -je- perhaps over erasure.
        .3 te of qe-te-se-u over erasure [[ta]]?

As(1) 625 + 5870 + 5942   (103)

   .1   ]i 1 DA 1 / ku-ru-no [   ] VIR 5 [
   .2   ] 1 DA 1 / pa-ta-u-na [   ] VIR 1[
   .3   ] VIR 1 DA 1 / pa-ta-u-na // ko-no-si-jo VIR[
   .4   ] 1 ke , ta-pa-da-no DA 1 / ke // si-to-po[
   .5   ]   no-do-ro-we DA[
lat. inf.   ]e-ne-o o-u[

24

.2 Trace at left, perhaps]r̤e̤. Perhaps -na̤// da̤-[..]] .

As(1) 645   (103)

    sup. mut.

.1   ]k̤i̤-ne-u V̤I̤R̤[

.2   sa-ma-ri-wa-ta VIR[

.3   a-re-ta-wo[

.4   inf. mut.

As(2) 1516   (101)

.1   ]-ru[

.2   ko-no-si-ja , ra-wa-ke-ja , a-nu-wi-ko VIR 1[

.3   a-ra-da-jo VIR 1   pi-ja-si-ro VIR 1   d̤a-[   ]   VIR 1

.4   ]-m̤e̤-ro VIR 1   po-to VIR 1   si-pu$_2$ VIR 1   pu-te VIR 1
                                                  i̤a̤-sa-no VIR 1

.5   qa-me-si-jo VIR 1   mi-ja-ra-ro VIR 1   mi-ru-ro   VIR 1

.6   a-ki-wa-ta VIR 1   u-ra-mo-no VIR 1   pi-ri-no   VIR 1

.7   qa-to-no-ro VIR 1   pe-te-ki-ja, VIR 1   ko-ni-da-jo VIR 1

.8   a-ko-ra-jo VIR 1   wa-du-[.]-to VIR 1   qo-te-ro   VIR 1

.9   i-te-u VIR 1   pu-to-ro VIR 1   ka-ri-se-u VIR 1
                                            a$_3$-ko-ta VIR 1

.10   ka-ke VIR 1   ru-na VIR 1   pu-wo VIR 1   a-ta-ze-u
                                                     [VIR 1

.11   a-ra-na-ro VIR 1   si-ja-pu$_2$-ro VIR 1   to-so X VIR 31

.12   ]-ti-jo , a-nu-to q̤a-si-re-wi-ja , VIR 1   su-ki-ri-to
                                                        VIR 1

.13   [.]ke-se-ra-wo VIR 1   qa[. .]-jo VIR 1   ne-o-ta   VIR 1

.14   o-pi-si-jo VIR [1]   a$_3$-wa-t̤o   VIR 1   a-ti-jo VIR 1   du-to
                                                             VIR 1

.15   a-de-we-[.] VIR 1   pa-na-re-jo VIR 1   sa-pi-ti-nu-wo
                                                         VIR 1

.16   du-to VIR 1   ka-*56-na-to VIR 1   a-qa-to   VIR 1

.17   du-ru-po VIR 1   qa-nu-wa-so VIR 1   ke-re VIR 1   pa-ti
                                                           VIR 1

.18   wi-ro VIR 1   su-mi VIR 1   i-wa-ko VIR 1   a-pi-wa-to
                                                           VIR 1

.19   pi-ja-se-me   VIR 1   to-so X VIR 23

.20   se-to-i-ja su-ke-re-o , qa-si-re-wi-ja VIR 1   ku-to   VIR 1

25

.21   sa-u-ri-jo VIR 1   du-ni-jo VIR 1   wi-ja-ma-ro VIR 1
                                                    a-pi-ra-wo VIR 1

.22   ]to VIR 1   pi-[.]-jo VIR 1
        ̤̤   ̤̤   wi-ra-ne-to VIR 1

.23   ]na-ro VIR 1   wa-ru-wo-qo VIR 1
                                    ̣

.24   ] VIR 1   a-ti-[.] VIR 1 to-so[
                                                      ̤̤

.25   ]vest.?[

    .3 Possibly da-na[(with na probably over another
               ̣   sign more or less erased).

    .8 wa-du-sa-to or wa-du-ni-to.
               ̣̣   ̣̣

    .12]ra-ti-jo or ku-]ta-ti-jo possible.
           ̣   ̣

    .17 pa-ti VIR 1 over erasure.

    .18 Perhaps su-/qa-// mi, but apparent qa may be an
                      ̣   accidental mark.   ̣

    .19 Probably erasure after 23.

    .22 Perhaps pi-ri-jo.
               ̣ ̣

As(2) 1517   (102?)

    .1   ]no , re-qo-me-no ,
                                    ̣

    .2 [.]si-re-u   1   a-di-nwa-ta   1

    .3 [.]-sa-ta   1   ti-qa-jo   1

    .4 da-wa-no   1   [. .]-wo   1

    .5 qi-qe-ro   1   wi-du[ ]   1

    .6 ku-ra-no   1   da-wi-[.]   1

    .7 e-ru-to-ro   1   ku-ta-i-jo   1
                                   ̣

    .8 ku-pa-nu-we-to 1   qa-ra-jo   1

    .9 ri-zo   1   pa-na-re-jo   1

    .10 ke-ka-to   1   to-so VIR 17

    .11 o-pi , e-sa-re-we , to-ro-no-wo-ko ,

    .12 po-to-ri-jo   1   pe-we-ri-jo   1

    .13 a_3-ni-jo   1

v.1   vacat

    .2 za-mi-jo   VIR 9

    .3   vacat

        reliqua pars sine regulis

    .1 After re-qo-me-no, numeral less probable than
            divider.

    .3 Possibly qo-sa-ta.
               ̣

26.

.5 Uncertain whether a narrow sign stood in the gap
    after wi-du[.

.10-.13 Erased and rewritten with traces of a previous
         ruling.

As(2) 1518 + 1529   (105)

.1   ]   VIR 5   to-ko[we-e-]wi-ja 1   [

.2   ]VIR 5   we-e[-wi-ja] , to-ko 1   [

.3   ]   VIR 5   we[-e-]wi-ja , to-ko 1   [

.4   ]re-we   VIR 5   we-e-wi-ja   , to-ko 1   [

.5   ] vacat   [   ]   vacat   [

     Probably complete at right.

     .3 Perhaps]re-we (but very faint).

As(2) 1519 + fr.   (101)

.0   sup. mut.

.1   ]   VIR 1

.2   i-we-ro   VIR 1

.3   ne-o-to   VIR 1

.4   qa-ti-ja   VIR 1

.5   o-pi-si-jo   VIR 1

.6   pa-ja-ro   VIR 1

.7   ki-ke-ro   VIR 1

.8   i-to   VIR 1

.9.10   vacant

.11 [.]-ri-ne-wo , wo-i-ko-de

.12 to-so   VIR 10

.13.14   vacant

.15   inf. mut.

     .1 Traces of 3 or 4 signs at left.

     .11 Possibly di-ri-ne-wo.

     .12 Over erasure.

27

.0   <u>sup. mut</u>.

.1   ]n̥o̥ ,

.2   ]1   a-ta-no   1

.3   ]wi-jo   1   a-te-mo   1

.4   ki-ma-ta   1   ri-zo   1

.5   ke-sa-do-ro   1   di-zo   1

.6   da-ko-so   1   si-za   1

.7   to-so   VIR 10

.8   <u>vacat</u>

.9   ] e-u-na-wo   1

.10   ] sa-zo   1

.11   ]o-*22-di   1

.12   ]pi-ma-na-ro   1

.13   ]a-*56-no   1

.14   <u>inf. mut</u>.

v.   <u>maior pars sine regulis</u>

.1   a-mi-ni-so   [

.2   a-ma-no 1 se[

.3   <u>inf. mut</u>.

         Probably same tablet as V 1526.

         .6 Erasure between <u>da</u> and <u>ko</u>.

.1   ]e̥-pi-ko-wo , e-qe-ṭa , e-re-u-ṭe̥[

.2   ]da-mo , / e-ro-pa-ke-u // VIR 1   ko-ki[

.3   ]-jo / ra-wo-po-qo , ze-ro[

     Missing: text from Evans' photograph.

.1   ]r̥o̥   <u>te</u> VIR 1[

.2   ] VIR[

     <u>inf. mut</u>.

28

As(1) 5549 + 8574 + fr.   (103)

.1   ]VIR 1 X

.2   ]to[ ]4   da-zo   VIR 2

.3]1 i[   ]2[   ] VIR 1 [

lat. inf.   ]1

     .1 Perhaps]wa VIR 1 X.

     .3 Perhaps no[instead of i[.

As(1) 5557   (103)

.1   ] VIR 2[

.2   ]a-re-te-re-u[

.3   ] vestigia [

     inf. mut.

          .1 Traces of small signs on either side of VIR:
             ]-tu VIR i-[.

          .3 Perhaps ne[.

As(1) 5605 + 5999 + frr.(3)   (103)

     sup. mut.

.1   ]   ko-ko[

.2   ]mi-dwe VIR[

.3   ]-ro   VIR 1[

.4   inf. mut.

          .3 Perhaps]ro₂.

As(1) 5609 + 6067   (103)

     sup. mut.

.1   ] vestigia [

.2   ]u-ko-ro VIR [

.3   ]-ke-u VIR 1[

.4   ] to-so VIR 10[

          .3 Possibly]pa-ke-u or]i-ke-u.

As(1) 5719   (103)

.1   ]ku-ka-so VIR 1[

.2   ] vacat   [

29

As(1) 5880 + 8221   (103)

  .1   ]VIR 1 [
  .2   ] VIR 1 [
  .3   ]ṭa VIR 1
  .4   ] vacat ? [
  .5   ] vac.? [

     inf. mut.?

       .2 Sign before VIR, perhaps m̤e, g̤i, k̤o or m̤o.
       Perhaps X after 1.

As(1) 5888   (103)

  .1   ]wa-je VIR 2 [
  .2   ]to , o-du[
  .3   ] vacat [

       .1 je over erasure.

As(1) 5908   (103)

     sup. mut.

  .1   ] vest. [
  .2   ] vacat [
  .3   ]   VIR 12[

As(1) 5932   (103)

  .1   sup. mut.
  .2   ]VIR 1   a-[.]-we   X̤[VIR
  .3   ]   X VIR 5   a-[
lat. inf.]su-*56-ta X VIR 1 [

       .2 Perhaps a-r̤o-we.
       .3 Sign at left, perhaps]ṭe or]p̤a.

As(1) 5941 + 8343 + fr.   (103)

  .1   ]VIR 1̣ 'e-re-ta' VIR[
  .2   ]VIR 1 'e-re-ta' V̤I̤R̤[
  .3   ] 'e-re-ta' [VIR

     inf. mut.

     Double rule between lines .2 and .3.

As(1) 5944 + 6013   (103)

  .1]me-ri-to <u>te</u> VIR 1
  .2   ] <u>vacat</u>

As(1) 5956   (103)

  .1]ma-jo , [
  .2   ] VIR[
  .3 <u>inf. mut.</u>
     .1 Trace at right consistent with VIR.

As(1) 5981   (103)

  .1 <u>sup. mut.</u>
  .2]   VIR [

As(1) 6038   (103)

  .1 <u>sup. mut.</u>
  .2]VIR 1 [

As(1) 8161   (103)

    <u>sup. mut.</u>
  .1]-u-to VIR 1[
  .2]1 o-ku 1   [
     .1 -<u>to</u> VIR 1 over erasure (perhaps [[V̤I̤R̤ 1̣]]).

As(1) 8342   (103)

    <u>sup. mut.</u>
  .1]V̤I̤R 3 a-[
  .2   ]-ẉẹ-ḍạ VIR 1 X[
<u>lat. inf.</u>   ]-ti VIR 1 X [
     <u>lat. inf.</u> Perhaps]*5̤6-ti.

31

B

B 41   (-)

  .1   ] 1 ra-ni   VIR 1

  .2   ] $\underline{vacat}$

B(4) 101   ("124")

  .1   ko-wi-ro-wo-ko VIR[ ] a_3-te-re VIR 8[

  .2 $\underline{vacat}$

B(4) 164 + 5666 + 7136 + 7544 + 8120 + $\underline{frr}$. (3)   ("124")

  .0 $\underline{sup. mut}$.

  .1   ]   VIR 37

  .2   ku-re-we[   ]ru-wo VIR 143

  .3   a-da-wo-ne[

  .4   i-ja-wo-ne[

  .5   ku-[   ]40

  .6   o-[   ]$\underline{vest}$.[   ]4

  .7   to-[/]to[   ]VIR 144

  .8   vacat

  .9   ] $\underline{vacat}$

     .1.2 Traces of erasure at end.

     .1   Traces at left before ideogram.

     .5 $\underline{ku\text{-}re\text{-}we}$[not impossible.

     .6   Third sign $\underline{ke}$ or $\underline{je}$?

B(4) 213   ("124")

    ]a_2-ta VIR 2

      Cut at right.

B(1) 755   (-)

    tu-ra-te-we VIR 15 [

      Perhaps cut at right.

B(1) 772   (-)

    sup. mut.

.1   ]-ṇu   VIR 1̣[

.2   ]ki-nu-wa , VIR[

B(1) 779   (-)

.1   ]re-ta   VIR [

.2   ]si-re-we   VIR[

B 798   (107)

    sup. mut.

.1   ]-ko̤ [

.2   ke-sa-do-ro   VIR̤[

.3   a-ke-ta   VIR[

.4   a-na-qo-ta   VIR 6

.5   ko-ma-we-ta   VIR 2

.6   pe-qo-no   VIR 1

.7   ra-wo-qo-no   VIR 1

.8   ko-a-ta   VIR 2

.9   ku-ni-ta   VIR 3

.10 o-pi-te-u-ke-we VIR 2

.11 i-se-we-ri-jo   VIR 3

       .9 ni over erasure.

B(5) 799 + 8306   ASHM/IR (104)

.1   da-i-pi-ta , ke-do-si-ja , [

.2 u-ra-jo , VIR wi-du-ro VIR ki-ri-[

.3   ]jo̤-si , VIR qo-ja-si , VIR , *56[

.4   ] , VIR pa-wi-no , VIR , di-de[

.5 e-u-da-mo , VIR qa-wo[   ]ka-ke , VIR ,   [

.6 pu₂-ra-ne-jo , VIR , a-ka̤-de , VIR , o-pe-ta VIR [

.7 a-ta-ma-ta , VIR e-ke-se , VIR , pu-ri , VIR ,   [

.8 a-tu-qo-ta , VIR i-ke-ta VIR[

.9   ]-si-jo VIR[

    inf. mut.

v.1   ] , sa-za-ro , VIR ku-pe-re-te , VIR

.2   ]me-ne-u , VIR e-u-na-wo   VIR

.3   ]ra-no , VIR me-ri-[

.4   ]me-ta-ra-wo[   ]ta , VIR a-me-ja-si VIR

.5   ]ko-me-no , VIR , na-su-wo VIR [[ke-ro VIR]]

.6   ][[   ]-so   VIR   ]]

.7   inf. mut.

       799 is in the Ashmolean, 8306 in Iraklion.
       Several readings are derived from SM II, pl.55
       (plaster now covers certain parts of the text).

       .6 a-ka-de and a-ge-de equally possible.

       v.4 After a-me-ja-si bottom of VIR on lat.dex.

B(5) 800 + fr.   (104)

.0   sup. mut.

.1   ]wo VIR

.2   ]jo , VIR

.3   ]a-wo-ro , VIR na-si-jo VIR

.4   ]VIR , ri-zo VIR me-de-i-jo VIR

.5   ]-do , VIR , [[ke-ro-te]]

.6   ]e , VIR 4   [[   ]]

.7   ]pa-no , VIR 30

.8   ]ke-re , o-pe

       .1 Traces of erasure.

       .4 Last VIR on right edge.

       .7 40 highly improbable.

B(5) 801 + 7593 + fr.   (104)

.0   sup. mut.

.1   ]ma-ma-ro , VIR[

.2   pu-sa-[.], VIR , ki-u-ro , VIR , do[

.3   a-ki-wa-ta , VIR , ki-ri-ja-si VIR   [

.4   a-pi-me-de , VIR , [

       .3 Trace at right (ro[?).

       .3.4 Traces of reworking at the bottom of the tablet
             (last rule erased and put higher in order to
             write the last entry?).

34

B(5) 802   (104)

.0   sup. mut.

.1   ra-ti-[

.2   e-u-ka-ri[

.3   e-ri-ti-qi[

.4   [.]-ka-ta[

      inf. mut.

      .1 Perhaps ra-ti-jo̧[.

B(5) 803   (104)

.0   sup. mut.

.1   ]-u , VIR , ko-ku-ro , VIR , to-na-ta , VIR,

.2   ]u , VIR , a-so-qi-jo , VIR , pi-ri-u̧-wo , VIR

.3   ]V̧I̧Ŗ ko-ru-[

.4   inf. mut.

      .2 pi-ri-jo̧-wo not completely impossible, but
          pi-ri-ţo̧-wo excluded.

B(5) 804   (104)

.1   ]ke-re , ke-do-si-ja , [

.2   ]wo-qo , VIR , do-qe-u , VIR , a-ki[

.3   ]e-i-ja-si , VIR , po-ti-jo , VIR [

.4   ] VIR , a-pa-re-[.] VIR pu-ra[

.5   inf. mut.

      .1 Trace at right.

      .4 Possibly a-pa-re-u̧.

B(5) 805   (104)

.1   pa-wi-no[   ]şa-me , VIR[

.2   ]pi-ja-to , VIR , to-pe-si VIR e-wi-ţạ[

.3   ]me-de , VIR , i-za-re , VIR [

.4   ] VIR ke-re , VIR mi-[

.5   inf. mut.

      .2 Probably no sign lost at left.

      .3 i-za- over erasure (za over [[i]]).

      .4 Trace at left.

35

4

sup. mut.

.1   ] V̤I̤R[

.2   ] , VIR , a-ra-ka-jo , VIR ko-[.]-no , VIR

.3   ]-wo-ta , VIR   po-ki-te ,   VIR

.4   ]se ,   VIR , ma-di-qo ,   VIR ,

.5   ]VIR , to-wa-no VIR

.6   ]VIR , pu-na-si-jo VIR

.7   ]e-wi-to-wo ,   VIR , ru-a̤2[ ] V̤I̤R

.8   ] , re-ka-ṭa ,   VIR [

.9   ]ma-ja-ro ,   VIR [

v.   sup. mut.

.1   vestigia[

.2   ko-[.]-ka-ra-te-ne VIR 2̤0̤[

          reliqua pars sine regulis

          .2.7 Last VIR on right edge.

          .1 Trace at left.

          .2 Trace at left. Probably ko-pi̤-no, but ko-wi̤-no not
              excluded.

          .3]pi̤-wo-ta or]e̤-wo-ta ?

          .8 VIR preceded by ⟦ VIR⟧ .

          .9 Trace of erased rule.

          v.1 Probably ko-wo̤-ka-ra-te-ne; less probably
               ko-e̤-ka-ra-te-ne or ko-pi̤-ka-ra-te-ne.

          sup. mut.

.1   tu-ṛi̤[-si-jo ?

.2   u-ta-ni-jo   VIR 237

.3   vacat

       reliqua pars sine regulis

       Cut at bottom.

       ra-sa-to / po VIR 2

       Cut at left.

B(1)   809   (107?)

  .a   ]me-no   VIR 2

  .b   ?ke-]sa-do-ro-jo

B(2)   810   (137)

      ]VIR 27 a-pe-o-te VIR[

          a-pe-o-te now a-[. .]-te: text from SM II.

B(1)   811   (-)

      ]-ma-da-jo VIR 1

        Cut at right.

B(1)   812   (-)

  .a   ]a-pi-ja-ko-ro-jo[

  .b   ]   VIR 4[

B(2)   813   (137)

  .A   ]   VIR [

  .B   ]21 o-pe-ṛọ[

        Line ruled after VIR was drawn.

        .A Perhaps VIR ḷọọ[.

B(3)   814 + 8067   (106)

      ]mi-jo / po̱ VIR 3[

B(3)   815   (106)

      ]jo / po-ku-ta VIR 1[

        Numeral probably at least 4.

B(3)   816 + 7636   (106)

      da-wi-jo / po-ku-ta VIR [

B(2)   817   (137)

      to-so / ku-su-to-ro-qa VIR [

        Perhaps traces of tens (two ?) at right.

37

B(2) 818   (137)

    a-]p̣u-do-si VIR 30 M 6 N 2[

B 822   (-)

.1a]   po-da̲-qe-re-ṣi̲-je-wo
.1b]p̣i̲-ro / si-ra-ko , qi-ri-ja-to // ku-te-ro / ku-ro$_2$-jo ,
                                    do-e-ro , VIR 1

.2   ]   <u>vacat</u>

    .1a <u>po-ṛo̲-qe-re-ṣi̲-je-wo</u> not entirely excluded; <u>ṣi̲</u> very
    doubtful.

B 823   (-)

    ]tu-wi-jo / ta-pa-e-o-te 'VIR 10' a-pe-o-te 'VIR 4['
    Possibly cut rather than broken at both ends.

B(3) 985   (106)

    e-ki-si-jo / po-ku[-ta

B(1) 988 + 7601 [+] 5761   (-)

.a   pa-qo-si[   ]-ra , qi-ri-ja-to , [
.b   ka-ra-na-ko , / ko-ma[   ] do-ẹ-ṛọ , VIR 2̣[
    Palimpsest.
    b. Trace of sign before <u>do-ẹ-ṛọ</u>. Perhaps only].̣[.

B(1) 1̣025 + 5718 + 7038 + 8065   (-)

.a   ]-o-me-no
.b   ]   wo-ro-ka-ne , a-ko-ro-da̲-mo-jo   VIR 3

v.   ]wo̲-ṛo̲-ka-ne / e-pi-ko
    .a]d̲e-o-me-no not compelling, but not excluded.

B 1055   (102?)

.1   ko-no-si-jo , e-qe-ta ,
.2   pi-sa-wa-ta , VIR[   ]-ṣẹ[
.3   wo-si-jo-ne   VIR[
.4.5   <u>desunt</u>
.6   ]VIR 1 e-ko-te[
.7   ]wi̲-[   ]VIR 1 me-ṭu̲[
.8   ]-ma-ro , VIR 1

.9   to-so , pa-te VIR 213[

          N.B. : .4 vest.[

                  .5 deest

          .8 Perhaps erasure at right.

B(5) 5025   (104)

   .0   sup. mut.

   .1   ]pe‑ri‑te‑u VIR[

   .2   ]e̤-qe-ra-wo VIR[

   .3   inf. mut.

B(5) 5026   (104)

   .1   sup. mut.

   .2   ]e-ri-ko[

   .3   inf. mut.

B(5) 5028   (104)

   .0   sup. mut.

   .1   ]ka-ra-i-no[

   .2   ] , VIR   [

          .2 Trace of sign at left.

B(5) 5029   (104)

   .0   sup. mut.

   .1   ]-wo , VIR a-du-[

   .2   ]-e , VIR   [

          inf. mut.

   v.0   sup. mut.

   .1   ] vestigia [

   .2   ]mi-[

          inf. mut.

B(5) 5132   (104)

          sup. mut.

   .1   ]-wa̤-[ ] , VIR [

   .2   we-ro-pa-ta VIR   e-re-ke[

   .3   ]ma̤-[
              inf. mut.

                        39

.1 Perhaps divider after VIR, but perhaps trace
    of an erased sign. Traces at right.

B(5) 5133   (104)

          sup. mut.
.1   ]vestigia[
.2   ]ri-jo , VIR [
.3   inf. mut.

B(5) 5134   (104)

          sup. mut.
.1   ke̤[
.2   to‑ke[
.3   vac. [

B(5) 5172   (104)

          sup. mut.
.1   [.]-wa-ta   VIR [
.2   wi-do-[.]-wi[
.3   e-re-ṳ-ta[
.4   vestigia [
          inf. mut.

B(2) 5584 + 7427 + fr.   (137)
       ]po̤-ni-ki-jo a̤-pu-do-si   VIR 3̤0̤ M̤[

B(3) 5749   (106)
       ]VIR 1

B(3) 5752 + 7039   (106)
       ka-pa-jo / po VIR 3
          Cut at right.

40

B(5) 5799   (104) ˙

  .0   <u>sup. mut.</u>

  .1   ]VIR [

  .2   ]<u>vac.</u>[

  .3   <u>inf. mut.</u>

B(1) 5984   (-)

  .a   ]-qo   [

  .b   ]-jo do-e-ro VIR[

       .a Trace of two signs before <u>qo</u>.

B 6042 + <u>fr.</u>   (-)

     ]VIR 12

       Units over erasure.

B(1) 7034 + 7705   (-)

     ]jo / to-so , o-re̦-i VIR 9̦00[

B(3) 7035 + <u>fr.</u> [+] 7704   (106)

     do[ ]ṭi̦-jo / po-ku-ta   VIR 10

       Cut at right.

B(1) 7036 + <u>fr.</u>   (-)

     ]te-re-ta VIR 1

B(1) 7037   (-)

     ]   VIR [

      Perhaps]0̦[.

B(1) 7041   (-)

     ]i-jo-te   VIR 130

B(3) 7042 + <u>fr.</u>   (106)

     ] VIR 10

       Cut at right.

B(3) 7043 + 7925   (106)

      ]-ra-so / po̲ VIR 2
         ]ka̤-ra-so or]q̤e-ra-so possible.

B(1) 7044   (-)
      ]VIR 4̣1[
      inf. mut.

B(5) 7859   (104)
   .0   sup. mut.
   .1   ]-wo[
   .2   ]V̤I̤R e̲[
         inf. mut.

B(3) 8006   (106)
      ]jo / po-k̤ṳ[-ta
         inf. mut.

B(5) 8206   ASHM (104)
   .1 ke-]d̤o̤-si-ja , [
   .2   ]ra-jo[
   .3   inf. mut.

   v.1] vacat [
   .2   ]me-za-wo[
   .3   inf. mut.
         .1 Trace at right, perhaps m̤o̤[.

                                   42

Ca

Ca 895   (-)

.1   i-qo   EQU^f 5   EQU^m 4   po-ro EQU[
.2   o-no   EQU^f 3   po-ro EQU 2   EQU^m 4   [

       .1 EQU^m is here shown by the mane instead of the usual two cross-bars as in line 2.

Ca 7788   (-)

    ]ta , o-no[
v.   ]EQU [

Cc

Ce 50   (124)

.1a   a-qi-ru OVIS^m 134   qa-ra$_2$-wo OVIS^f 43
.1b   te-pa-ra , pe-re-qo-ta
.2   a-nu-ko OVIS^f 51   ro-ru OVIS^f 32

v.1a a-qi-ru OVIS^m 190   qa-ra$_2$-wo OVIS^f 144
.1b   o-pa
.2   a-nu-ko OVIS^f 133[ ] ro-ru OVIS^f 150
lat. sup.   we-ka-ta BOS^m 6

    .1b On both sides written in smaller signs between the first signs of 1a.

    .1b te-pa-ra over erasure (pa over [[si]]).

    lat. sup. 6 written as 4 + 2 (the two strokes under the first two have almost certainly been accidentally deleted).

Ce 59   ASHM ("124"c)

.1   ]ma-sa / we-ka-ta BOS^m 6 // da-wo / we-ka-ta BOS^m 6
.2a   ta-ra-me-to   [.]-mo
.2b   ku-]ta-to / we-ka-ta BOS^m 10 // da-*22-to / we-ka-ta BOS 6
.3a   [.]-mo
.3b   ] tu-ri-so / we-ka-ta BOS^m 6 // ku-do-ni-ja / we-ka-ta BOS^m 50

    .2b 10 over [[6]] .
    .3 Whole line over erasure.
    .3a da-mo almost impossible (perhaps re-mo).

Ce 61 (124)

.0   sup. mut.

.1   me-*86-ta   BOS 1[

.2   ra-wo-ti-jo   BOS 1 [

.3   re-u-ka-ta   BOS 1 [

.4   ti-ri-sa-ta[

.5   inf. mut.
       .4 Possible trace of the "ear" of BOS at right.

Ce 76 ("124")

       ]ka-ti   OVIS^m[

Ce 113 ("124")

       ]o   SUS 7 [
           ]o or]o̲.   Trace at right.

Ce 139 + fr. ("124")

.1   a-ku-na̠-i   OVIS 21̣[

.2   do-ti-ja   OVIS 30[

.3   vacat   [

Ce 144 (124)

.0   sup. mut.

.1   e-re-pa-ṛọ BOS ZE [

.2   a-pa-ta-ẉạ[

.3   inf. mut.
       .1 e-re-pa-ṭọ less likely.

Ce 152 + 8256 ("124")

.1   je-[

.2   ja-sa-[   ]B̲O̲S̲ 1   OVIS 1   ÇAP̣[

.3   ta-ta-ta   BOS 1   OVIS 1   [

.4   da-na   OVIS 1   CAP 1   [

.5   vacat   [

v.1   ạ-re-ko-to-re   BOS 1   OVIS 1   CAP 1

.2   ]ọ-ne   BOS 12   OVIS 12   CAP 12

.3   ]-na-i   BOS 12   OVIS 12   CAP [

.4   inf. mut.

44

.1 je-da̤[possible.

.2 Perhaps ja-sa-ro̤[.

.4 Trace at right.

v.3 Possible trace of 10 after CAP.

Ce 156   ("124")

.0   sup. mut.

.1]-na-zo BOS [

.2 te-wa-jo   BOS 3 [

        .1 One or two signs missing before]-na-zo.

Ce 162   ("124")

    OVIS 10000

v.   [[SUS^f   ]]

        Many traces of erasure on both sides. On recto OVIS
        10000 is followed by a large number (9000 +) partially
        erased. Tablet possibly used for rough working.

Ce 163   ("124")

.1 OVIS^m 7̣0[

.2 CAP^m 44[

.3.4 vacant[

        .1 Possible traces of units (6?) after tens.

Ce 283 [+] 7250   ("124")

    ]200   e-po   60[   ]   10   OVIS 40

v.   [[i-w̤e̤]][   ][[ja]]   [

        283: -po̱ 60[over erasure. 7250: Probably over erasure.

        v. Less probably [[i-q̤e̤]][.

Ce 7061   ("124"?)

.0   sup. mut.

.1]BOS   ZE 1

.2]BOS   ZE 1

.3   inf. mut.

Ce 8345 + <u>fr.</u>   ("124")
    ]BOS^x 6 [

      <u>inf. mut.</u>

Ce 8346 + 8644   ("124")
    ]SUS^x 4

Ch

Ch 896   (110)
    ta-za-ro / a$_3$-wo-ro 'ke-ra-no-qe' <u>ne</u> , <u>we</u> BOS^m <u>ZE</u> 1

Ch 897 + 7639   (110)
    e-po-ro-jo / 'to-ma-ko' wo-no-qo-so-qe BOS^m <u>ZE</u> 1

Ch 898 + 7912 + 8069   (110)
    a$_3$-]wo-ro-qe , to-ma-ko-qe BOS^m <u>ZE</u> 1

Ch 899   (110)
    ]k̥o̤ 'po-da-ko-qe' BOS^m <u>ZE</u> 1[

Ch 900   (110)
    ']k̥o̤-so-u-to-qe' BOS^m <u>ZE</u> 1

<u>Ch</u> 972   (110?)
    au-to-a$_3$-ta [

Ch 1015 + 8344   (110)
    ]no / wo-no-qo-so 'to-ma-ko-qe' BOS^m <u>Z̤E̤</u>[

Ch 1029 + 5760 + 7625   (110)
    pu-r̥i̤ / a$_3$-w̤o̤-r̥o̤-qe , po-da-ko-qe BOS^m <u>ZE</u> 1[

Ch 1034   (110)
    ] a$_3$-zo-ro-qe w̤o̤[

Trace of large sign at left (]to?).

Ch 5724 + 6005 + <u>frr</u>.   (110)

]qe , wa-no-qe BOS^m <u>ZE</u> 1   [

Ch 5728   (110)

']pa-ko-qe' BOS^m[

Ch 5754 + 5975 + 6009 + <u>fr</u>.   (110)

]wi-du-ru-ta / a$_3$-wo-ro[
        Nothing lost at left.

Ch 5938 + <u>fr</u>.   (110)

a$_3$-]wo-ro-qe BOS^m[

Ch 7047   (110)

]no-qe BOS [
        Apparently not BOS^m; perhaps BOS <u>ZE</u>[.

Ch 7065   (110)

]qe BOS^m <u>ZE</u> [

Ch 7066   (110)

]no-qe BOS^m <u>ZE</u> 1[

Ch 7100 + 7703   (110)

]a-ko-ro-we-i BOS <u>ZE</u> 1 [

v.   ]a$_3$-ku-ta [
        Probably same tablet as Ch 7937.
        v. Probably nothing lost at left.

<u>Ch</u> 7937   (110?)

]ni-to[

v.   ] [[BOS^m]] [
        Probably same tablet as Ch 7100.

47

Ch 8222 (110)

<u>sup. mut.</u>

]-qe BOS^m [

Co

Co 903 (107)
.1   wa-to / a-ko-ra-ja   OVIS^m 60   OVIS^f 270   CAP^m 49
.2   CAP^f 130   SUS^m 17   SUS^f 41   BOS^m 2   BOS^f 4

Co 904 + 8008 (107)
.1   ku-do-ni-ja / a-ko-ra-ja   OVIS^m 117   OVIS^f 100[
.2   CAP^m 54   CAP^f 151   SUS^f 87   BOS^m[

Co 906 (107)
.1   ka-ta-ra-i / a-ko-ra-ja   OVIS^m 100   OVIS^f 650
.2   CAP^m 40[ ] CAP^f 150   SUS^f 80 [[BOS^m]] BOS^f 6
       Cut at right.

Co 907 (107)
.1   si-ra-ro / a-ko-ra-jo OVIS^m 202   OVIS^f 750
.2   CAP^m 125   CAP^f 240   SUS^m 21   SUS^f 60   BOS^m 2   BOS^f 10

Co 909 + 7133 + 7835 (107)
.1   a-pa-ta-wa , / a[-ko-ra-]ja   OVIS^m [
.2   CAP^f 120   SUS^m 3   SUS^f[
       Possibly same tablet as Co 8347.

Co 910 (107)
.1   o-]du-ru-wo / a-ko-ra-ja[
.2   ] CAP^f 190   SUS^f[
       Probably same tablet as Co 7056.

Co 7056 (107)

  .1   ] OVIS^f 600[

  .2]SUS^f 50 BOS^m 2 BOS^f[

       Probably same tablet as Co 910.

Co 8347 (107?)

     sup. mut.

    ] BOS^f [

       Possibly same tablet as Co 909.

C

C 33 (-)

     sup. mut.

  .1   ]^f 2[

  .2]OVIS^f 6[

  .3] OVIS^f 1 [

  .4] vacat   [

    .3 Perhaps ni[, but more likely X[.

C 394 (-)

  .1   vacat[

  .2 qe-[

  .3 BOS^m 1 sa OVIS^m[

  .4 pa-ja-o-ne / pa-de[

  .5   ]vest.[

    inf. mut.

  v.1   ]no

  .2   ]sa OVIS^m 1 sa CAP^m 1[

  .3]we pa OVIS^m 1 [

  .4] vestigia   [

  .5   inf. mut.

    .4 pa-ja-wo-ne very difficult.

C 767 (-)

  .1] SUS^f [

  .2] vest.[

    inf. mut.

.1 Perhaps 3.
.2 Perhaps SUS^x.

C(1) 901 + 7661 + 8049   (107)

    e-wo-ta-de   BOS^f 20   ta BOS 1

C 902   (201)

  .0   sup. mut.

  .1   mi-ru-ro / si-pe-we   BOS   ne *170 12

  .2   o-du-ru-wi-jo / ko-re-te BOS   ne *170 12

  .3   wa-to / ko-re-te   BOS   ne *170 12 // wa-to / da-nu-wo 'BOS'
                                                           *170 12

  .4   si-ra-ro / ko-re-te   BOS 1 ne *170 12

  .5   *56-ko-we / e-ra-ne   BOS 1 ne *170 12

  .6   o-du-ru-we / u-wo-qe-we   BOS 1 ne *170 12

  .7   ri-jo-no / ko-re-te   BOS 1 ne *170 12

  .8   ru-ki-ti-jo   BOS 1 ne *170 12

  .9   a-pa-ta-wa / ko-re-te   BOS 1 ne *170 12

  .10 ku-ta-i-to / ko-re-te   BOS 1 ne *170 12

  .11 re-ri-jo / e-re-ta   BOS 1 ne *170 12

  .12] wa-to /we-re-we   BOS 1 ne *170 12

  .13 inf. mut.

    .12 Probably nothing lost before wa-to.

    .13 Bottom line probably uninscribed.

    Verso ruled (9 lines) but uninscribed.

C(3) 905   (109)

    ] SUS 1 [

C(2) 908   (112)

    ]pa-ro , / de-ki-si-wo   CAP^f 1 [

C(4) 911   (111)

  .1   ma-mi-di-zo / pi-ri-to-jo   OVIS^f 40[

  .2   [. .]-ro , da-nu-wo   OVIS^f 100[

  .3   po-ri-wo ,/ su-ki-ri-ta-jo , wo-we-u   CAP^m 180

  .4   ja-ru , / pa-ta-ti-jo , do-e-ro ,   CAP^f 230

  .5   a-du-po-to ,/ qi-ko-we-e , do-e-ro ,   CAP^f 90

.6 qa-di-ja , / po-ku-te-ro , da-mo , 'do-e-ro' CAP^f 70

.7 da-[. .] / po-ku-ta CAP^f 130

.8 ra-wa-ni̭ , / po-ku-ta , ra-ri-di-jo OVIS^m 190

.9 o-mi-ri-so , / ṭa-so , do-e-ro OVIS^m 50

.10 [. .]-so , / a-pi-me-de-o , po-ku-ta 'ra-ri-di-jo' OVIS^f 140

.11 ku-jo[/]ṭa-so // do-e-ro OVIS^f 100

.12 a-*56-da-ro̭ / ka-ta-mi-jo , do̭-ḛ-ro̭ OVIS^x[

.13 a-ra-ko , / ra-ṛi-di̭-jo , do̭-e-ro̭ OVIS^m 100[

.14-.17 <u>vacant</u>

> .2 First sign possibly pḛ.
>
> .8 ra-wa-m̭o not impossible; the fragment bearing the <u>first two</u> signs in this line has now been lost (see SM II, pl.70).
>
> .10 [.]-ṛo-so or [.]-ḍa-so ?
>
> .12 Probably OVIS^f[ ]1̭0̭0̭ .
>
> .13 Possibly 12̭0̭[.

C(4) 912 + 5027 (111)

.1] re-ko-no-jo

.2 pu-wo / po̭-ku-ta // da-we-ro OVIS^m 270

.3 wa-du-na-ro , / po-ku-ta OVIS^m 110

.4 [.]-qa-to , / pḁ-[ ]te-re[ ]OVIS^x 140[

.5 pu-na-to , do-e-ro , e-te-wa-tu-wo [[OVIS^m]] OVIS^m 80

.6 i-ro-to , [ ]na̭-jo OVIS^m 80

.7 qa-sa-ko , / [.]-wa-so OVIS^m 170

.8 ka-sa-ro , / a-da-wa-si-jo OVIS^m 60

.9 ḍi̭-[ ] OVIS^m 140[

.10 a-nu-no[/]jo-ṭe[ ] OVIS^m 80

.11 ko-to , / po-ku[ ] OVIS^f 100[

.12]ṛe-to / ka-[

.13 <u>inf. mut.</u>

v.1 su-pu-wo / do-e-ro-jo OVIS^x[ ]7̭0 CAP^f 40

.2 to-so OVIS^m 900 [

.3-.9 <u>vacant</u>

<u>inf. mut.</u>

> .4 Perhaps <u>a-qa-to</u> and probably over erasure.
>
> .7 Perhaps <u>a</u>-wa-so.

51

5

.10 Perhaps 90.

.11 po over erasure, perhaps [[ṭa]] or [[ṣu]] .

v.1 Probably OVIS^f[.

C(2) 913   (112?)

.1   pa-ro , e-te-wa-no , a̱₃ CAP^m 1[

.2   pa-ro   ko-ma-we-te CAP^m 1 pa[

     .2 CAP^m over [[CAP^f]] .

C(2) 914   (112)

.A   pa-ra-ti-jo OVIS^m 50

.B   a-ka-wi-ja-de / pa-ro ,   CAP^m 50

     Left end of central line (under pa-ra-ti-jo) erased.

C(2) 915   (112)

.A   ]   OVIS^f 10   [

.B   ] pa-ro , a-pi-qo-ta / pa-ro , do-e-ro CAP^f 10 [

C(4) 917 + 7729 [+] 918   (111?)

.1   re-ko-no , / to-sa , qe[   ] OVIS^m 1700[

.2   OVIS^f 1200 [   ]40   ÇAP^x 500[

.3   to-sa , pa-ta[

v.1   [[re-ko-no-jo , po]][

.2   [[po-ku-ta   ]][

.3   [[vestigia]][   ] vacat [

      Cut at left.

      .1 Traces before OVIS^m.

      .1-.2: Right-hand part of 918 damaged: text of recto
              from SM II, pl. 65, text of verso from Handlist.

      v.1 1 or 2 dividers between -jo and po[? (on the
           original, only re-ko-no[survives).

C(2) 922 + 5764   (112)

     ]te-ru-wo-te   CAP^f 1   [

52

C(2)   941 + 1016 + <u>fr</u>.   (112)

  .A   OVIS^m 8[

  .B   pa-ro / a-pi-qo-ta , sa-pa-ka-te-ri-ja OVIS^f 10 [

v.A   [[   ]] [

  .B   [[wi-ja   ]] [

      .B Traces at right.

C   954 + <1632> + 5016   (-)

  .1   ]OVIS^f 1 mo-ro-qa OVIS^f 1 ke-to-ro OVIS^f 1 we-wo-ni-jo

                                                                          CAP^f [

  .2   ]ku-no-o CAP^f 1 pe-ri-te-u OVIS^f 1 me-tu-ro CAP^f 1

                                                                                si-[

  .3   ]CAP^f 1 di[   ]po-ro-i CAP^x 1[

v.1   ]-ne-wa CAP^f 1

        <u>reliqua pars sine regulis</u>

           <1632>: missing; text from SM II, pl. 62.

           .3 <u>di[-pte-ra-]po-ro-i</u> ?

<u>C(3)</u>   967   (109?)

      pu-na-so , [

        Trace at right.

C   973   (-)

      te-re-wa-ko / a$_3$-wa !   tu-ma-ko   BOS[

C(3)   979 + 1032 + 7051 + 7052 + 7657   (109)

      do-ti-ja , / ra-ja , pu-na-so-qe , 'ra-su-to-qe' a-to-mo

                                                                       SUS 1

C(1)   989 + 5744 + 7997   (107)

      ]re-[.]-ja / ku-do-ni-ja   BOS^f 14[

        ]<u>re-[.]-ja</u>: neither mo, qi nor ki satisfactory.
        Perhaps trace at left, but certainly no more than
        one sign lost before <u>re</u>.

C(3)   1030 + 7055   (109)

      e-ko-so , / du-ma   SUS 1

        Cut at right.

C(3) 1039

.a   ]   e-ra-wo , du-ma   [
.b   *56-]ko-we-qe   SUS^x[

C 1044 + 7053   (-)

.a   ] , we-ka-ta-e   [
.b   ]   ke-u-po-da-o   BOS^m ZE 1 [

C 1561   (-)

.a   ]ka-te-ri-ja   [
.b   ]wo   OVIS^f[

C 1582   (-)

.a   ]we-ka-ta   [
.b   ]-au-a$_3$-ta   BOS^m[

C <1902>   (-)

.1   ]68   CAP^f 2
.2   ] CAP^f 45
.3   ]   vacat
        Missing; text from Evans' Notebook 1905, p.9a.

C 5089   (-)

        ] BOS^f [
        Palimpsest: [[u-.-.]] visible after ideogram.

C(1) 5544

        ] BOS^m 91[

C 5669   (-)

.0   sup. mut.
.1   ]*150   12   CAP^f 1[
.2   ]*150   12   CAP^f[
.3   inf. mut.
        .1 Possibly *258 not *150.
        .2 Reading of the first ideogram very uncertain.
           Perhaps CAP^f 2[.

C 5734 + 8224   (-)

   we-]ka-ta   BOS $\underline{ZE}$ 20
          Cut at right.

C(1) 5753 + 7046 + 7630   (107)

   ko-no-so-de BOS^f 5 BOS^m 8
          BOS^m 8 over erasure and the numerals unusually
          arranged.

C(2) 5765 + $\underline{fr}$.   (112)

   ] CAP^f[

C 5985   (-)

   ] BOS^m [

C 6021   (-)

   .1   ]no-re CAP^m $\underset{.}{1}$[
   .2   ]ra-zo[

C 7048   (-)

          $\underline{sup.\ mut.}$
   .1   ]$\underline{vest.}$[
   .2   ]-je-re-u   OVIS [
   .3   ]$\underset{.}{t}a$ $OVIS^x$[
          $\underline{inf.\ mut.}$

C 7054   (-)

   ]24 $CAP^{\underset{.}{m}}$ 20
          CAP^m roughly corrected from CAP^f.

C(3) 7057   (109)

   ]ma   SUS $\underset{.}{1}$[

C(3) 7058 + 7922   (109)

   ]$\underset{.}{d}a$-mo-ko-ro   SUS 1[

C 7059 + 7877   (-)

  .A   ]ka-ma-o [ ]^f[

  .B   ]-no   CAP^f 20[

        .B Perhaps]o̭-no ̭ .

C 7060   (-)

  .1   ]2 <u>WE</u> 1

  .2   ]   <u>vacat</u>

       <u>inf. mut.</u>

  v.   ri   [

       <u>inf. mut.</u>: Or cut at bottom ?

       v. Perhaps [[<u>ri</u>]] .

C 7062 + 8348   (-)

       ] 1   OVIS 2   'e-u-[.]-m̭a-[.]-jo   OVIS 1'

       Trace at left (OVI̭S̭^{f} ?). <u>e-u</u>-[.]-<u>m̭a</u>-[.]-<u>jo</u>:
       third sign could be ḓa or ṱa, fifth w̭i or s̭i.

<u>C(2)</u> 7064 + 7543 + 8226   (112?)

  .1   a-ki-ri-ja   CAP^m 2̭6   CAP^f [

  .2   <u>vacat</u>   [   ]k̭ḙ   3[

C 7067   (-)

  .1   ]<u>mo</u> BOS^m [

  .2   ] <u>vacat</u> [

       .1 <u>mo</u> apparently adjunct.

C 7088   (-)

       ]C̭A̭P̭^{f} 50 <u>ki</u> CAP 20

       Cut at right.

C 7515   (-)

       ]BOS 1 [

       Possibly]<u>mu</u> 1. Traces at right.

C 7516   (-)

  .1   ]57 <u>PO</u> 7 CAP[

.2]3 SUS^x[

.3]vest.[

C 7698 + 7892 + 8223 + frr. (-)

tu-zo BOS ZE 1[

Over erasure.

C(2) 8225 + fr. (112)

] CAP^f 1[

C(2) 8578 (112)

]pa-ro , [

Da

Da 1078 (117)

    e-ki-no / a-ka   OVIS^m 200

Da 1079 + 7192 (117)

    a-ko-ro-qo-ro / a-ka   OVIS^m 200

Da 1080 (117)

    .A   OVIS^m 200

    .B   au-ri-jo / a-ka

Da 1081 (117)

    e-ne-ke-se-u , / a-ka   OVIS^m 200

Da 1082 (117)

    .A   OVIS^m 200

    .B   o-ku-no / a-ka

Da 1083 (117)

    .A   OVIS^m 200

    .B   po-i-te-u / a-ka

Da 1087 (117)

    .A   ]   OVIS^m 100[

    .B   ]-jo / a-ka   [

Da 1091 + 1413 (117)

    ]ri-sa-ta , / ri-jo-no ,   OVIS^m 300

        v.: two lines (.1.2) with vestigia.

Da 1098 (117)

    .A   OVIS^m 110   [[o̲ OVIS^m 1]]

    .B   ru-na-mo / qa-ra ,   X

lat. inf.   [[ki-ṛe-i-ṣo , qa-ra   OVIS^m 100   ]]

        .A 10 of 110 over [[9]] .

        .B m̲o̲ over erasure (perhaps [[s̲o̲]] ?).

        lat. inf. Perhaps ki-ṇe-i-ṣọ.

Da 1108   (117)

.A   OVIS^m 200

.B   ki-ta-ne-to , / su-ri-mo

Da 1114 + 5216   (117)

.A   ]   OVIS^m 50[

.B   ]ri-wi-so / ku-ta-to , [
                  .
        Text doubtless complete at left.

        .A 50[probably complete.

Da 1116   (117)

.a   da-mi-ni-jo

.b   au-ri-jo , / ku-ta-to   OVIS^m 50[

        .b 50[almost certainly complete (tablet ends shortly
            after).

Da 1123 + 7178   (117)

        a-qi-ro / ku-ta-to   OVIS^m 100

        a-qi-ro / ku-ta-to over erasure.

Da 1127   (117)

.a   u-ta-jo,

.b   mi-ru-ro / da-*22-to , OVIS^m 100 [

Da 1132 + 6023   (117)

.a   u-ta-jo

.b   *56-du-nu-ka , / do-ti-ja OVIS^m 100

Da 1134   (117)

.a   u-ta-jo   [

.b   ke-to , / *56-ko-we   OVIS^m 100[

Da 1135 + 7182   (117)

.A   u-ta-jo-jo   OVIS^m 100

.B   ke-to , / *56-ko-we ,

Da 1137 + 1437   (117)

.a   ]   u-ta-jo   [

.b   ]po-ru-qo-to , / e-ko-so   OVIS^m 100[

Da 1143 + 5707 + 7222 + 7684   (117)

.a   u-ta-jo-jo ,

.b   du-ri , / ri-jo-no   OVIS^m 100

Da 1147   (117)

          sa-ma-ri-jo / da-*22-to   OVIS^m 100

              Palimpsest; previous text upside down:
              [[po-ri-[   ] / da-*22-to   ]]

Da 1156 + 7236   (117)

.A   we-we-si-jo   OVIS^m 100

.B   a-re-ke-se-u , / pa-i-to

Da 1161 + 7187   (117)

.A   ]   we-we-si-jo   OVIS^m 300[

.B   ]ku-tu-qa-no / pa-i-to[

Da 1162   (117)

.a   we-we-si-jo-jo

.b   e-ro-u-ta , / su-ri-mo   OVIS^m 200

Da 1163 + 1400   (117)

.A   we-we-si-jo   OVIS^m 100

.B   wi-je-so , / pa-i-to ki-ri-jo-te

          .B wi over erasure, perhaps [[je]] . pa-i-to over
              [[su-ki-ri-ta]] .

60

Da 1164 + 1421 + 7169   (117)

  .A   ·   we-we-si-jo   OVIS^m 130[

  .B   da-i-qo-ta / pa-i-to

            .A Probably no more than 140.

Da 1170 + <u>fr</u>.   (117)

  .A   OVIS^m 100

  .B   o-ku / pa-i-to

Da 1172 + <u>frr</u>.   (117)

  .A   OVIS^m 100[   ] <u>vacat</u>

  .B   ru-*56-ra-so / pa-i-to , pe-ri-qo-te-jo

Da 1173 + 7121   (117)

      du-pu$_2$-ra-zo , pa-i-to   OVIS^m 200

<u>lat. inf.</u> ku-ru-me-ni-jo , ke-to

        Palimpsest.

Da 1189 + 6065   (117)

      a-me-a / ra-su-to   OVIS^m 100

Da 1194   (117)

  .a]   ki-ri-jo-te

  .b]-de-u , / ra-su-to   OVIS^m 30

Da 1195   (117)

      a-ke-e-to / ra-su-to   OVIS^m 100

Da 1197   (117)

  .a   ki-ri-jo-te

  .b wi-na-jo , / ra-su-to   OVIS^m 40

Da 1202   (117)

      ku-mi-so / ra-ja   OVIS^m 100

        <u>ku-mi-so</u> over erasure.

Da 1221 + 8200   (117)

.A   OVIS^m 200

.B   a$_3$-ta-ro-we , / *56-ko-we ,

Da 1238   (117)

.A   OVIS^m 100[

.B   ku-ka-ro , / ti-ri-to[

            .B ti-ri-to over erasure.

Da 1253 + 7153 + fr.   (117)

.A   tu-ni-ja[   ]OVIS^m 100

.B   *34-zo , / pe-ri-qo-te-jo ,

            .B Erasure before pe-ri-qo-te-jo.

Da 1268   (117)

.A   ]   OVIS^m 100[ ] [

.B   ] vest.,/qa-ra , se-wo-to   [

            .A 100 probably complete, but just room in damaged
            area for 10.

Da 1273 + 1440   (117)

      ]ne-u / e-ko-so   OVIS^m 100[

        Tablet originally divided horizontally: dividing
        line later erased.

Da 1275 + 7687   (117)

.A   OVIS^m 100

.B   ka-ma-to /   e-ko-so

Da 1276 + 2018   (117)

.A   OVIS^m 150

.B   to-tu-no / e-ko-so

Da 1277 + 5247   (117)

      ]na-mo / e-ko-so   OVIS^m 100[

Da 1288   (117)

.A   OVIS^m 100

.B   mo-ni-ko / ru-ki-to

Da 1289   (117)

.A   OVIS^m 100

.B a-no-qo-ta / ru-ki-to

Da 1293   (117)

.A   OVIS^m 110

.B ka-mo-ni-jo / ru-ki-to

Da 1299   (117)

.a   ki-ri-jo-te   [

.b e-u-ko-ro / do-ti-ja OVIS^m 100[

Da 1313 + 1395 + 5590   (117)

.A   OVIS^m 100

.B ku-mo-no-so / da-wo

Da 1314   (117)

.a   te-ra-po-si-jo

.b po-i-ti-jo , / da-wo , OVIS^m 50

Da 1315 + 1458 + 5311 + fr.   (117)

.A   OVIS^m 100

.B u-ra-mo-no / da-wo

Da 1317 + 5316 + 5397   (117)

  da-i-ze-to , /qa-mo , u-ta-jo-jo , OVIS^m 110 [

Da 1321 + 5101 + 5773   (117)

.A   OVIS^m 200   [

.B su-ta-no , / ra-to , pe-ri-qo-te-jo , [

Da 1323 + 5243 + 5325 + fr.   (117)

.A   a-no-qo-[ ] OVIS^m 100[ ] vacat

.B ke-ti-ro , / e-ra[   ] vestigia ?

Da 1333 + 2015   (117)

  .A   ]   'e-ra'   OVIS^m 100[

  .B]pu-to-ro , / pe-ri-qo-te-jo , [

           Text probably complete at left.

           .B <u>pe-ri-qo-te-jo</u> over erasure.

Da 1338 + 1448 + <u>fr.</u>   (117)

      te-mi-ro , / di-ro ,   OVIS^m 100   [

Da 1339 + 5289 + <u>fr.</u>   (117)

  .A   OVIS^m 100

  .B si-ki-to / pu-so

Da 1341   (117)

  .a da-mi-]ṇi-jo

  .b   ku-]ṭa-to   OVIS^m 400

Da **1343 + 7637**   (117)

  .A   OVIS^m 200

  .B ta-pe-ro ,/ e-ṛạ

Da 1350 + 1452 + <u>frr.</u>   (117)

  .A   OVIS^m 200

  .B ka-ne-u-ta / a-ka

Da 1351 + 5255   (117)

      ]qa-na-no-to   OVIS^m 2ṣ0

Da 1352 + 5634   (117)

  .A   ]   u-ta-jo-jo ,   OVIS^m 200[

  .B]ḳẹ-jọ , / pa-i-to ,   [

Da 1353 + 1467 + <u>fr.</u>   (117)

  .A   [[OVIS^m 100[   ]] OVIS^m 100

  .B a-ri-ko , / da-*22-to ,

Da 1355   (117)

    ] di-ro OVIS^m 100

      Trace of sign at left.

Da 1363   (117)

    ]so / qa-ra OVIS^m 100

Da 1365 + 7256 + 8730   (117)

.A]jo OVIS^m 100

.B]   ki-ri-jo-te

Da 1378 + 1405   (117)

.a   u-ta-jo

.b wi-ja-ma-ro / pa-i-to , OVIS^m 50

Da 1379 + 5207 + 5305   (117)

    i-ne-u , / ri-jo-no OVIS^m 50

Da 1382 + 1482   (117)

.a]   u-ta-jo

.b]mi-ni-to , / ri-jo-no OVIS^m 110

Da 1384 + 5684 + 5702 + 7247 + 8548 + <u>fr</u>.   (117)

.A   u-ta-jo , OVIS^m 100[

.B ti-ri-jo-ko-so / [ ]*56-ko-we [[?]] [

Da 1390 + 5351 + 5382 + 5417 + <u>frr</u>.   (117)

.A   [ ] OVIS^m 200

.B e-u-mo / ra-to

Da 1392 + 1619 + 7112 + <u>fr</u>.   (117)

.A   a-te-jo OVIS^m 100

.B ku-ke-to , / se-to-i-ja ,   [?]

      .B At the end of line, probably two damaged (but
         not erased) signs, perhaps <u>au-to</u>, (or even
         <u>au-to</u>-[.]).

Da 1396 + 5249 + 5339   (117)
.A   OVIS^m 100   [
.B   ku-ne-u / da-wo   [

Da 1401 + 7998 + <u>fr</u>.   (117)
        ]-wi / da-*22-to   OVIS^m 150
            Perhaps]t̞o-wi (and probably no other sign lost at left).

Da 1415 + 7074   (117)
.A   u-ta-jo
.B   ri-ma-zo , / tu-ni-ja   OVIS^m 200

Da 1435 + 2023 + 7220   (117)
        ]ki-ki-jo / ku-ta-to   OVIS^m 100
            Text probably complete at left.

Da 1445 + 5807   (117)
.A   OVIS^m 100
.B   wa-du-ka-sa-ro

Da 1461 + 7091   (117)
        ma-ri-ti-wi-jo , / *56-ko-we   OVIS^m 100

Da 1485 + 2022   (117)
        ]sa-nu-mo , / ri-jo-no , OVIS^m 100   [

Da 1495 + 5175 + 5563   (117)
.A   OVIS^m 200
.B   qo-te-ro / pa-i-to

Da 1509 + 7077   (117)
.A   we-we-si-jo-jo   OVIS^m 1̞10[
.B   o-ki-ro /   pa-i-to,   [

Da 1588 + 5705 + 7233   (117)
.A   OVIS^m 100   [
.B   ta-*49-ro / pu-na-so   [

Da   2005 + 5366   (117)
    ]ṛọ / a-ka   OVIS^m 200[

Da   2027 + <u>fr</u>.   (117)
    ]*22 / ku-ta-to   OVIS^m 100

Da   5038 + 5039   (117)
  .A   ]   OVIS^m 100   [
  .B   ]tu-ni-ja   [

Da   5179 + 5674 + 7257 + 8556   (117)
    ]ṭị-ko-ro / ku-ta-to   OVIS^m 100[

Da   5192 + 5572 + <u>fr</u>.   (117)
    su-se , / ra-to   OVIS^m 100

Da   5195 + 5596 + 8227   (117)
    po-ka-ro , / pu-so ,   OVIS^m 100[

Da   5204 [+] 5345 + <u>fr</u>.   (117)
  .a   ki[-ri-jo-]te
  .b   a-nu-mo / [   ]   OVIS^m 200
    .b   Trace at right on 5204.

Da   5205 + 5208   (117)
    ]-wa-ta / ri-jo-no   OVIS^m 100   [

Da   5214 + <u>fr</u>.   (117)
    ]-so / ri-jo-no   OVIS^m 100

Da   5217 + 5230 + <u>fr</u>.   (117)
    pi-ki-nu-wo / ra-to   OVIS^m 100
    <u>ki</u> perhaps over erasure.

Da   5218 + 6064 + <u>fr</u>.   (117)
    ze-ro / e-kọ-so   OVIS^m 100

Da 5220 + 5330 + 5355   (117)

>]ṛọ / ku-ta-to   OVIS^m 100

Da 5223 + 7184 + 7898 + 8269   (117)

> .A   OVIS^m 100
> .B   a-da-ra-ro / da-wo , ki-ri-jo-te

Da 5225 + fr.   (117)

>]-to   OVIS^m 100

Da 5234 + frr.(3)   (117)

> wi-ro-jo / pu-na-so   OVIS^m 80

Da 5244   (117)

>]OVIS^m 200

Da 5245 + 5299   (117)

> .a]   ki-ri-jo-te
> .b]ṛọ / e-ko-so   OVIS^m 200

Da 5251   (117)

>]to   OVIS^m 100

Da 5270   (117)

>]OVIS^m 120

Da 5295 + 5384 + fr.   (117)

> .A   ]   OVIS^m 50
> .B   ]me-to-re / ra-su-to

Da 5308 + 5332   (117)

>]te-u / ku-ta-to   OVIS^m 100[

Da 5317   (117?)

> .A   ]OVIS^m 100 [
> .B   ]ra-ja ,   [

Da 5354   (117)
    ]OVIS^m 100[

Da 5356 + 5369   (117)
    a-]ka   OVIS^m 200[

Da 5427   (117)
    ]OVIS^m 100 [
      inf. mut.

Da 5576 + 7160   (117)
.A]   OVIS^m 100
.B]ki-so / e-ra , u-ta-jo-jo

Da 5709   (117)
.A]u-ta-jo-**jo** , OVIS^m 100[
.B]   inf. mut.   [

Da 6061 + fr.   (117)
    a$_3$-to / ri-jo-no OVIS^m 100[
      Perhaps 130[or more.

Da 7080   (117)
    ]ro / *56-ko-we OVIS^m 100[

Da 7081   (117)
.a ki-]ri-jo-te
.b   ]ja ,   OVIS^m 100

Da 7090   (117)
.A]vac.[   ]OVIS^m 100
.B] da-*22-to

Da 7109 + 7166   (117)
.A]te , OVIS^m 60   [
.B   ]   u-ta-jo-jo [

Da 7165 + 7271   (117)

.A   ]si-jo'-jo'   OVIS^m 100
.B   ] <u>vacat</u>

Da 7185   (117)

.A   ]OVIS^m 100   [[OVIS^f]] [
.B   <u>inf. mut.</u>

Da 7186   (117)

        <u>sup. mut.</u>
        ] OVIS^m 100   [

Da 7213   (117)

        ] OVIS^m 100[

Da 8201 + <u>fr.</u>   (117)

.A   we-we[-si-jo   ] OVIS^m 100
.B   ta-za-po / pa-i-to
        .B Perhaps ta-za-so.

Da 8228 + <u>fr.</u>   (117)

.a   u-ta-jo-jo   [
.b   [.]-nwa-jo / da-wo   OVIS^m 100[

Da 8355 + <u>fr.</u>   (117)

.A   OVIS^m 100
.B   [.]-ki-si-wo , / ra-su-to

Da 8377 + 8399   (117)

        ]-to   OVIS^m 100
            Perhaps]<u>ja-to</u>   or   ]<u>so-to.</u>

Da 8400   (117)

.A   ] 100
.B   ] <u>vacat</u>

Db

Db 1097 ⁽¹¹⁷⁾
.A $\quad$ OVIS^m 48 $\quad$ OVIS^f 2
.B $\quad$ ta-za-ro / u-ta-no $\qquad$ X

Db 1099 ⁽¹¹⁷⁾
.A $\quad$ OVIS^m 90 $\quad$ OVIS^f 10
.B $\quad$ a-wa-so / qa-mo $\qquad$ X

Db 1105 + 1446 ⁽¹¹⁷⁾
.A $\quad$ OVIS^m 52 $\quad$ OVIS^f 28
.B $\quad$ a$_3$-ku-pi-ti-jo , / su-ri-mo

Db 1110 ⁽¹¹⁷⁾
$\quad$ qa-si-da-ro , / ku-ta-to $\quad$ OVIS^m 190 $\quad$ OVIS^f 5

Db 1115 ⁽¹¹⁷⁾
$\quad$]ku-ta-to , $\quad$ OVIS^m 80 $\quad$ OVIS^f 20
$\qquad$ 80 certain; small mark after 80 not deliberate.

Db 1126 + 5303 + 7208 ⁽¹¹⁷⁾
$\quad$]no-ta-na / ku-ta-to $\quad$ OVIS^m 134 $\quad$ OVIS^f 16

Db 1140 + 1499 + 5700 ⁽¹¹⁷⁾
.A $\quad$ OVIS^m 165 $\quad$ OVIS^f 35 [
.B $\quad$ qi-ja-to , / qa-ra , u-ta-jo-jo , $\qquad$ [
$\qquad$ Text doubtless complete at right.

Db 1155 + 5378 + 5688 ⁽¹¹⁷⁾
.A $\quad$ we-we-si-jo $\quad$ OVIS^m 86 $\quad$ OVIS^f 14
.B $\quad$ wi-jo-ka-de / da-wo

Db 1159   (117)

.A   we-we-si-jo-jo   OVIS^m 144   OVIS^f 55[

.B   du-ta-so , / pa-i-to   [

  .B pa-i-to over [[e-ra ,]] .

Db 1160 + 8428 + 8671   (117)

.A   we-we-si-jo-jo OVIS^m 94 OVIS^f 6[

.B   a-qe-mo / pa-i-to

Db 1165 + 7110 + 7226   (117)

.A   ]   we-we-si-jo   OVIS^m 49   OVIS^f 51

.B   ]ra-ko , / da-ra-ko

Db 1166   (117)

.A   we-we-si-jo   OVIS^m 46   OVIS^f 4

.B   au-ta$_2$, / di-ro ,   •

Db 1168 + 7168 + fr.   (117)

.A   we-we-si-jo-jo   OVIS^m 91   OVIS^f 9

.B   ma-di , / e-ko-so   [

Db 1185   (117)

  ro-ru / ra-to   OVIS^m 62   OVIS^f 36

        Possibly pa-ru.

Db 1186 + fr.   (117)

  i-mi-ri-jo , / ra-to , OVIS^m 40   OVIS^f 60

Db 1196 + 8233   (117)

  ]pa-u-ro / ra-su-to   OVIS^m 93   OVIS^f [

Db 1198 + 5710   (117)

  ta-na-po-so / ra-su-to   OVIS^m 82   OVIS^f 18

Db 1204 + 5306   (117)

  qe-ro / ri-jo-no   OVIS^m 72   OVIS^f 28

72

Db 1208 + 5488   (117)

.A]   OVIS^m 72   OVIS^f 28

.B]ra-so , / ri-jo-no

Db 1211 + 5389   (117)

.A]   OVIS^m 71   OVIS^f 29[

.B]ru-ka-*18 / ri-jo-no   [

Db 1212 + 1375   (117)

      da-wi / ri-jo-no OVIS^m 132 OVIS^f 18

Db 1225 + 5177 + 5703   (117)

      wi-na-jo / *56-ko-we OVIS^m 90 OVIS^f 10

          wi-na-jo over [[te-[. .]-jo[ ]] .

Db 1227 + fr.   (117)

.a   OVIS^m 50   OVIS^f 50

.b sa-nu-we-ta / *56-ko-we

Db 1232   (117)

.A   OVIS^m 23   OVIS^f 27

.B na-pu-ti-jo , / ti-ri-to , pe-ri-qo-te-jo

          .B pe-ri-qo-te-jo possibly over erasure.

Db 1236   (117)

.A   OVIS^m 64   OVIS^f 36

.B a-ra-ko / ti-ri-to

Db 1241   (117)

.A   OVIS^m 81   OVIS^f 19

.B o-te-se-u , / tu-ri-so ,

Db 1242   (117)

.A   OVIS^m 80   OVIS^f 20

.B wa-du-na-ro , / tu-ri-so ,

Db 1245 + 7216   (117)

.A   OVIS^m 186   OVIS^f 14

.B ra-wi-zo , / tu-ri-so ,

        .A Erasure before OVIS^f ([[O̤V̤I̤S̤^{f}]] ?).

        .B Perhaps [[O̤V̤I̤S̤^{m}]] .

Db 1246   (117)

.A   OVIS^m 89   OVIS^f 11

.B a-wa-so / tu-ni-ja   [

Db 1247   (117)

        ]ta-za / tu-ni-ja   OVIS^m 88   OVIS^f 12

        Text almost certainly complete at left.

Db 1250 + 1606   (117)

.a   ]   OVIS^m 99

.b   ] tu-ni-ja   OVIS^f 7

Db 1261   (117)

.A   OVIS^m 89   OVIS^f 11

.B a-no-ke-we / qa-ra

Db 1262 + 1486 + 7162   (117)

.A   OVIS^m 68   OVIS^f 32

.B sa-ze-ro / qa-ra

Db 1263   (117)

.A   ]   te-ra-po-si-jo   OVIS^m 90   OVIS^f 10

.B   ]ka-mo / qa-[.]

        .b Either qa-mo or qa-ra possible.

Db 1265 + 1477   (117)

.A   OVIS^m 142   OVIS^f 8

.B u-ra-jo / qa-ra ,

74

Db 1274 + 8376   (117)

.A]   OVIS^m 47   OVIS^f 3[

.B   ]je-zo / e-ko-so   [

Db 1279   (117)

.A   OVIS^m 97   OVIS^f 3

.B   tu-qa-ni-ja-so , / ru-ki-to

        Much of tablet erased and reused; tu-qa-ni-ja-so over
        [[ ]wo-ro-to]] (perhaps no sign before wo).

Db 1282   (117)

     wi-na-jo / ru-ki-to   OVIS^m 50   OVIS^f 50

Db 1295 + 5409   (117)

.A   OVIS^m 96   OVIS^f 4

.B   a$_3$-ke-wa-to / ru-ki-to

Db 1297   (117)

.A   OVIS^m 78   OVIS^f 22

.B   qa-da-so / ru-ki-to
            .B to looks very much like so.

Db 1302   (117)

.A]   OVIS^m 44   OVIS^f 56

.B   ]da-nwa-re / do-ti-ja

Db 1304   (117)

.A   OVIS^m 41   OVIS^f 59

.B   na-ru , / do-ti-ja ,

Db 1305   (117)

.A   OVIS^m 52   OVIS^f 48

.B   wi-jo-qo-ta / do-ti-ja

Db 1324   (117)

.A   OVIS^m 93   OVIS^f 7

.B   da-na-jo , / su-ki-ri-ta

Db   1327 + 1345 + 7681 + 7992   (117)

        ki-mu-ku / su-ki-ri-ta   OVIS^m 120   OVIS^f 80

Db   1329 + 5698 + <u>fr</u>.   (117)

.a   ]   a-te-jo
.b   ]u-ra-jo , / qa-sa-ro-we   OVIS^m 40   OVIS^f 10

Db   1340 + 5263   (117)

.A   ]   OVIS^m 75   OVIS^f 5
.B   ]ra-ro , / su-ri-mo
            Erased dividing rule below existing rule.

Db   1344 + 6017 + 7268 + 7950 + 8235   (117)

.A   ]   we-we-si-jo-jo   OVIS^m 170   OVIS^f 30
.B   ]-tu-to ,/ pa-i-to[   ]   <u>vacat</u>
        .B   Perhaps]ṭị-tu-to.

Db   1367 + 1391 + 1513   (117)

.A   OVIS^m 95
.B   e-wa-ra-jo / do-ti-jạ[   ]OVIS^f 5
        .B   Traces before OVIS^f: more likely erased units
             than adjunct.

Db   1368 + 5906 + <u>frr</u>.   (117)

.A   ]   OVIS^m 78   OVIS^f 22
.B   ]ma-da-ro / da-wo

Db   1372   (117)

.A   ]OVIS^m 76   OVIS^f 24̤[
.B   da-]wo   [

Db   1373 + 1475   (117)

        pa-ra-to / da-*22-to ,   OVIS^m 72   OVIS^f 28

Db   1389 + 1590 + 7197   (117)

.A   ]   OVIS^m 82   OVIS^f 18̣[
.B   ]e-u-ko-ro / ti-ri-to
            Text almost certainly complete at left.

76

Db 1423 + 5320   (117)

.A   OVIS^m 87   OVIS^f 13

.B   *56-ri-to / ru-ki-to

Db 1426 + 5847 + 7225   (117)

.A   OVIS^m 78   OVIS^f 12

.B   de-ke-se-u , / do-ti-ja ,

          .A OVIS^f over [[OVIS^f]] slightly more to the left.

Db 1464 + 7070   (117)

.A   we-we-si-jo-jo   OVIS^m 38   OVIS^f 62

.B   a-nu-ko / pa-i-to   ki-ri-jo-te

          .B nu probably over erasure.

Db 1507   (117)

.A   OVIS^m 38   OVIS^f 62

.B   na-wi-ro / pa-i-to   [   ] vacat

          .B Perhaps traces of erasure at end.

Db 1610   (117)

        OVIS^m]37   OVIS^f 33

Db 2020 + 5314 [+] 5423   (117)

.A   ]   OVIS^m 40[   ] OVIS^f 20[

.B   ]ru-wo-i-ko , /   su-ri[-mo] vacat [

          .A Perhaps 20 over [[OVIS^m]] .

Db 5041   (117)

.A   ]OVIS^m 110   OVIS^f 10

.B   ]   vacat

Db 5212 + 5257 + 7237   (117)

        ]ra / ra-to   OVIS^m 77   OVIS^f 23

Db 5231 + 5394   (117)

        *49-wo / ra-to   OVIS^m 81   OVIS^f 19

          Not du-wo.

77

Db   5272   (117)
.A   ]   ki-ri-jo-te
.B   ] OVIS^m 40   OVIS^f 60

Db   5274 + 8238 + 8681 + <u>frr</u>.   (117)
      ]OVIS^m 195   OVIS^f 5

Db   5310 + 6062 + 8375   (117)
.A   OVIS^m 76   OVIS^f 24
.B   e[?]jo , / ku-ta-to ,
         .A 24 corrected from 2$\underset{.}{5}$?

         .B Perhaps only <u>e-jo</u>, if the mark between <u>e</u> and <u>jo</u>
             is accidental; if not, perhaps <u>e-qa-jo</u>.

Db   5352 + 5589 + 7095 + 7275 + <u>fr</u>.   (117)
      ko-ti ,/ ku-ta-to   OVIS^m 80   OVIS^f 20

Db   5359 + 5565 + 7214   (117)
.A   u-ta-jo   OVIS^m 111   OVIS^f 19
.B   [.]-ma-na-so , / ra-su-to

Db   5367 + 6063   (117)
      u-ro$_2$ / ra-to   OVIS^m 57   OVIS^f 23
         57 certain.

Db   5385   (117)
      ]OVIS^f 44
         Trace of a half-erased ruling.

<u>Db</u>   5390   (117?)
      ]OVIS^f 32

Db   5399   (117)
.a   ]O$\underset{....}{VIS}$^{m} 45   OVIS^f 5
.b   ]ra

Db 5680   (117)

.A]   OVIS^m 125   OVIS^f 25

.B]   e-ra

Db 5714   (117)

.A] OVIS^m 58   OVIS^f 2

.B]su-ri-mo

     .A Or 56.

Db 5715 + 7274 + 7942 + 8374 + <u>fr</u>.   (117)

.a   OVIS^m[   ]

.b   . .]-ti-jo / da-*22[-to   ]OVIS^f 15

Db 7107 + 8380 + 8427   (117)

.A   ]   OVIS^m[ ]31   OVIS^f 9

.B da-]wo ,   [[<u>pa</u> OVIS^m [   ]]]

     .A Room in the lacuna for 91.

Db 7108 + 8417   (117)

.A] OVIS^m [ ]4   OVIS^f 24

.B   ]ja

Db 7118 + 7229 + 7881   (117)

.A]   OVIS^m 78   OVIS^f 22

.B]ma / qa-na-no-to

Db 7164 + <u>fr</u>.   (117)

.A   ]   OVIS^m 100   OVIS^f 11

.B u-]ta-jo-jo

     .A Trace before OVIS^m :]to ?

Db 7172 + 8364 + <u>fr</u>.   (117)

.A   OVIS^m 89   OVIS^f 11

.B i-pa-[.] / ra-su-to

Db 7211   (117)

      ] OVIS^f 12

         Traces of erasure.

Db 8352   (117)

      si-ra-ko / ra-ja   OVIS^m 176   OVIS^f 24

      OVIS^f perhaps over [[OVIS^m]].

Db 8360 + <u>fr</u>.   (117)

      ]-zo , / ra-su-to   OVIS^m 92 / OVIS^f 8

Dc

Dc 926   (117)

  .A   ] OVIS^m 129   <u>pe</u> OVIS 1 [

  .B   ]pu-so   [

      .A OVIS changed from [[OVIS^f]] (intended for OVIS^m?).
           129 perhaps over erasure ; erasure after 1.

      .B <u>so</u> over [[<u>ri</u>]] .

Dc 1117   (117)

  .A   da-mi-ni-jo   OVIS^m 50

  .B   wa-*86-re / ku-ta-to   <u>pe</u> OVIS^m 50

Dc 1118   (117)

  .A   da-mi-ni-jo   OVIS^m 77

  .B   wa-du-na-ro / ku-ta-to ,   <u>o</u> OVIS^m 23

      .B <u>du</u> possibly over erasure.

Dc 1122 + 7685 + <u>fr</u>.   (117)

  .A   da-mi-ni-jo ,   OVIS^m 30

  .B   a-nu-ko / ku-ta-to ,   <u>pe</u> OVIS^m 20

Dc 1129   (117)

  .A   u-ta-jo   OVIS^m 37

  .B   po-ro-u-te-u / da-*22-to ,   <u>o</u> OVIS^m 63

      .A 37 corrected from 38.

Dc 1130   (117)

.A   u-ta-jo   OVIS^m 80

.B   ta-ra-to-no , / da-*22-to ,   o̱ OVIS^m 20

Dc 1148   (117)

.A   ]   OVIS^m 95   p̱e̱ OVIS^m 5

.B   ]ma-ro , / da-*22-to

        Traces of erasure ; perhaps palimpsest.

Dc 1154 + 7683   (117)

.A   we-we-si-jo-jo   OVIS^m 91

.B   wo-*82-ni-jo , / da-wo , o̱ OVIS^m 9

Dc 1167 + 7194 + 7666   (117)

.A   we-we-si-jo-jo   OVIS^m 157   [

.B   da-ja-ro , / di-ro ,   o̱ OVIS^m 1 [

        .A we-we-si-jo over erasure.

Dc 1203 + 1476 +5358   (117)

     pa-ja-so , / ra-ja   OVIS^m 130   o̱ OVIS^m 3̱0

        3̱0 : perhaps only 2̱0, but this a little less likely.

Dc 1220 + 5811 + 7277   (117)

     da-ra-mu-ro , / *56-ko-we   OVIS^m 89   p̱e̱ OVIS^m 11

Dc 1228 + 1455   (117)

.A   OVIS^m 7̱1

.B   no-da-ro / *56-ko-we , p̱e̱ OVIS^m 29

Dc 1270   (117)

.A   OVIS^m 92

.B   a-ku-di-ri-jo / e-ko-so   o̱ OVIS^m 4̱8

        .B 5̱8 not impossible, with the fifth ten on the rim
           o̱f the edge (possible trace).

81

  .a   ki-ri-jo-te

  .b   a-te-mo , / e-ra ,   OVIS^m 93 <u>pe</u> OVIS^m 7

Dc 1303   (117)

  .A   a-te-jo   OVIS^m 50   [

  .B   de-ni-mo , / do-ti-ja , <u>o</u> OVIS^m 50   [

             Text doubtless complete at right.

Dc 1337 + 1393   (117)

  .A   a-te-jo   OVIS^m 70[

  .B   ku-ka-no , / pu-na-so , <u>o</u> OVIS^m 30 [

Dc 1359 + 1387   (117)

  .A   OVIS^m 87 <u>pe</u> OVIS^m 13 [

  .B   e-ra-to , / *56-ko-we ,   [

Dc 1364 + 1397   (117)

  .A   OVIS^m 99 <u>pa</u> OVIS^m 1[

  .B   se-me-tu-ro / e-ra   [

Dc 1369 + 7156   (117)

  .a   ] u-ta-jo

  .b   ] ra-ja , OVIS^m 80 <u>o</u> OVIS^m 20

Dc 1419 + 5078   (117)

  .A   OVIS^m 42 <u>pe</u> OVIS^m 58

  .B   da-*83-jo

Dc 1515 + 5682 + 5713 + 8237 + <u>fr.</u>   (117)

  .A   OVIS^m 48 <u>o</u> OVIS^m 2

  .B   qi-nwa-so , / da-wo , ki-ri-jo-te

Dc 5030   (117)

     ]OVIS^m 50 <u>o</u> OVIS^m 80[

Dc 5190 + 7157 + 8194   (117)
  .A   ]   OVIS^m 80   [
  .B   ]de-a-ta , / *56-ko-we   pe OVIS^m 20   [

Dc 5228 + 5261 + 5419 + 5571   (117)
  .A   OVIS^m 46
  .B   wo-wo , / ku-ta-to   pa OVIS^m 4
            pa over [[o]] .

Dc 5250 + 5396   (117)
        ]OVIS^m 128   pa OVIS^m[

Dc 5392 + 5410 + 5676   (117)
  .A   ]   OVIS^m 70   [
  .B   ]o OVIS^m 130[

Dc 5587 + 7217 + 7234   (117)
  .A   ]   OVIS^m 93   [
  .B   ]*56-ko-we ,   pe OVIS^m 7   [

Dc 5677 + 5706 + fr.   (117)
  .A   OVIS^m 60   pe OVIS^m 40
  .B   pu-ra-so / ru-ki-to

Dc 5687 + 7154 + 7209 + 8414 + 8683   (117)
  .A   ]   a-te[-jo] OVIS^m 35
  .B   ]to-ro / se-to-i-ja ,   o OVIS^m 65
         .B]to-ro probably complete at left.

Dc 5771   (117)
        ] , *56-ko-we ,   OVIS^m 90   pe OVIS^m 10

Dc 7161 + 7179 + 8365 + fr.   (117)
  .A   u-ta-jo-jo ,   OVIS^m 94   [
  .B   [.]-to , / ku-ta-to   o OVIS^m 6
         .B Trace of erased numerals under and after 6.

83

7

Dc 7163 + 7210   (117)

.a   ki-]ri-jo-te
.b   ]OVIS^m 90   o̲ OVIS^m 10

Dc 8080   (= 7067 bis)   (117)

.A   ] [[OVIS^m]] pe-ko   OVIS^m 20
.B   ] ru-ki-to   p̲a̲ OVIS^m 10
          .B Perhaps 2̲0̲.

Dc 8354   (117)

.A   OVIS^m 97   p̲e̲ OVIS^m 3
.B   du-to / r̲u-ki-to

Dd

Dd 659 + 1252 + 7278   (117)

.A   ]   <OVIS^m> 69   OVIS^f 30 [
.B   ]ke-me-de , / tu-ni-ja , p̲a̲ OVIS^m 1

Dd 1106 + 1489 + 5591   (117)

.A   ]   OVIS^m 175   OVIS^f 15 [
.B   ]re-me-to , / su-ri-mo   p̲a̲ OVIS^m 10

Dd 1144 + 8416 + 8513   (117)

.A   ] OVIS^m 70   OVIS^f 210[
.B   ]̣, e-r̲a , u-ta-jo-jo , p̲a̲ OVIS^m 1[
lat. inf.]   ki-ri-jo-te[

Dd 1149   (117)

.A   OVIS^m 34   OVIS^f [
.B   e-u-ko-ro , / da-*22-to , p̲a̲ OVIS^m 1[
          .A 34 over another erased number (tens and units);
              OVIS^f probably also over erasure.

Dd 1150   (117)

.A   ]   OVIS^m 70   OVIS^f 29
.B   ]qa-ra-su-ti-jo / da-*22-to   p̲a̲ OVIS^m 1

Text doubtless complete at left.

.A Further 30 erased at right of 70 ; 70 altered from 90?

Dd 1157   (117)

.A   we-we-si-jo-jo   OVIS^m 56   OVIS^f 42

.B   a-wo-ti-jo / pa-i-to ,   pa OVIS^m 2

     .A 42 corrected from 44.

Dd 1171   BM (117)

.A   OVIS^m 20   OVIS^f 72

.B   po-ro / pa-i-to   pa OVIS^m 8

Dd 1193 + 5370   (117)

.A   ]   OVIS^m 132   OVIS^f 56

.B   ]du-ro , / ra-to ,   pa OVIS^m 12

Dd 1201   (117)

.A   OVIS^m 34   OVIS^f 60

.B   du-ni , / ra-ja   pa OVIS^m 6   [[pe OVIS^m 4]]

     .A 60 over [[OVIS^f [ ]2]].

Dd 1207 + 2024   (117)

.A   OVIS^m 77   OVIS^f 22[

.B   o-ne-u , / ri-jo-no ,   pa OVIS^m 1 [

     Nothing lost at right.

Dd 1218   (117)

.A   OVIS^m 48   OVIS^f 46

.B   o-wi-ro / *56-ko-we   pa OVIS^m 6

Dd 1244 + fr.   (117)

.A   ] OVIS^m 74   OVIS^f 25

.B   ] , tu-ri-so   pa OVIS^m 1   [

     Complete at left, but surface completely burnt.

     .A 5 of 25 over erasure.

Dd 1271 + 1356   (117)

  .A   OVIS^m 86   OVIS^f 13

  .B   du-ni , / e-ko-so ,   <u>pa</u> OVIS^m 1

Dd 1281   (117)

  .A   OVIS^m 87   OVIS^f 11

  .B   pa-ti , / ru-ki-to , <u>pa</u> OVIS^m 2

Dd 1283   (117)

  .A   OVIS^m 69   OVIS^f 36

  .B   qa-ṣa-ko / ru-ki-to <u>pa</u> OVIS^m 5

     .B <u>qa-ṇi-ko</u> not completely excluded, but less likely.

Dd 1284   (117)

  .A   OVIS^m 71 OVIS^f 27

  .B   wi-su-ro , / ru-ki-to , <u>pa</u> OVIS^m 2

        .A 27 corrected from 28.

Dd 1286   (117)

  .A   OVIS^m 74   OVIS^f 20

  .B   u-wa-ta / ru-ki-to , <u>pa</u> OVIS^m 6

        Traces of erasure all over tablet.

Dd 1291   (117)

  .A   OVIS^m 50   OVIS^f 46

  .B   qi-zo / ru-ki-to   <u>pa</u> OVIS^m 14

Dd 1296 + 7158   (117)

  .A   OVIS^m 97 OVIS^f 12

  .B   ma-ra-pi-jo / ru-ki-to <u>pa</u> OVIS^m 1

 v.   a

     .A OVIS^f 12 over erasure.

Dd 1300   (117)

  .A   OVIS^m 34 OVIS^f 60

  .B   ra-u-ra-ta / do-ti-ja   <u>pa</u> OVIS^m 6

Dd 1306   (117)

.A   OVIS^m 43   OVIS^f [

.B   ku-ke-so / do-ti-ja   <u>pa</u> OVIS[^{m}

Dd 1342   (117)

.A   ]ra-to-jo   OVIS^f 30

.B   ]pa-i-to   OVIS^m 267   <u>pa</u> OVIS^m 3

Dd 1366 + 5360   (117)

.A   ]   OVIS^m 72   OVIS^f 27

.B   ]na / da-wo   <u>pa</u> OVIS^m 1

Dd 1374   (117)

.A   ]   OVIS^m 72   OVIS^f 24

.B   ]ri-jo-no   <u>pa</u> OVIS^m 4

Dd 1376 + 5288   (117)

.A   OVIS^m 70   OVIS^f 51[

.B   po-me , / pu-na-so   <u>pa</u> OVIS^m 21[

         Small circular mark, apparently deliberate, visible
         between <u>po-me</u> and OVIS^m.

         .B Faint mark to left of <u>po</u>, but probably accidental.

Dd 1380 + 7151 + 8608   (117)

.A   ]   OVIS^m 108   OVIS^f 8

.B   ]te-ru-ro / da-*22-to   <u>pa</u> OVIS^m 4

         Text almost certainly complete at left.

Dd 1402 + 1593 + 2007   (117)

.A   OVIS^m 52   OVIS^f 46[

.B   wi-da-ka-so , / su-ri-mo   <u>pa</u> OVIS^m 2   [

Dd 1425 + 5388 + <u>fr</u>.   (117)

.A   OVIS^m 80   OVIS^f 16

.B   ke-*83-*18   <u>pa</u> OVIS^m 4

         .A 16 corrected from 17.

87

Dd 1429 + 5264 + 5327   (117)

.A]   u-ta-jo   OVIS^m 54   OVIS^f 43

.B   ]za-ra-ro / pa-i-to   <u>pa</u> OVIS^m 3

Dd 1468 + 5210 + 7123   (117)

      a-te-i-ja-ta / ku-ta-to   OVIS^m 40   OVIS^f 51[ ]/ <u>pa</u> OVIS^m [

        <u>pa</u> OVIS^m written below 51[; 51[over [[OVIS^f]] .

Dd 1579 + 1586 + <u>fr</u>.   (117)

.A]   we-we-si-jo   OVIS^m 62   OVIS^f 36 [

.B   ]ti / da-ra-ko   <u>pa</u> OVIS^m 2 [

Dd 1592 + 5199 + 5598   (117)

.A   OVIS^m 32   OVIS^f 62

.B u-ta-no / ra-to   <u>pa</u> OVIS^m 6

        .A 32 corrected from 34 ; 62 corrected from 66.

        .B Perhaps divider after u-ta-no.

Dd 2010 + 5180 + 5266   (117)

.A   OVIS^m 57   OVIS^f 28

.B di-ka-ta-ro / su-ri-mo ,   <u>pa</u> OVIS^m 15

Dd 5012   (117)

.A OVIS^m]20   OVIS^f 79   [

.B   ]ra <u>pa</u> OVIS^m 1   [

Dd 5174 + 5215   (117)

.A]   OVIS^m 78   OVIS^f 10[

.B   ]da-na-ro , / pa-i-to   <u>pa</u> OVIS^m 6 [

Dd 5262 + <u>fr</u>.   (117)

.A] OVIS^m 75   OVIS^f 24

.B] ,   <u>pa</u> OVIS^m 1

Dd 5268   (117)

.A]3   OVIS^f 40[

.B   ] <u>pa</u> OVIS^m 1[

88

Dd 5344 + 5408   (117)

.A   ] OVIS^m 90[ ] OVIS^f 22

.B   ] su-ri-mo <u>pa</u> OVIS^m 2

Dd 5383 + 8411   (117)

.A   OVIS^m]88 OVIS^f 10[

.B   ]ja   <u>pa</u> OVIS^m 1   [

Dd 5692   (117)

.A   ]OVIS^m 34   OVIS^f[

.B   ]   <u>pa</u> OVIS^x[

      .A OVIS^m over [[OVIS^f]] .

Dd 7105 + 7159   (117)

.A   ]   OVIS^f 27

.B   ]so OVIS^m 101   <u>pa</u> OVIS^m 2

      Whole tablet over erasure.

Dd 7106   (117)

.A   ]36   OVIS^f 8   [

.B   ]<u>pa</u> OVIS^m 6   [

Dd 7170   (117)

.A   ] OVIS^m 38   OVIS^f 60[

.B   ] <u>pa</u> OVIS^m 1   [

De

De 1084   (117)

.a   a-ka-i-jo

.b   ko-ti / pa-i-to ,   OVIS^m 34   OVIS^f 4   <u>o</u> OVIS^m 2

De 1109   (117)

.A   ]   u-ta-jo   OVIS^m 79 OVIS^f 21[

.B   ]te-to / ku-ta-to   <u>o</u> OVIS^m 100

De 1112   (117)

  .A   OVIS^m 57   OVIS^f 23

  .B a-ko-mo-ni-jo , / ku-ta-to   <u>o</u> OVIS^m 20

De 1136 + 1358 + 5202   (117)

  .A]   u-ta-jo   OVIS^m 58   OVIS^f 32

  .B]we-ra-to , / e-ko-so   <u>o</u> OVIS^m 10

          Text probably complete at left.

De 1138 + 7645   (117)

  .A   u-ta-jo-jo OVIS^m 103   OVIS^f 88

  .B si-ta-ro / da-wo   <u>o</u> OVIS^m 9

De 1141   (117)

  .A]OVIS^m 188 OVIS^f[

  .B]ra , u-ta-jo-jo , <u>o</u>[OVIS^m

De 1151   (117)

  .A   we-we-si-jo OVIS^m 264   OVIS^f 22

  .B su-di-ni-ko , / da-*22-to , <u>o</u> OVIS^m 14

De 1152   (117)

  .A   we-we-si-jo-jo OVIS^m 46 OVIS^f 22

  .B ko-ro , / da-*22-to ,   <u>o</u> OVIS^m 12

De 1153 + 7212   (117)

  .A   we-we-si-jo-jo , OVIS^m 75 OVIS^f 3

  .B da-ta-ja-ro / da-*22-to <u>o</u> OVIS^m 2

De 1231   (117)

  .A   OVIS^m 81   OVIS^f 17

  .B da-i-ta-ra-ro , / ti-ri-to , pe-ri-qo-te-jo , <u>o</u> OVIS^m 2

De 1254   (117)

  .A   OVIS^m 69   OVIS^f 19

  .B ku-ja-ro / qa-ra   <u>o</u> OVIS^m 12

De 1260 (117)

.A $OVIS^m$ 277 $OVIS^f$ 14

.B   ka-mi-ni-to / qa-ra   o͝ $OVIS^m$ 9

De 1264 + 5424 + 8234 (117)

.A $OVIS^m$ 48 $OVIS^f$ 41[

.B   qi-si-ta / qa-ra   o͝ $OVIS^m$ 11   [

De 1269 + 1408 (117)

.A $OVIS^m$ 48 $OVIS^f$ 44[

.B   ta-u-na-so / qa-ra ,   o͝ $OVIS^m$ 3[

De 1287 (117)

.A   ] $OVIS^m$ 80 $OVIS^f$ 38

.B   ]ka-wa-ro / ru̜-ki-to   o͝ $OVIS^m$ 82

      Text very probably complete at left.

De 1294 + 7221 (117)

.A $OVIS^m$ 20 $OVIS^f$ 10

.B   qe-da-do-ro , / ru-ki-to ;   o͝ $OVIS^m$ 70

     .B   qe-da-do-ro over erasure (and [[ro̜]] after -ro ,).

De 1301   ASHM (117)

.A   a-te-jo , $OVIS^m$ 28 $OVIS^f$ 22

.B   ja-ti-ri , / do-ti-ja,   o͝ $OVIS^m$ 50

De 1307 + 5685 + 8424 + frr. (3) (117)

.A   a-te-jo $OVIS^m$ 63[   ] $OVIS^f$ 14̤[

.B   a-ra-ko , / do-ti-ja   o͝ $OVIS^ṁ$ [   ]   vacat

De 1322 (117)

.A   pe-ri-]qo-te-jo $OVIS^m$ 59 $OVIS^f$ 7

.B   ]   o͝ $OVIS^m$ 34

De 1361 + 8240 (117)

.A   te-]ra-po-si-jo , $OVIS^m$ 80 $OVIS^f$ 8

.B   ]da-wo   o͝ $OVIS^m$ 12

91

De 1362 + 1473   (117)

.A   OVIS^m 170   OVIS^f 20
.B   a-nu-mo / qa-ra   o̲ OVIS^m 10
         .A 170 over erasure.

De 1371 + 1480 + 7115   (117)

.A   ]   te-ra-po-si-jo , OVIS^m 80   OVIS^f 8
.B   ]-to-ro-qa , / da-wo   o̲ OVIS^m 12

De 1381 + 1497 + 7963   (117)

.A   e-me-si-jo , OVIS^m 192 OVIS^f 8
.B   mo-qo-so / pu̲[   ]   o̲ OVIS^m 20
         .A OVIS^f 8 over [[OVIS^x]] .

De 1383 + 5679   (117)

.A   ]   u-ta-jo-jo ,   OVIS^m 66   OVIS^f 19
.B   ]r̲o̲ / ku-ta-to ,   o̲ OVIS^m 25

De 1398 + 7148 + 7155 + 7199   (117)

.A   OVIS^m 75   OVIS^f 5
.B   se-do , / ra-ja[   ]u-ta-jo ,   o̲ OVIS^m 20

De 1409 + 1617 + 5791   (117)

.A   OVIS^m 71   OVIS^f 2
.B   ta-de-so / e-ko-so   o̲ OVIS^m 47
         Most of tablet over erasures (probably [[e̲]] before
         the present one, certainly [[OVIS^m 40[ ]]] written
         full height between e̲-k̲o̲-s̲o̲ and OVIS^m).

De 1424 + 5023   (117)

.A   OVIS^m 57   OVIS^f 42
.B   ja-ra-to / qa-ra   o̲ OVIS^m 1

De 1510 + 7068 + 7265   (117)

.A   ]   a-te-jo   OVIS^m 93   OVIS^f 20
.B   ]o-ra / do-ti-ja   o̲ OVIS^m 7
         Text probably complete at left.
            .B Perhaps divider after]o̲-r̲a̲.

92

De 1585   (117)

.A   ] OVIS^m 110   OVIS^f 3

.B   ] ,   o̱ OVIS^m 37

       .A.B Traces at left; perhaps]t̤o̤ in .B.

De 1618 + 7171 + 7174 + fr̲.   (117)

.A   [   ]j̤o̤[ ]OVIS^m 47   OVIS^f 37   [[3]]

.B   ta-na-to , / e-ko-so ,   o̱ OVIS^m 16   [[2]]

      .A Perhaps [u̲-]t̤a̤-j̤o̤-j̤o̤.

De 1648   ASHM (117)

.A   we-we-si-jo-jo ,   OVIS^m 58 OVIS^f 2

.B   a-te-mo , / ku-ta-to   o̱ OVIS^m 50

De 5018 + 7980   (117)

.A   ]   OVIS^m 78   OVIS^f 14

.B   ]-so / do-ti-ja   o̱ OVIS^m 8

De 5032 + 5426 + 5564 + fr̲.   (117)

.A   OVIS^m 68   OVIS^f 31

.B   ta-di-*22-so , /   qa-ra ,   o̱ OVIS^m 1

De 5336 + 7201 + 7263   (117)

.A   ]   OVIS^m 6   OVIS^f 29̤[

.B   ]vest̲./ su-ri-mo , u-ta-jo-jo ,   o̱ OVIS^m 84[

De 5353 + 5380 + 5420   (117)

.A   ]5   OVIS^f 21[

.B   ku-]ta-to   o̱ OVIS^m 20

De 5405   (117)

.A   ]21   OVIS^f [

.B   ]   o̱[OVIS^m

      .B Traces to right consistent with OVIS^m.

De   6060   (117)
.A   pe-ri[-qo-te-jo]OVIS^m 165   OVIS^f 33
.B   pe-po-ro , / ri-jo-no[   ] o OVIS^m 2   [

De   7096 + 7653 + 7903   (117)
.A   OVIS^f 1
.B   a-ke-u / ra-ja   OVIS^m 97 [ ] OVIS^m 2 [
       .B Probably o OVIS^m.

De   7203 + 8230 + 8418   (117)
.A   ]u-ta-jo-jo OVIS^m 2   OVIS^f 13[
.B   ]e-ra   o OVIS^m 85   [

Df

Df   1119   (117)
.A   da-mi-ni-jo   OVIS^m 56   OVIS^f 16
.B   de-ke-se-u / ku-ta-to , pe OVIS^m 28

Df   1120 + fr.   (117)
.A   ]   da-mi-ni-jo   OVIS^m 40   OVIS^f 36
.B   ]u-*56 , / ku-ta-to ,   pe OVIS^m 24
         Text probably complete at left.
         .B 24 possibly over erasure.

Df   1121 + 7689   (117)
.A   da-mi-ni-jo ,   OVIS^m 143   OVIS^f 36
.B   ti-mi-za / ku-ta-to ,   pe OVIS^m 21
         .B pe over erasure, possibly [[o]].

Df   1187 + 7191   (117)
     ]ri-jo , / ra-to ,   OVIS^m 54   OVIS^f 42   pe OVIS^m '2['
         pe OVIS^m 4[not impossible.

94

Df   1210 + 8372   (117)

.A   OVIS^m 64   OVIS^f 20[

.B   ku-do / ri-jo-no ,   pe OVIS^m 1[

       .A Perhaps 30[.

Df   1219   (117)

.A   OVIS^m 8   OVIS^f 23

.B   ka-*56-no / *56-ko-we ,   pe OVIS^m 19

Df   1222 + 5393   (117)

.A   ]   OVIS^m 24[ ] OVIS^f 35

.B   ]de-a-ta / *56-ko-we   pe OVIS^m 40

Df   1223   (117)

.A   ]   OVIS^m 37   OVIS^f 51[

.B   ] vest. / *56-ko-we   pe OVIS^m 12 [

Df   1229 + 5222 + 5342   (117)

.A   OVIS^m 25   OVIS^f[

.B   a-ra-si-jo / *56-ko-we ,   pe OVIS^m[

Df   1230 + 1453   (117)

.A   OVIS^m 62   OVIS^f 20[

.B   ka-pte / *56-ko-we , pe OVIS^m 11[

       .B pe probably over erasure. 11 probably complete.

Df   1233   (117)

.A   OVIS^m 70   OVIS^f 27

.B   pu-nu-so / ti-ri-to   pe OVIS^m 3
                Palimpsest.

Df   1285   (117)

.A   OVIS^m 50   OVIS^f 24

.B   ta-de-so / ru-ki-to , pe OVIS^m 26

Df   1290   (117)

.A   OVIS^m 56   OVIS^f 4

.B   sa-sa-jo / ru-ki-to ,   pe OVIS^m 40

Df   1325 + 1494 + 5191 + 5267   (117)
 .A   OVIS^m 68   OVIS^f 25
 .B   a-re-ta$_2$ / su-ki-ri-ta ,   pe OVIS^m 3[
          .B 3[: perhaps 4̣[(i.e. 7 or 8 possible).

Df   1360 + 5304 + 7679   (117)
 .A   OVIS^m 36   OVIS^f 56
 .B   qe-ri , / do-ti-ja   pe OVIS^m 8

Df   1469 + 1584   (117)
 .A   OVIS^m 70   OVIS^f 3
 .B   a-si-wi-jo / ru[-ki-]to   pe OVIS^m 17

Df   1589   (117)
 .A   ]   OVIS^f 56[
 .B   ] pe OVIS^m 7
          .A Probably 5̣7.

Df   <1591>   (-)
 .A   ]pe OVIS^m 50   OVIS^f 8
 .B   ]   vacat
          Missing; text (suspect) from Evans' papers.

Df   1602 + 5196 + 5229 + fr.   (117)
        te-mi , / ra-to   OVIS^m 48   OVIS^f 44   pe OVIS^m 8

Df   5182 + 5783   (117)
 .A   ]   OVIS^m 23   OVIS^f 69
 .B   *56-]ko-we ,   pe OVIS^m 8
          .A 23 corrected from 25 or 26.

Df   5211 + 5313 + 5381   (117)
        ku-jo , / ra-to ,   OVIS^m 40   OVIS^f 52   pe OVIS^m 8

96

Df 5238 + 5269   (117)

.A]OVIS^m 32   OVIS^f 61   pe OVIS^m 5[

.B]   ki-ri-jo-te

   .A 7 possible at end.

Df 5260 + 5348   (117)

.A   ]18   OVIS^f 52[

.B] tu-ni-ja ,   pe OVIS^m 10   [

   .B pe over erasure, perhaps [[pa]] ; 10 over [[1]] ,
       perhaps [[2]] or [[3]] .

Df 5275 + 5581 + 7078   (117)

   ]ti / ri-jo-no   OVIS^m 81   OVIS^f 16   pe OVIS^m 3

Df 5391 + 5395 + 5658   (117)

.A] OVIS^m 110   OVIS^f 40[

.B] su-ri[-mo]   pe OVIS^m 4   [

   .B Perhaps pa[or o[.

Df 5406 + 8371   (117)

.A]   pe OVIS^m [

.B]jo-[.]/, ra-su-to OVIS^m 31   OVIS^f 62[

Df 7173 + frr.   (117)

.A   OVIS^m 62   OVIS^f 24

.B   si[   ] / [. . .]   pe OVIS^m [   ] 4

Df 7188 + fr.   (117)

.A]1   OVIS^f 44[

.B]   pe OVIS^m 2 [

Dg

Dg 1101   (117)

.A   OVIS^m 29   OVIS^f 45

.B   qa-i-po , / su-ri-mo , pe OVIS^m 2   o OVIS^m 24

Dg 1102   (117)

.A   OVIS^m 47   [ ] OVIS^m 52[
.B   a-tu-ko / su-ri-mo   pa OVIS^m 1

Dg 1107   (117)

.A   ]   OVIS^m 76   OVIS^m[
.B   ]to / su-ri-mo ,   pa OVIS^m 1   pe OVIS^m[
        .B Possibly]u / . Over erasure, from su- to end.

Dg 1158   (117)

.A   we-we-si-jo ,   OVIS^m 63   OVIS^f 25
.B   a-ni-ja-to , / pa-i-to ,   pa OVIS^m 2 o OVIS^m 10
            .B 10 corrected from 12.

Dg 1235 + 5400   (117)

.A   OVIS^m 66   OVIS^f 16
.B   qa-ra$_2$-ti-jo / ti-ri-to   pe OVIS^m 16   o OVIS^m 2

Dg 1278   (117)

.A   OVIS^m 55   OVIS^f 11
.B   ti-ja / ru-ki-to   pa OVIS^m 4   pe OVIS^m 30
            .A 55 apparently changed from [[66]] : scribe first
            included OVIS^f with OVIS^m?

Dg 1280   (117)

.A   OVIS^m 39   OVIS^f 11[
.B   si-ni-to / ru-ki-to   pa OVIS^m 10   pe OVIS^m 40 [

Dg 1316   (117)

.A   OVIS^m 60   OVIS^f 30
.B   si-ta-ro , / qa-mo , pa OVIS^m 8   pe OVIS^m 2[

Dg 1318   (117)

.A   ]   OVIS^m 92 pa OVIS^m 4
.B   ]ta-ro, / qa-mo   o OVIS^m 4

Dg 1438 + 1604 + 5387   (117)

.A   OVIS^m 50   OVIS^f 15

.B   ru-ma-no / su-ri-mo   pa OVIS^m 2   pe OVIS^m 3

Dg 5280 + 5401   (117)

.A   ]31   OVIS^f 50[

.B   ] pa OVIS^m 7   pe OVIS^m 1[

    Probably same tablet as Dv 5200.

Dh

Dh(1) 1240   (117)

.A   ne ki OVIS^m 82   pe OVIS^m 18

.B   ko-ku , / ti-ri-to ,

Dh(1) 1243   (117)

.A   ]   ki OVIS^m 100   [[OVIS^f]]

.B   ]e-to , / tu-ri-so

Dh(1) 1406 + 5678 + 8046 + fr.   (117)

.A   ki OVIS^m 75   pe OVIS^m 10[ ] vacat

.B   su-ma-no /ti-ri-to [vestigia ?   ] vacat

Dh(2) 1646 + 7919   ASHM/IR (120)

    ka-ni-to , / e-ko-so , ki OVIS^m 10[

    1646 Ashmolean ; 7919 Iraklion.

    Cut at left.

Dh(2) 7128 + 8618   (-)

    ] u-ta-no , ki OVIS^m [

Dh(2) 7231   (120)

    ]-so , ki OVIS^m[

Dk

Dk(1)   671   (120)

     OVIS^m] 120   LANA 28 o̱ LANA 1[
     Perhaps traces of OVIS^m at left.
     Graffito on verso.

Dk   727   (117?)

  .A   ]   e-ko-so OVIS^m 100   LANA [
  .B   ]da-ro , /   X   LANA [

<u>lat. inf.</u>   ]a$_3$ [
     .B Traces after LANA possibly 10[.

Dk(1)   920 + 7294 + 7330   (120)
  .a   ]   ko-ma-we-to
  .b   ]ni-ja-so / da-*22-to   OVIS^m 60   LANA 8   o̱ LANA 7

Dk(1)   925   (120)

     ]ko-we-jo   OVIS^m 1̤0̤[
     Trace of sign at left, probably majuscule.

Dk(1)   931 + 7293   (120)
  .a   ]   ko-ma-we-to
  .b   ]da / sa-jo ,   OVIS^m 100   LANA 28
     Cut at right.

Dk(1)   936   (120)

     qi-ta-ro , / da-ra-ko   OVIS^m 25   LANA 1[
     Cut at left.

Dk(1)   945   (120)

  .a   ]   <u>vestigia</u>
  .b   ] <u>vest.</u> /ku-mo-no pa-ro   OVIS^m 110 LANA 8   o̱ LANA 19
     Cut at right.
     .a Perhaps]we̤-r̤o̤ or]we̤-t̤o̤.
     .b 10 after 100 looks like an afterthought.

Dk(1) 951   (120)
       ] OVIS^m 130   LANA 26   o̲[LANA

Dk(1) 964   (120??)
.A   v̲a̲c̲.[
.B   da-to-ro / su-r̤i[-mo
                Cut at left.
                .B d̲a̲-̲t̲o̲-̲r̲o̲ over erasure.

Dk(1) 969   (120??)
.A   ]   si-ja-du-we , [
.B   ]ki-to / a-ko-ra[
                .A Over erasure . Trace at left.

Dk(1) 1049   (120)
.a   ] ko-ma-w̲e-te[
.b   ] ra-su-to   [

Dk(2) 1064   (119)
.A   X OVIS^m 100   LANA 7 M 1
.B   a-te-i-ja-ta / ku-ta-to   LANA 17 M 2

Dk(2) 1065   (119)
.A   X OVIS^m 100   LANA 11 M 1   [
.B   ka-da-no / ku-ta-to   o̲ LANA 13 M 2   [

Dk(2) 1066   (119)
.A   ]   k̲i̲ n̲e̲ X OVIS^m 200   LANA 19
.B   ]t̤e-u / ku-ta-to [   ] v̲a̲c̲a̲t̲

Dk(2) 1067 + 5189   (119)
.A   k̲i̲ n̲e̲ X OVIS^m 100   LANA 6 M 2
.B   a-ko-mo-ni-jo / ku-ta-to   [v̲e̲s̲t̲i̲g̲i̲a̲]
                Cut at left.
                .B o̤ L̤A̤N̤A̤ K̲T̲^2 (Bennett); upright stroke after
                    k̲u̲-̲t̲a̲-̲t̲o̲ consistent with o̲ ; this is followed
                    by a disturbed area, and marks perhaps consistent
                    with LANA are detectable in the upper and lower
                    part of this ; possibly [[o̲ LANA]] , but perhaps
                    no trace of following numer̄al.

                                101

Dk(2) 1068   (119)

  .A]   ku-ta-to   OVIS^m 114   LANA 26

  .B]-*49-so /   X   o̲ LANA 2

        .B *49̲ over erasure.

        Perhaps traces on the verso.

Dk(2) 1069   (119)

  .A]   X̲ OVIS[^{m} 100]LANA 19

  .B]ku-ta-to   [ ] o̲ LANA 6

Dk(2) 1070   (119)

  .A]   X OVIS^m 100   LANA 7

  .B]za-ra-ro / ku-ta-to   o̲ LANA 18

        .B Perhaps]-za-ra-ro̲.

Dk(2) 1071   (119)

  .A   X OVIS^m 50   LANA 6

  .B wo-wo / ku-ta-to   o̲ LANA 6 M 1

Dk(2) 1072   (119)

  .A   X OVIS^m 100 LANA 13 M 1

  .B ka-te-u / ku-ta-to   o̲ LANA 11 M 2

        .B ka-te-u̲ over erasure.

Dk(2) 1073   (119)

  .A   X OVIS^m 50   LANA 6 M 2

  .B ka-mi-ni-to / ku-ta-to   o̲ LANA 5̣ M 2

        .B Perhaps 5̣ corrected from 6.

Dk(2) 1074   (119)

  .A   X OVIS^m 100   LANA 19

  .B e-ru-to-ro / ku-ta-to ,   o̲ LANA 6

Dk(2) 1075   (119)

  .A   X OVIS^m 100   LANA 10[

  .B di-ra-qo / ku-ta-to   o LANA 12[

          Cut at left.

Dk(2) 1076   (119)

  .A   X OVIS^m 200   LANA 31[

  .B ti-mi-za / da-mi-ni-jo   o LANA 16[

          .A Perhaps 3̣2[.

Dk(2) 1077 + 5292   (119)

  .A   X OVIS^m 100   LANA 5[

  .B i-ke-se-ra / da-mi-ni-jo   o LANA 10[

          .A Perhaps 6̣[.

Dk(2) 1320   (119)

  .A] X OVIS^m 100   [

  .B] da-mi-ni-jo   o [LANA

Dk(2) 1399   (119)

  .A]   X OVIS^m[

  .B]se-u , / da-mi-ni[-jo

Dk(2) 1491   (119?)

      wa-du-na-ro[

Dk(2) 1565   (119)

  .A]LANA 24   [

  .B]LANA 2   [

Dk(2) 1567   (119)

  .A]   LANA 6[

  .B] o LANA 12[

Dk(2) 1613 + 5597 + fr.   (119)

  .A]ku-̣ta-to OVIS^m 123   LANA 30 M 1[

  .B]   X   [

Dk(1)   2129   (120?)

      ]o LANA 9[

Dk(1)   5183   (120)

      ? LANA]1   o LANA 20[

Dk(2)   5201 + 5281   (119)

  .A   ]   X OVIS^m 100[

  .B   ]ka-ta-wo / da-mi-ni-jo o[LANA

             .A Perhaps 102[or 103[.

             .B Perhaps o LANA[.

Dk(2)   5233   (119)

  .A   ]   X OVIS^m [

  .B   ]ku-ta-to [

Dk 5403 + 5562   (117?)

  .A   ] OVIS^m 98   LANA 19 M 2

  .B   ]OVIS^m 2 o LANA 4[

          .A Perhaps only LANA 16.

Dk(1)   5464   (120)

      ]5   LANA [

      Trace at left (perhaps]35).

Dk(2)   5566   (119)

  .A   ]OVIS^m 100   LANA 9

  .B   da-mi-]ni-jo   o LANA 16

Dk(1)   5731   (120)

      ]1 o LANA 38 [

Dk(1)   5733   (120)

      ]8   LANA 21   o LANA[

Dk(1)   5768   (120)

      ]70   LANA 14 / o LANA[

Dk(1) 7117   (120)

   ]OVIS^f 80   LANA[

Dk(1) 7144   (120?)

   .A]40   LANA 14[
   .B]   OVIS^m 20   [

Dk(2) 7204 + 8534   (119)

   .A]   OVIS^m 50[
   .B da-]mi-ni-jo   [

Dk(1) 7295   (120)

   ]OVIS^m 100   LANA 18[

Dk(1) 7297   (120)

   ]4   o LANA 7[
           Possibly cut at right.

Dk(1) 7299   (120)

   ]45   LANA 4
           Cut at right.

Dk(1) 7300   (120?)

   ]ru-wo   LANA [

Dk(1) 7301   (120)

   ] LANA 21[

Dk(1) 7303   (120)

   ]LANA 9 [

Dk(1) 7304   (120)

   ]OVIS^m 50   LANA[

Dk(1) 7306 + 7831   (120)

   ]56   LANA 9[
           Or perhaps only 4[if the two lower strokes are
           accidental or erased.

105

Dk(1) 7308   (120)
    ]50   LANA 10[

Dk(1) 7311   (120)
    ]OVIS^m 200   LANA [

Dk(1) 7313   (120)
    ]4   LANA 4̣[

Dk(1) 7314   (120)
    ]OVIS^m 100   LANA 1̤0[

Dk(1) 7315   (120)
    ] o̲ LANA 4
        4 over erasure.

Dk(1) 7316   (120)
    ]30   LANA 1̤4[
        Perhaps]7̣0.

Dk(1) 7322   (120)
    ]4̣5   LANA [

Dk(1) 7323   (120)
    ]6   LANA[

Dk(1) 7325   (120)
    ]o̲ LANA 3

Dk 7327   (-)
    ]LANA 12 o̲ [LANA

Dk(1) 7328   (120)
    sup. mut.
    ] o̲ LANA [

Dk(1) 7329   (120)
    ]2̤0̤   LANA [

Dk(1) 7781   (120)
    ] LANA 20[

Dk(1) 7899   (120?)
    ]LANA 2̤   o̲[LANA

Dk(1) 7902   (120?)
  .a]   a[
  .b]-ki-ro / <u>vest</u>.[

Dk(1) 8018   (120?)
    ]LAN̤Ạ̤ 7

Dk(2) 8209   ASHM (119)
  .A]   X OVIS^m 30[
  .B]a-nu-ko / da-mi-ni-jo [

Dk(2) 8403   (119?)
  .A]2̤2
  .B] <u>vacat</u> ?

Dk(1) 8463   (120?)
    ]4̤   o̲ LANA 4̤[

Dk(1) 8464   (120)
    ]LAṆ̤Ạ̤ 20 /   o̲ LANA[

D1

D1 47   ASHM (-)
  .1]e-ke , e-u-da-i-ta   OVIS^f 39̤[
  .2]ki-u-ro , / su-ki-ri-ta-pi <u>o ki</u> OVIS 15 [
      .1 [[O̤V̤ỊS̤^{x}]] under <u>e</u> of <u>e-u-da-i-ta</u>.
      .2 <u>o ki</u> OVIS 15 over erasure.

107

v. Graffito

lat. inf. Traces of erasure.

D1(1) 412   (118)

.A   ]   sa-qa-re-jo   OVIS^f 50   [
.B   ]da̤ / ka-ru-no   o ki̤ OVIS^m 50   [
     .B]ṛọ less likely.

D1(1) 413   (118)

.A   ] ki̤ OVIS^m 30   LANA 2[
.B   ]   o LANA 2[
     .A Perhaps erased units before LANA.

D1(1) 414 + 6016   (118)

.A   ]OVIS^f 140   LANA 12   [
.B   o]OVIS^f 60   o ki̤ OVIS^m 200   o LANA [

D1(1) 463   (118?)

.A   OVIS^f 46   ki̤ OVIS 5   LANA 5 M 1
.B   mi-ti / ku-ta-to o OVIS$^{f.}$ 35   o ki̤ OVIS 45 o LANA 10 M 2
     Cut at right. Most numerals on this text indistinct,
     some possibly erased.
     .A Perhaps 4̤5̤, 5̤5̤ or 6̤5̤.

D1(1) 790   (118)

.A   ] OVIS^f 60   [[   ]] WE [
.B   ]e-ko-so   ki̤ OVIS^m 25   o ki̤ OVIS^m 32[
     .A Possibly [[o ỌVỊṢ^{f}]] .

D1(1) 791   (118)

.A   ] OVIS^f 70   o OVIS^f 10   WE̤[
.B   ]e-ko-so   ki̤ OVIS^m 35   o ki̤ OVIS^m[

D1(1) 792 + 7619   (118)

.A   ]   OVIS^f 50   [?   ] vacat [
.B   ]o-ku / e-ko-so   ki̤ OVIS^m 44   o ki̤ OVIS$^m_.$[

108

D1(1)   794 + 7069 + 7292   (118)

.A   ]sa-qa-re-jo   OVIS^f 43   LANA 3 M[

.B   ]*56-ko-we-e o̱ OVIS^f 7   o̱ ki̱ OVIS^m 50   o̱[LANA ?

D1(1)   916   (118)

.A   OVIS^f 50   [[   ]] WE̱[

.B di-ta-ka-so / e-ko-so ki̱ OVIS^m 10   o̱ ki̱ OVIS^m 40[

        .A Perhaps [[o̱ OVIS^x [ ]]].

D1(1)   928   (118)

.A   ]   ra-wo-qo-no-jo   OVIS^f[

.B   ]*56-na-ro /   da-wo   ki̱ OVIS^x[

        .A qo̱ over erasure.

        .B]a̱-na-ro less likely. Probably OVIS^f[or
           OVIS[(cf. D1 1060).

D1(1)   930 + 7284 + 7290 + 7333 + 8002   (118)

.A   ]   po-ti-ni-ja-we-jo OVIS^f 50   LANA 3 M [

.B   ]ma-di-qo / si-ja-du-we   o̱ ki̱ OVIS^m 50   o̱ LANA 6 M 2[

D1(1)   932 + 963 + 7291 + 7871   (118)

.A   sa-qa-re-jo / a-ko-ro , e-pe-ke OVIS^f 40 [ ] LANA[

.B qa-ra$_2$-ro / ma-so-mo   o̱ ki̱ OVIS^m 40
                                             o̱ LANA 5 [

D1(1)   933 + 968 + 975   (118)

.A   ]   po-ti-ni-ja-we-jo OVIS^{f}40   LANA 3 o̱ LANA 9

.B   ]-*83-re-to,/ si-ja-du-we   o̱ OVIS^{f}20   o̱ ki̱ OVIS^m 60

        .B Perhaps]ko̱-*83-re-to.

D1(1)   934 + 7082   (118)

.A   ]   OVIS^f 17   o̱ OVIS^f 19   WE̱ 6

.B   ]ja / e-ko-so ki̱ OVIS^m 6   o̱ ki̱ OVIS^m 24
        .A Perhaps only 16 corrected from 17.

D1(1)   935 + 942   (118)

.A   ]   sa-qa-re-jo   OVIS^f 27   LANA 2   o̱ LANA 11[

.B   ]nu-ka , / da-ta-ra-mo o̱ OVIS^f 43   o̱ ki̱ OVIS^m 70   [

109

D1(1)   938   (118)

.A   ]re-jo   OVIS^f 50   <u>ki</u> OVIS^m 40   LANA 7
.B   ]   <u>o</u> <u>ki</u> OVIS^m 10   <u>o</u> LANA 3
     .B   Trace at left, perhaps]<u>to</u> .

D1(1)   939   (118)

.A   ]LANA 2   M 2
.B   ]<u>o</u> LANA 5   M 1

D1(1)   940   (118)

.A   ]   sa-qa-re-jo   OVIS^f 60   LANA[
.B   ]so / ẹ-ra   <u>o</u> <u>ki</u> OVIS^m 60   LANA[

D1(1)   943   (118)

.A   po-ti-ni-ja-we<-jo>   OVIS^f 90   LANA 11
.B   a-ko-i-da / qa-nwa-so   <u>o</u> <u>ki</u> OVIS^m 90 <u>o</u> LANA 7̣
     .B   7̣ perhaps corrected from 8 (or eighth stroke
          accidentally erased).

D1(1)   944   (118)

.A   sa-qa-re-jo OVIS^f 60   LANA 5 M 2   <u>o</u> ḶAṆ̣Ạ̣[
.B   ta-mi-de-so ,/ e-ra   <u>o</u> OVIS^f 40   <u>o</u> <u>ki</u> OVIS^m 100   [

D1(1)   946 + <u>fr</u>.   (118)

.A   po-ti-ni-ja-we-jo   OVIS^f 70   LANA 7
.B   ke-u-sa / si-ja-du-we ,   <u>o</u> <u>ki</u> OVIS^m 70   <u>o</u> LANA 7

D1(1)   947 + 7626   (118)

.A   e-se-re-e-jo   OVIS^f 80   <u>ki</u> OVIS^m 10   LANA 11 [
.B   si-da-jo / ma-ri   <u>o</u> <u>ki</u> OVIS^m 70   <u>o</u> LANA 5 [

D1(1)   948 + 977   (118)

.A   sa-qa-re-jo   OVIS^f 20   LANA 2[ ] <u>o</u> LANA 8
.B   pa-za-ti / ma-ri   <u>o</u> OVIS^f 30 <u>o</u> <u>ki</u> OVIS^m 50

D1(1)   949 + 7145 + 7660   (118)

.A   e-se-re-e-jo   OVIS^f 40   LANA 2   [
.B   i-pe-ta / su-ri-mo   o OVIS^f 20   o ki OVIS^m 60   [
        .A Trace at right, perhaps o[LANA .

D1(1)   950   (118)

.A   po-ti-ni-]ja-we-jo OVIS^f 50   LANA 5   [
.B   si-ja-du-]we o ki OVIS^m 50   o LANA 5   [

D1(1)   952   (118)

.A   ]jo   OVIS^f 40   LANA 5
.B   ] o ki OVIS^m 40   o LANA 3

D1(1)   1046 + 7281   (118)

.A   ]e-se-re-e-jo   OVIS[^{f}]20   LANA[
.B   ]ra-su-to   o ki OVIS^m 50   LANA 3[

D1 1060   (215)

.A   ]   OVIS^f 50 ki OVIS 10   LANA 6[
.B   ]-ra   o ki OVIS 15   LANA 1   [

D1 2021   (215)

.A   ] 27   LANA 1[
.B   ] o OVIS^f 23   LANA 2[
        .A Trace at left consistent with OVIS or OVIS^f.
        .B Trace at left.

D1 5530   (-)

.1   ]   LANA [
.2   ] vacat   [
        .1 Trace of signs, perhaps erased, at left.

D1 5535   (-)

.1   ]2   LANA 12[
.2   ] vacat [
        .2 Perhaps [[LANA]] .

111

D1 7071 -   (218)

.A]   ri-jo-no OVIS^f[   ] LANA [   ] <u>vac.</u>
.B]no /   <u>o</u> OVIS^f 30   <u>o</u> LANA 4

D1(1) 7072   (118)

.A] <u>WE</u> 40
.B]4 <u>o</u> <u>ki</u> OVIS^m 26

D1 7075   (-)

.A]   OVIS^f 100[
.B]-u-ko / u-ta-no   <u>ki</u>[

D1(1) 7076   (118)

.A]   <u>WE</u> 20
.B]9 <u>o</u> <u>ki</u> OVIS^m 41
        Probably erasures before <u>WE</u>.

D1(1) 7085 + 7332   (118)

.A] LANA 3 M 2   <u>o</u> LANA 11[
.B   ]<u>ki</u> OVIS^m 77
        .A LANA 3 over erasure.

D1(1) 7086   (118)

.A]OVIS^f 80   <u>WE</u> 40[
.B]ẹ-ko-so <u>ki</u> OVIS^m 60 [[to-sa-wa]] <u>o</u> <u>ki</u> OVIS^m[
        .A Over erasure.

D1(1) 7092   (118)

.A] <u>WE</u> 70
.B] <u>o</u> <u>ki</u> OVIS 25
        Cut at right.
        .B 5 over erasure.

D1 7114 + 7129   (218)

.A]no OVIS^f 20 [ ] <u>vac.</u>[
.B]   <u>o</u> OVIS^f [   ] <u>o</u>[

112

D1 7116   (-)

  .A   ] OVIS^f 50 LANA[

  .B   ] ki OVIS^m 20[

         .B Trace at left, probably]to ( ]o less likely).

D1 7125   (-)

  .A   ]   OVIS^f 40[

  .B   ]to / ri-jo-no o OVIS^f 20 o[

D1(1) 7132 + 7279   (118)

  .A   ] OVIS^f 50   LANA 6

  .B   ]OVIS^m 50 o LANA 4

D1(1) 7138 + 7671 + 7864   (118)

  .A   sa-qa-re-jo OVIS^f[

  .B a-ko-ro / ra-ja   o ki OVIS^m[

D1(1) 7141 + 7264 + 7971 + 7984   (118)

  .A   ]   sa-qa-re[-jo   ]vest.[

  .B   ]ti-za / *56-ko-we-e   o ki OVIS^m 50[

      .A vest. : perhaps foot of OVIS^f.

      .B Trace of an erased sign before ti, which is itself
         over [[i]].

D1(1) 7147 + 7851   (118)

  .A   ] po-ti-ni-ja-we-jo OVIS^f[

  .B   ] ka-ru-no   o ki OVIS^m[

      .B Trace at left.

D1(1) 7238   (118)

  .A   ] OVIS^f 30[

  .B   ] OVIS^x 10[

     inf. mut.

D1(1) 7249 + 7282   (118)

  .A   ]OVIS^m 20 LANA 6 M 1

  .B   ] o LANA 3 M 2

D1(1) 7283   (118)
.A   ] LANA 6 [
.B   ]o̱ LANA 3 M[
          .A Trace at right, possibly M̱[.

D1(1) 7287   (118)
.A   ] <u>vacat</u>   [
.B   ]LANA 6 M 2 [

D1(1) 7288   (118)
.A   ]5   [
.B   ] o̱ LANA[

D1(1) 7503 + 7683 + 7847   (118)
.A   po-ti-ni-ja-we-jo   OVIS[^f
.B   te-wa-jo , / si-ja-du-we   o̱[

D1(1) 7721   (118)
.A   ]e̱-se-ṟe̱-e̱-jo̱   OVIS^f [
.B   ]ma̤-so-mo   o̱ ki̱ OVIS[^m

<u>D1(1)</u> 7771   (118?)
.A   ]   po-ti-ṇi̱[-ja-we-jo
.B   ]qo-ta , / ra-ja   [

D1(1) 7905   (118)
          <u>sup. mut.</u>
.A   ]<u>vest</u>.[
.B   si-]ja̱-du-we   o̱[

D1(1) 7959   (118)
.A   ]   sa-q̱a[-re-jo
.B   ]o̱ / [
          <u>inf. mut</u>.

D1(1) 8103   (118)
.A   ]   OVIS^f 60[
.B   ]ṟo̱ / e-ko-so [
          .B Or]da̱. Traces to right consistent with ki̱ OVIS^m.

<u>D1(1)</u> 8177   (118?)
.A   <u>vac</u>.[
.B   pa-re / e[-ko-so

114

D1 8216   BM (215)

.A   ]   LANA 3 M [
.B   ]18 <u>ki</u> OVIS^m 25 [

     V-shaped mark crossing central dividing line to left:
     probably the remains of a deleted <u>ki</u>.

D1(1) 8217   BM (118)

.1   ]6 [
.2   ]1 M 1 [

     .1 Trace of sign at left, possibly]LANA.

D1 8229   (215?)

    ] LANA 12[

    <u>inf. mut.</u>

Dm

Dm 1174 + 5265   (117)
.A   a$_3$-mi-re-we   OVIS^m 2
.B   ri-jo-no / e-ka-ra-e-we ,   OVIS^m 20

Dm 1175 + 1456   (117)
.a   a$_3$-mi-re-we   OVIS^m 4
.b   ra-su-to , / e-ka-ra-e-we   OVIS^m 10

Dm 1176 + 5375 + 5616 + 5833   (117)
.A   a$_3$-mi-re-we ,   OVIS^m 5 [
.B   ku-ta-to , / e-ka-ra-e-we ,   OVIS^m 61[

Dm 1177   (117)
.A   a$_3$-mi-re-we ,   OVIS^m 3
.B   ru-ki-to / e-ka-ra-e-we   OVIS^m 24

v.   OVIS^m 100   6
    v. Lower line of possible six on edge.

9

Dm 1178   (117)

  .A   ] a_3-mi[-re-we

  .B]vest./ e-ka-ra-e-we[

Dm 1179 + 5364   (117)

  .A   ] a_3-mi-re-we OVIS^m 5

  .B ku-]ta-to , / e-ka-ra-e-we OVIS^m 67

Dm 1180 + 5048   (117)

  .A a_3-mi-re-we , OVIS^m 4

  .B pa-i-to / e-ka-ra-e-we OVIS^m 20

Dm 1181 + 1431   (117)

  .A a_3-mi-re-we , OVIS^m[

  .B do-ti-ja , / e-ka-ra-e-we OVIS^m [

      .B e-ka over erasure.

Dm 1182   (117)

     to-u-na-ta , / e-ka-ra-e-we OVIS^m 21

Dm 1183 + 5227   (117)

     e-ka-ra-e-we / ku-ta-to [

Dm 1184 + 8408   (117)

  .a   e-ka-ra-e-we

  .b]to , / o-we-to , o-pa , OVIS^m 15

Dm 5181   (117)

     *56-ko-we-i / e-ka[-ra-e-we

Dm 5226 + 5290 + 8189   (117)

     e-ko-so , / e-ka-ra-e-we OVIS^m 10

Dm 5237 + 5277   (117)

  .A] a_3-mi-re-we OVIS^m 4

  .B]ra-to / e-ka[-ra-e-]we OVIS^m 24

     .A Or 3.

Dm 5323 + 5374 + 8629 + <u>frr</u>.   (117)

.A   ]   a₃-mi-re-we   OVIS^m 2
.B   ]e-ka-ra-e-we   OVIS^m 15

Dn

Dn 1088   (117)

    ]OVIS^m 19300[

Dn 1089 + 1414 + 5373   (117)

    ]su-ri-mo   OVIS^m 2390

Dn 1090   (117)

.1   ] OVIS^m 2040[
.2   ] OVIS^m 2040[

        .2 Second thousand over erasure; fourth (lowest) ten
            stroke shows trace of erasure, perhaps accidental.

Dn 1092 + 5379 + <u>fr</u>.   (117)

.1   e-ko-so   OVIS^m 2252   [
.2   su-ki-ri-ta OVIS^m 517   [

        Text doubtless complete at right.
            .1 2252 or 2262.

Dn 1093   (117)

.1   da-*22-to   OVIS^m 1370
.2   *56-ko-we-i OVIS^m 2003

        Perhaps palimpsest.

Dn 1094 + 1311   (117)

.1   pa-i-to OVIS^m 1509
.2   da-wo   OVIS^m 2440

        .1 Last hundred and 9 over erased numerals
            (certainly [[80]] and probably units).

117

Dn 1095   (117)

  .1   ]1222   [

  .2   ]2290   [

Dn 1096 + 1336   (117)

  .1   ra-ja   OVIS^m 904

  .2   pu-na-so   OVIS^m 330

Dn 1200   (117)

  .1   do-ti-ja [OVIS^m

  .2   ra-su-to [OVIS^m

Dn 1209   (117)

  .1   ri-jo-no   OVIS^m 2000[

  .2   ra-to   OVIS^m[

Dn 1319 + 5307 + 5568   (117)

      a-]mi-ni-si-ja , <u>ne</u> OVIS^m 11900[

Dn 2016 + 8407   (117)

      ]-jo-jo OVIS^m [

        Shape of break perhaps favours]<u>si</u>-jo-jo[. Perhaps
        2000 after OVIS^m.

Dn 5014 + 5386   (117)

      ] OVIS^m 3103[

        Perhaps trace of sign at left, not incompatible with]<u>to</u>.

Dn 5015 + 5194   (117)

  .1   ti-ri-to ,   OVIS^m 1000[

  .2   qa-ra ,   OVIS^m 1000[

Dn 5286 + 5362   (117)

      ]ka-ta   OVIS^m 4000   [

Dn   5318 + 8388   (117)

.1   ru-ki-to   OVIS^m 4140[

.2   pu-ṣo   OVIS^m 1034   a-ka OVIS^ṃ[

   .1   Traces between 4000 and 40 unclear; perhaps 100
      rather than another 1000.

   .2   Certainly not e-.

Dn   5559   (117)

.1   u-ta-no[OVIS^m

.2   qa-mo [OVIS^m

Dn   5668 + fr.   (117)

   ]qo-te-jo   OVIS^m 3300[

Do

Do   919 + 921   (106)

.A   ki pe OVIS^m o [OVIS^m

.B   wi-da-ma-ro / se OVIS^f 100   za OVIS^m [

Do   923   (106)

.A   ki OVIS^x[

.B   to-wi-no /   se OVIS^f 100   o OVIS^m [

Do   924 + 7563 + 7869   (106)

.A   ki pe OVIS^m o OVIS^m 20[

.B   tu-da-ra /   se OVIS^f 100   za OVIS^m [

Do   927   (106)

.A   ]   pe OVIS^m 19

.B   ]se OVIS^f 100   ki za OVIS^m 30   o OVIS^m 31

   Cut at right. Second half of text probably over erasure.
   ki larger sign than za; it extends well above the centre
   of the tablet, and evidently qualifies both registers
   which follow.

Do 929   (106)

  .A]   <u>ki</u> <u>pe</u> OVIS^m <u>o</u> OVIS^m 80
  .B]OVIS^f 100

        Cut at right.
        .B 100 over erasure.

Do 996 + 7235   (106)

     ]i-mi-so <u>se</u> OVIS^f 100[

     Palimpsest.

<u>Do</u> 1054   (106?)

  .a   se-to-i-ja   [
  .b ko-te-u / ka-to-ro , OVIS^f[

     Cut at left.

Do 5010 + 7084   (106)

  .A   <u>ki</u> <u>pe</u> OVIS^m 10 <u>o</u> OVIS^m 30
  .B wo-ro-to / <u>se</u> OVIS^f 100 <u>za</u> OVIS^m

        .A <u>pe</u> OVIS^m and <u>o</u> OVIS^m over erasure.
        .B <u>se</u> over erasure, [[<u>da</u>]] or [[<u>se</u>]] .

Do 5720   (106)

  .A]   <u>ki</u> <u>pe</u> OVIS^m[
  .B] OVIS^f 100   <u>za</u> OVIS^m[

     Traces of erasure at left.

Do 5740   (106)

     ] OVIS^f 100   [

     <u>inf. mut.</u>

Do 5770   (106)

     ]OVIS^f 100   <u>ki</u>[

Do 7079   (106)

     ]OVIS^f 100   <u>ki</u> OVIS 50

     Cut at right.

Do 7087   (106)

.a   se-to-]i-ja
.b   ]ro̤   OVIS^f 100   k̲i̲ OVIS 50
          Cut at right.
          .b Possibly]d̤a̤. Text from OVIS^f to end over erasure.

Do 7093 + 7253   (106)

.A   ]   k̲i̲ OVIS^x[
.B   ]s̲e̲ OVIS^f 100   o̲[

Do 7120   (106)

.A   ]   k̲i̲ OVIS^m 2[
.B   OVIS^f]1̤0̤0̤   z̲a̲ OVIS^m 5   [

Do 7239   (106)

      ] OVIS^f 100[

D̲o̲ 7613   (106?)

.a   se-to-i̤[-ja
.b   a-di-ri-jo / ka-to-r̤o̤[

D̲o̲ 7740   (106?)

.a   ]   se-to-i-j̤a[
.b   ]-ta / ka-to-r̤o̤[
          .b]k̲e̤̲-ta or]d̲e̤̲-ta.

Dp

Dp 43   (-)

      ]ta-re-wo OVIS^m LANA[
          ]t̲a̲-r̲e̲-w̲o̲ probably over erasure.

Dp 699   (-)

.a   ]ku-su-pa-ta , n̲e̲   [
.b   to-]s̤a̤   OVIS^m LANA[

121

<u>Dp</u> 937 + 8047   (-)

    ]   LANA 180

    Traces at left, perhaps $OVIS^f$, but rather doubtful.

    Traces of erased ruling ([[.1.2]]).

<u>Dp</u> 997 + 7206   (118)

  .a]   po-ti-ni-ja-we-ja   [

  .b]to-sa , / ne-wa , po-ka $OVIS^f$[LANA

<u>Dp</u> 1061   (117?)

    ?to-]sa / pa-i-ti-ja $OVIS^x$ LANA 456[

    $OVIS^f$ not impossible ($OVIS^m$ impossible).

<u>Dp</u> 2004 + <u>fr</u>.   (215?)

    ]-jo $OVIS^m$ LANA 2[

  v.   ]   [[90]][

<u>Dp</u> 5508   (117?)

    ? to-]sa / ko-no-si[-ja ?

    Possibly same tablet as X 2011, cf. Dp 1061.

Dp 7135   (-)

    <u>sup. mut.</u>

    ] $OVIS^m$ LANA 10[

Dp 7280   (120)

  .1]$OVIS^m$ LANA 50   [

  .2]$OVIS^f$ LANA 36[

Dp 7742   (-)

  .1   ? pe-ru-si-]nwa , po-ka   [

  .2   ]po-ti-ni-ja-we-i-jo[

Dq

Dq(3)   42   (217)

  .a   ]   pe-ri-qo-ta-o   [

  .b   ]jo , / ma-sa ,   OVIS^m[

Dq(3)   45   (217)

  .a   ]   a-ṇọ-qo-ta-o   [

  .b   ]mo , / e-ra   OVIS^m[

Dq(3)   46   (217??)

  .A   ]   pe-ri-qo-ta-o [

  .B   ]ṇọ / e-ko-so   [

Dq(4)   438   (106)

  .a   ]   se-to-i̯-ja

  .b   ]to-i-ja , / ka-to-ro   OVIS^m 100

          Cut at right.

Dq(1)   439 + 5469 + 5762   (121)

  .A   da-*22-to   OVIS^m 50

  .B i-ti-nu-ṛị / o-re-te-wo o͟ OVIS^m 50

       .B -ṛị abnormal and doubtful, perhaps unfinished.

Dq(1)   440   (121)

  .A   ]   e-ra OVIS^m 120[

  .B   ]ka-mo / a-no-qo-ta o͟ OVIS^m[

Dq(1)   441   (121)

  .A   ]   da-*22[-to

  .B   ]qo-si-jo / o-re[-te-wo ?

Dq(3)   442 + 5991   (217)

  .a   ]ke-u-po-da-o   [

  .b   ]ku-ta-to   OVIS^m 100[

          Traces at right.

123

Dq(3) 445   (217?)

.a   ]ko-we-jo   [
.b   ]d̤ạ-*22-to   OVIS^m[

Dq(1) 447   (121)

.A   ]   da-mi-ni-jo   OVIS^m 40[
.B   ]-ta-wo /   o̱ OVIS^m 34[
         .B]ḵạ-ta-wo and]g̤e-ta-wo possible.

Dq(1) 448   (121)

.A   ]   u-ta-no[
.B   ]ni-to   [

Dq(1) 449   (121)

.A   ]-jo   OVIS^m 70
.B   ]OVIS^m 30

Dq(1) 672   (121)

.A   ]OVIS^m 130   [
.B   ]   o̱ OVIS^m 10 [

Dq(4) 686   (106?)

.a   se-to-i-ja   [
.b   te-ki-ri-ne-to / ka-to-ro OVIS^m[
         Cut at left. Traces of erasure.
         .b -r̲i̲- inserted after the rest of the word was written.

Dq(3) 1026 + 7273   (217)

.a   wi-]jo-qo-ta-o   [
.b   ]ta   OVIS^m 100[

Dq(2) 1234 + 7261 + 7266   (216)

.A   ]   OVIS^f 122
.B   ]ro-ru / ti-ri-to OVIS^m 75   o̱ OVIS 3
         .A Trace of ruling (erased) immediately above existing
             ruling.
         .B Text certainly complete to left. o̱ OVIS error for
             o̱ OVIS<m>?

124

Dq(2) 1377 + <u>frr</u>.(3)   (216)

      pa-[.]-to / ti-ri-to   OVIS^m 50

Dq(2) 1603 + 7083   (216)

.A   ]   OVIS^m 26 OVIS^f 34

.B   ] <u>vest</u>. , / ti-ri-to   <u>pa</u> OVIS^m 10

      .B <u>pa</u> possibly over erasure (perhaps [[<u>o</u>]]).

Dq(1) 1803   (= 47 bis)   (121)

.A   da-mi-]ni-jo OVIS^m 30[

.B   ]<u>o</u> OVIS^m 30[

      .B Possible traces of two further tens after 30[.

<u>Dq(2)</u> 5595 + 5638   (216?)

      ] ti-ri-to OVIS^m 151[

<u>Dq(2)</u> 7113   (216?)

.A]30 OVIS^f 30[

.B] <u>vacat</u>

      .B Perhaps]<u>ro</u> or, less likely,]<u>wo</u>.

Dq(3) 7119   (217)

.a]ta-o   [

.b]   OVIS^m 30[

      .b Trace at left; probably not]<u>wo</u>, possibly]<u>no</u>.

Dq(3) 7126   (217)

.a   ]ko-ta-o [

.b pa-]i-to   OVIS^m[

Dq(3) 7137   (217)

.a]ta-o   [

.b]to OVIS^m[

    <u>inf. mut.</u>

<u>Dq(2)</u> 7177   (216?)

    ] OVIS^f 2

125

<u>Dq(2)</u> 7260   (216?)

  .A   ]**2** OVIS^f 20   [
  .B   ]2

<u>Dq(3)</u> 7852   (217?)

  .a   ] wi-jo-qo[-ta
  .b   ]pa-i-to [

<u>Dq(1)</u> 8208   ASHM (121)

  .A   ]OVIS^m 110   [
  .B   ]jo <u>o</u> OVIS^m 20[

<u>Dq(3)</u> 8351   (217?)

  .a   ] pe-ri-qo[-ta-o
  .b   ] ,   qa-sa[

Dv

Dv 1085   (117)

  .a   a-ka-i-jo
  .b ki-mu-ko , / pa-i-to   OVIS^m 36   OVIS^f 10[

Dv 1086   (117)

  .A   ]   OVIS^m 100   OVIS^f[
  .B   ]ro / da-*83-ja , a-ka-ta-jo[

Dv 1100 + 8389 + 8430   (117)

  .A   OVIS^m]35 OVIS^f 25
  .B   ]   X
        .B Possible traces to left.

Dv 1103   (117)

  .A   ]   OVIS^m 110[
  .B   ]au-ri-jo / su-ri-mo[
        Text doubtless complete to left.

126

Dv 1104

.A $\qquad$ OVIS^{m} [

.B da-to-ro , / su-ri-mo[

$\qquad$ .A Probably traces of tens at right.

$\qquad$ .B Possible traces of erasure.

Dv 1111

.a $\qquad$ OVIS^{m} 44 / OVIS^{x}[

.b ri-wi-so , / ku-ta-to $\qquad$ [

Dv 1113 + 5221

.A $\qquad$ da-mi-ni-jo , OVIS^{m} 36[

.B ka-ta-wo / ku-ta-to , $\qquad$ [

Dv 1124

.A] OVIS^{m} 40[

.B]ta / ku-ta-to[

$\qquad$ .A Possibly over erasure.

Dv 1125 + 5321

$\qquad$ e-qa-ro / ku-ta-to [

$\qquad$ Perhaps trace of OVIS^{m} at right.

Dv 1128 + 5567

.A $\qquad$ OVIS^{m} 66 [ ]OVIS^{x}[

.B ka-da-no / ku-ta-to , $\qquad$ [

Dv 1133

.a] u-ta[-jo

.b]a-ke-u / e-ko-so OVIS^{m} 70[

$\qquad$ .b ke probably over erasure.

Dv 1139

.a] u-ta-jo-jo $\qquad$ [

.b]-ta , / da-*22-to , OVIS^{m}[

Dv 1142   (117)

.A   ]   u-ta-jo-jo   OVIS^m[

.B   ]-jo-ko / e-ko-so   [

Dv 1145   (117)

.a   ]   u-ta-jo-jo,   [

.b   ]ṣọ , / da-wo , OVIS^m 81   OVIS^f 11[

Dv 1146 + 1498   (117)

.A   ]   u-ta-jo-jo OVIS^m 40[

.B   ]-mo-ni-ja-ro / da-wo ,   OVIS^f 109 [

Dv 1169   (117)

.A   we-we-si-jo   OVIS^m 36   OVIS^f 16

.B   ka-to / da-ra-ko ,   ọ OVIS^f 68

v.   68̣
           .B Error for ọ OVIS^m?

Dv 1188 + 1484   (117)

.a   OVIS^m 30[

.b   sa-ma-ri-wa-ta , / ra-to[
           .a OVIS^m over erasure (possibly [[ụ̣]]).

Dv 1190 + 1444   (117)

      a$_3$-ke-wa-to , / ra-to   OVIS^m 84   OVIS^f 10[

Dv 1191 + fr.   (117)

.A   OVIS^m 110

.B   *56-du-nu-ka ,̣ / ra-to
           .B Possibly vestigia to right.

Dv 1192   (117)

.A   ]pẹ-ri-qo-te-jo   OVIS^m 6̣8̣   OVIS^x[

.B   ]ra-to   [

Dv 1199   (117)

      u-ra-jo / ra-su-to   OVIS^m 40[

Dv 1205 + 5206   (117)

   ]wi-ra-ne-to , / ri-jo-no   OVIS^m 130[
         Text certainly complete at left.

Dv 1206 + <u>fr</u>.   (117)

   .A   OVIS^m 63[ ]OVIS^f 20[
   .B   e-u-na-wo , / ri-jo-no [

Dv 1213   (117)

   .A   ]   OVIS^m 82[
   .B   ]-so / u-ta-no , [
            .B Traces to left: <u>to</u>, <u>po</u>, <u>jo</u> all possible.

Dv 1214 + 5273 + 5298   (117)

   .A   OVIS^m 52   OVIS^f 44[
   .B   mo-re / u-ta-no   [
            .A OVIS^m probably over erasure.

Dv 1215   (117)

   .A   ]   OVIS^m 90 [
   .B   ] <u>vest</u>. / u-ta-no ,   [

Dv 1216   (117)

   .A   OVIS^m [
   .B   *22-ri-ta-ro / u-ta-no[

Dv 1217 + 5331   (117)

   .A   ]   OVIS^m 78 [
   .B   ] <u>vest</u>. / u-ta-no ,   <u>o</u>[OVIS^m

Dv 1226 + 1357   (117)

   .A   OVIS^m 62   OVIS^f 10
   .B   a-ze-o , / *56-ko-we , OVIS^m 28
   v.   ȧ
            .B Error for <u>o</u> OVIS^m?

                          129

Dv 1237   (117)

  .A   OVIS^m 40[

  .B   ku-ta-si-jo / ti-ri-to [
                                 ..

Dv 1239   (117)

  .1   ]*34-so , 'da-*22-to'   OVIS^m 50   [

  .2   ] ti-ri-to   OVIS^m 50   [

            Text certainly complete at right.

Dv 1248   (117)

  .A   OVIS^m 84   OVIS^m 11[

  .B   ki-ri-ne-to / tu-ni-ja   pe OVIS^m 5

   v.   ru   ka
       .A OVIS^m 11[: apparently error for OVIS^f or o OVIS^m
           11[. Probably 11 [.

Dv 1249   (117)

  .A   OVIS^m 82   OVIS^f 12[

  .B   ra-o-no / tu-ni-ja   [

Dv 1255   (117)

  .A   OVIS^m 30[

  .B   me-ri-wa-ta , / qa-ra   [

Dv 1266   (117)

  .A   OVIS^m[

  .B   wi-je-mo / qa-ra[
                     ..
            .B -je-mo possibly over erasure.

Dv 1267 + 7175 + 7215   (117)

  .A   OVIS^m 93   OVIS^f 7[
                                 .
  .B   ko-ri-jo /   qa-ra ,   [

Dv 1272 + 5411   (117)

  .A   ko-ma-we-to   OVIS^m 19[
                                     .
  .B   a-ti-ro , / e-ko-so ,   o OVIS^m 71

                            130

Dv 1292 + 5701   (117)

.A   OVIS^m [   ] <u>vacat</u>
.B   mi-ta-qo , / ru-ki-to   [   ] <u>vacat</u>

Dv 1308 + 7686   (117)

.A   OVIS^m[
.B   te-ru-sa , / do-ti-ja[

Dv 1309   (117)

.A   ]   a-te-jo [
.B   ]wo-no , / do-ti-ja , [

Dv 1310   (117)

     ko-ru-to / da-wo[

Dv 1312 + <u>fr.</u>   (117)

.A   [
.B   su-ru-so / da-wo [

Dv 1328 + <u>fr.</u>   (117)

     ]*49-so , / ku-ta-to ,   OVIS^m 114 [
v.   ]   90   [

Dv 1330 + 1404   (117)

.A   OVIS^m 72[
.B   wi-na-jo , / e-ra , u-ta-jo[

Dv 1331   (117)

.a   ]   a-ka-ta-jo[
.b   ]mu-da / e
         .b <u>e</u>: word apparently left incomplete.

Dv 1332   (117)

.A   e-ra   OVIS^m[
.B   ta-we-si-jo , / pe-ri-qo-te[-jo

131

10

Dv 1334 + 5324 + 8393   (117)

.A   ]   ki-ri-jo-te   [
.B   ] vest. , / pe-ri-qo-te-jo , [
          .B Perhaps]ja.

Dv 1370 + 1488 + 7189   (117)

.a   u-ta-jo
.b   tu-*56-da-ro / e-ra[ ] OVIS^m 15   OVIS^m 85
          Perhaps traces of erasure.

Dv 1386   (117)

.a   vest.[
.b   ti-ri-to /qa[
          .a vest.:not OVIS^m, perhaps u[.

Dv 1388   (117)

.A   OVIS^m 76   OVIS^f[
.B   e-u-me-ta / ra-ja , pe-ri-qo-te-jo[

Dv 1394   (117)

.A   vac.[
.B   ku-ta-si-jo / [

Dv 1403   (117)

.A   vac.[
.B   wi-*65-te-u , / da[

Dv 1410 + 1514   (117)

.A   OVIS^m 91[
.B   ta-na-po-so , / pu-so   pe OVIS^m 2[
          Erased rule visible above existing rule.

Dv 1411   (117)

        ]ri-ja-ta , [

Dv 1412   (117)

        ]ri-di-ne-to[
          Over erasure.

<u>Dv</u> <1416>   (-)

      po-ro-ko[

        Missing; text from SM II.

Dv 1417 + 7097   (117)

  .A   ]   OVIS^m 49 <u>o</u> OVIS^m 30[

  .B   ]po-to / ru-ki-t<u>o</u> , u-ta-jo ,   [

Dv 1418   (117)

      po-ri-[

Dv 1420 + 7241   (117)

  .a   we-we-si-jo , [

  .b   da-ja-ro /   ru-ki[-to

Dv 1422   (117)

  .A   OVIS^m[

  .B   *56-ro$_2$ / s<u>u</u>[

      .B Not <u>ja</u>[(line in the middle accidental).

Dv 1427   (117)

  .a   pe-ri[-qo-te-jo

  .b   ke-me-u /   [

Dv 1428 + 5683   (117)

      ]ki-*18-i-s<u>o</u>[

        <u>inf. mut</u>.

        <u>ki</u> probably first sign of tablet.

Dv 1430   (117)

  .a]   we[

  .b]do-ro , / da-ra-ko[

Dv 1434 + 5691   (117)

  .a   o-pa-we-[

  .b   me-ki-ti , / ma-no-we[

        .a Possibly <u>o-pa-we-n̥o</u>[or <u>o-pa-we-r̥i̥</u>[.

133

Dv 1436 (117)

    ki-sa[

Dv 1439 (117)

 .a   te-ra̤[-po-si-jo
 .b ru-na-so , / qa[

Dv 1441 (117)

    ru-na[
        Possibly joins Da 1277.

Dv 1442 (117)

    ru-na-so[

Dv 1443 (117)

    a_3-ke-[

Dv 1447 + 7258 + 8379 (117)

    i-je-ro , / e-ko-so , [

Dv 1449 (117)

    ka-ni-to [
        Trace of a dividing line at right.

Dv 1450 + frr. (117)

 .A   vac.[
 .B ka-sa-ro / vest.[

Dv 1451 (117)

    ka-jo / ku[-ta-to
      ka-jo altered from ka[[-te-u]].

Dv 1454 (117)

 .a]   vest.[
 .b]no-qa-ta / vest.[

Dv 1457   (117)

  .A   ]   we[

  .B   ]ra-ne-to /   [

Dv 1459   (117)

    ra-wo[

Dv 1460 + 7150   (117)

  .a   u-ta-jo   [

  .b   ma-di-qo / da-wo   OVIS^m 30[

        .b Trace on right edge, perhaps another 10, so as to
        make a minimum of 50[.

Dv 1462   (117)

    a-wo-i-[

Dv 1465   (117)

    a-du-ru-po[

    Traces to right, perhaps of division into two lines.

Dv 1466   (117)

  .A   OVIS^m 40[

  .B   a-ze-ta /   e-ra[

Dv 1470   (117)

    a-ti[

    Perhaps <u>a-ti</u>-[or <u>a-ti</u> and beginning of division into
    two lines.

Dv 1471 + 5404   (117)

  .A   OVIS^m 42   OVIS^f 54

  .B   a-na-ki-ti , / ra-to , [   ]<u>pa</u> OVIS^m 4

Dv 1472   (117)

    a-ko-mo-ni[

<u>Dv</u> 1478   (117 ??)

    ]ta-u-na-[

      Perhaps]<u>ta</u>-u-na-<u>so</u>[.

135

Dv 1479 + fr.   (117)
     to-u-[
          Perhaps to-u-na̤[or to-u-to̤[.

Dv 1487   (117?)
     ko-no-si-ja , [

Dv 1490   (117)
     qa-si-da-ro / ku-ṭa̤[-to

Dv 1492 + 7099   (117)
     .A   OVIS^m 86   OVIS^f 4
     .B wo-*65-ṛọ / ru-ki-tọ [
          .A 4 corrected from 6 or 8.

Dv 1493   (117)
     ]ọ-ta₂[
          Probably complete at left.

Dv 1496 + 7228 + 7244   (117)
     .A   da-ṃị-ṇị-jo   OVIS^m[
     .B i-ke-se-ra , / ku-ta-to ,   pe OVIS^m[

Dv 1500 + 8316   (117)
     .A   vest.[
     .B qi-ja-zo / [
               .A a̤[or da̤[?

Dv 1501   (117)
     di-*79-nu[

Dv 1502 + 2017   (117)
     di-ki-nu-wo , / ra-ja[

Dv 1503 + 7183   (117)
     .A   da-*22-to OVIS^m 150[
     .B di-wo , / u-ta-jo-jo   [

                          136

Dv 1504 + <u>fr</u>.

.A   [OVIS^m]37   OVIS^f 3 [

.B   di-de-ro / <u>vestigia</u>

      .A Perhaps]67 and OVIS^f 6.

      .B Perhaps e[.

Dv 1505

    di-za-so[

      Perhaps <u>di-za-so</u> , [.

Dv 1506

    di-za[

Dv 1511 + 7193 + 7198 + <u>fr</u>.

.A   OVIS^m 51   OVIS^f 40[

.B   o-na-jo / tu-ni-ja ,   [   ]9   [

v.   si   [

Dv 1601

.A   ]   OVIS^m[

.B   ]we-wa-do-ro , / qa[

Dv 1607 + 5978 + 7276 + <u>fr</u>.

.A   ]   we-we-si-jo   OVIS^m 27   OVIS^f[

.B   ]ti-ro / pa-i-to   [

     .A Probably 37 or 47.

Dv 1621 + 5116

.a   pe-ko   [

.b   tu-ti / e[   ] OVIS^x[

Dv 2019 + 5681

.A   OVIS^m 40[

.B   de-we-ra , / ra-to   [

     Possibly same tablet as Dv 5412.

Dv 5049   (117?)

      po-ro-[
        Perhaps po-ro-ko[.

Dv 5052   (117)

  .A   ]50
  .B   ti-]ri-to
        .A Trace of probable base of OVIS^{m}.

Dv 5054 + 5080 + 7255   (117)

      sup. mut.
      sa-ma-ja-so / tu-ni-ja[

Dv 5075   (117)

  .A   ]   we-we-si-jo OVIS^{m} [
  .B   ]mo / pa-i-to ,   o[OVIS^{m}

Dv 5178   (117?)

      ]qa-sa[

Dv 5193 + 7205 + 7521   (117)

      wi-ra-ne / ku-ta-to[

Dv 5197   (117)

      ki-sa[

Dv 5198   (117)

  .A   ]   [
  .B   ]wi-na-jo , / ra[

Dv 5200 + 8601   (117)

  .A   [
  .B   ta-so / su-ri[-mo
        Probably same tablet as Dg 5280.

Dv 5203   (117)

    ]ki̤-sa-qo[

Dv 5209   (117)

    ]-jo / pu-so   OVIS^m[

v.   ]   60   [

    v. Perhaps over [[8ọ]] .

Dv 5213   (117)

.a   ]ki-r̤i̤-jo-te   [

.b   ]   ra-su-to   OVIS^m[

Dv 5219 + 5574   (117)

.A   ]   OVIS^m 290[

.B   ]ta-za , / su-ri-mo   [

Dv 5224 + f̲r̲.   (117)

.A   ]   OVIS^m[

.B   ]a-pa-ni-jo / [

Dv 5232 + 5686 + 8386   (117)

.A   ]   vestigia   [

.B   ]a-*56-no , / su-ki̤-ri-ta   [

Dv 5235 + 7196   (117)

    ]ku-ta-to   OVIS^m 123

Dv 5236 + 5329   (117)

.A   ]   OVIS^m 60[

.B   ]-jọ , / ra-to

    .B Perhaps]q̲ạ-j̲ọ or]w̲ọ-j̲ọ.

Dv 5241 + 5293   (117)

    a-pi-je-t̲ạ[

Dv 5248   (117)
     OVIS^m]100[

Dv 5252   (117)
     ] 100

Dv 5253 + <u>fr</u>.   (117)
     ]pu-so   OVIS^m 60[

Dv 5256 + 5300 + 5347   (117)
     a-ka-to , / ra-to   OVIS^m 48   OVIS^f 23[
          Perhaps 33[.

Dv 5258 + 8600   (117)
          <u>sup. mut</u>.
     ]pu-so   OVIS^m 50

Dv 5259 + <u>frr</u>.   (117)
     .A   ] OVIS^m 50
     .B   ] ru-ki-to

Dv 5271   (117)
     .A   ]6   OVIS^f 23
     .B   ]41
               .A 3 perhaps over erasure.

Dv 5278 + 5338   (117)
     .A   ]   OVIS^m 46 [
     .B   ]ma-we / qa-mo [

Dv 5279 + 5585   (117)
     .A   ]   OVIS^m 84   OVIS^f 14
     .B   ]jo / ri-jo-no [   ] OVIS^m 2

Dv 5285   (117)
     qa-ra-i[

Dv 5287   (117)
     ka-to , [

Dv   5291 + 5588.   (117)

   .A   ]   OVIS^m 64[

   .B   ]ri-ro / su-ri-mo [

            .B Trace of erased sign after -ro?

Dv   5294   (117)

      ru-ta$_2$ / ra[

Dv   5296 + 5365   (117)

   .a   u-ta-jo-jo ,   [

   .b   ru-*18 / e-ko-so , OVIS^m 100   OVIS^f 30[

            .b Perhaps 34[, and perhaps division into .A.B at the
                end of the tablet.

Dv   5297   (117)

   .A   ]   OVIS^m 80[

   .B   ]ti-jo / qa-mo   [

Dv   5301 + 7089 + 7958   (117)

      ]sa-zo / da-wo   OVIS^m 86[

Dv   5302   (117)

      ]wo-ti-jo / ku-ta-to[

Dv   5312   (117)

      wo-jo[

Dv   5315   (117)

      ]pu-so   OVIS^m 130[

Dv   5322 + 5377   (117)

      ]ro / [   ]to ,   OVIS^m 74[

Dv   5328 + 5376   (117)

   .A   ]   OVIS^m 62[

   .B   ]-ro , / ku-ta-to , [

141

Dv   5335   (117)

      <u>sup. mut.</u>

    ] , ku-ta-to[

    Trace at left.

<u>Dv</u>   5346   (117?)

    ta-pa[

Dv   5349   (117)

    ]nwa , / pu-so[

 v.   ]30   [

Dv   5350   (117)

      <u>sup. mut.</u>

 .A   ]<u>vest.</u> [

 .B   ]<u>vest.</u>/ su-ri-mo[

Dv   5357 + <u>fr.</u>   (117)

    u-ra-jo / ra-su-to   OVIS^m 200

Dv   5368 + 5371   (117)

 .A   ]34   OVIS^f 11

 .B   ] OVIS^m 25

         .B Trace of adjunct before OVIS^m.

Dv   5372 + 7230   (117)

 .A   ]99   OVIS^f 11 [

 .B   ]   <u>vacat</u>   [

Dv   5398 + 7207 + 8749 + <u>fr.</u>   (117)

 .A   ]   OVIS^m 66   OVIS^f 32[

 .B   ]ro , / ku-ta-to   [

        .A Possibly 67.

Dv   5407 + 8359 + <u>fr.</u>   (117)

    ] OVIS^m 100[

    <u>inf. mut.</u>

Dv 5412 + 8431   (117)

  .A   ] OVIS^f 8

  .B   ]<u>o</u> OVIS^m 10[
              Possibly same tablet as Dv 2019.

Dv 5413   (117)

     ]39[

Dv 5414   (117)

  .A   ]5

  .B   ] <u>vacat</u>

Dv 5416   (117)

  .A   ]4

  .B   ] <u>vacat</u>

<u>Dv</u> 5512   (117?)

     tu-ni̤[

Dv 5517   (117)

  .A   ]   OVIS^m[

  .B   ]-jo / ku[-ta-to

Dv 5579   (117)

     a$_3$-[

<u>Dv</u> 5580   (117?)

     *34̤[

Dv 5593   (117)

  .A   ]90 OVIS^f[

  .B   <u>inf. mut.</u>

<u>Dv</u> 5603   (117?)

     <u>sup. mut.</u>

     ta̤[

Dv   5618   (117)

    <u>sup. mut.</u>
    ]ku-i[

<u>Dv</u>   5640   (117?)

    ru[

Dv   5663   (117)

    si-pa-ta-do , [

Dv   5667   (117)

.A   ]   u-ta-jo-jo   OVIS^{m}[
.B   ]<u>vest.</u>/ tu-ni-ja   [

Dv   5675   (117)

.1   ]6
.2   ]2

Dv   5689   (117)

    ]ma-jo [
        Probably complete at left.

Dv   5690   (117)

    du-ni-[

Dv   5694 + <u>fr.</u>   (117)

.A   ]   OVIS^{m} 91 [
.B   ] ru-ki-to   [

Dv   5696 + 8331   (117)

.A   ][[OVIS^{m}]]   OVIS^{m} 106[
.B   ] u-ta-jo-jo   [
    .A Probably 108[.

Dv   5704 + 7180 + <u>fr.</u>   (117)

.A   OVIS^{m} 80[ ] OVIS^{f} 15
.B   ri-pa-[.] / ra-ja ,   [   ]3

144

Dv 5735   (117?)
    ku[

Dv 5775   (117)
    sup. mut.
    di[

Dv 5812 + 7993   (117?)
    su-po[
    inf. mut.
        Possibly su-po [or su-po-[.

Dv 5826   (117?)
    ]so[

Dv 5839   (117)
    ]so[

Dv 5841 + 7951 + fr.   (117)
    ]pẹ-ri-mo / da-wo OVIS^m[

Dv 5843   (117)
.A]   OVIS^m[
.B]ṭị / da-wo[

Dv 5934   (117)
    ] u-ta-jo [
    inf. mut.

Dv 5989 + 7224 + frr.   (117)
.A   we-we-si-jo[
.B je-zo , / da-ra-ko ọ OVIS^m 20[
        .A we-we-si-jo probably complete.

Dv 6018 + 8358 + fr.   (117)
.A   vac. [
.B ḳe[ ]na-ro , / tu-nị[-ja

145

Dv 6022   (117)

       <u>sup. mut.</u>

.a]   u[
.b]ṇo-to / da-[

       <u>inf. mut.</u>

Dv 6025   (117)

    ]da-wo   OVIS^m[

Dv 6045   (117)

    pu-ma-[

Dv 6054 + 8397   (117)

.A]OVIS^m 195   OVIS^f 35
.B] OVIS^m 70

Dv 6056   (117)

    ] pu-so   OVIS^m[

      Traces at left.

Dv 6057   (117)

    ] e-ko-so   OVIS^m [

      <u>e-ko-so</u> possibly over erasure.

Dv 6059   (117)

    no-sa-ro , / e-ko̤[-so

Dv 7098 + 7111 + <u>fr.</u>   (117)

.A] pe-ko   OVIS^m 42   [
.B   ]ṭi̤-ri-to ,   [

      Traces of erasure in both lines.

Dv 7124   (117)

.A] OVIS^f 60 <u>pe</u> OVIS^m[
.B   ] OVIS^x[

      <u>inf. mut.</u>

Dv 7140   (117)

  .A   ]   OVIS^m[
  .B   ]wo / e-ra   [
              .B Trace at right ($\underset{\cdot\cdot}{pa}$[?).

Dv 7142   (117)

        ]34 $\underline{pa}$ OVIS^m 3

Dv 7149   (117)

        ]OVIS^m 160[

Dv 7152   (117)

  .A   ]   OVIS^f 34
  .B   ]OVIS$\overset{m}{\underset{\cdots}{\cdot}}$ 6

Dv 7167   (117)

  .A   ]7   OVIS^f 46
  .B   ]7
              .B Traces to left perhaps consistent with OVIS^m.

Dv 7176 + 8281   (117)

  .a   ko-]ma-we-to   OVIS^m 20 [
  .b   ]e-ko-so   [

Dv 7181 + 7227   (117)

  .A   ]   OVIS^m 82   OVIS^f 14[
  .B   ]qa-na-no-to   [

Dv 7190 + 8704   (117)

  .A   ]OVIS^m 23   12[
  .B   ]$\underline{o}$ OVIS^m 50   [
              .A <OVIS^f> before 12[.

Dv 7195   (117)

        ]$\underset{\cdot\cdot}{12}$ OVIS^f 26[

147

11

Dv 7200   (117)

  .A   ]58 OVIS^f [

  .B   ]OVIS^m 30   [

       <u>inf. mut.</u>

Dv 7202 + 8231 + <u>fr</u>.   (117)

  .A   ] OVIS^m 89   OVIS^f 11

  .B   ]   <u>vacat</u>   [

<u>Dv</u> 7223   (117?)

  .A   ]220[

  .B   ]<u>vacat</u>[

Dv 7240 + 7688 + 7946   (117)

      ta-ja-no , / e-ko[-so

Dv 7245   (117)

  .A   ]-jo OVIS^m 100[

  .B   ] OVIS^x[

       <u>inf. mut.</u>

       .B Perhaps <u>o</u> OVIS^x[.

Dv 7246   (117)

       <u>sup. mut.</u>

  .A   ]3

  .B   ]OVIS 7

Dv 7248 + 7885   (117)

      ]qa-na-no-to OVIS^m 60[

Dv 7262   (117)

      ]OVIS^m 30[

Dv 7267   (117)

      <u>sup. mut.</u>

.A   ]<u>vest</u>.[

.B   ]pu-na-so[

Dv 7269   (117)

       <u>sup. mut.</u>

   ]na-ta / do-ti[-ja

      <u>inf. mut.</u>

Dv 7270   (117)

.A]OVIS^m [

.B <u>inf. mut.</u>

<u>Dv</u> 7272   (117?)

     <u>sup. mut.</u>

  ]OVIS^m 200[

Dv 7617 + <u>fr.</u>   (117)

.A   [

.B   te-jo / e-ko-so [

Dv 7678   (117)

   a$_3$[

<u>Dv</u> 7690   (117?)

   wa[

<u>Dv</u> 7694   (117?)

   si[

<u>Dv</u> 7697   (117?)

   pu[

<u>Dv</u> 7736   (117?)

.A   ]OVIS^m 5 o [

.B   ]15 o [

Dv 7777   (117?)

   ]me-tu[

Dv 7785   (117)

            sup. mut.
   .a   we-]we-si-jo[
   .b   da-]wo   [
            inf. mut.

Dv 7863 + 8373 + 8402 + fr.   (117)

   .A   ]   vestigia [
   .B   ]wo-ro-to / ru-ki-to [
            Perhaps cut at left.
            .A Perhaps OVIS^{m} 9.

Dv 7904   (117?)

       ]ko-ro-da[
            Uncertain whether]ko-ro-da-[or]ko-ro-da [and
            beginning of division into .A and .B .

Dv 7908   (117?)

            sup. mut.
       ]ta-we-si[

Dv 7911   (117?)

       ]da-ma[
       inf. mut.

Dv 7934   (117)

            sup. mut.
   .A   ]   vac.[
   .B   ]ri /   e[

Dv 8151   UCL (117)

   .a   vac.[
   .b   ma-ta-u-ro / vest.[
                .b Possibly ga[, ri[or ku[.

150

Dv 8193   (117)

    ]su-ti-jo , / a[

Dv 8197   (117?)

    ]ka-ta$_2$[

Dv 8203   (117)

.A   ] OVIS^m 70[
.B e-]ko-so   [

Dv 8232   (117)

    ]43 OVIS^f 2
    inf. mut.

Dv 8236   (117)

    sup. mut.
    ] o OVIS^m 30[
    inf. mut.

Dv 8239   (117)

.A] OVIS^f 40[
.B]4   [

Dv 8241   (117)

    ] we-we-si-jo[
    inf. mut.

Dv 8278   (117)

    ]ke-u [

Dv 8280 + 8710   (117)

    qa-mi-ni[

151

Dv 8287   (117)

    <u>sup. mut.</u>

    qa-]na-no-to[

    <u>inf. mut.</u>

     Small fragment bearing <u>to</u> lost at right; text from
     photograph BSA 58, plate 23.

<u>Dv</u> 8288   (117?)

    ]ṣi̦-no-u-ṛo̦[
     Probably trace of erasure.

Dv 8289   (117)

    o-to-ṛo̦[

Dv 8290   (117)

    pa-ja[

Dv 8294   (117)

    ]po-[

    <u>inf. mut.</u>

     Probably p̲o̲-[.

Dv 8302   (117)

     <u>sup. mut.</u>

    ]-ri-jo̦ , [

<u>Dv</u> 8308   (117?)

    <u>sup. mut.</u>

    ta-ṛo̦-[

Dv 8332 + 8412   (117)

    ] OVIS^{m} 300[

     <u>inf. mut.</u>

Dv 8356 + <u>frr.</u>   (117)

  .A   OVIS^{m} [ ]9 OVIS^{f} 11

  .B <u>vest.</u> / <u>vest.</u>   pa OVIS^{m}[

      .B p̲a̲ or o̲ .

Dv 8357 + fr.   (117)

.A   OVIS^m 48   OVIS^f [ ]

.B   ta-u-na-so , / su-ri-mo pe-ri-qo-te-jo

Dv 8361 + fr.   (117)

.A   ]   [   ]   OVIS^m 44   OVIS^x [

.B   ]-to , / da-wo , [   ]41[

Dv 8362 + fr.   (117)

.A   ]   OVIS^m 141   OVIS^x [

.B   ]so , / ra-ja   [

v.   ]   80   [

Dv 8363 + fr.   (117)

.A   ]   vest. [

.B   ]-u /   vest. [

     .B Possibly da-wo [.

Dv 8366   (117)

.A   ]   vest. [

.B   ]-*56-wo / su-ri-mo [

Dv 8367   (117)

.A   ]   vac. [

.B   ]qe-u / vac. [

Dv 8368   (117)

     ]-ko-so [

Dv 8369   (117)

     o-po-da [
          Alternatively o-po-mu [or o-po-ja [.

Dv 8370   (117)

     ]ko , [

Dv 8381   (117)

    <u>sup. mut.</u>
    ] , ḍa[

Dv 8382   (117)

    <u>sup. mut.</u>
    ]ṭu-ni-ja , [

Dv 8383 + 8415 + 8426 + 8547   (117)

.A   ]   [?] O̤V̤I̤S̤^{m}[   ] OVIS^f 5[
.B   ]ko-sọ / ra-to   [
      Text perhaps complete at left.
.A ụ-ṭạ-jọ ? ; perhaps <u>vestigia</u> on verso.

Dv 8384 + <u>fr.</u>   (117)

.A]O̤V̤I̤S̤^{m}[
.B] <u>vest.</u>[

v.] 20 [

Dv 8385   (117)

.A] <u>vest.</u> [
.B]tu-ri-so [

<u>Dv</u> 8387   (117?)

    ] ti-ri-to O̤V̤I̤S̤.^{m}[
      Perhaps O̤V̤I̤S̤^{m} 9̤0[.

Dv 8391   (117)

.A] OVIS^m 5[
.B] OVIS^m 22[

Dv 8392 + <u>fr.</u>   (117)

.A   ]14̤0̤
.B] <u>vestigia</u> ?

154

Dv 8394   (117)
    ] OVIS^m 20[

Dv 8395   (117)
 .A]60   o OVIS^m 40
 .B] vacat ?

Dv 8396   (117)
 .A   ] vacat
 .B ki-ri-]jo-te

Dv 8398 + fr.   (117)
 .A   ] OVIS^m 30[
 .B ru-]ki-to

Dv 8401   (117)
    ]80   o OVIS^m 20

Dv 8404   (117)
    ] OVIS^m 30 [

Dv 8405   (117)
 .A]OVIS^m 100 [ ]OVIS^m 3[
 .B] vestigia   [

Dv 8406   (117)
    ]50[

Dv 8409   (117)
 .A]OVIS^f 20[
 .B] vacat [

Dv 8410   (117)
      sup. mut.
 .A]jo-jo OVIS^m 10[
 .B   inf. mut.

Dv 8413   (117)

      <u>sup. mut.</u>
     ]   OVIS^{x}[
      <u>inf. mut.</u>

Dv 8419   (117)

      <u>sup. mut.</u>
     ]OVIS^{m} 50[
      <u>inf. mut.</u>

Dv 8420   (117)

      <u>sup. mut.</u>
     ] OVIS^{m} [

Dv 8421   (117)

      <u>sup. mut.</u>
.A   ]3 OVIS^{f}[
.B   <u>inf. mut.</u>

Dv 8422   (117)

      <u>sup. mut.</u>
.A   ]OVIS^{m} 2[
.B   ]OVIS^{m} 20[
      <u>inf. mut.</u>
       .A Perhaps]22[.

Dv 8423   (117)

      <u>sup. mut.</u>
     ] <u>o</u> OVIS^{m} 20[
      <u>inf. mut.</u>

Dv 8429   (117)

.A   ]47   [
.B   ] OVIS^{m} 1[
      <u>inf. mut.</u>

<u>Dv</u> 8432   (117?)

     ]26   [

     <u>inf. mut.</u>

<u>Dv</u> 8433   (117?)

     <u>sup. mut.</u>

     ]2

Dv 8434 + <u>frr.</u>   (117)

  .A   ]100

  .B   ] <u>vacat</u>

<u>Dv</u> 8585   (117?)

     <u>sup. mut.</u>

     ]qa-[

     <u>inf. mut.</u>

Dv 8636   (117)

     *83[

Dv 8637   (117)

     ]au[

Dv 8715   (117)

  .A   ]9

  .B   ] <u>vacat</u> ?

Dv 8716 + <u>fr.</u>   (117)

  .A]   OVIS^{m} 33 OVIS^{f}[

  .B]ja-se / <u>vestigia</u>

Dv 8717   (117)

  .A   ]1

  .B   ] <u>vestigia</u>

       ]to[

          Or]wo[? Perhaps .a and .b, with vestigia in .a .

D

D 411 + 511   (–)

       di-ko-to / e-ma-a$_2$-o   OVIS^f 60   WE 30[

          -ma- and perhaps e$_{\overline{z}}$ over erasure. Perhaps to be read
          as e-ma-a$_2$ o OVIS^f. Perhaps traces after 30[.

D 747   (–)

.a   ]a-di-je-wo   [

.b   pa-]i-to   OVIS^m 40 [

D 1615   (–)

.A   ]   OVIS^m 190[

.B   ]   o OVIS^m 10 [

D 1650   ASHM (118?)

.a   ]   ra-wo-qo-no-jo

.b   ]pa / da-wo   OVIS^m 68

D 2130   (–)

.A   ]ra   OVIS^m 100[

.B   ]   vacat   [

       .A 100 over erasure (perhaps [[90]]).

D 5094   (–)

.A   ]50   OVIS^f[

.B   ] OVIS^m 40 [

D 5519   (–)

       ] OVIS^m 77

          Cut at right.

D 5520   (-)
  .a]wo   [
  .b]ja OVIS^m 100[

D 5545   (-)
  .A]OVIS^f 50 [
  .B]   <u>o</u> [
       .B Perhaps trace of OVIS^m at right.

D 5810   (-)
  .A]   OVIS^f 2[
  .B]OVIS^m 70 <u>o</u> OVIS^m[

D 5919   (-)
  .A] OVIS^f 20[
  .B]<u>o</u> OVIS^m [

D 5954   (-)
     <u>sup. mut.</u>
    ]ke̦-mo / <u>sa</u> OVIS̤^{m}[

D 7101   (-)
    ]OVIS^x 68 [
      Trace at right, very faint, perhaps LA̦NA̦[.

D 7102   (-)
  .A][[50 O̦V̦I̦S^f 2̦0]]
  .B] <u>vacat</u>

D 7103   (-)
  .a] <u>vest.</u>   [
  .b]to OVIS^m 94[

D 7122   (-)
    ]ko-we O̦V̦I̦S̤^{m}[

D 7127   (-)

      ]OVIS^m 4 [

          Traces of erasure.

D 7130   (-)

  .1   ]   OVIS 110[

  .2   ]te-we   OVIS 100   sa[

D 7134 + 7724   (-)

  .A   ] do-ti-jo OVIS^m 100   LANA[

  .B   ]   a-te-jo   [

D 7146   (-)

      ] OVIS^m 34[

D 7242   (-)

      ]OVIS^m 81[

D 7243   (-)

      ] OVIS^m 30[

      inf. mut.

D 7251   (-)

  .A   ]LANA 3 M[

  .B   ] 1   M[

      .B Traces at left consistent with]LANA.

D 7252   (-)

  .1   ] OVIS^m VIR 1 [

  .2   ]OVIS^x VIR[

      inf. mut.

D 7254   (-)

      ]OVIS^m 200[

      inf. mut.

D 7334   (-)
    .A   ]   a-no-qo[-ta
    .B   ]ni-to / e-ra   [

D 7541   (-)
    .A   ] OVIS^m 60[
    .B   ]   o̭ OVIS^m [

D 7727   (117??)
    .1   ]a-ka   OVIS^m [
    .2   ]   vacat   [
          .1 Perhaps (though very doubtful) OVIS^m 1̤0̤0[.

D 8174   (-)
    .1   ]-si-jo-jo   OVIS^m[
    .2   da̤-te-we-ja   [

D 8333   DESB (-)
          ]da-wo   OVIS^f 60[

D 8349   (-)
          ] [[vest.]]
    v.   OVIS^m [
              Perhaps [[ ]q̭e 1]]   or [[   ]q̭e Z̤Ë]] .

D 8350   (-)
    .1   ]   o̭ OVIS^m 26[
    .2   ] vestigia   [

E

E 36   (-)

      pi-ra-me-no , / pa-i-to   GRA 10[

E(1) 71   ("124")

      ka-pa   GRA[

     .Possibly same tablet as F 7360. Palimpsest.

E(1) 132   ("124")

      <u>sup. mut.</u>

.1   <u>vest</u>.[

.2   GRA 202[

      Over erasure. A sign such as <u>o</u> appears to be ligatured
      with GRA (if not part of deleted text).

E(1) 165   ("124")

.1   ]2   GRA 5[

.2   ] 3   GRA 4 [

.3   ]   GRA T[

      <u>inf. mut.</u>

E(1) 288   ("124")

      ra-wa-si-jo   GRA[

E(2) 668   (103)

.1   ru-ki-ti-jo   GRA 246   T 7

.2   tu-ri-si-jo   GRA 261   ra-ti-jo   GRA 30 T 5

E(2) 669   (103)

.1   ]ti-jo   GRA 195   OLIV+<u>A</u> 43   OLIV+<u>TI</u> 45

.2   ]i-jo   GRA 143   da-*22-ti-jo   GRA 70   OLIV 45

E(2)   670   (103)

  .1   ]da-*83-ja-i   GRA 302   OLIV 89[
  .2   ru-ki-ti-jo   GRA 73 o-na-jo   GRA[
        .1 Probably nothing lost at left.

E   749 + 5532 + <u>fr</u>.   (136)

  .1   qa-ra-jo ,   GRA 25
  .2   ru-ki-ti-jo   GRA 23[
  .3   ti-ri-ti-jo   GRA [
  .4   [su-]ri-mi-jo GRA[   ] T 2 'V 3'
  .5   qa-mi-jo ,   GRA 12 T 5
  .6   u-ta-ni-jo , GRA[
  .7   pu-si-jo ,   GRA 6[
  .8.9   <u>vacant</u>
  .10   <u>vacat</u> [

E   777   ASHM (-)

  .1   ko-no-si-ja / ki-ri-te-wi-ja-i   LUNA 1   GRA 100[
  .2   a-mi-ni-si-ja   LUNA 1   GRA 100 [
  .3   pa-i-ti-ja   LUNA 1   GRA 100[

  v.1   a-ze-ti-ri-ja   GRA[
      <u>reliqua pars sine regulis</u>
        Cut at left.

E   842   (-)

  .1a]   di-wo [
  .1b]ra , te-o-i / me-a-de[
  .2   ]OLIV 24 T 4   PYC[ ] T 2   me-na   GRA 2 T 4[
  .3   ]pe-ro$_2$-i   ] 2 T 4 ki-da-ro GRA 20[   ]to-so   GRA[
      .3 Trace before] 2 consistent with GRA.

102

E 843

.1   e-me-si-jo[

.2   pa-na-so   GRA 100[

.3   ta-ra-qo   GRA [

.4   ta-u-pa-du-we   G̣R̤Ạ[

.5   a-r̥o-ja[

.6   <u>inf. mut.</u>

First line uninscribed.

.5   a-p̣a-ja not impossible, but unlikely.

E 845   (-)

.a   ]   a-ma   [

.b   ]r̥o , /   da-mo   GRA [

E 846   (-)

.1   ]ra-wa-e-si-jo , / to[

.2   ṭo-so   GRA 22[

.1 Probably nothing lost at left.

E 847 + 5739 + 7341   (-)

.1   ]no-so / a-no-qo-ta-o   LUNA 1   GRA 10 [

.2   ] LUNA 1 · GRA 12 T 7̣   da-na-mo   LUNA 1   GRA 1̣1̣[

Traces of erasure.

E 848   (102?)

.1   ]q̣a-sa-ro-we[

.2   ] GRA 6̣2[

.2 Probably 7̣2[or 8̣2[.

E 849   (136?)

.1   pu-ta-ri-ja , pe-ra[

.2   to-so   GRA 130[

E 850   (-)

]ma-si-jo a-ma   GRA 132 T 5

T is apparently written with an extra cross-bar (= <u>to</u>).

E 971   (-)
 .a   ]vest.   [
 .b   ]to-i-ja , o-pa   GRA[
           .a Perhaps]10 or even]GRA 10.

E 1035 + 5747   (-)
         o-ta-re-wo / a-ma   GRA 100[

  v.   wi
             Cut at left. Traces of erasure.

E 1569 + 7349 + 7843 + 8004   ASHM/IR (-)
 .1   ]do-ti-ja   GRA 48   pe-ma   [
 .2   ]ra-wa-ke-si-jo   GRA 10   T 3
           1569: Ashmolean; 7349 + 7843 + 8004: Iraklion. Text
           complete at left.

E 1574   (-)
 .1   ]GRA 4   T 2
 .2   ]   vacat

E 4466   (-)
 .1   ]ri-mi-jo   GRA 10[
 .2   ] GRA 35   ri-[
 .3   ]ri-jo   GRA[
           .2 Trace at left.

E 5000 + 7853 + 8041   (-)
 .1   ]67
 .2   ]GRA 181   T 5
 .3   ] ,   GRA 102   T 5
 .4   ]   vacat
           7853 + 8041 + <fr.> = 1630 (photograph in SM II, pl.57).
           .3 Trace at left.

165

E 5556   (-)

  .1   <u>sup. mut.</u>

  .2   ]GRA 2

  .3   ] GRA 2

  .4   <u>inf. mut.</u>

E 7338   (-)

      ] GRA 100[

      <u>inf. mut.</u>

E 7339   (-)

  .1   <u>sup. mut.</u>

  .2   ]ro   GRA[

E 7340   (-)

  .1   ]GRA 200[

  .2   <u>inf. mut.</u>

E 7350   (-)

      ]3   GRA 1[

      <u>inf. mut.</u>

E 7354   •   (-)

      ] 33 T 5 [

        Shape of break favours GRA. The arrangement of 5 is
        abnormal.

E 8040   (-)

  .1   ] a-ma

  .2   ] 8

        .1 Trace to left.

        .2 Trace to left possibly GRA.

E(1) 8122   ("124")

      ]e-pi-ke-to   GRA 30[

E(1) 8435   ("124"?)

      sup. mut.

.1   ] vacat [

.2   ]GRA Z[

      inf. mut.

        .2 Or]GRA 100[?

Fh

Fh 339   (141)

    o-pa-wo-ne-ja / to-qa   OLE 24

Fh 340   (141)

    ka-ro / a-pu-do-si '<u>te</u>' OLE 23 S 2

Fh 341   (141)

    pe-da-i-ra / du-ni-ja   OLE 4 S 2 V 1

Fh 342   (141)

    a-ne-ra-to   OLE 2   do-re-we   OLE 2

Fh 343   (141)

    du-pu$_2$-so / zo-a   OLE 15   e-pi-ko-wa   O̤L̤E̤ 1̤ S 1 V 3

Fh 344   (141)

    ka-pa-ri-jo-ne   OLE 1

Fh 345   (141)

    du-ru-po   OLE V 1

Fh 346   (141?)

    a$_3$-ki-pa-ta   OLE   2[
        Probably 3[̤.

Fh 347   (141)

  .1 ma-ro-ne / ku-pi-ri-jo   OLE 6 S 2 <u>MU</u> 5
  .2 we-we-r̤o̤ , /o-no   OLE 1 a-ri-to-[.]j̤o   OLE V 2
        Cut at left. .2 V 2 corrected from V 4.

Fh 348

   .1   o-no , i-su-ku-wo-do-to ,   OLE 1 S 1

   .2   qe-te-o , [[te-o-.]]   OLE 1

          Cut at both ends.

            .2 Perhaps [[te-o-i]] , but i very doubtful; uncertain
whether this word was erased intentionally or
accidentally.

Fh 349

     ]ru-ki-to / a-pu-do-si   OLE 53[ ]vest.[

     vest.: S or V?

Fh 350

     po-ro-ko-wa   OLE 2

     Cut at right.

Fh 351

     *47-so-de   OLE V 3

     Cut at right. V over [[S]].

Fh 352

     de-u-jo-i   OLE S 1

Fh 353

     ra-ma-na-de / de-ma-si 'OLE' S 1

     Cut at right.

Fh 355

     qa-ti-ja / zo-a   OLE 30

     Cut at right.

Fh 356

     o-mi-ri-jo-i   OLE 1[ ]

     Cut at right. Probably only 1.

Fh 357   (141)

 .1 *47-so-de OLE 2 S 1

 .2 e-ra-de   OLE 2 V 1

   Cut at left.

Fh 358   (141)

  ] , to-ro-qa OLE 10

   Cut at right. Trace at left.

Fh 359   (141)

 .a   zo-a[

 .b ku-do-ni-ja / e-te-ja[

Fh 360   (141)

 .a   ki-ra-*56-so , u[

 .b ma-si-dwo / me-[

   Cut at left.

   .b ma- perhaps over erasure. Perhaps me-sa-to[.

Fh 361   (141)

 .a   OLE 21 S 2 [

 .b ku-pi-ri-jo / o-no zo-a OLE 2[

Fh 362   (-)

 .1 [[ne-wo OLE 83]] [

 .2   tu-[   ] 7 V 2[

   Text badly damaged.

   .1 OLE not at all sure. After 83 : S 2 Bennett, V 4
     Ventris; perhaps S 4.

   .2 tu-ni-ja OLE S 7 Bennett, tu-ni-ja [ ] OLE 7
     Ventris; perhaps V 4[.

Fh 364   (141?)

 .a]-ke , a-ku-tu-ru-wo[

 .b]u-te-si   OLE[

   .a]do-ke is possible.

Fh   365   (141?)

  .a   ]wo-ja-de   OLE V 1

  .b   ]da-so-de   OLE V 1

        Cut at right.

       .b Two more or less vertical strokes above]da-so-.

Fh   366   (141)

      to-so / a-pu-do[-si

        Probably [+] Fh 5503. Cut at left.

Fh   367 + 5460   (141)

      to-so-ku-su-pa   OLE 330 S[

        Cut at left. Traces of erased units beneath 30.

Fh   368 + 5499   (141)

      o-pi , du-ru-po   OLE S 1 [

        Text probably complete.

Fh   369   (141)

      zo-a / a-ra-si-jo   OLE[

Fh   370   (141)

  .a   ]   ko-no-so[

  .b   ]mu-to / de-ka-sa[

        Possibly same tablet as Fh 5473.

Fh   371 + 5448   (141)

      ]o-se-ko-do / ku-pi-ri-jo   OLE 13 S 1   MU 10

        MU 10 written below 13.

Fh   372 + 5474   (141)

      ku-pi-ri-jo / o-no   OLE [

Fh   373 + 5489   (141)

      tu-ni-ja-de , / te[

Fh <374>   (141??)

    a-pu-do[

        Missing; text from SM II.

Fh 375   (141)

    ]ne-wo   OLE 10[

Fh <376>   (141??)

    ?to-]ro-qa   OLE 1[

        Missing; text from SM II.

Fh 377   (141)

    ]si   OLE 152 V 2

Fh <378>   (141??)

    ]ma-qa-to   OLE[

        Missing; text from SM II.

Fh <379>   (141??)

    a-]pu-do-si   OLE 17   S 2[

        Missing; text from SM II.

Fh 380 + 2006 + 5445 + fr.   (141)

    ]jo-te / zo-a   OLE 33 S 1   e-pi-ko-wa[

Fh <381>   (141??)

    ]po-ro-ko-wa , / a[

        Missing; text from SM II.

Fh <382>   (141??)

    ko-ro-ja-ne   OLE [

        Missing; text from SM II.

Fh <383>   (141??)

    ku-do[

        Missing; text from SM II.

Fh <384>   (141??)

    ]re-pi-ru-nu-we[

      Missing; text from SM II.

Fh <385>   (141??)

    do-ni-ja[

      Missing; text from SM II.

Fh 386 + 5462 + 5495   (141?)

    ka-ke-we   OLE   S 1   V 1

      Trace between OLE and S.

Fh <387>   (141??)

    ]te-o[

      Missing; text from SM II.

Fh <388>   (141??)

    tu-ri[

      Missing; text from SM II.

      Probably tu-ri-[(Ventris conjectured tu-ri-so[ )
      and not tu-ri 1[.

Fh <389>   (141??)

    ]qa-nu-we[

      Missing; text from SM II.

Fh <390>   (141??)

    e-ri-nu[

      Missing; text from SM II.

Fh <391>   (141??)

    ]ro-to-qa   OLE 20[

      Missing; text from SM II.

      Probably to be emended to]to-ro-qa.

Fh <392>   (141??)

        u-ru-pi-ja[
            Missing; text from SM II.

Fh 393   (141)

        *47-so-de[
            Cut at left. Traces at right.

Fh 462 + 2008 + 5470   (141?)
    .1   ]-si-ja V 1   a-ri-ja-wo-ne   [   ]
    .2]si-ja / e-to-wo-ko V 3   *47-so-de S 1

  v.1   ]de   V 3
    .2] vacat
            .1 Perhaps]-pa-si-ja. -si- over erasure.

Fh 1056   (141?)

        ra-pte-re   OLE V 3
            Cut at right.

Fh 1057   (141?)

        *56-i-ti   OLE S 1
            Cut at right.

Fh 1059   (141?)

        wi-na-jo / e-ra-jo   OLE V 1
            Cut at right.

Fh 2013   (141)

        ]jo / pe-da-i-je-[
            Possibly pe-da-i-je-ro[. Divider after pe-da not excluded.

Fh 2014 + 5439   (141)
        ]de   OLE [[S   ]]   OLE   S 2

  v.   ]ra-i / ko-[   ] OLE   S 1
            OLE S 2 over erasure.

<u>Fh</u> 5246   (141?)

   ]100 [

      Possibly]O̤L̤E̤ 100 [.

<u>Fh</u> 5337   (141?)

   <u>sup. mut.</u>

   ke-[

      Cut at left. Perhaps <u>ke-ta̤</u>[.

Fh 5428 + 5500   (141)

   wi-ri-ne-we   OLE 12 S 1

Fh 5429   (141?)

   wa-po   OLE [

Fh 5430   (141)

   *47-so-d̤e̤[

Fh 5431   (141)

   ]o-na-de[

   <u>inf. mut.</u>

Fh 5432 + 5461   (141)

   ]pte-si / [.]-u-pi-ri-[

 v.]de-ma-si   OLE 2[

      Perhaps <u>n̤a̤-u-pi-ri-j̤o̤</u>[.

Fh 5434 + 5438   (141)

      <u>sup. mut.</u>

   to-]s̤o̤ / a-pu-do-si   OLE[

Fh 5435 + 7987   (141)

   wi-ri-ne-we[

Fh 5436 + 5441 + 7335   (141)

   ]-de , zo-a   OLE 23 S 1

Fh   5437   (141)
      ] S 2

Fh   5440   (141?)
      ]50
            Cut at right.

Fh   5442   (141)
      a-]mi-ni-si[
       inf. mut.

Fh   5443 + 5454   (141)
      ro-ru[

 v.   u-ta-no , [
         r. Perhaps erased.
         v. Trace of sign at right.

Fh   5444   (141?)
         ]pu-do[

Fh   5446   (141)
   .1   ku-pi-ri-jo / u-ne[
   .2   to-ro-qa / a-ṇu-[
            .2 Perhaps a-ṇu-ẉẹ[.

Fh   5447 + 7787   (141)
      ] ku-pi-ri-jo[
            Trace of sign at left.

Fh   5449 + 7896   (141)
      ]-jo   OLE 2 S 2

Fh   5450   (141?)
      ]me-no   OLE 2   S 2

Fh 5451 + 5496   (141)
  .a   za-we-te   [
  .b   a-mi-ni-si-ja / a-pu-do-si   OLE 30[

Fh 5452   (141)
     ] MU 7

Fh 5453   (141)
  .a   ko[
  .b   zo-a / a[
          Cut at left.

Fh 5455   (141)
        sup. mut.
     ]no   OLE V 1[

Fh 5456   (141?)
     ta-nu[
          Cut at left.

Fh 5457   (141)
     ]OLE 70
          Cut at right.

Fh 5458   (141)
     ] OLE V 2 [

Fh 5459 + 5482   (141)
     a-]pu-do-si   OLE 37 S 1

Fh 5463   (141?)
     qa-to-no-ro[

Fh 5465 + 5484 + 5491   (141)
     ko-ki-de-jo / qa[

177

Fh   5466   (141)

>   ]9 S[

inf. mut.

        Probably]OLE 9 S[.

Fh   5467   (141)

.a   ]   di-ka-ta-de[
.b   ]de / i-je-[   ]OLE 1 [
      .a Perhaps di-ka-ta-de S 1.
      .b Perhaps i-je-ro[.

Fh   5468   (141?)

>   ]to-de[

Fh   5471   (141?)

.1   ]si-na-jo[
.2   ]-ni-ja[

Fh   5473   (141)

>   ] OLE 70
        Possibly same tablet as Fh 370. Cut at right.

Fh   5475   (141)

sup. mut.
qe-ra-si[-ja?

Fh   5476   (141)

.1   ku-pi-ri-jo[
.2   si-ja-ma[
      inf. mut.

Fh   5477   (141)

sup. mut.
]ra-u-to [

Fh   5479   (141?)

>   ]*47-so-de / wa-u-so[

178

Fh 5481   (141?)

      sup. mut.
     ]OLE S[

Fh 5483   (141)

     ] S 1
     inf. mut.
        Cut at right.

Fh 5486   (141)

     sup. mut.
     ]ko-pe-re-we[
     inf. mut.

Fh 5487   (141?)

     *56-ro-[
        Perhaps *56-ro-u[.

Fh 5490   (141)

      sup. mut.
     ]ku-pi-ri[-jo
      inf. mut.

Fh 5493   (141?)

     ]no OLE [
     inf. mut.

Fh 5494   (141?)

     *56[
     inf. mut.
        Reading very doubtful.

Fh 5497   (141)

     to-ro-qa   OLE 5
        Cut at both ends. Palimpsest.

13

Fh 5498 + <u>fr</u>.   (141)

.a   ]   OLE [
.b   ]OLE S 1   ru-do-ro-ṇọ[
          .b   ru-do-ro-ị[not excluded.

Fh 5501   (141?)

      ]-so-de   OLE 1
          ]*47-so-de possible.

Fh 5502   (141)

      ku-ru-me-ne-jo / de-u-jọ-ị̣   ỌḶẸ[

Fh 5503   (141)

      ]ỌḶẸ 339 V 5
          Probably same tablet as Fh 366.

Fh 5505   (141)

      me-ra-de [

Fh 5506   (141)

.a   <u>vestigia</u> [
.b   [. . .]-ra-de / ne-wo-jo [
          .a Perhaps ṭẹ-[.]-ṛọ or ṭẹ-[.]-ị̱.
          .b Perhaps wọ-[.]-wọ-ra-de.

<u>Fh</u> 5614   (141?)

.1   ]55[
.2   <u>inf. mut.</u>

Fh 5722   (141?)

      qa-ra , a[

Fh 5723   (141?)

      me-na-wa-te[
          Cut at left.

180

Fh 5970   (141?)

        <u>sup. mut</u>.
     ]no , ma-ṛi[
        ma-ṛi[over erasure. Vestigia at top from a line .a or
        even .A.

Fh 6001   (141?)
     ]wa-ja , / qa-ṣa[

Fh 7336   (141?)
     ]1 S 2

Fh 7571   (141?)
     qo-pa-ra[

Fh 8297 + <u>fr</u>.   (141?)
     qe-ṛa[-si-ja?

Fh 8299   (141?)
     <u>sup. mut</u>.
     ]q̣o-ta[

Fh 8436   (141)
     <u>sup. mut</u>.
     ]   V 1[
       Traces at left: Ṣ or OḶE?

Fh 8504   (141?)
     ]ạ-ẓe-ti-ri-[

Fh 8646   (141?)
     ]2̣

Fp

Fp(1) 1 + 31   (138)

.1   de-u-ki-jo-jo   'me-no'
.2   di-ka-ta-jo / di-we   OLE   S 1
.3   da-da-re-jo-de   OLE   S 2
.4   pa-de   OLE   S 1
.5   pa-si-te-o-i   OLE   1
.6   qe-ra-si-ja   OLE   S 1[
.7   a-mi-ni-so , / pa-si-te-o-i S 1[
.8   e-ri-nu ,   OLE   V 3
.9   *47-da-de   OLE   V 1
.10   a-ne-mo , / i-je-re-ja   V 4
.11   vacat
.12   to-so   OLE 3 S 2 V 2

        .2 <u>ka</u> perhaps over erasure.
        .6.7 The numeral on one of these lines must be
             restored as 2 to produce the total.

Fp(1) 5   (138)
.1   di-wi-jo-jo 'me-no' qe-ra-si-ja   OLE S 1
.2   pa-si-te-o-i   OLE   S 1
.3   vacat
        Cut at left. Verso ruled (2 lines) but not inscribed.

Fp(1) 6   (138)
.1   ka-ra-e-ri-jo / pa-si-te-o-i   S 1
.2   qe-ra-si-ja   OLE   S 1
        .1 <u>e</u> possibly over erasure.

Fp(1) 7   (138)
.1   ka-ra-e-ri-jo , 'me-no'   [
.2   di-ka-ta-de ,   OLE   S 1[
        .1 Probably nothing lost at right.

Fp(1) 13   BM (138)

  .1   ra-pa-to 'me-no' , *47-ku-to-de   OLE V 1   pi-pi-tu-na
                                                                V 1
  .2   au-ri-mo-de OLE V 4   pa-si-te-o-i S 1   qe-ra-si-ja S 1
  .3   a-ne-mo-i-je-re-ja OLE 1 u-ta-no , 'a-ne-mo-i-je-re-ja'
                                                              S 1 V 3

          .1 ra- over erasure.
          .2 pa- probably over erasure.
          .3 OLE 1 to end over erasure.

Fp(1) 14 + 27 + 28 + frr.   (138)
  .1a   me-no   OLE
  .1b a-ma-ko-to ,/   jo-te-re-pa-to , // e-ke-se-si V 1
  .2   qe-ra-si-ja S 1   a-mi-ni-so-de ,/ pa-si-te-o-i S 2   a-re
                                                                V[

Fp(1) 15   (138)
  .1   ka-ra-e-ri-jo , / me-no
  .2   *56-ti S 2 , pa-si-te-o-i S 1

Fp(1) 16   (138)
  .1   wo-de-wi-jo, 'me-no' , pa-si-te-o-i S 1
  .2   qe-ra-si-jo   OLE S 1
          Cut at left.

Fp(1) 18   (138)
  .1   ]-jo-de , / ka-ra-e-ri-jo , me[-no
  .2   ]jo S 1   pa-si-te-o-i S 1 [

Fp(1) 30   (138)
          to-so ,[
  v.   ko-no[

Fp(1) 48   (138)
  .1   wo-de-wi-jo , 'me-no' / si-ja-ma-to OLE   S 2
  .2   pa-de , S 1   qe-ra-si-ja S 1   pa-si-te-o-i S 1
  .3   a-mi-ni-so-de , / pa-si-te-o-i OLE   S 1

Fp(2) 354   (222?)
    .1   ]ka-ra-e-i-jo   OLE 1 S 2
    .2   ]jo   OLE V 1   pa-ja-ni-jo   OLE V 1
          Cut at right.

Fp(2) 363   (222)
    .1   qe-te-a , te-re-no   OLE [
    .2   da-*83-ja-de / i-je-ro S 2   ki-ri-te-wi-ja , [
    .3   di-wo-pu-ka-ta   S 2   [
    .4   ]   vacat   [
          Possibly same tablet as Fp 5472.

Fp(2) 5472   (222?)
                 sup. mut.
    .1   ]su-ko-ne   OLE [
    .2   ]   OLE 1 S [
    .3   ]de   OLE 2 [
    .4   ]   vacat   [
          Possibly same tablet as Fp 363.

Fp(2) 5504   (222?)
          a-ka-ta-ra-te-so-de   OLE 10
          Cut at right.

Fs

Fs 2   (139)
    .A   HORD T 1   NI V 3   OLE Z 2
    .B   sa-na-to-de , FAR V 1   VIN V 1

    v.   ME+RI Z 1
          Perhaps traces of erasure.

Fs 3   (-)
    .A   HORD T 1   NI V 3
    .B   a-*65-ma-na-ke / me-na FAR V 1   OLE Z 1
          Perhaps traces of erasure.

184

Fs 4   (139)

    .A   HORD T 1   <u>NI</u> V 3   FAR V 2   VIN V 2
    .B   a-ro-do-ro-o , / wa-ke̤-ta , HORD T 1   <u>NI</u> V 3   OLE V 1

  v.   <u>ME+RI</u> Z 2
            .B Or wa-de̤-ta.

Fs 8   (139)

    .A   HORD T 1   <u>NI</u> T 1[
    .B   pa-de , FAR V 2[

  v.   <u>ME+RI</u>   *211^{VAS}+<u>PO</u> 1[

Fs 9   (139)

    .A   ]   [[HORD]] HORD[
    .B   ]ki̤-to , / o-ja-de , [

  v.   ]Z 1   [
            .B Trace at right probably VIN. <u>o-ja-de</u> plainly
                written after the deletion of the first HORD
                (<u>de</u> over [[HORD]] and beginning of central rule).

Fs 11   (139)

    .A   ]   HORD T 1   <u>NI</u> T 1   FAR V 2   VIN V 2
    .B   ]qe-sa-ma-qa , / ta-mi-te-mo , HORD T 1   OLE V 1

  v.   ]<u>ME</u>[+<u>RI</u>] Z 2

Fs 12   (139)

    .A   ]1   <u>NI</u> V 3   VIN V 1
    .B   ]2̤   OLE Z 2

Fs 17   (139)

    .A   ]i , HORD T 1   <u>NI</u> V 3   OLE Z 2   [
    .B   ]FAR V 1   VIN V 1   [

  v.   ]Z 1   [

185

Fs 19   (139)

    .1   e-ti-wa , HORD T 1   <u>NI</u> V 3
    .2   FAR V 1   OLE Z 2   VIN V 1

    v.   <u>ME+RI</u> Z 1
             Whole tablet erased and reused?

Fs 20   (139)

          a-*65-ma[
           .
    v.   <u>ME+RI</u> Z 1[

Fs 21   (139)

    .1   ka-u-da ,   HORD , T 1 [
    .2   FAR V 1   VIN V 1[

Fs 22   (139)

    .A   ]   HORD T 1   <u>NI</u> V 3 [
    .B   ]na-to-de , FAR V 1   VIN V 1 [
            ..
             .B 1 in VIN V 1 over [[2]].

Fs 23   (139)

    .1   ja-pe-re-so , HORD T 2   <u>NI</u> V 3   VIN V 2
    .2   FAR V 1   OLE V 1

    v.   <u>ME+RI</u> Z 1
             .2 V in OLE V 1 over [[Z̦]].

Fs 24   (139)

    .A   ] HORD T 1   <u>NI</u> V 3   FAR V 1
    .B   ] , OLE Z 2   VIN V 1

    v.   ] Z 1
             Trace at left.

Fs 25   (139)

    .A   ]   HORD T 1   <u>NI</u> V 3   VIN V 1
    .B   ]de , FAR V 1   OLE Z 2

Fs 26   (139)

  .1   ]ki-ri-jo-de[

  .2   ]FAR V 1   [

  v.   ] ME+RI Z [

Fs 29   (139)

  .A   ]   [

  .B   ]de , [

  v.   ]1̣   [

          .B Trace at right.

<u>Fs</u> <32>   (-)

        da-da-re[

          Missing; text from SM II.

F

F(1) 51   ("124"d)

          HORD T 7 V 5 Z 3̣[

  v.1   wa HORD T 1 V 3   po-ro-de-̣qo-no V 2 Z 2

    .2   di-we HORD T 1 HORD T 4 Z 1   ma-q̣e HORD V 6

          r. Whole surface deleted and reused (trace of a central
              rule; [[.1]] [[pa-wị[ ]] at beginning; numerals at end).

          v.1 Absolutely no trace of sign before <u>wa</u>. Accidental
               scratch, or divider, between <u>po-ro-de</u> and <u>qo-no</u>?

            .2 Traces of deletion and overwriting. ma-ḳạ not
                excluded. V 6 over [[T]].

187

F(1)   153 + 7348 + <u>fr</u>.   ("124")

        <u>sup. mut.</u>

.1   a-ta-ti-nu   T[ ]V[

.2   a-e-da-do-ro   T 3 [[V 2]]

.3   a-me-ja   T 3 V 2

.4   ]   T 4

.5.6   ]   <u>vacant</u>

v.   <u>sup. mut.</u>

.1   ]-me-no

.2   [.]-pi

.3   ta-pa-no

.4   ne-je-ta[

.5   a-ka-i-jo[

.6   a-ri-we-we[

        <u>inf. mut.</u>

    [+] F 7748 but position unknown.

    .2 Perhaps [[V 4]] .

F(1)   157 + <u>fr</u>.   ("124"d)

.1   e-ko-so , / to-so   GRA 400[

.2   CYP+<u>KU</u> 5 T 3   CYP[+?] 1[

.3.4   <u>vacant</u>

v.1] <u>vacat?</u>

    <u>reliqua pars sine regulis</u>

F(1)   193 + 7361   ("124")

    te-ra-po-ti HORD 9 T [

    HORD over [[GRA]] .

F 452   (-)

.1   ]ka-da-ra-so OLE 2   [

.2   ]qa-ka OLE 1 pu-ri   OLE S 2[

.3   ]-jo OLE S 3 o[

    Traces of erasure over the whole tablet.

    .3 Traces after <u>o</u>[, but both <u>o</u>-[and <u>o</u> (adjunct
       or ideogram) are possible.

F 726   (-)

.1   ]wi-jo-jo   e-ra[

.2   ]w̤o̤   OLE+A̲   V 1 [

      .1 Trace of another sign at right, perhaps w̤o̤.

F(3) 741   (-)

          sup. mut.

.1   ]to[

.2   ] 'da-*22-to' HORD 2

.3   ]-r̤o̤ 'da-*22-to' HORD 2

.4   ]-ri 'da-*22-to' HORD 2

.5   ]   vacat

          inf. mut.

          Probably same tablet as F 8242.

          .1 Traces at right.

          .2 Trace at left?

F(2) 841 + 867   (-)

.1   ]-ti-ja , sa-pi-ti[-ne-]we-jo   [

.2   a-di-*22-sa   GRA+PE̲ T 5̤   NI̲ 8[

.3   ]n̤o̤-di-mi-zo-jo[   ] , GRA+PE̲ 2 NI̲ 34[

.4   pa-i-to , mi-sa-ra-jo , sa-pi-ti-ne-we-jo[

.5   su-za ,   NI̲ 75   ka-po , e-[

.6   ]wa , OLIV 46   e-ra-wa[

.7.8   ]   vacant   [

      .3 Probably no other sign before]n̤o̤. Traces after
          -j̲o̲ probably smaller sign (possibly ko or dwe).

F(2) 844   (-)

.A   ]ja GRA 20   T 5   [

.B   ]   OLIV+A̲   10 T 2 [

lat. inf.]1 OLI̤V̤ 10 T 2   [

              Palimpsest

F(2) 851   (-)

  .1a   ]   e-pi-ke-re   [

  .1b]i̞ /   a-ma   GRA [

  .2   ]   OLIV+A̱ 46[

  v.1   ][[940]][

  .2   ] [[117]][

F(2) 852   (-)

  .1   da-wo / a-ma , e-pi-ke-re   GRA   10000[

  .2   OLIV+A̱ 70   OLIV+T̲I̲ 20 O̤L̤E̤[

          Cut at left.

          .2 Or P̤Y̤C̤[.

F(2) 853 + 5947 + 6035   (-)

  .1   ] GRA 500[

  .2   ] OLIV+T̲I̲ 3 T [

          .1 Trace at left.

F(2) 854   (102)

          sup. mut.

  .1   ]vest.[

  .2   ]na-r̤o̤   GRA 5

  .3]-do-we-i , ma-so-qe   GRA 8

  .4   ] vacat

  .5   ] GRA 402   OLIV+A̱ 52

          reliqua pars sine regulis

F(2) 866   (-)

     ]n̤i̤-jo / di-ka-ta-de N̲I̲ 10 ma-s̤a̤[

       Less likely]s̤a̤-jo.

F(2) 5001 + fr.   (-)

  .1   sup. mut.

  .2   ]80   OLIV+A̱ 3̤0[

  .3   ] vacat   [

  .4   ]GRA 3   OLIV+A̱ 2 N̲I̲[

  .5.6   ] vacant   [

F(2)   5005   (-)

   ]8   OLIV+<u>A</u> 12

F(2)   5043   (-)

.0   <u>sup. mut.</u>

.1   ]T 4   OLIV 4[

.2   ]T 9   OLIV 29[

    Palimpsest (the 3 on the <u>lat. inf.</u> is very likely the
remains of the previous text running over the edge).

F(1)   5079 + 8259   ("124"d)

.1   ka-ma[

.2a   di-pa-te[

.2b   ka[

.3a   i-je[

.3b   [?]ka-ma[

.4a   sa-i-[

.4b   i-je[

v.1   ]30

.2   ]i̤ ,   CẎP̣+O̲ 6

.3   ]mo̤ ,   CẎP̣+O̲ 5

.4   ] ,   CẎP̣+O̲ 5

.5   ]   4

    Signs in lines .b are small and **alternate** with large
signs in lines .a (cf. Cе 50).

    .3b Perhaps nothing lost before <u>ka</u>.

    v. CẎP̣+O̤: perhaps *1̤8̤O̤; perhaps simply <u>O</u> or <u>o</u>.

    .2.3.4 Perhaps <u>not</u> dividers (they are very large; in
        .2, perhaps d̤a̤?).

    .5 Perhaps CẎP̣+]O̲ 4.

F(2)   7050 + 7342   (-)

.1   ]104   OLIV 120 [

.2   ]GRA 4̤5̤3   [

    <u>inf. mut.</u>

    .1 Unidentifiable trace at right (ideogram ?).

    .2 4̤5̤3 is the minimum certain figure.

191

F 7337   (-)
     ]24 S[

F(2) 7343   (-)
  .1   ]44[
  .2   ]80 NI[

          .1 Traces at left, perhaps not part of the numerals.
          .2 Traces of erasure (perhaps originally 5 tens in
              the second column of tens).

F(2) 7345   (-)
  .1   ] T 3   OLIV+A 53   OLIV+TI 6 T 7[
  .2   ]   vacat

F(2) 7346   (-)
     ] NI 612[

F(1) 7356   ("124")
  .1   ]OLIV 82 T 4
  .2   ]T 7
  .3   inf. mut.

  v.1 a-ko-ra-ja   [

          reliqua pars sine regulis
          inf. mut.
          v.1 Trace at right, perhaps /ku[.

F(2) 7357   (-)
     ]4   OLIV 30[
          Perhaps]6 or]T 4.

F(1) 7359   ("124")
     ]T 1 V 4

F(1) 7360 + 8028   ("124")
     ]1 T 6
          Possibly same tablet as E 71.   Palimpsest.

F(1)   7362   ("124")

    T 2 V 1   [

v.   ke-ki[

       Perhaps cut at right.

F   7542   (-)

.1   ]31   KO 25

.2   ]6 Ṣ 1   OLE 9

F(1)   7748 + 8529   ("124")

      sup. mut.

.1   ]vest.[

.2   e-u-ko-me[

.3   [.]-qe[ ]vac.[

      inf. mut.

      Same tablet as F 153, but uncertain where it should
      be placed. Verso ruled but not inscribed.

      .3 or [.]-qe-[? or even [.]-qe-u[??

F(3)   8242   (-)

.0   sup. mut.

.1]da-*22-to   HORD [

.2 da-]*22-to   [

      inf. mut.

      Probably same tablet as F 741.

      .2 Trace at right, possibly HORD[.

F(1)   8437   ("124")

    ]OLIV [

    inf. mut.

Ga

Ga(2)   <34>   (136 ?)
.1   pu-na-si-jo / ti-mi-nu-wo[
.2   <u>KO</u> T 5   [
        Missing (destroyed in 1899); text from Evans' photograph.
        .1 <u>ti-mi-*56-wo</u>[not entirely excluded.

Ga(2)   415   (136)
        ru-ki-ti-jo 'ko-ri-ja-do-no'   AROM 1 T 6

Ga(2)   416   (136)
        a-ka-re-u / pa-i-to   AROM 9 T 2

Ga(2)   417   (136)
.A   po-ni-ki-jo M 5
.B   qa-mo / ko-ri-ja-do-no   AROM 1 [
<u>lat. inf.</u> ta-u-na-so   <u>KO</u> V 1[

Ga(2)   418   (136)
.A   po-ni-ki-jo M 3
.B   su-ri-mi-jo / ko-ri-ja-do-no T 5
        .A Over erasure.
        .B T 5 over erasure.

Ga(2)   419 + 5806   (136)
.1   a₃-ta-jo / ku-ta-ti-jo[   ]AROM 1
.2a   ri-wi-so[ ] ko-ri[-ja-do-no   ]
.2b tu-to / ku-ta-ti-jo   [   ]AROM 1

Ga(2)   420   (136)
.A   ]   po-ni-ki-jo [
.B   ]pu-na-si-jo   [

194

Ga(2)   421   (136)

  .a   ]   a-pu-do-si ko-ri-ja-do-no   T 5
  .b   ]-ṭi-jo

Ga(2)   422   (136)

  .a   ]   ko-ri-ja-do-no
  .b   ]jo   AROM 1

Ga(2)   423 + 7366   (136)

  .A   po-ni-ki̱[-jo
  .B   qa-ra-jo / ko-ri-ja-do-no   AROM 2̣ [

  v.   da-wa-no , e-we-de-u [
              .B Second unit fainter, perhaps added later.

Ga(2)   424   (136)

  .a   po-ni̱-ki-jo
  .b   *56-ko-we-i-jo / a-pu-do-si M 5

Ga(2)   425   (136)

  .A   ]'pa-ra-u-jo' a-pu-do-si 'po-ni-ki-jo' M 1
  .B   ]   <u>vacat</u>
              .B Trace of large sign at left.

Ga(2)   426   (136)

  .A   ] po̱-ni-ki-jo   M 4 N 1
  .B   ] du-ni-jo   [
              .B <u>du</u>- over erasure.

Ga(2)   427 + 8102   (136)

  .1   da-wi-jo / a-pu-do-si po-ni-ki-jo di-ta-ka-so   M 8   N[ ]o̱[
  .2   e-pu$_2$-no / po-ni-ki-jo   M 8 N 1   o̱ M 1 N 1
              .1 -<u>ta-ka</u>- over erasure (<u>ta</u> over [[ka̱]]).

Ga(2)   428   (136?)

  .a   a[
  .b   ti-ri-ti[

<u>Ga(3)</u> 454   (223?)

    ku-ta-to , / ku-pa[-ro

<u>Ga(3)</u> 456   (223?)

 .1   ]2   pa-de ,   PYC T[
 .2   ][[wa-du-ri]][

Ga 461   (-)

 .a   ]te-ra   [
 .b   ]do-si   CYP 10   o-pe-ro[

<u>Ga(3)</u> 464   (223)

 .1   da-*22-to , / o-pe-ro , *<u>171</u> 4[ ]   PYC 26 T 3
 .2   ku-ta-to , / o-pe-ro , *<u>171</u> 4   PYC 15
          Cut at right.

<u>Ga(3)</u> 465   (223)

 .1   ]*83-re-jo-de   T 1
 .2   a-mi-]ni-so-de , / ku-pa-ro   T 1
          Cut at right.

<u>Ga(1)</u> 517   (135)

 .a   ku-pi-ri-jo
 .b   tu-wi-no , / ku-pa-ro   AROM+PYC 1 [
          Probably nothing lost at right.

<u>Ga(1)</u> 518   (135?)

 .a   ]za-we-te-ra   [
 .b   a-]pu-do-si   AROM+PYC 10[
          .b AROM+PYC over erasure.

<u>Ga(1)</u> 519   (135?)

 .1a   ]   ku-pa-ro   *<u>171</u> 2[
 .1b   ]to   a-pu-do-si   [
 .2   ]4 T 5   o-[
 .3   ]   <u>vacat</u>   [
          .2 o-pe[possible.

                          196

Ga(2) 673   (136)

.1   ku-ta-ti-jo[

.2   ko-ri-ja-do-no[
                    ··

Ga(1) 674   (135)

.a   ]   pe-ma

.b   ]ma-ri-ne-we , / ko-ri-ja-do-no , AROM 10
         ··

Ga(1) 675   (135)

      wa-na-ka-te , / [[ko]] pe-ma   AROM 10

Ga(1) <676>   (135)

.a   ko-ri-ja-do-no

.b   tu-wi-no-no / ku-pi-ri-jo   AROM 6
            ·
         Missing; text from SM II, pl. 60.

Ga(1) 677 + 7769   (135)

      ]ni-jo , / ku-pi-ri-jo   AROM 5

Ga(1) 678   (135)

      ]ko-ri-ja   AROM 5   [
         ·· · ··

Ga(1) 679   (135)

      ]-do   AROM 6
         Trace to left consistent with ja; cf. Ga 680.1b.

Ga(1) 680   (135)

.1a   ]pe-ma

.1b   ]ja-do   AROM 1   T[
                            ·
.2   ]-ni-jo , AROM[

lat. inf.   ]mi-dwe , AROM 10[

Ga(1) 685   (135)

      ko-sa-ma-to , / ko-ri-ja-do-no   T 2

                            197

Ga   738   (-)

.a   ] a-ka-wo   [
.b   ]   <u>ko</u>   AROM[
          Trace of large sign at left.

Ga(4)   834   (137)

     ]po̤-ni-ki-jo , ko-no-si-ja M 34 [
         -<u>si-ja</u> over erasure.

Ga   953 [+] 955   (219)

.1   wo-de-wi̤-jo-jo , / me[-no //]ri-jo-de ,
.2   ko-no , <u>MA</u> 3   ko-r̤i[   ]2 pa-de-i , ko-no <u>MA</u> 2 <u>KO</u>
                                                           T 1[

.3a   [   ] pa-si-te-o-i ,
.3b pa-sa-ja , ko-no , [   ]   a-mi-ni-so-de , <u>MA</u> 2 <u>KO</u>
                                                           T 4

     .2 Perhaps T 2̤[.
     .3 Trace of sign after <u>ko-no</u> (perhaps m̤a[in .a and
         r̤i[in .b).
     .3b <u>MA</u> has here the extra stroke which distinguishes
         <u>LANA</u>, probably in error.

Ga(4)   992 + 8582   (137)

     ]pu-si-jo / po-ni-ki-jo , a-pu[-do-si

Ga(4)   1020   (137)

     ]jo / po-ni-ki-jo , a-pu-do[-si

Ga(4)   1021 + 7428   (137)

     ]po̤-ni-ki-jo , a-pu-do-si[

Ga(4)   1040   (137)

.a   ]   a-pu-do[-si
.b   ]we-i-jo / po-ni-ki-jo[

Ga   1058 + 5671   (135?)

     te-o-po-ri-ja / ma-sa   PYC T 1

198

Ga(2) 1335   (136)

.a   ]wo-ne-we [

.b   ]po-ni-ki-jo[

Ga(5) 1530 + 1531   (221)

            sup. mut.

.1   ]-si-jo / o-pe-ro[

.2   da-wi-jo , / ki[-ta-no

.3a   [a-pu-]do-si

.3b   [.]-je-[   ] / [ki-ta-]no   AROM 11 o 2

.4a   a-pu-do-si

.4b   pu-na-si-jo / ki-ta-no   AROM 11 o 1[

.5   vacat

.6   to-sa   AROM 58

.7   to-sa-de / o-pe-ro   AROM 31

.8   vacat?

        .1 ku-ri[Bennett; tu-ri[Ventris.

Ga(5) 1532   (221)

.0   sup. mut.

.1a   ] a-pu-do-si

.1b   ]ki-ta-no   AROM 13 o AROM 1[

.2   ]65

.3   ]AROM 35 [

.4   ] vacat?

        .1b Perhaps 2[.

        .3   Perhaps nothing else at right and line complete,
             but possibly vestigia.

Ga(5) 1533   (221)

     e-]ki-si-ja , AROM 12   [

Ga(5) 1534   (221)

     ]-ni-ja AROM 5

                          199

Ga(5)   1535   (221)
    ] AROM 12
        Cut at right.

Ga(5)   1536 + 5776   (221)
  .1   pa-i-ti-ja AROM 34[
  .2   _vacat_ [ ] _vacat_ [

Ga(5)   5020   (221)
    ]AROM 4
        ....

Ga(5)   5021   (221)
    ] AROM 100[
    inf. mut.

Ga   5088   (-)
    ]do-si PYC+QA 9[

Ga   5672   (-)
  .1   ]me-no , [
  .2   ]MA 2   pa[
  .3   ] , pa-ra[
      .2 MA: possibly LANA or even]ma. Perhaps PA 2[or
           pa-[(pa-ṣa[not entirely excluded).
      .3 Trace at left.

Ga(4)   5736   (137)
    ]30 M 2[

Ga(5)   5780   (221)
    ] AROM 30
        Cut at right.

Ga(2)   7286   (136?)
  .1   ] M 8
  .2   ] _vacat_
      .1 Traces before M, perhaps badly written]o.

Ga 7344   (-)

    ]PYC 4 T 2[
      ...
    <u>inf. mut</u>.

Ga 7347   (-)

.1   ] PYC 3 <u>o</u> PYC 1[
                 ·
.2   ] PYC 6 <u>o</u> PYC 2[

      .2 Last numeral probably more than 2.

Ga 7358   (-)

.a   ]   T 3
.b   ] PYC+QA 3

      Palimpsest (traces of numerals before T, trace of
      ruling in the middle).

      .a T 3 perhaps corrected from T 4 (but interference by
      the previous text possible).

      .b Trace of sign at left ( ]<u>ro</u>, or]<u>pa</u> ,).
                               ··   ··

<u>Ga(1)</u> 7365   (135?)

    ]jo , AROM 20

<u>Ga(2)</u> 7367 [+] 7368 + 7874   (-)

.1   ]-ti-jo , ka-to[ko-ri-]ja-do-no T 6
.2   ]<u>o</u> T 3 ta-si-ko[   ]<u>o</u> T 3
      ·
.3   ]T 7 <u>o</u> T 3[   ][[   ]][
      ·
.4   ]2   [

      <u>inf. mut</u>.

      .2 Perhaps ideogram before T 3, rather than <u>o</u>.
      <u>ta-si-ko</u>-[or <u>ta-si-ko</u> 2[possible (<u>ta-si⁻KO</u> 2[not
      likely, given the spacing).   ·

      .3 Trace (ideogram?) before T 7.
                            ·

<u>Ga(2)</u> 7425   (136)

.1   ']<u>si</u>' po-ni-ki-jo M 2
       ··
.2   ]   <u>vacat</u>

Ga(2)   7426   (136)
  .a   po-ni-]ki-jo M 14[
  .b   ] <u>vacat</u>
           .b Trace at left ( ]<u>si</u> ?).

Ga(2)   7429   (136)
  .1   po-]ni-ki-jo M[
  .2   ] <u>vacat</u>   [

Ga(2)   7431   (136)
  .a   ]2 N 1
  .b   ]   <u>o</u> M 1 N 1
           .a N 1 over erasure.

Ga(2)   7446   (136)
  .1   ]41 M 2
  .2   ] <u>vacat</u>

Ga 7496   (219)
  .1   ] , <u>MA</u> 1   <u>KO</u> T 2[
  .2   ]<u>MA</u> 2   <u>KO</u> T 4   [
  .3   ]   <u>vacat</u>   [
           .1 Trace at left, possibly]<u>u</u>.

Ga(1)   7594   (135)
         ma-ri[

<u>Ga(3)</u>   8005   (-)
         ku-]pa-ro <u>PYC</u>[
            <u>inf. mut.</u>

Ga(4)   8438   (137)
         po-]ni-ki-jo[

<u>Ga(2)</u>   8439   (136?)
            <u>sup. mut.</u>
         po-]ni-ki[-jo

                          202

Gg

Gg 10   (138)

.1   ]*209^{VAS} 2   [

.2   ]te-o   ME+RI   *209^{VAS}1[

.3   ]   vacat   [

.2 Over erasure.

Gg 521 + 712   (-)

to-so / e-te-jo   *209^{VAS} 542   *172[

Gg 701   (-)

]i-to , /da-nwa   ME+RI   *209^{VAS}+A 16   *172 8

Gg(1) 702   (103)

.1   pa-si-te-o-i   /   me-ri   *209^{VAS} 1

.2   da-pu$_2$-ri-to-jo , / po-ti-ni-ja 'me-ri'   *209^{VAS} 1

Gg 703   (-)

]1   ME+RI   *209^{VAS}+A 34[

v.   ]80[

Traces at right (after and above 34[ ).

Gg(1) 704   (103)

.1   ]   me-no

.2   ]o-ne   me-ri   *209^{VAS}+A 1

Gg(3) 705   (140)

.1   ]   a-mi-ni-so , / e-re-u-ti-ja   ME+RI   *209^{VAS} 1

.2   ]pa-si-te-o-i   ME+RI   *209^{VAS} 1

.3   ]o-ne   ME+RI   *209^{VAS} 1

Gg(4) <706>   (220)

]to / o-pe-ro   *209^{VAS} 'ME+RI' 20

Missing; text from SM II, pl. 37.

Gg(4) 707 + 5022   (220)

    ]ra   *209^{VAS} 'ME+RI' 2

v.]180

Gg(4) 708 + 7718   (220)

    ]to / o-pe-ro   'ME+RI' *209^{VAS} 20

v.]580

        Perhaps trace of sign immediately after o-pe-ro, in a
        break.

Gg 709   (-)

.a]-na   [
.b]   *209^{VAS} 2 [

        .b Trace of a sign at right edge, probably an ideogram
            (perhaps AES).

Gg 710   (-)

    ]'ME+RI' *209^{VAS} 6 [

Gg 711   (-)

    ] [[*209^{VAS}+A 270]] [

v.]290   KE 200[

lat. inf.] ku-do-ni-jo , [

        v. First numeral rather doubtful.

Gg(2) 713 + 994   (135)

    ma-ri-ne-we , / do-e-ra   'ME+RI' *209^{VAS}+A [
        Perhaps *209^{VAS}+A 1[.

Gg(3) 717   (140)

.1] , me-na , pa-si-te-o[-i
.2]si-da-o-ne , ME+RI [
        .2 Traces at right.

Gg(2)   995 + 7370 + 7591 + 7764   (135)

   ma-ki-ro-ne , / ku-pi-ri-jo , 'ME+RI' *209^{VAS}+A 6[

   *209^{VAS}+A over erasure. 6[perhaps over erasure.

   verso: streaked impressions corresponding to fingermarks
   on the recto.

Gg 5007   (-)

   ] ME+RI *209^{VAS}+A 10[

   Traces at left.

<u>Gg(2)</u> 5184   (135?)

   ]*209^{VAS}+A 4[

   Basketry (?) marks on verso (cf. Gg 995).

Gg(3) 5185   (140)

   .1   ]-to , a-pa-to[

   .2   ]o-ne ME+RI[

Gg 5548   (-)

   [[*209^{VAS}+A]] [

   v.   ku[

Gg(1) 5552   (103)

   .1   ]me-no

   .2   ]2

Gg 5637 + 8243   (-)

   .1   ]ru 1 [

   .2   ] za-we-[.] *209^{VAS} [

<u>lat. inf.</u>]me-zo-e *209^{VAS} [

      .2 Trace at left. One or two signs after <u>we</u>:
      certainly not <u>ta</u> (te-ro, o, nu, or *56?; perhaps
      one sign over another erased).

205

Gg(4) 7232   (220?)

   ] 5 [

        Trace of ideogram at left, perhaps *209^{VAS}?

Gg(1) 7369   (103)

.1   ka-]ra-e-ri-jo-jo me-no[

.2   ] LANA 1 M 1   me-ri S[

Gg(2) 7371   (135?)

   ]6   *209^{VAS} 1[

     Trace of a ruling in the middle.

Gg(2) 7372   (135?)

   ]*209^{VAS}+A   24

Gg(1) 8053   (103)

.1]me-no

.2] vacat

Gm

Gm 840   (-)

.1   ]ni-jo , / a-pu-da-se-we

.2   ]1   VIN 168

.3   ]   VIN 100

.4   ]25   VIN 75[

.5]to   [   ]125   VIN 155

       reliqua pars sine regulis

    Cut at bottom. Palimpsest.

Gm 5788   (-)

.1]si-jo , VIN[

.2] vacat   [

Gv

Gv 862   (-)

.1   ]su-za   ARB 1770

.2   ]jo   ARB 405

.3   ']i-po-qa'   ARB 10[   ]   ARB 17   *<u>174</u> 20

.4   ][[4]]

.5   ]365   *<u>174</u> 225

.6   ]   <u>vacat</u>

    .1-.3 Four varieties of the sign ARB are used, each
            associated with a different introductory word.

    .3 Trace of sign before the second ARB (perhaps
            ]me). 20 over erasure?

    .5 Over erasure.

    .6 Probably over erasure.

    v. Tallying (10 or 11 tens).

Gv 863   (-)

.1   ]qa-ra , / jo-e-ke-to-qo , wo-na-si , si[

.2   ] we-je-we   *<u>174</u> 420   <u>su</u> ARB 104[

    .1 <u>jo-e-ke-to-qo</u>, <u>wo</u> over erasure.

Gv 864   (-)

.1   ]   *<u>174</u> 69[

.2   ]su-za   ARB 53[

.3   ]   pu-ta *<u>174</u> [

    Many traces of erasure.

G

G 760   (-)

.a   ]no   <u>HORD</u> 1   a[

.b   ]ni-ja-we-jo   [

    .a <u>a</u>-[or <u>A</u> 1[.

G 820   ASHM (-)

.1]ṇa , e-ko-si , a-pi , ku-do-ni-ja / to-sa 'ki-ri-ta' LUNA 1

.2]ja-qe , *56-ko-we-i-ja-qe   LUNA 4

.3]ti-ja , ku-ta-ti-ja-qe , po-ti-ni-ja-we-ja , a-pu , ke-u-po-
                                                            de-ja

.4]   LUNA 4

      .1 Possibly]dị. Trace of erasure after to-sa.

      .3 Probably over erasure down to po-; -pu, ke-u- over
         erasure.

G 5528   (-)

.1 sup. mut.

.2] vacat

.3]T 9 [

.4 inf. mut.

G 7352   (-)

    ] 3 T 2 [

        Shape of break at left favours PYC. The 2 is abnormal
        owing to lack of room. Traces of another sign at right.

G 7355   (-)

    ]o T 5

        Cut at right.

G 7364   (-)

    ]37 T 5[

        Perhaps 6̣[or 7̣[.

G 7509 + 7879   (-)

.1]   di-ka-ta-de[

.2]   CỴP+Ọ 6[

G 7525   (-)

.1]ko 1 HORD T 1 [

.2 inf. mut.

        .1 Possibly KO̲.

208

K

K 93   ("124")

$*226^{VAS}$ 2 $*226^{VAS}$[

First $*226$ over erasure. Second = $*205^{VAS}$+$*200^{VAS}$.

K 434   (-)

.1   ]sa , $*208^{VAS}$ 1 $*229^{VAS}$ 1

.2   ]de-wa-pi , ko-no-ni-pi , $*217^{VAS}$ 1

The division into two lines ends after $*229^{VAS}$ 1 and $*217^{VAS}$ occupies the full height of the tablet.

K 700   (-)

.1   ]   300 $*210^{VAS}$+KA 900[

.2   ]   300 $*210^{VAS}$+KA 900 da-mi[

In both lines the traces preceding 300 are not consistent with with numerals.

K(1) 740   (102?)

sup. mut.

.1   ] vestigia[

.2   di-pa   AES $*214^{VAS}$ 30[

.3   qe-ro$_2$ 'AES' $*255$ 16

.4   ku-ru-su-$*56$ $*207^{VAS}$1

.5   pi-ri-je   ZE 1

.6   ] 'me-no-no['

inf. mut.

.3.4.5 Large dots after $*255$, before $*207^{VAS}$, and before ZE.

.6 Trace of at least two large signs at the beginning of the line.

K(2) 773 + 1809   (224?)

.A   ]   ke $*202^{VAS}$ 7

.B   ] ku-pi-ri-jo /ke $*202^{VAS}$ 1

.B $*202^{VAS}$ differs from form in .A; more like $*205^{VAS}$ but without handle.

K(2) 774   (224)

  a-ro-we   *212^{VAS}+<u>u</u> 1

K(2) 775   (224)

  ]*47-ti-jo   *212^{VAS}+<u>u</u>[

K(2) 776   (224)

  ]jo   *212^{VAS}+<u>u</u> 5

K 778   (-)

.1   ]ka-ra-re-we   *210^{VAS} 180
.2   ]pi̧-ja-qe
.3   ] <u>vacat</u>
.4   ]no , VIR 1
.5   ]to̧ , VIR 1
.6   ]do-ke-u ,

      .1 Trace (of large sign?) at left.

K(1) 829 + 874   (102)

.1   ] <u>vacat</u>   [
.2   ]*202^{VAS}+<u>DI</u> 75 / me-wi-jo-e , [ ]4 *202^{VAS}+<u>DI</u> 40[
.3   ]35 / me-wi-jo-e[   ]*202^{VAS}[+<u>DI</u>
.4   ] <u>vacat</u>   [

      .2 Traces of strokes, perhaps tens, above]4.
      .3 Perhaps trace of *202^{VAS} on left edge.

K(1) 872   ASHM (102)

.1   ]ke-ra-a ,   *227^{VAS} [
.2   ]me-no , ne-qa-sa-pi , *227^{VAS} 1
.3a   ]-te-te , ku-ru-so , [[ku̧-ru̧-so̧]]
.3b ne-]qa-sa-pi ,   *218^{VAS} 3
.4   <u>inf. mut.</u>

      .3a]-<u>te-te</u> :]pi̧-te-te possible.
      .3b Erased word under *218^{VAS} ([[<u>we</u> . . . <u>no</u>]]).

<u>K(1)</u> 873   (102?)

.1   ]we u-do   *<u>211</u>^{VAS}+<u>PO</u> 32[

.2   ]-we   *<u>211</u>^{VAS}+<u>PO</u> 25[

.3   ]we   *<u>211</u>^{VAS}+<u>PO</u> 22 [

    .2 Perhaps]-<u>ṛo</u>-we.

K(1) 875   (102)

.1   ] ,   qa-si-re-wi-ja , di-pa , a-no-wo-to [

.2   pe-ri-ta ,   qa-si-re-wi-ja , di-pa , a-no-wo-to , [

.3   wi-na-jo ,   qa-si-re-wi-ja , di-pa , a-no-wo-to [

.4   i-da-i-jo ,   qa-si-re-wi-ja , di-pa , a-ni-wo-to [

.5   sa-me-ti-jo , qa-si-ṛe-wi̤-ja , di-pa , a-no-wo-to   [

.6   i-je-re-wi-jo , qa-si-ṛe[-wi-]ja̤ , a-no-wo-to   *<u>202</u>^{VAS} 10
                                             po-ti-[

    .6 10 over [[5]] . <u>po-ti-ṇi̤</u>[possible.

<u>K(1)</u> 877   (102?)

   ] , ma-te-u-pi̤ , *<u>212</u>^{VAS}+<u>U</u>[

K(2) 1810   (= 776 bis b)   ASHM (224)

   ] *<u>212</u>^{VAS}+<u>U</u> 1

K(2) 5526   (224)

   ]jo *<u>212</u>^{VAS}+<u>U</u>[

K 7353   (-)

   ] *<u>2̣1̣3̣</u>^{VAS} 1̣0̣[

K 7363   ("124")

   ] *<u>155</u>^{VAS}+<u>DI</u> [

K 8244   (-)

   ] *<u>207̣</u>^{VAS}[

K(2) 8440   (224)

   ]-jo   *<u>212</u>^{VAS}+<u>Ṳ</u>[

    One or two signs before <u>jo</u> , the second probably <u>ni</u> or <u>sa</u>.

Lc

Lc(2)   446   (113?)

  te-ra-po-si-jo[

Lc(2)   481   (113/115)

 .A] 'pa-we-a' TELA^3 30[

 .B] , ku-do-ni-ja LANA[

 v. to-]u-ka LANA[

    .A TELA^3 over erasure.

    .B Trace of large sign at left, perhaps jo.

Lc(2)   483 + fr.   (113/115)

 .A]ne TELA^3 26 2

 .B] LANA 12 M 1 [

 v.]LANA 7

    A. Isolated 2 at end of line, cf. Lc 7377, Lc 7433.

Lc(2)   504   (113/115)

 .A]   pa-we-[

 .B]ru-so-no , / me-zo[

 v.] to-u-ka LANA[

    .A Trace at right consistent with a.

Lc(2)   512   (113/115)

  si-ra-ri-ja[

 v. to-u[-ka

Lc(1)   525   (103)

 .a   'wa-na-ka-te-ra' TELA^3+TE 40 LANA 100[

 .b se-to-i-ja , / tu-na-no TELA^1 3 LANA [

    Right half over erasure.

    .b Erased tens after TELA^1 3. Traces after LANA,
    probably numerals (units?).

Lc(1)   526   (103)

 .A]   'pe-ko-to' TELA^1+TE 10 TELA^2+TE 14[

 .B]da-wi-ja / tu-na-no TELA^1 3 LANA[

Lc(1)   527 + 7143 + 7331   (103)
.A   ]   'pe-ko-to' TELA^1+$\underline{TE}$ 2   TELA^2+$\underline{TE}$ 19   LANA 153
.B   ]e-ki-si-ja / tu-na-no   TELA^1 2   LANA 6

Lc(1)   528   (103)
.A   'pa-we-a' ko-u-ra   TELA^x[
.B   e-ra-ja / tu-na-no   TELA^1 1[

Lc(1)   529 + 545   (103)
.A   TELA^2+$\underline{TE}$ 30   [
.B   ri-jo-ni-ja / tu-na-no   TELA[^{1}

Lc(1)   530 + 7384   (103)
.A   ]   pa-we-a ko-u-ra   TELA^1 40   LANA 60[
.B   ]ja / tu-na-no   TELA^1 3 LANA 12   TELA+$\underline{TE}$ 7   LANA[
        .A Perhaps divider after pa-we-a.

Lc(1)   531 + 542   (103)
.A   ]   'pa-we-a ko-u-ra'   *$\underline{161}$ TELA^1 15[
.B   ]a-ra-ka-te-ja /   tu-na-no   TELA^1 1 [

Lc(1)   532 + 554   (103)
.A   ]   'pa-we-a' ko-u-ra TELA^1 16 LANA 26 M 1 [
.B   ]ku-wo / tu-na-no TELA^1 1 LANA 3   TELA+$\underline{TE}$ 4 LANA 28[
        .B]o-wo not entirely excluded. Plain TELA+$\underline{TE}$.

Lc(1)   533   (103)
.A   TELA^1+$\underline{TE}$ [
.B   tu-ri-si-ja [

Lc(1)   534 + 7647 + 7818   (103)
.A   pa-we-a , ko-u-ra *$\underline{161}$ TELA^1 10[
.B   e-ro-pa-ke-ja /   tu-na-no   TELA^1 1[
        .B e-ro-pa-ke-ja over erasure.

213

Lc(1)   535 + 538   (103)

.A   ta-ra-si-ja   pa-we-a   [
.B   ke-ri-mi-ja   tu-na-no [
.C   to-sa /   pe-ko-to [
          .C Trace at right consistent with TELA.

Lc(1)   536 [+] 7383   (103)
.A   ] 'ta-ra-si[-ja']pa-we-a[ ]TELA^x 200
.B   ] 'vest.['   ]   tu-na-no[ ]TELA^1 48   a-ro-zo 'ki-to'
                                                                    TELA^1 1
.C   to-]sa /   pe[-ko-to TELA^1+TE]18   TELA^2+TE 267

Lc(1)   540 + 8075   (103)
.A   'pa-we-a' ko-u-ra   TELA^1 3[
.B   da-te-we-ja /   [
         .A 3[: arrangement suggests 9.

Lc(1)   541 + 7104 + 8045   (103)
.A   TELA^1+TE 22   LANA 154
.B   ja-pu$_2$-wi-ja
         .A 154 : fourth unit damaged, probably accidentally.
         .B]pu$_2$-wi-ja still legible on original; text derived
             from drawing in SM II.

Lc(1)   543   (103)
.A   TELA^1+TE 11[
.B   qa-mi-ja /   tu[-na-no

Lc(1)   546   (103)
     pa-i-ti-ja[

Lc(1)   547   (103)
     tu-ni-ja[

Lc(1)   548   (103)
     ko-no-so , / ko[-u-re-ja ?

214

Lc(1)   549   (103)

      ko-no-so , / te[-pe-ja ?

Lc(1)   550 + 7381   (103)

.A   'pa-we-a['

.B   a-mi-ni-so / ko-u-re-ja[

Lc(1)   551 + 5507 + 7397   (103)

.A   'pa-we-a' [ko-u-ra] TELA^x 110 LANA 140[

.B   e-me-si-jo-jo ,/ tu-na-no TELA^1 3 LANA 9 pe TELA^x+TE 2

                                          TELA^1[ ]+TE 10[

lat. inf.   LANA 250[

Lc(1)   552   (103)

.A   ]LANA 77

.B   ]TELA^1 1   LANA 3

Lc(1)   553 + 7379   (103)

.A   pa-we-a ko-]u-ra TELA^1 50 LANA 82[

.B   tu-na-no TELA^1]2 LANA 6   TELA^1+TE 10 LANA 70[

      .B 70[probably complete.

Lc(1)   555   (103)

.A   ]LANA 178[

.B   ]2 LANA 6

Lc(1)   557   (103)

.A   ] TELA^1 80   LANA 130[

.B   ]TELA^1 7   LANA 11[

Lc(1)   558   (103)

.a   ]tu-na-no   TELA^2 1   LANA 3

.b   ]   TELA^2+TE 20[ ]

      Traces of erasure. Possible large sign at left.

Lc(1)   560 + 7587 + 7815   (103)

.A   pa-we-a , ko-ụ[-ra
.B   ne-we-wi-ja /   [

Lc(1)   561   (103)

.a   [[po-pu]] e-pi-qe ṛe-si
.b   e-ra-ja /   TELA^{1}+$\underline{TE}$ 1
     .b TELA^{3} ($\underline{KT}^{3}$) unlikely.

Lc(2)   581   (113/115)

.A   ]   'pa-we-a' TELA^{4} 40[
.B   ]no , / ko-u-re-ja LANA 30[

v.   ]   to-u-ka L̲A̲N̲A̲[
        .B k̲o̲-u̲-r̲e̲-j̲a̲ over erasure.

Lc(1)   582   (103)

.A   ]T̲E̲L̲A̲^{x} 30 LANA [
.B   tu-]na̤-no TELA^{1} 6[

Lc   646 + 662 + 6015 + 8517 + $\underline{fr}$. [+] 5875   (103)

.A   o-pi-si-ri-ja-we [pe-ko-]to '$\underline{re}$'TELA^{1}+$\underline{TE}$ 1
                                                         LANA 20[
.B   [ ] e-qe-si-jo   [TELA^{x}] LANA 140   [
.C   i-ja-pu$_{2}$-we / [   ]tu-na-no   [TELA^{1}]1̣ LANA 3   [

v.   ] o̲ [ ]T̲E̲L̲A̲^{x} 6   TUN+$\underline{KI}$ 2[ ] $\underline{vacat}$
        Palimpsest.
        .A Traces at right of 646 consistent with pẹ.
        .B Traces at right of 646 consistent with T̤E̤L̤A̤.
        .C Traces at right of 646 consistent with T̤E̤L̤A̤.

Lc(1)   1580   (103)

.A   ]L̲A̲N̲A̲ 56
.B   ] LANA 3

Lc(1)   5053   (103)

     a-mi-ni-so[

                        216

<u>Lc(1)</u> 5612 + 5885   (103?)

.1   ]   TELA^4 [[+<u>ZO</u>]] 1   [

.2   ]LANA   M 1[

v.   ][[-a- .]]ra[

<u>lat. sup.</u>   [[to-]so   LANA   ]]   [

        Possibly same tablet as Lc 7394.

        .1 TELA^4: fourth "fringe" very small.

<u>Lc(1)</u> 5746   (103)

.A   ] TELA^1+<u>TE</u> 4   TELA^2+<u>TE</u> 10[

.B   ]tu-na-no   TELA^1 2   LANA[

<u>Lc(1)</u> 7285   (103)

.A   ]30   LANA 100[

.B   ]   <u>vacat</u>   [

        Possible traces on verso and <u>lat. sup.</u>

<u>Lc(1)</u> 7289 + 7395   (103)

.A   ] TELA^1 13[ ]LANA 30   [

.B   tu-na-]no   TELA^1 1   LANA 3   [

<u>Lc(1)</u> 7318   (103)

.A   ]LANA 14[

.B   ] <u>vacat</u> [

<u>Lc(2)</u> 7319   (113)

.A   ]5   [

.B   ]5 M 1 [

        Trace on left edge of verso.

<u>Lc(1)</u> 7321   (103)

.A   ] LANA[ ]100[

.B   ]TELA^1 2   LANA 1[

217

Lc(1)   7376   (103)

.A   ]   'pa-we-a' ko-u-ra *<u>161</u> TELA^1 10[

.B   ]ja /   [

Lc(2)   7377 + 7385 + 8016   (113/115)

.A   ]   'pa-we-a'   TELA^3 12   3

.B   ]we̤-ri-jo-jo , / ku-do-ni-ja   LANA 18

v.   ]to-u-ka   LANA 4

        .A Isolated 3 at end of line, cf. Lc 483.

Lc(1)   7392 + 7398   (103)

.A   ']p̤a-we̤[-a]' ko-u[-ra   ]230[

.B   we-]we-si-jo-jo [tu-na-no] TELA^1 10[

        .A Perhaps]240[.

Lc(1)   7394 + 8684   (103?)

.1   ]ja TELA^2 1 [

.2   ]-ja-i L̤A̤N̤A̤[

        Possibly same tablet as Lc 5612.

Lc(2)   7433   (113?)

.A   ]T̤E̤L̤A̤ 20   5

.B   ]LANA 16 M 1 N 2

        .A For 5 cf. Lc 483, Lc 7377.

Lc(2)   7438   (113/115)

.1   ] 5[

.2   ] 2 M[

v.   ] M 1 [

        v. Trace at left (numerals or L̤A̤N̤A̤).

Lc(1)   7549   (103)

.A   ]   [

.B   ]da-wi-ja / tu[

218

Lc(1) 7901   (103)

    da-]*22-ti-ja [

Lc(1) 8572   (103)

    ]ne-ja [

        Perhaps]ne-ja , and beginning of a division into .A and .B.

Ld

Ld(1) 571   (116)

.a   pe-ne-we-ta a-ro$_2$-a   *$\underline{158}$ 1
.b pa-we-a , / e-qe-si-ja , re-u-ko-nu-ka ,   TELA^3 25
      .b 5 over erasure.

Ld(1) 572   (116)

.a   pe-ne-we-ta , a-ro$_2$-a   *$\underline{158}$ 1
.b pa-we-a / e-qe-si-ja re-u-ko-nu-ka   TELA^2 25
      .b 5 over erasure.

Ld(1) 573   (116)

.a   e-ru-ta-ra̤-pi
.b pa-we-a , / ke-se-nu-wi-ja , re-u-ko-nu-ka TELA^3 35   *$\underline{158}$ 1
      .b 35 *$\underline{158}$ 1 probably over erasure.

Ld(1) 574   (116)

.a   re-u-ko-nu-ka [
.b pa-we-a , / ke-se-nu-wi-ja [

Ld(1) 575 + 580   (116)

.a   e̤-qe-si-ja
.b pa-we-a , / pa-ra-ku-ja   TELA^2 30 *$\underline{158}$ 1

Ld(1) 576   (116)

    ]TELA 10 [[   ]] *$\underline{158}$ 1

219

Ld(1) 577   (116)
     ]TELA^x 40[[ ]] *<u>158</u> 1

Ld(1) 579   (116)
.a   po-ki-ro-nu-ka , o-[
.b   pa-we-a / o-re-ne-ja ,   [
     .b Trace at right, possibly <u>e</u>-[.

Ld(1) 583 + 6024   (116)
.a   ]o-re-ne-ja , a-ro$_2$-a   [
.b   e-]qe-si-ja , re-u-ko-nu-ka[

Ld(1) 584   (116)
.1   po-]ki-ro-nu-ka 'o-pi-qi-na' TELA^2 4
.2   pa-]ro , e-ta-wo-ne-we 'o-nu-ka' TELA^2 5
<u>lat. inf.</u>]to-sa   TELA 15
     .1 Possibly <u>o-pi qi-na</u> (but certainly no divider).

Ld(1) 585   (116)
.a   ] re-u-ko-nu-ka e-ru-ta-ra-pi
.b   ] ke-se-nu-wi-ja ,   TELA^2 25
     Traces of erasure. .b written before .a .

Ld(1) 587 + 589 + 596 + 8262   (116)
.1   to-sa , po-ki-ro-nu-ka TELA^2 24   re-u-ko-nu-ka TELA^2 372
.2   ko-ro-ta$_2$ TELA^2 14 *56-ra-ku-ja TELA^x 42 po-ri-wa
                                                        TELA^2 1
<u>lat. inf.</u>   <u>vacat</u>   [   ]to-<u>s</u>a TELA 149
     All numerals, except the last on .2, completely or
     partly over erasure.

Ld(1) 591   (116)
.1   ]   re-u-ko-nu-ka[
.2   e-]ta-wo-ne   o-nu-ka   [

Ld(1) 595   (116?)

.1   ]e-ro-pa-ke-ja   <u>o</u> TUN+<u>KI</u> 1[

.2   <u>pe</u> TUN+<u>KI</u> 8   [

     .1 Probably nothing lost before <u>e-ro-pa-ke-ja</u>.

Ld(1) 598 + 661   (116)

.1   wi-jo-qo-ta-o po-ki-ro-nu-ka   TELA 1   [

.2   re-u-ko-nu-ka TELA^1 37   ko-ro-ta$_2$ TELA 2 [

<u>lat. inf.</u>   to-sa   TELA 40 <u>o</u> TELA^1 6[

Ld(1) 599   (116?)

.a   ]   pa-we-a   [

.b   ]ko-ro-ta$_2$ TELA^2 [

     Traces of erasure at right.

Ld(1) 649 + 8169   (116)

.a   ]   e-ru-ta-ra-pi   [[re-ụ]][

.b   pa-we-]a / ke-se-ne-wi-ja , / re-u-ka[

     .b Trace at right perhaps TELA.

Ld(1) 656   (116?)

.1   pe-ki-ti[

.2   re-u-k̤o[

Ld(2) 785   (114)

.1   po-]ki-ro-nu-ka , '*<u>161</u>' TELA^2 3   ki-ri-ta ,/ e-ru-ta-ra-pi ,
                                            *<u>161</u> TELA^3 [

.2a]   e-ru-ta-ra-pi   [

.2b]TELA^x 2 ke-ro-ta , / *<u>161</u> ki-to-na   TELA^x[

     Trace of a previous ruling.

     .2b TELA^x[: at least TELA^1[, probably TELA^3[.

Ld(2) 786   (114)

.A   ]   a-*35-ka   TELA^3+<u>PA</u> [

.B   pa-we-]a$_2$, / ke-ro-ta , *<u>161</u> ki[

221

Ld(2)   787 + 1009 + 7378   (114)
 .A   a-*35-ka   TELA^3+$\underline{PA}$ 1 [
 .B   pa-we-a$_2$, / o-re-ne-ja   *$\underline{161}$ ki-to-pi[
           Cut at left.

Ld(2)   788   (114)
 .A   ]   ti-ri[
 .B   pa-we-]a$_2$, / ke-ro-ta[
              .A Over erasure.

Ld(1)   5601   (116)
        sup. mut.
         pa-we[
        inf. mut.

Ld(1)   5607 + 8247   (116?)
 .1   ]TELA^2 1   [
 .2   e-]ta-wo-ne   TELA^2 1[
            .2 Perhaps 2̣[.

Ld(1)   5615 + 5873 + 8248 + $\underline{fr}$.   (116?)
 .1   re-u-]ko-nu-ka   TELA^2 13   [
 .2   ]o-nu[   ] TELA^2 7   [

Ld(1)   5647   (116?)
        sup. mut.
        ] *$\underline{158}$[

Ld(1)   5845   (116?)
 .1   ]   po-ki-ro[
 .2   ']nu-ka' ọ[
            .2 Traces of erasure (no divider).

Ld(1)   5894   (116)
 .1   ]nu-ka [
 .2   inf. mut.

Ld(1) 5916   (116?)

  .1a]   o-nu[

  .1b]TELA^1 13   pa-ro , e[

  .2   ]   <u>vacat</u>   [

Ld(1) 5955   (116?)

  .1   da-*22-ti[

  .2   pa-ro , e[

Ld(2) 8192   (114)

  .A   <u>sup. mut.</u>

  .B   ]*<u>161</u> *35-ka[

Ld(1) 8245 + 8691 + 8729   (116?)

  .1   ]TELA^1 15

  .2   ] <u>vacat</u>

      .1 TELA^2 not impossible. Perhaps X̣ after 15.

Le

Le 641 + <u>frr.</u>   (103)

  .1   o-a-po-te , de-ka-sa-ṭọ , a-re-i-jo , o-u-qe-po[

  .2   pa-i-ti-ja , '<u>pe</u>' TELA+<u>TE</u> 2 <u>mi</u> TELA^1+<u>TE</u> 14 da-wi-ja ,
                                          <u>pe</u> TELA^X+<u>TE</u> 1[

  .3   do-ti-ja <u>mi</u> TELA+<u>TE</u> 6   qa-mi-ja TELA^1+<u>TE</u> 1[

  .4   ko-no-so , / te-pe-ja '<u>mi</u>' TELA+<u>TE</u> 3 tu-ni-ja TELA^1+<u>TE</u> 1 [

  .5.6 <u>vacant</u> [   ] <u>vacant</u>   [

Le 642 + 5950   (103)

  .1   ]ra-wo , de-ko-to 'ṭa-ra-si-ja' ne[

  .2   ]ja TELA^1+<u>TE</u> 2   ri-jo-ni-ja TELA^1+<u>TE</u>[

  .3   ]ri-jo TELA^1+<u>TE</u> 6   da-mo-ko[

  .4   ] <u>vacat</u>   [

Le 654   (103)

 .1   sup. mut.

 .2   ]si̥-ja [

 .3   a-mi-ni-si-ja [

 .4   se-to-i-ja 'wa' 2[

 .5   tu-ni-ja 2[

 .6   we-we-si-jo 1̣[

Le 5629 + 5867 + 8446 + 8522 + 8559 + frr. [+] 8512   (103)

 .1   e-ki[-si-]ja   TELA^1+TE [

 .2   vest.[ ]j̣a / a-pu-do-si TELA^1+TE [

 .3   pa-i-to̥ / ko-ma-we-to̤   TELA^1+TE [

Le 5646 + 5912 + 5993 + 6012   (103)

 .1   o-pi , [']e-ko-so' [

 .2A   [. .]   TELA^x+TE 1̣   [

 .2B *56-ko-we / o-pi   TELA+TE 1   // tu-ni[-ja

        .1 Perhaps TELA̤[at end.

        .2A Perhaps p̥o̤-m̤e before TELA^x+TE.

Le 5903 + 5937 + frr.   (103)

 .1a]a̤-pu-do-si   [

 .1b]wa-de   TELA^1+TE 1 [

 .2   ]   vacat   [

        .1a Perhaps]ja / .

Le 5930 + 6003   (103)

 .1   ]-ko-si-[

 .2   ]ja mi̤ TELA+TE 11[

 .3   ]vest.[

 .4   ]   TELA^1+TE[

 .5   ]   vacat

        .2 Perhaps TELA^1.+TE.

Le 6014   (103)

 .1   sup. mut.

 .2   ]TELA^1+TE 6 [

 .3   ]1̣6   [

224

Ln

Ln 1568 (103)

```
.1a                    mi-ja-ro , e , pa , 4     e , pa 6           e , pa 12
.1b  *56-po-so 1 wa-wa-ka 1 TELA¹+TE 1  ru-ki-ti-ja  pe TELA+TE 1  wi-da-ma-ta₂ , mi TELA¹+TE 1
.2a       e , pa 12                e  pa 4                     e , pa 4            e , pa 8
.2b  po-po  pe  TELA¹+TE 1   ta-su  mi TELA+TE 1 ko-re-wo  mi TELA+TE 1  di-*65-pa-ta mi TELA+TE 1
.3a       pa 12                       pa 11                        pa 12
.3b  ru-sa-ma pe TELA¹+TE   na-e-ra-ja  pe TELA+TE 1  qe-pa-ta-no   pe TELA+TE 1
.4a       pa 8
.4b  ]tu-na-no , ru-nu TELA¹ 1 [     ]TELAˣ 1
.5                               no-si-ro  TELAˣ+TE 3
.6   da-wo   to-sa te-[    ]    pa-ra-ja 'mi'TELAˣ+TE 7  [
lat. inf. .a    a-ze-ti-ri-ja     ne-ki-ri-de  [
       .b  o-pi , ma-tu-we  o-nu-ke  LANA 1  o-pi , po-ni-ke-ja[
```

Tablet now much damaged; several readings from Ashmolean photograph.

.3a pa 11 perhaps over erasure.

.4b Traces after TELA¹ 1, before lacuna.

.6 Traces at right (possibly LANA[ ).

lat. inf. a-ze-ti-ri-ja : ri damaged by a blow.

L

L 104   ("124")

  .a]pa-we-pi   [

  .b]ro   TELA^2 [

        .a Perhaps] , <u>pa-we-pi</u>.

        .b Perhaps traces of erased numerals after TELA^2
          (at least [[2]]).

L 178 + 281   ("124")

     we-we-e-a   *<u>161</u> TELA^3+<u>PA</u> 6 / u-po-we   TUN+<u>RI</u> 2

L 192 + 8022   ("124")

     ]-da-na / to-ni-ja   TELA^2 2

L 433   (-)

     ] TELA^3+<u>ZO</u> 1[

L(3) 455   (207)

  .1]o-pe-ro [

  .2]sa-me-u[

        Probably same tablet as L 1616.

        .2 Trace of upright at left.

<u>L(6) 460</u>   (210?)

     a-du[

L(6) 469   (210)

  .a   me-[.]-ta   [

  .b po-ku-ta / pa-i-to   TELA^3+<u>PU</u> 34[

        .a <u>me-ki-ta</u> and <u>me-ko-ta</u> both possible.

L 470   (-)

  .a]-ta

  .b]   TELA^2+<u>PU</u> 415

  v.   90   [

        v. Perhaps 60 over [[90]] .

L(7) 471   (211)

 .a   ]   me-zo-e
 .b   pu-]ka-ta-ri-ja , / re-u-ka   TELA^4+$\underline{PU}$ 10

L(6) 472   (210)

      ]ko-ru-we-ja   TELA^2+$\underline{PU}$ 84
         84 over erasure.

L(2) 473   (207)

 .A   o-pe-ro $\underline{pe}$ TELA^2+$\underline{PU}$ 30[
 .B   qa-ra / i-se-we-ri-jo   [
         Traces of erasure.

L(7) 474 + $\underline{fr}$.   (211)

      po-pu-re-ja , / pu-ka-ta-ri-ja   TELA^3+$\underline{PU}$ 21

L(4) 475   (208)

      do-ti-ja   TELA^2+$\underline{PU}$ 5̣0[

L(4) 480   (208)

 .a   ]   ka[
 .b   ]pi   qo-u-qo-ta [

L(4) 484   (208)

      do-ti-ja / ọ[

L(4) 489   (2̣08?)

      ka-to-ro [
         Trace at upper right.

L   491   (-)

 .1   ] TELA^3 50
 .2   ] $\underline{vacat}$
         Traces of erasure.
         .2 Perhaps trace at left.

L   501   (209?)

      ]ta   TELA^2+$\underline{PU}$ 34̣[

227

16

L(5) 513   (209)

  .a   qe-te-o TELA^2 [

  .b po-po TELA^2 4   [

v.   [[a-mi-si-ja TELA^1 12]][

       v. Possibly erased accidentally. Perhaps TELA^2.

L 514   (-)

  .1]ro , TELA^2+KU 14   a-[

  .2   ] TELA^3 18 [

      .2 Trace of sign at left.

L(4) 515 + 7412   (208)

    ]-mo TELA^1+PU 29 TELA+KU 2[

    Traces before mo consistent with ri. 9 over erasure.

L(4) 516   (208)

    ]2 TELA^2+KU 2

L 520   (-)

  .1   do-ti-ja ,   LANA 18 pe-re-ke *164 3

  .2 ka-ma   LANA 12   *164 2

  .3 sa-mu-ta-jo   LANA 24   *164 4

      Cut at right.

L 523   (-)

  .a]qe-re-jo   [

  .b]ku-da-ra-ro   TELA^x+PA[

lat. inf.]   ka[

L 564   (-)

    e-ko-so / po-ki-ro[

L 565   (-)

  .1 ']si' te-jo , ka-[

  .2]TELA^2 66   [

L(1) 567   (103)

.1   o-pi / po-po [

.2   o-pi / a$_3$-ka-ra 'ri-ta['

L 578   (-)

]ra-wo   *158 2 [

Traces at right, perhaps TELA[.

L 586   (103?)

.Aa   a-ro$_2$-a TELA^2 3 [

.Ab   LANA 3   TELA^x[

.B   ]ru-wo-we-ja /   [

v.   ]15   3 [

L 588 + 644 + 5777 + fr.   (-)

.1   i-ku-tu-re , ru-si-qe , a-pa-i-ti-jo , ze-me-qe[

.2   a-qo-ta , TELA^1 8   zo-ta-qe , TELA^1 13 [

.3   po-[   ] , e-[.] , ku-do-ni-ja-de , di-du-me , o-qo-o-ki-te [

      .3 Probably divider after di-du-me, possibly after
          o-qo-o. po-[   ] : 2 or 3 signs in the lacuna,
          last perhaps qe or ka.

L 590   (103)

.1   po-]ki-ro-nu-ka   *161 TELA^1[

.2   ]re-u-ko-nu-ka *161 TELA^1[

lat. inf.]ke M 1 P 3

L(7) 592 + 663 + 8310 + frr.   (211?)

nu-wa-i-ja , / 'pa-we-a'   *161 TELA^3 30[[ ]]

L(2) 593 + 5992 + 8587   (103)

.Aa] vac. [   ]o-pe-te-wo-qe   *161[

.Ab] vac. [   ]si-ja , o-re-ne-a   TELA^1[

.B   ko-]pu-ra ,/ e-ni-qe , pe-ne-we-ta *161 TELA^1 4 TUN+KI 2
                                                      TUN+KI[

      .B Oblique stroke after TUN+KI 2 indicating that
          following entry belongs to A.

229

L(1)   594   (103)

.a   ]   ri-ta , pa-we-a
.b   ]da-te-we-ja   TELA^1 1   TUN+<u>KI</u> 1

L(2)   647 + 2012 + 5943 + 5974   (103)
.A   ]   'nu-wa-ja , <u>pe</u> TELA^1['   ] TELA^1 17   TUN+<u>KI</u> 3
.B   ]ra , / e-ni-qe e-ra-pe-me-na 'nu-wa-ja' TELA^1[   ]-ra$_2$
                                              TELA^1 ^{2}$_1$

<u>lat. inf.</u>]   [[e-ri-[   ] TELA 1   ]]

         .A Trace of one or two signs before the second TELA^1
            (probably neither *<u>161</u> nor <u>mi</u>) [cf. the end of line .B].

         .B Traces of erasure : -<u>ni</u>- over [[<u>qe</u>]] and perhaps
            <u>e</u>[[-<u>qe</u> e-<u>ra</u>-<u>pe</u> ...]] (the <u>e</u>- now immediately follows
            the -<u>qe</u>); also other traces of erasure on the tablet
            (<u>ex. gr.</u> above]<u>ra</u>).

L(1)   648   (103)

.a   ri[-ta pa-we-a
.b   o-pi , / po-po[
         .b -<u>pi</u> , / <u>po</u>- over [[<u>po-po</u> ,]] .

L 651   (103)

.1   ]o , pa-we-o , 'e['
.2   ]nu-we-jo , / pa-we-o[

L 693   (103)

.1   ri-no , / re-po-to , 'qe-te-o' ki-to , AES M 1 [
.2   sa-pa P 2 Q 1   e-pi-ki-to-ni-ja   AES M 1[
         .2 <u>ni</u> over [[ja]] ; AES over erasure.

L 695   (103)

.1a]ti-jo   e-ta-wo-ne-wo
.1b]   o-pa   TELA^1 6
.2.3]   <u>vacant</u>
.4   ]2 P 2   e-ne-ro   're-u-ko' N 2

                          230

L 698   (103)

  .1]ne-we , pe-ko-to   *$\underline{164}^{1}$[

  .2]i-jo-te , 'ku-su-a-ta-o' 11[

  .3]jo-du-mi 'wo-ke' P 1[

         Possibly same tablet as Od 696.

L(10) 735   (214)

  .1]a-ro$_2$-e TELA^3+$\underline{PU}$ [

  .2]me-sa-ta , TELA^x+$\underline{PU}$[

         .2 TELA^x : at least TELA^1.

L 758   (-)

  .a ?o-]re-ne-o , po-pu-ro$_2$

  .b   ]o-no   TELA^2+$\underline{PU}$ 2

L 759 + 8023   (-)

      ]ta$_2$ TELA^3+$\underline{PU}$ 70

  v.]ku-ta-mi [[po-ma-no-ri]]

L(9) 761   (213)

      ra-su-ti-jo , / to-mi-ka[

L(9) 764 + 8015   (213)

      ]jo,/ to-mi-ka   TELA^3 50

         50 over erased numeral probably ending in 5.

L 771 + $\underline{fr}$.   (-)

  .1 ka-ta-ni-ja , po-ro-[. .] pa-we-a [

  .2]ka-ta-ni-ja , ki-to-ne , [. .]-to   [

         .2 Perhaps [.]-me-to.

L 868 + 5712   (-)

      ] , sa-de-so , TELA^2+$\underline{PU}$ 15 *$\underline{146}^{2}$[

lat. inf.   ]   11   [

         Trace at left.

231

L(3) 869   (207)

.A   o-pe-ro   pe̱ TELA^2+P̱U̱ 3
.B   ti-ri-to / p̣i̱[   ] vacat
        Palimpsest.

L 870   (114?)

    o-]da̤-ku-we-ta / we-we-e-a   TELA^3 1   TUN+ḴI̱ 1
        Cut at right.

L 871   (114?)

.a   ]   pa-ro , re-wa-jo
.b   ]ra , pe-ne-we-ta , / e-qe-si-ja , te-tu-ko-wo-a TELA^4 6
        Cut at right.

L <1599>   (-)

    ]TELA^2+P̱U̱[
        Missing; text from Myres' papers (= 1595.2?).

L(3) 1616   (207)

.A   ] 'pe̱' TELA^3+P̱U̱ 3
.B   ] vacat
        Probably same tablet as L 455.

L(8) 1647   ASHM (212)

.A   ']LANA' 6 TELA+ḴU̱ 5   TELA^3+P̱U̱ [
.B   ]   X   [
        Palimpsest.
        .A 5 corrected from 6.   TELA^3+P̱U̱ 1̣[?

L 1649   ASHM (103?)

.0   sup. mut.
.1   ]TELA^1̣ 4   ḴI̱ 2   e[
lat. inf.]-ja-o̱ 1   TELA^1 [

v.   ]a-ko-we-i-ja   [
            inf. mut.
            .1 4 over erasure. Perhaps E̱ 1[, but more probably e̱-[
               (e-ra̤[?).
            lat. īnf. Perhaps (less likely)]-ja-r̤o̱ 1.

232

L 2127   (-)

.1   ]o-pi , TELA^6+[?] [

.2   ]   TELA^x+<u>PU</u> [

       verso ruled (2 lines) but not inscribed.

       .1 TELA^6+<u>TE</u> or TELA^6+<u>ZO</u> possible.

L 5090   (-)

.1   ]pe-ko-[

.2   ]te-pa[

       Perhaps nothing lost at left.

       .1 Possibly]pe-ko-to[.

L(5) 5092   (209)

.a   ]   qe-te[-o

.b   ]so   TELA^1 [

L(2) 5108   (103)

.A   ] o-re-ne-ja *<u>161</u>[

.B   ] pe-ne-we-te   [

<u>lat. inf.</u> to-]sa   TELA^1 8[

       .A Traces at right not incompatible with TELA[.

L 5284   (114?)

       <u>sup. mut.</u>

.a   ]so   [

.b   ] , TELA^3 2 ru[

<u>lat. inf.</u>]-ka-ma [

       .b Perhaps [[<u>ru</u>]][.

L 5561   (-)

.1   ] TELA^3+<u>PU</u> 980[

.2   ]   <u>vacat</u>   [

       .1 Traces at left (perhaps numerals, but possibly
          ]wa or]si).

L 5569   (-)

     ]   TELA^4+<u>PU</u> 1[

233

L 5582   (-)
     ]   TELA^3+$\underline{PU}$ 4[
         Traces (of numerals?) at left.

L 5599   ("124")
         $\underline{\text{sup. mut.}}$
  .1   ]TELA^3+$\underline{PU}$ 10 [
  .2   ]TELA^x+$\underline{PU}$ 30 [
         $\underline{\text{inf. mut.}}$

L 5660   (103)
  .1 $\underline{\text{sup. mut.}}$
  .2   ] TELA^3+$\underline{TE}$ [

L 5745   (-)
     ]wa-ja , / ki-to[

L 5757   (209?)
  .a   ]TELA^3+$\underline{KU}$ 3
  .b   ]TELA^x+$\underline{KU}$ 4

L 5805   (221?)
     ]we   TELA^1[

L(2)   5909 + 5939 + 6007   (103)
  .1a   ]-ke-me-na , a-ro-za[
  .1b   ]o-re-ne-ja [
  .2   ] 'a-ro-za'   TELA^x 4 [
              .1a]ke-ke-me-na not impossible, but rather unlikely.

L(2)   5910 + 5920   (103)
  .1   ] , e-ni-qe , nu-wa-i-ja , [
  .2   ]a 'a-ro$_2$-a' *$\underline{161}$ TELA^1 12   po[
              .2 Perhaps TELA^2.

L 5914   (116?)
     ]TELA^1[ ] 40

234

L 5917   (103)

  .a   ] a-pu-do-si[
  .b]   TUN+<u>KI</u>   [

L(2) 5924 + 6000   (103)

  .A]   zo-[
  .B] , e-ni-qe [
         .A Perhaps zo-<u>ṭạ</u>[.

L(1) 5927   (103)

  .a]   ri-ta , pa-we[-a
  .b]te-we , / e-me[

L(1) 5949   (103)

  .a   ] , pa-we-a[
  .b]a$_3$-tu-ti-ja[
       .a Trace at left compatible wịth]<u>ṭạ</u>.
       .b <u>ti</u> over [[<u>ṭạ</u>]] . -<u>ẉạ</u>[not impossible.

L(2) 5961   (103)

  .1] ẹ-ni-qẹ[
  .2] TUN+<u>KI</u> 3[
      <u>inf. mut.</u>
       .2 3[: probably at least 5.

L 5987   (103?)

      <u>sup. mut.</u>
  .1   ]si[
  .2]re-ja <u>TELA</u>^{x}+[?][
  .3]ḍọ-si [

L(2) 5998   (103)

  .A   pa-we-ạ[
  .B ko-pu-ra , / e-ṇị[-qe

235

L 6002   (103?)

.1   <u>sup. mut.</u>

.2   ]TELA^1 1[

.3   ] TELA^x 1[

        <u>inf. mut.</u>

L(5)   7380 + 7500   (209)

.a   ]   qe-te-o   TELA^1 2[

.b   ]-ra /   TELA^x 4   <u>po</u> TELA^x[

L 7382   (103)

.a   ]-za   TELA^1[

.b   ]re-ja   [

L 7387   (-)

      ]TELA^3+PA 1

L 7389   (-)

      ]   *<u>161</u> TELA^2[

L 7390   (-)

      ]   TELA^1 12

      Cut at right. Possibly TELA^2 (but second "fringe" very low).

L 7391   (-)

      ]ka   TELA^2 20[

<u>L(5)</u>   7393   (209?)

.a   ] 3

.b   ] TELA^1 1

L 7396   (-)

      ]TELA 30[

      <u>inf. mut.</u>

L 7399   (116??)

        sup. mut.
    ]   TELA^2 2[

L(9) 7400 + 7402 + 8250   (-)
        ]to-mi-ka   TELA^2 12[
            12 corrected from 22[.

L 7401   (-)
    ] TELA^3 60[

L 7403 + 8199   (-)
        ]-so   TELA^3+PU 100 [
            100 over [[80]] .

L(8) 7404   (212)
    .1]TELA+KU 10   TELA^3+PU 100[
    .2] vacat   [

L 7405   (-)
        ]2   TELA^2+PU 90

L 7406   (-)
    ]   TELA^1+PU 130[

L 7407   (-)
    ]   TELA^2 20[

L 7408   (-)
    .a   ]te-ro   [
    .b   ]-jo-ne-we   TELA^2+PU[

L(10) 7409 + 8304   (214?)
    .A   ]   a-ro$_2$-e   TELA^3+PU 60[
    .B   to-]sa / me-sa-ta   TELA^2+PU 100 [
lat. inf.]   to-sa o[
            lat. inf. to-sa TELA[less probable.

                              237

L 7410   (-)
    ] TELA+$\underline{PU}$ 9
      Cut at right.

L(8) 7411   (212)
  .1]TELA^x 6 TELA^2+$\underline{PU}$ 100
  .2] $\underline{vacat}$

L(4) 7413   (208)
    ]TELA+$\underline{KU}$ 1

L 7414   (-)
    ]TELA^2+$\underline{PU}$ 13[

L(4) 7415   (208?)
    ]TELA^3+$\underline{PU}$ 1 [

L(4) 7416   (208?)
    ] TELA^x+$\underline{PU}$[

L 7497   (-)
    ] TELA^3[

L 7514   (-)
  .a   ]so , pa-ke-we
  .b]ki-to-ni-ja   63

L(4) 7578 + 8442   (208?)
    ]e-ra-ja TELA^x 3[

L 7833   (-)
    ]TELA^1 3 TELA^1+$\underline{PU}$[

L(5) 7834   (209)
  .a]qe-te-o [
  .b] TELA^x [
    $\underline{inf.\ mut.}$

238

L   7866   (103?)

      sup. mut.

.1   ] <u>vest.</u>[

.2]re-ne[

      .1 Perhaps $\underset{....}{\text{TELA}}^{x}$[.

L   8058   (-)

   ]$\underset{....}{\text{TELA}}$ 20 [

L   8105   (103)

.a] o-pi-si-ri-ja-we pe-ko-to [

.b] 2 <u>ko</u> TELA^{1} 2 <u>re</u> TELA^{1}[

    .a Trace to right consistent with $\underset{....}{\text{TELA}}$.

    .b First 2 corrected from 3.   Trace to left consistent
        with $\underset{....}{\text{TELA}}$.

L(1) 8159 + 8165   (103)

.a   ]   ri-ta , [

.b]e-me-s̤i̤-jo-jo   [

    .a Perhaps <u>p̤a</u>[-we-a.

L   8160   (103)

      sup. mut.

.1   ]TELA^{2}+<u>TE</u> 1[

.2] <u>vacat</u>   [

      inf. mut.

    .1 Perhaps TELA^{3} , but not very likely.

L   8163   (103)

      sup. mut.

.1]<u>vestigia</u>[

.2]TELA^{x} 15[

      inf. mut.

L 8246   (103)

.1] TELA^{1} 4[

.2 <u>inf. mut.</u>

239

L(5) 8441   (209)

  .a   ]   qe-ṭẹ-o   [

  .b   ]-u   TELA 2   [

L 8443 + 8445   (103)

       sup. mut.

  .1   ]   TELA^x [

  .2   ]   TELA^x 1 [

  .3   inf. mut.

L 8503   (103)

      ]a-rọ-zo[

      inf. mut.

Mc

Mc 1508 + 1564   (132?)

   .A   *150 16   CAP^f 10 [

   .B   da-*22-ti-jo   CORN 12   *142 M 6[

   v.   OVIS^f 50 o   o-pi CORN   [

            .v Perhaps traces at right. Possibly neither CORN nor
            *253, but a new ideogram.

Mc 4453 + 5798   (132)

   .A   ]ja-*18   *150 24[ ] CAP^f 17

   .B   ]   *142 M 12   CORN 24

Mc 4454 + 4458 + fr.   (132)

   .A   'da-wa-no'   *150 29   CAP^f 16

   .B   u-qa-mo /   da *150 1   *142 M 13   CORN 26

Mc 4455 + 8449 + 8554 + fr.   ASHM/IR (132)

   .A   'a-pa-sa-ki-jo' *150 28   CAP^f 17

   .B   ku-ta-to /   *142 M 12   CORN 24

           4455 : Ashmolean; 8449 + 8554 + fr. : Iraklion.
           .B M over [[12]] .

Mc 4456 + 4477 + fr.   (132)

   .A   ]   'si-nu-mo-ro' *150 16   CAP^f 10 [

   .B   ]da-*22-to /   *142 M 7   CORN 14   [

Mc 4457 + 5098 + 8264   (132)

   .1   to-sa *150 345   CAP^f 208[

   .2   ke[   ] *142 L 5 M 4   CORN 345[

           .1.2 Right end : numerals probably complete.

Mc 4459 + 5786 + frr.   (132)

   .A   ]   'a-ko-ro-ta' *150 23 CAP^f 15   [

   .B   ku-]ta-to /   qe-wa-ra   *142 M 10   CORN 20 [

Mc 4460 + <u>frr</u>.   (132)

  .A]   a-wa-so ,   *<u>150</u> 14   CAP^f 7[

  .B]-so /   *<u>142</u> M 6   CORN 12[

Mc 4461 + 5781   (132)

  .A   *<u>150</u>[

  .B ja-qo , / da-wa-no ,   *<u>142</u>[

  v.   160[

Mc 4462 + 5792 + 5808 + 5816 + 8450 + <u>fr</u>.   (132)

  .A   ']ra-wo-qo-no'   *<u>150</u> 61   CAP^f 30

  .B ti-]ri̤-ṭo / ·   a-re   *<u>150</u> 1   *<u>142</u> M 26   CORN 52[

Mc 4463 + <u>fr</u>.   (132)

  .A]   'a-pa-u-ro'   *<u>150</u> 10[

  .B]jo /   *<u>142</u> M 5   CO̤R̤N[

Mc 4464 + <u>fr</u>. [+] 8305 + 8613   (132)

  .A ·   ']te-rṳ-ṛo'   *<u>150</u> 12   CAP^f[

  .B se-to-i[-]ja /   *<u>142</u> M 5   [

Mc 5107 + 5123 + 5693   (132)

      *<u>150</u> 354   CAP^f 200[

Mc 5118   (132)

  .A]CAP^f 15 [

  .B]C̤O̤R̤N̤ 20 [

Mc 5187   (132?)

  .A]5 o̤ *<u>150</u> 1̤7̤ [

  .B] CAP^f 8   *<u>142</u> M 20 [

      .B Perhaps]1̤ at left.

Mc 5809 + 8703 + <u>frr</u>.   (132)

  .A   ]C̤A̤P̤^{f} 16[

  .B] CORN 26   [

Mc 5818 + fr.   (132)

  .A]te[   ]*150 15[

  .B   ] Ṃ 3[

Mc 5820   (132?)

    ]ri-na-jọ[

Mc 8447 + fr.   (132)

  .A]CAP^f 10

  .B]10[ ] vacat

Mc 8448 + fr.   (132)

  .A] 14   [

  .B]10   CORN[

Mc 8452 + fr.   (132)

  .A]   e-[. .]-dạ[

  .B]i / [

Mc 8705   (132?)

  .0 sup. mut.

  .1]10

Mc 8708 + fr.   (132?)

    sup. mut.

    ]6̣[

M

M 467   (-)

    ]2 *146 2

M(1) 559   (103)

  .1 ']ke' o-no o-na   LANA 2

  .2   ]da-wi-jo *146 2

      .1 Between o-no and o-na, more likely divider than right
         hand part of no.
      .2 2̣ or 1.

M(1) 683   (103)

.1a]   a-ze-ti-ri-ja
.1b]te-o   o-nu-ke   LANA 9 M 2
.2   ]ti-mu-nu-we   *146 30

M 719   (140)

.1   a-mi-ni-so ke-re-na , re-ne , [
.2   e-ne-si-da-o-ne , su-ja-to, *146 1[

        .1 -na over erasure (explains the wide spacing between
            ke-re- and -na). Sign at right perhaps pe[, but
            this is rather doubtful.

        .2 *146 1 over erasure.

M(1) 720   (103)

.a   o-re-o-po TELA^x[
.b   ze-ne-si-wi-jo /   *146 1[

M 724   (-)

.1   ]me-no   *146
.2   ] vacat

M 729   (-)

.1   ]ma-wo ,   *146 1[
.2   ]po-ti-ni-ja[

        .1 Trace before ma-wo, perhaps divider.
        .2 Erasure between po and ti. Perhaps 1[after
            po-ti-ni-ja ; further traces at end.

M 757   (-)

     ] *146^2 250[
lat. inf.   ] *181 10[
            lat. inf. : Perhaps (rather doubtful, but cf. U 736)
                       ] 110 [.

M(1) 1645   ASHM (103)

.1   ka-]ra-e-ri-jo-jo , me-no
.2   ]-wi-jo-do   pe *146 1

M 7373   (-)

       ]   *146+PE [

v.   ]50[

        Perhaps trace of numeral at left.

M 8170   (-)

   .1   ]   *146^2 24[

   .2   ]-na M 58   [

   .3   ]   vacat   [

        Possibly same tablet as X 8171.

        .1 Trace at left.

Nc

Nc 4470   (133)
    pu-ru[

Nc 4473 + 5779   (133)
    zo-wa 'tu-ri-jo' [

Nc 4474 + <u>frr.</u> (3)   (133)
    e-ri-sa-ta   M 1 [

<u>Nc</u> 4475   (133?)
    me-[

Nc 4479   (133)
    ]da-so / <u>SA</u> M 1
       <u>so</u> over erasure.

Nc 4480 + 8252   (133)
    a-na-ka   Ṃ[

Nc 4484   (133)
    to-so , a-pu-do-so[

Nc 4485   (133)
    ]di-mi-zo[

Nc 4488   (133)
    a-]mi-ni-so [
       Perhaps Ṃ[on right edge.

Nc 4489 + 8185   (133)
    ]qa-ra-su-ti-jo[

Nc 4490 + 5099   (133)
    ]si-da-jo   M 1

Nc   5100 + 8184   (133)
      ] M 8 <u>o</u> M 4
<u>lat. inf.</u>   ]2 <u>KE</u> M 10   *146 6
                         Probably same tablet as Nc 8175.

Nc   5103 + 8180   (133)
      wi-pi-o   N 3[

Nc   5109   (133)
      ]ta [

Nc   5110   (133)
         <u>sup. mut.</u>
         ]-e   [

<u>Nc</u>   5112   (133?)
      ku-[

Nc   5117   (133)
      ]-ta , M 1 [

Nc   5120   (133)
      ]   M [

Nc   5121   (133)
      ]wa-ko   <u>SA</u>[

Nc   5122 + <u>fr.</u>   (133)
      ] M 1 [

Nc   5126   (133)
      ]   M [

Nc   5128   (133)
         <u>sup. mut.</u>
         ]   M [

247

Nc 5129 + frr.   (133)
      ] M 1

Nc 5130 + 8179 + fr.   (133)
      ]-jo   M 1

Nc 5772 + fr.   (133)
      ]ta-jo   M 1 [

Nc 5787 + 8178   (133)
      sa-na-so[

Nc 8106   (133)
      ]jo   M 1[

Nc 8144   (133)
      sup. mut.
      ]sa   M [
      inf. mut.

Nc 8145   (133?)
      sup. mut.
       du-[

Nc 8146   (133)
      ]ko-ri-jo   [

Nc 8172   (133)
      ] M 3

Nc 8173 + fr.   (133)
      ]zo   M 3[

Nc 8175   (133)
      e-si-[
lat. inf.   o-pe[
              Probably same tablet as Nc 5100.

248

Nc 8176   (133)

    ]jo , 'i-we' [

      <u>we</u> smaller than <u>i</u>.   Trace at right.

<u>Nc</u> 8181   (133)

    ] M [

<u>Nc</u> 8183   (133?)

    ]ro[
    <u>inf. mut.</u>

<u>Nc</u> 8186   (133?)

      e[
    <u>inf. mut.</u>

<u>Nc</u> 8187   (133?)

    <u>sup. mut.</u>
    ]-ri[
    <u>inf. mut.</u>

Nc 8188   (133)

    <u>sup. mut.</u>
    ]M [

Nc 8276   (133)

    [.]-jo [
    <u>inf. mut.</u>

Nc 8300   (133)

    ]-ra-ma[
    <u>inf. mut.</u>

<u>Nc</u> 8309   (133?)

    <u>sup. mut.</u>
    ]te-we   [

Nc 8313   (133?)

     ]tu-[

    inf. mut.

       Probably tu-[.

Nc 8315   (133)

    sup. mut.

    ] Ṃ   [

Nc 8317 + fr.   (133)

    ]M 1   [

Nc 8318   (133)

    ] Ṃ [

    inf. mut.

Nc 8453   (133?)

    ] M [

Nc 8454   (133)

    sup. mut.

    ]M   [

Nc 8455   (133?)

     ]jạ[

    inf. mut.

Nc 8456   (133)

    ]1   [

Nc 8586   (133?)

    ]ra-rọ̣[

Nc 8728   (133?)

    sup. mut.

    jạ-[

      Perhaps jạ-rọ̣[.

Np

Np(1)   85 + 5047 + 7938 + 8057   ("124"e)
        ka-ta-ra   CROC QI 6

Np(1)   267   ("124"e)
        sa-ma-da   CROC RO[

Np(1)   268   ("124"e)
        ]to   CROC RO 1

Np(1)   269   ("124"e)
        ]ni-ja   CROC [
            Trace at right (QI or RO possible).

Np(1)   270   ("124"e)
        ]ja   CROC P 2 QI 4

Np(1)   271   ("124"e)
        ]CROC RO 1 QI 1

Np(1)   272 + 7419 + fr.   ("124"e)
        da-wo   CROC Q 1

Np(1)   273   ("124"e)
        ]ti-ja-no   CROC P 5[
            ]ti-ja-no in small signs under CROC.

Np(1)   274   ("124"e)
        ]CROC N 1 P 1

Np(1)   276   ("124"e)
        ]so   CROC[

Np(1)   277   ("124"e)
        ]CROC QI 4

Np(1)   278 + 7436 + <u>fr</u>.   ("124"e)
        ] CROC P 2
            Trace of majuscule sign at left.

Np(1)   286   ("124"e)
        ]na-pi   CROC N[
            ]<u>na-pi</u> in small signs below CROC.

Np(2)   855 + 7434   (134)
        ]jo-zo   CROC P 3̣ o̱ P 6[

Np(2)   856 + 7915 + 7917   (134)
        ]nṳ-po , / a-nu-ko   CROC N 1
            Cut at right.

Np(2)   857   (134)
        ]jo / sa-ma-ri-jo   CROC [

Np(2)   858   (134)
        ]ma-ki-nu-wo   CROC [
            Perhaps]-<u>ma-ki-nu-wo</u> or possibly]<u>vest</u>. / <u>ma-ki-nu-wo</u>.

Np(2)   859   (134)
        ]-wo , CROC P 9 o̱ [

Np(2)   860   (134)
        ]   CROC P 4   o̱ P 2[

Np(2)   861   (134)
        ]r̤o   CROC N 1
            Cut at right.

Np(2)   1000 + 5004   (134)
        ]-si-du-wo   CROC N[

Np 2138   (-)
   .1   ] CROC N[
   .2   inf. mut.
              Strange trace at left.

Np(2)   5002   (134)
          ]CROC N 1
              Cut at right. N over [[P]] .

Np(2)   5008   (134)
          ]o P 10[

Np(1)   5013   ("124"e)
          ]CROC P 1[

Np(2)   5725 + 5886   (134)
          ]na-wo   CROC N 1
              Cut at right.

Np(2)   5945   (134)
          ] CROC N[

Np(2)   5980   (134)
          ]P 7 [

Np(2)   5982   (134)
          sup. mut.
          ]N 1
              Cut at right.

Np(2)   7417   (134)
          ]   CROC[

Np(2)   7418   (134)
          ]CROC N 1
              Cut at right.

Np(2)   7420   (134)
        ]   CROC[

Np(2)   7421   (134)
        ]   CROC[

Np(1)   7422   ("124"e)
        ]CROC[
            Trace at left ? (perhaps]ṛa).

Np(1)   7423 + 7641   ("124"e)
        wa-to   CROC[

   v.   ri-no   M [
            Probably same tablet as Np 7445.

Np(1)   7424   ("124"e)
        ]CROC[
        inf. mut.
            Trace of sign before CROC ? (perhaps]g̱a ?).

Np(2)   7439   (134)
        ] N 1
            Cut at right. Trace at left possibly CROC.

Np(1)   7441 + fr.   ("124"e)
        ]2̣ P 1

Np(2)   7442   (134)
        ]CṚOC̣ P [

Np(1)   7445   ("124"e)
        ]N 2 [

   v.   ] P 2[
            Probably same tablet as Np 7423.

Np(2)   7447   (134)
        ]ọ P [

254

Np(1)   7508   ("124"e)
             ]   Q 1 [

Np(1)   7923 + 8461   ("124"e?)
             ]qa-sa-ro-we[

Np(1)   7967   ("124"e?)
             ]-ra-to[

Np(2)   8003   (134)
             ]N 1
          Cut at right.

Np(1)   8059   ("124"e?)
             ] 2
               Trace at left (not a part of the numeral; possibly]Ṇ).

Np(1)   8123 + 8460   ("124"e)
             ]1̣ P 1   [

Np(2)   8249   (134)
             ]CROC N[

Np(2)   8457   (134)
             ] P 10̣[
          inf. mut.
               Bottom now missing (seen on Bennett's photograph of 1950).

Np(1)   8458   ("124"e)
             ]j̣o̱   CROC[

Np(1)   8459   ("124"e)
             ]C̣ṚOC̣ P[
          inf. mut.

Np(1)   8462   ("124"e)
             ]P̣[
          inf. mut.

                              255

Oa

Oa 730   (-)

    ]*<u>167</u> 60   L 52   M 2

        Cut at right.

Oa 731   (-)

    ]L   [[   ]][

        Numeral in erasure (perhaps [[6̣]]).

Oa 732   (-)

    ]re-o   L[

Oa 733   (-)

    ]*<u>167+PE</u>   1o   L 6̣[

Oa 734   (-)

    ]jo   AES   *<u>167+PE</u>[

Oa 878   (-)

.1   ]   *<u>166+WE</u> 18

.2   ] e-to-ro-qa-ta 16

        Palimpsest.

Oa 1808   (= 734 bis)   (-)

    <u>sup. mut</u>.

    ]*<u>166+WE</u> 1

        Perhaps cut at right.

Oa 7374   (140?)

.1   ]-jo-jo , me-ṇo[

.2   ]pọ-ti-ni-ja   <u>ri</u> *<u>166+WE</u> 2̣2[

        .1 Trace of 2 or 3 signs before]-<u>jo-jo</u> , the second
        perhaps a <u>ri</u> badly drawn and incomplete.

Od

Od 485   (115)

.a   ]   ko-ro[-to?

.b   ]o-nu-ka   LANA [

Od 486   (115)

.a   ?ko-]ro-to   [

.b   ]-ta-ma-[

     .b Perhaps]a-ta-ma-si[, but ma possibly LANA and
         following trace a numeral.

Od 487   (115)

.a   ?ko-ro-]to   LANA M 1   [

.b   ]-ka LANA 2   [

     .b Traces to left consistent with nu.

Od 502   (-)

.a   pa-i-to   [

.b   we-we-si-jo-jo X LANA 11[

         Cut at left; this tablet was a sort of label (mark of
         a cord inside).

         .b Over erasure. Check-mark inscribed after drying.

Od(1) 539 + 7296 + 7602   (103)

       o-pi ti-mu-nu-we   LANA 2[

Od(1) 562   (103)

.1   ]o-pi , no-nu-we , 'a-ti-pa-mo' pe-re   LANA 91

.2   ]si-da-jo , pe-re 'po-ro-to'   LANA 42

.3   a-po-te , pe-re   LANA 69

Od(1) 563   (103)

.1   ri-jo-ni-jo , / e-ze-to , to-ro-qo

.2   a-to-mo-na , / su-mo-no-qe   LANA 14

257

Od(1) 570   (103)

.a   o[

.b   o-pi ki-si-[

          .b Over erasure (-pi over [[pi]]). Sign after si
              perhaps wi or pi.

Od 666   (115)

.a   ]   to-so o LANA 14

.b   ]ke-me-no / au-u-te , a-pe-i-si

v.   ]ke-re-wa LANA 9 M 1 P 6

lat. sup.] o-mu-ka-ra LANA 3 N 2 P 2

          .a to- over erasure, perhaps [[o]] . Reading to-so-o LANA
              not excluded.

          v. -wa over [[ja]] ? Perhaps [[9]] after -re-.

Od(1) 667   (103)

.1   ]LANA 1 M 2 P 4[

.2   ]ja M 2 P [

lat. inf.] 1 qo-ja-te P 1[

          .1 4[half-obliterated, but probably not deleted.

          .2 P over erasure, probably erased units.

Od(1) 681   (103)

.a   'e-na-po-na , o-nu , pa-i-ti-jo' e-ti-wa-ja-qe LANA[

.b   qo-ja-te a-pu-do-ke , ti-ra [

       Traces of erasure.

Od(1) 682   (103)

.1   ] o-nu-ke   LANA 5

.2   ]   vacat

Od(1) 687   (103)

.a   ti-ra

.b   a-mi-ke-te-to / ne-ki-ri-si   LANA 1

258

```
Od(1)  688                                           (103)
   .a     ]                e-ki
   .b    ri-]jo-ni-ja , / to-sa    LANA 30


Od(1)  689                                           (103)
   .a               ne-wo
   .b    o-pi , po-po    LANA 4


Od(1)  690                                           (103)
   .1    o-pi  a-to-mo-na    LANA 2
   .2    o-pi , po-ro-i-ra    LANA 2


Od(1)  696                                           (103)
   .1    ]e-pi-ro-pa-ja , / o-du-we 'te-o-po-ri-ja' M 2[
   .2    ]  LANA 2 M 1
   .3    ]  vacat
              Possibly same tablet as L 698.


Od(2)  714                                           (103)
   .a               a-*65-na           [
   .b    e-re-u-ti-ja           LANA 1  [


Od(2)  715                                           (103)
   .a               e-re-u-ti-ja
   .b    ta-wa-ko-to       LANA 1


Od(2)  716                                           (103)
   .a    ]e-re-u-ti-ja
   .b    ]               LANA 4


Od(2)  718                                           (103)
         a-mi-ni-so[
              Over erasure.


Od   765 + 7320                                      ( - )
   .a    ]to                    [
   .b    ]     a-me-a    LANA M  [
```

259

18

Od(3) 1062   (-)

     LANA <u>PE</u> 200 [

       Trace of third hundred sign (erased) below two
       existing signs.

Od(3) 1063   (-)

     ]LANA <u>PE</u> 500
     ····

Od 2026   (-)

  .1]wi-ri-za LANA [
  .2] <u>vacat</u>   [

Od 5003   (-)

  .A] ki-ri-ta-i   LANA 2[
  .B] <u>vacat</u>   [

Od 5082   (-)

  .1]ni-ki-jo LANA[
                 ····
  .2] <u>vacat</u>   [

Od(1) 5511   (103)

     ] LANA 1

Od 5558   (-)

       sup. mut.
     ]nu-we , o-na LANA[
     ··

Od 5620   (-)

       <u>sup. mut.</u>
     ]LANA 1[
         ·

Od 5711   (-)

  .1]LANA 1[
  .2]LANA 1[

Od 5758   (-)

     ]<u>o</u> LANA 12

260

Od   5846   (-)
   .1.2] <u>vacant</u>   [
   .3   ]10   LANA[

Od(1)   5966   (103)
        <u>sup. mut.</u>
   .1   ]<u>vest</u>.[
   .2   [.]-jo[
   .3   LANA   M 2[

Od   7298   (-)
      ]LANA 250

Od   7302   (-)
      ]-ri   LANA 2   [
          Cut along upper edge.   2 corrected from 4.

Od   7305   (115?)
      ]2̣   LANA 12[

Od   7307   (-)
   .1   ]1̣
   .2   ]3   ọ LANA 10
          Cut at right.
          .1   ]1̣ perhaps over [[ḶAṆA̤]] .

<u>Od(1)</u>   7309   (103?)
      ]4̣   LANA 32[
   v.   ]8
          32 over erasure ?

Od(1)   7310   (103)
   .a   ]ṛạ   [
   .b   ] LANA 5[

Od   7312   (-)
      ]ṇẹ   LANA M 4̣[

                           261

Od 7317   (-)
   .1   ]15   LANA 3 [
   .2   ]   vacat [

Od(1) 7324   (103?)
   .a   ] LANA 30[
   .b   ] vacat [

Od 7326   (-)
        sup. mut.
        ]-we   LANA M[

Od 7388   (-)
        ]ta   LANA 1 [
lat. inf.]   da-i-ra [
            Ideogram possibly MA.

Od 7779   (-)
        ] LANA M 1[
        inf. mut.

Od 7927   (-)
        ]110   LANA[
        inf. mut.

Od 8202 + fr.   (-)
   .A   ] wi-ri-za
   .B   ] su-ri-mo   LANA 1
            End of ruling erased and LANA written full height. Trace
            of a large sign at left.

Od 8465   (-)
   .1   ]LANA   [
   .2   ]LANA 5   o LANA[
            .1 Traces of numerals and other signs after LANA.
            .2 2[?

                          262

Od 8722   (-)

.1   ] <u>vacat</u>

.2   ]LANA [ ] <u>vacat</u>

    .1 Perhaps]jo.

    .2 Trace of numerals (20?) after ideogram.

Og

Og(1) 180   ("124")

.1   pa-i-ti-ja   M 130[

.2   da-wi-ja   M 60[

v.1   ]-to   M 40[

.2   M   4[

    .1.2 Possible trace of units after tens.

    v.1   Perhaps]te-to.

Og 833 + 959   (-)

.0   <u>sup. mut.</u>

.1   [su-]ri-mi-jo[

.2   [u-]ta-ni-jo[

.3   [ti-]ri-ti-jo   M 6

.4   qa-mi-jo   M 6

.5   pu-si-jo   M 5

.6   ru-ki-ti-jo   M 9

.7   tu-ri-si-jo   M 4

.8   qa-ra-jo   M 9

.9   to-so   M 47

Og 1527   (221?)

    <u>sup. mut.</u>

.1   ]mo-ri-wo-do M 3

.2   ]2   mo-ri-wo-do M 3

.3   ]N 2 mo-ri-wo-do M 3

.4   mo-ri-]wo-do M 1[

    <u>inf. mut.</u>

Traces of a previous ruling, about 4 mm below the present
one, and of erasure.

263

Og(1) 1804   (= 58 bis)   ("124")
    .a   ]   RO 2
    .b   ]ra-jo / qa-ra-o P 1
            .a Not AES; possibly RO [[ ]] 2.
            .b Perhaps qa-ra o.

Og(2) <4467>   (-)
    .1   jo-a-mi-ni-so-de , di-do-[
    .2   ku-pe-se-ro M 30   me-to-re M [
    .3   ne-ri-wa-to M 15   pi-ri[
           Missing; text from SM II, pl. 18.
           .1 Traces at right consistent with si (perhaps
               di-do-si[ ).

Og 5019   (-)
    .1   ]   P 4   [
    .2   ]no P 4

Og(1) 5095   ("124")
        ]P 1   Q 1

Og 5515 + 5518 + 5539   (-)
        ]ka-te-ro   L 4 M[
           Text probably complete at left.

Og 5551   (-)
        ] M 10
           Trace at left.

Og 5778 + fr.   (-)
    .A   ] ri-no M 1[
    .B   ]   vacat   [

Og 7430   (-)
        ] M 6   [
           Trace at left, possibly numeral 1.

Og(1) 7432   ("124")

       ] P 12 [ ] / P 20

            Probably palimpsest, except for the small P 20 at the
            end, perhaps not erased by omission; traces between P 12
            and P 20 more probably [[ ]] than [ ]. 12 consists
            of 10 and 2 written underneath.

Og 7435   (-)

.1   sup. mut.
.2   ]ne-a   M 1[

Og 7440   (115?)

.a   ]to M [
.b   ]ke   [

Og 7443   (-)

      ]P 5[

Og 7504 + 7844   (-)

      e-re-pa-ta ,   L M 30   ka[
           Cut at left.

Og(1) 8038   ("124")

      ] 46

v.   ] M 80

           Trace to left possibly AES (less likely BOS or su).

Og(2) 8150   (-)

      sup. mut.?
.1   ]o-no M 12 [
.2   ]-u   M 9 [
.3   ]   vacat [

Og 8466   (-)

.1   ]vestigia[
.2   ]   P 6 [

Pp

Pp 493 + 500 + 5813   (119)

    ]ti-ri-to / di-za-so   *168+<u>SE</u>[

Pp 494 + 7448   (119)

    ] su-ri-mo / a-na-re-u   *<u>168</u>+<u>SE</u> 14[

Pp 495   (119)

    ]qa-ra / re-me-to *168+<u>SE</u> 28

Pp 496   (119)

    ]u-ta-no / ṭẹ-*5̣6̣[   ]   *<u>168</u>+<u>SE</u> 2̣3

        Perhaps division into .A .B. Possibly pạ-*5̣6̣[.

Pp 497   (119)

    ]qa-mo [   ]*<u>168</u>+<u>SẸ</u> 6

        Complete at right on SM II photograph (now 6[ ).

Pp 498   (119)

    .1   e-ra / ta-si-[   ] *<u>168</u> 3̣0[

    .2   mu-ka-ra / pạ-i-to *<u>168</u>[

        .1 Last sign before *<u>1̣6̣8̣</u> perhaps <u>we</u>.

Pp 499   (119)

    ]to-so *<u>168</u>+<u>SE</u> 217

Ra

Ra(2)   984 + <u>fr</u>.   (127)

  .1   ]pa-te , de-de-me-na , [

  .2   ]zo-wa , e-pi-zo-ta , ke-ra , de-de-'me-na' PUG[

         .2 <u>e-pi-zo-ta</u> over erasure. PUG inverted.

Ra(2)   1028   (127)

  .A   ]   e-re-pa-te[

  .B   ]qo-jo , / zo-wa[

         .B Probably no other sign immediately following <u>zo-wa</u>,
            cf. Ra 984.

Ra(1)   1540   ASHM (126)

      to-sa / pa-ka-na   PUG 50[

Ra(1)   1541   (126)

      ka-si-]ko-no , pa-ka-na , a-ra-ru-wo-a   PUG 1[

Ra(1)   1542   (126)

      ]wo-a   PUG 1[

Ra(1)   1543 + 1560 + 1566   (126)

  .a   de-so-mo

  .b   a-mi-to-no / pi-ri-te , a-ra-ru-wo-a   PUG[

Ra(1)   1544   (126)

      ]   PUG 2[

Ra(1)   1545   (126)

      ]na , a[

Ra(1)   1546   (126)

      ka-si-]ko-no   PUG 2

Ra(1) 1547   (126)
        da-zo / pi-ri-je-te[
            Possibly same tablet as Ra 1814.

Ra(1) 1548   (126)
  .A   de-so-mo
  .b   ku-ka-ro / pi-ri-je-te pa-ka-na a-ra-ru-wo-a   PUG 3

Ra(1) 1549   (126)
        ]no / pi-ri-je-te , pa-ka[-na

Ra(1) 1550   (126)
        ]te , pa-ka-na , a-ra[

Ra(1) 1551   (126)
  .a   ]   a-ra-ru-wo-a [
  .b   ka-si-]ko-no , pa-ka-na   [
            .a wo over incomplete ja.
            .b Over erasure.

Ra(1) 1552   (126)
        pa-]ka-na , a-ra-ru[-wo-a

Ra(1) 1553   (126)
  .a   a-]ra-ru-wo-a   [
  .b   ]pa-ka-na   PUG[

Ra(1) 1554   (126)
        ]pa-ka-na , a-ra-ru[-wo-a

Ra(1) 1555   (126)
        ]wi-jo / ka-si-ko-no [

Ra(1) 1556   (126)
        ]ka-si-ko-no   PUG[

Ra(1) 1557   (126)
        ka-]si-ko-no   [

268

Ra(1) 1558   (126)

     o-wa-si-jo [

Ra(1) 1559   (126)

     ]u-ta-jo / ka-si-ko[-no

Ra(1) 1814   (= 1547 bis)   (126)

    ]   PUG 5

      Possibly same tablet as Ra 1547. Cut at right.

Ra(2) 7498   (-)

  .1   ]ri   PUG 18

  .2   ]me-na , PUG 99

R

R 1562 + 1563   (-)

    ]je-ne   ZE 12

      ZE possibly ideographic.

R 1815   (= 4481 bis)   (-)

    e-]ke-a / ka-ka re-a   HAS 12

      ka-ka re-a over erasure (possibly ka-ka-[[re]] corrected
      to make two words, but final intention unclear).

R 4482   (-)

  .1   ]   SAG 6010

  .2   ]   SAG 2630

    .1 10 over erasure.

    .2 Trace of erasure at left.

Sc

Sc 103 + 5069 + 5145   ("124"i)

      ki-ra$_2$-i-jo   TUN 2   BIG 1   EQU

         Cut at both ends. ki- over erasure.

Sc 135 + 5149   ("124")

      qa-mi-si-jo [[TUN]]   BIG[

         BIG[over erasure (not [[TUN]]).

Sc 217   ("124")

      ]ta   TUN 2   BIG 1   EQU   ZE 1

  v. a-]mi-ni-si

         .v -si half-formed.

Sc 218   ASHM("124"f)

      ] EQU   ZE 1

Sc 219   ("124"k)

      ] [[TUN]]   BIG 1 [

Sc 220 + fr.   ("124")

      ] 1   EQU 'MO 1'

Sc 221 + 5147   ("124"i)

      ]TUN   BIG 1   EQU   MO 1

         Perhaps [[TUN]] .

Sc 222   ("124")

      me-za-wo   TUN 2   EQU   ZE 1

Sc 223   ("124")

      ]DA 1   BIG   AES [

         Perhaps]da 1 ?; AES written underneath BIG.

Sc 224 + 228   ("124"m)

    pa-di-jo   TUN+QE   2   EQU   ZE 2
        Erasure at end (perhaps [[TUN]] ?).

Sc 225   ("124"f?)

    ]BIG   1   EQU   MO   [

 v.   ]   *166   1   [

Sc 226   ("124"i?)

    ti-ri-jo-qa BIG   1   TUN   EQU   1 'e-ko 1'
        Cut at right. 'e-ko 1' written above dividing line
        beginning after EQU 1.

Sc 227   ("124"m)

    ]   TUN+QE   2   EQU   'MO 1'
        Cut at right. Traces at left.

Sc 229   ("124"m)

    ]ri-jo TUN+QE   2   MO[

Sc 230   ("124"f)

    o-pi-ri-mi-ni-jo TUN 1 BIG   1   EQU ZE[
        1 rather doubtful.

Sc 231   ("124"g)

    ]TUN 2 BIG 1   EQU ZE 1
        Cut at right.

Sc 232   ("124"g)

    ]2   BIG   1   EQU   ZE[

Sc 233   ("124")

    ]a-qa-ro   TUN [

Sc 234   ("124")

    ]   TUN   2   BIG[

271

Sc 235   ("124"g)
      po-*34-wi-do   [[TUN]]   BIG[

Sc 236   ("124"k)
      ku-ru-me-no   [[TUN]]   BIG
          Cut at right.

Sc 237   ("124"k)
      a-e-da-do-ro   [[TUN]]   BIG[
  v.   a-mi-ni-si[
      a-e-da-do-ro probably over erasure (a- certainly over [[si]]).

Sc 238   ASHM("124"h)
      me-nu-wa   TUN[   ]   BIG [

Sc 239   ("124")
      a-ko-to   TUN [

Sc 240   ("124")
      ta-pa-no   BIG[

Sc 241   ("124")
      ]EQU MO 1
          Cut at right. Over erasure, (with MO over [[ZE 1]]).

Sc 242   ("124")
      ]BIG 1   EQU ZE 1
  v.   a-*47[
          Cut at right.

Sc 243   ("124"f)
      ]jo / pu₂-re-o̥   TUN 1   BIG 1   EQU[

Sc 244   ("124")
      ]no̤ / e-ro-e   BIG[

272

Sc 245 + 5064   ("124"f?)

      ]re-o   BIG 1
        Cut at right. -o over [[TUN]] .

Sc <246>   ("124")

      qe-ra-di-ri-jo   *165[
        Missing; text from SM II, pl. 29. *165 over [[TUN]] .

Sc 247   ("124"f)

      pa-re   *165 1[
        *165 over [[TUN]] .

Sc 248 + 7484   ("124")

      ]BIG 1   *165   1
        Cut at right. *165 over [[EQU]] .

Sc 249 + 265   ("124")

      ]pa-re   BIG 1   *165[

Sc 250 + 7691   ("124"f)

      a-ko-to   TUN[

Sc 251   ("124")

      ]*47-u   TUN   BIG[
        ]je-u possible.

Sc 252 + fr.   ("124"j?)

      we-wa-do-ro   TUN[

  v.   a-mi-ni-[
        TUN over [[TUN]] .

Sc 253   ("124"k)

      i-sa-wo   [[TUN]]   BIG[

Sc 254 + 7465   ("124"i)

      pa-wa-wo   TUN 2   BIG[

                            273

Sc 255   ("124"j)
        di-so   TUN 2   BIG[
    v.   po-*34[

Sc 256   ("124"j)
        a-ka-to   TUN 2   BIG[
    v.   a-re-ka[
            Possibly same tablet as Sc 5163.

Sc 257   ("124"h)
    .1 ka-ro-qo   BIG 1   [
    .2 qa-*83-to   DA 3   [
    .3   vacat   [

Sc 258   ("124")
    .a]pa-ra'-ko'   1 pa-wa-so 1   TUN 1 [
    .b]TUN 1 i-ka-se   1 di-ka[
    v.   ku-ne[

        .a ra and ko both squeezed in as an afterthought, ko
            above ra.

        .a.b Perhaps divider and not 1 after]pa-ra'-ko',
             pa-wa-so and i-ka-se.

Sc 259   ("124")
        ]EQU ZE 1   TUN 2

Sc 260   ("124")
        ]jo   TUN   1   BIG[

Sc 261   ("124"f)
        a-*64-jo   TUN[

Sc 262   ("124")
        ]BIG 1   EQU 1   [

Sc 263   ("124"f)
        si-mo   TUN[

                        274

Sc   264   ("124")
     ]BIG   1   EQU   <u>ZE</u>   1

Sc   266   ("124"m)
     ]TUN+<u>QE</u>   1   <u>QE</u>   <u>ZE</u>   1
          Cut at right.   QE apparently added as an afterthought.

Sc   1644   ASHM("124")
     ]   TUN 2   BIG[

Sc   1651   ASHM("124")
     ]BIG   1   EQU[

Sc   5046   ("124")
     ]si-jo   [[TUN]]   BIG[

Sc   5057   ("124"g)
     ]BIG 1
          Cut at right.

Sc   5058 + 7800 + 7825   ("124")
     ]da-nwa-re   BIG   1   [

Sc   5059   ("124")
     ]   BIG[

Sc   5060 + 5140   ("124"f)
     ]   TUN 2   BIG   1   EQU   <u>ZE</u>   [

Sc   5061 + 5067   ("124"i)
     ]BIG   1   EQU
          Cut at right.

Sc   5062 + 5143   ("124")
     ]BIG   1   EQU <u>MO</u> 1
          Cut at right.

275

Sc 5065 + <u>frr</u>.   ("124"f)
        ]BIG 1   EQU [

Sc 5066   ("124"i)
        ˙]EQU   [

Sc 5068   ("124")
        ]BIG[

Sc 5070   ("124"f)
        ]   TUN[
             Perhaps trace of erasure.

Sc 5071   ("124")
        ] EQU   <u>ZE</u>[

Sc 5072   ("124"k?)
        ]   EQU <u>ZE</u> 1

Sc 5073   ("124")
        ]wa   BIG[
         ˙˙

Sc 5083   ("124"i)
        ]   BIG   [
            Trace at right.

Sc 5084   ("124")
        ]   TUN[
            Trace at left.

Sc 5085   ("124")
        ]TUN   2   BIG   1   EQU   <u>ZE</u>   1[

Sc 5086   ("124"i)
        ]TUN   1   BIG   1   EQU
             Cut at right.

Sc 5087   ("124")
    ]EQU <u>ZE</u> [
        Traces below <u>ZE</u>.

Sc 5136   ("124"g)
    ]EQU 1   [

Sc 5137   ("124"k)
    ] [[TUN]]   BIG 1
        Cut at right.

Sc 5138   ("124"g)
    ] [[TUN]]   BIG 1
        Cut at right.

Sc 5139   ("124")
    ]TUN   BIG 1   EQU
     ...

Sc 5141   ("124"g)
    ]BIG 1   EQU [
  v.   ]*<u>166</u> 1   [

Sc 5142   ("124")
    ]1   BIG [
     .

Sc 5144 + 5152 + 7482 + <u>fr</u>.   ("124"f)
    ]BIG 1   EQU [

Sc 5146   ("124"g)
    ]BIG   EQU[
  v.   ]pa   [

Sc 5148   ("124"f)
    ]BIG 1   EQU[

Sc 5150   ("124"f?)

      ] BIG[
         Perhaps trace at left.

Sc 5151   ("124")

      ] EQU[
         Trace at left.

Sc 5153   ("124")

      ] BIG[
         Trace at left.

Sc 5154 + 8048   ("124"f)

      ]EQU ZE 1

Sc 5155   ("124"k)

      ]TUN   BIG 1
       ...
          Cut at right.

Sc 5156   ("124")

      ]zo   TUN   2
       ..

Sc 5157   ("124"f)

      ] BIG[
         Trace at left.

Sc 5158   ("124"g)

      ] EQU ZE 1
         Cut at right.

Sc 5159   ("124"g)

      ]EQU ZE 1
         Cut at right.

Sc 5160   ("124"g?)

      ]BIG 1 EQU ZE 1
       ...
         Cut at right. ZE looks erased, but probably only by
         accident.

278

Sc 5161   ("124"f)
     ]BIG 1   EQU[

Sc 5162   ("124"i)
     ][[TUN]]   BIG[
        .   .

Sc 5163   ("124"j?)
     ]1   EQU ZE 1

  v.   ]-wo T
             .
             Possibly same tablet as Sc 256.
             Cut at right.
             v. Perhaps]ru-wo .
                            .

Sc 5164   ("124"i)
     ]jo   [[TUN]]   BIG[
                          . . .

Sc 5165   ("124")
     ]   BIG [

Sc 5166 + 8642   ("124")
     ]BIG 1   EQU 1

Sc <5167>   ("124"?)
     ] EQU 1 [
             Missing; text from Bennett's 1950 drawing.

Sc 5168   ("124")
     ]EQU ZE '1'
             1 above and to the left of ZE.

Sc 5169 + 7477 + 7536   ("124"i)
     ][[TUN]]   BIG 1   EQU MO 1
             Probably whole tablet over erasure.

Sc 5170   ("124")
     ]BIG 1   EQU[

                        279

Sc 7444   ("124")
    ]TUN   2

Sc 7452   ("124"i)
    ]BIG   1   EQU   ZE [

Sc 7453   ("124")
    ]ta-o   EQU   ZE [

Sc 7454   ("124"k?)
    ]BIG   1   EQU[

Sc 7455 + 7458   ("124")
    ]BIG   1   EQU   ZE 1   [

Sc 7456   ("124")
    ]ọo   TUN   2   [

Sc 7457   ("124")
    ]BIG   1   EQU[
        inf. mut.

  v.   ]   tọ   [

Sc 7459   ("124"g)
    ]   BIG[
    inf. mut.

Sc 7460   ("124"g)
    ]BIG   1
        Cut at right.

Sc 7461   ("124")
    ]   *165[
        *165 over [[TUN]] . Trace at left.

280

Sc 7462   ("124"g?)
        ]BIG[

   v.   ] *165[
                ...

Sc 7463   ("124")
        ]EQU 'ZE' 1
             Cut at right.

Sc 7464   ("124")
        ] EQU[

Sc 7466   ("124")
        ]jo TUN[

Sc 7467   ("124"i)
        ]BIG 1
             Cut at right.

Sc 7468   ("124")
        ]2 BIG[

Sc 7469 + 7472   ("124")
        ] TUN   BIG[

   v.   ]a-*47-wi[
              .

Sc 7470 + 8473   ("124")
        ]BIG[

Sc 7471 + 8620 + 8633   ("124")
        ]BIG 1   ZE

   v.   ']-ja' ka-wo
             .   ..
             v. ka very doubtful. Traces of erasure at left of wo.

Sc 7473   ("124"f)
        ]BIG 1 EQU[
        inf. mut.

281

Sc 7474   ("124")
    <u>sup. mut.</u>
    ]BIG[

Sc 7475   ("124")
    ]wa   TUN 1[

Sc 7476   ("124")
    <u>sup.mut.</u>
    ]   BIG[
v.   a-mi-]ni-si-jo[
    <u>inf. mut.</u>

Sc 7478   ("124")
    ]EQU <u>ZE</u> 1[

Sc 7479   ("124"m)
    ]EQU <u>ZE</u> 1 [

Sc 7480   ("124"1)
    ]jo , to-wo   TUN[

Sc 7481   ("124"1)
    ]u   TUN 2
       Cut at right.

Sc 7483   ("124")
    <u>sup. mut.</u>
    ]EQU 'ZE' 1[

Sc 7772   ("124")
    ] [[TUN]]   BIG[
v.   a-mi-]ni-si-jo[

282

Sc 7782 + 8568 + <u>fr</u>.   ("124")

   ]t̤a̤   [[TUN]] BIG[

v.   a-]mi-ni-si-j̤o̤[

Sc 7798   ("124")

   ] EQU <u>ZE</u>[

Sc 7821   ("124")

   <u>sup. mut.</u>
   ] TUN[

Sc 7849   ("124")

    <u>sup. mut.</u>
   ]-j̤a̤ BIG[

Sc 7882   ("124")

   ]ni-k̤o̤ [[TUN]] [

      Probably]d̤a̤ / ni-k̤o̤ or]r̤o̤ / ni-k̤o̤, though in either
      case there may have been a further minuscule sign
      before ni-k̤o̤.

Sc 7889   ("124")

    <u>sup. mut.</u>
   ]B̤I̤G̤ 1 E̤Q̤Ṳ[

Sc 8081   (= 7475 bis)   ("124")

   <u>sup. mut.</u>
   ]EQU 1

      Cut at right. It is possible that a <u>ZE</u> written above
      the line stood between EQU and 1.

Sc 8124   ("124"f)

   ]w̤o̤ TUN[
   <u>inf. mut.</u>

Sc 8125   ("124"m)
     ]   TUN+QE[
         Trace at left.

Sc 8253 + fr.   ("124")
     ]BIG 1 [

Sc 8271   (-)
     e-wo[   ]TUN+QE[
         Perhaps small sign between wo and TUN.

Sc 8467   ("124")
     ]TUN   [

Sc 8468   ("124")
     sup. mut.
     ]   TUN[

Sc 8469   ("124"j?)
     ]   TUN[
     inf. mut.

Sc 8470   ("124")
     sup. mut.
     ]TUN   [

Sc 8471   ("124")
     ]2 BIG[
     inf. mut.

 v.   sup. mut.
      ]si-jo[
         Perhaps]TUN 1 or even]TUN 2 on recto.

Sc 8472   ("124")
     ]   BIG[

Sc 8474   ("124")
    ] BIG[
    <u>inf. mut.</u>

Sc 8475   ("124")
    ]BIG[
    <u>inf. mut.</u>

Sc 8476   ("124")
    <u>sup. mut.</u>
    ]BIG   [

<u>Sc</u> 8478   ("124"?)
    ]BIG   [
    <u>inf. mut.</u>

Sc 8479   ("124")
    ]BIG   EQU[

Sc 8480   ("124")
    <u>sup. mut.</u>
    ]BIG 1   EQU[

Sc 8481   ("124")
    ]EQU 1

Sc 8482   ("124")
    ]EQU 'ZE'[
    <u>inf. mut.</u>

Sc 8483   ("124")
    ]'ZE' 1 [

Sc 8723   ("124")
    <u>sup. mut.</u>
    ]TUN[
    <u>inf. mut.</u>

Sd

Sd 4401   (128)

.a]a-ra-ru-ja , a-ni-ja-pi , wi-ri-ni-jo , o-po-qo , ke-ra-ja-pi ,
                                                    o-pi-i-ja-pi CUR[

.b]i-qi-jo ,/ a-ja-me-no , e-re-pa-te , a-ra-ro-mo-te-me-no
                                                    po-ni-ki[-jo

    Signs of erasure in the centre of the tablet between
    the two lines.

    .b i-qi-jo corrected from -ja.

Sd 4402 + fr.   (128)

.a] a-u-qe , a-re-ta-to , o-u-qe , pte-no , o-u-qe , au-ro ,
                                        o-u-qe , 'pe-qa-to' CUR[

.b]i-qi-ja , / a-ra-ro-mo-te-me-na , po-ni-ki-ja , o-u-qe ,
                                        a-ni-ja , po-si ,   [

Sd 4403 + 5114   (128)

.a] e-re-pa-te-jo , o-po-qo , ke-ra-ja-pi , o-pi-i-ja-pi
                            'ko-ki-da , o-pa'   CUR 3

.b i-]qi-ja [,]/ a-ja-me-na , e-re-pa-te , a-ra-ro-mo-te-me-na ,
                                                    a-ra-ru-ja [

    Right-hand section of Sd 4403 now missing; text from
    SM II, pl. 14.

Sd 4404 + fr.   (128)

.a   ]jo , i-qo-e-qe , wi-ri-ni-jo , o-po-qo , ke-ra-ja-pi[,]
                                        o-pi-i-ja-pi   CUR[

.b]i-qi-ja , / ku-do-ni-ja , mi-to-we-sa-e , a-ra-ro-mo-te-me-na [

lat. sup. po-ni-ki-ja BIG 1   [

Sd 4405 + 4410 + fr.   (128)

.a wi-ri-ni-jo , o-po-qo , ke-ra-ja-pi , o-pi-i-ja-pi , o-u-qe ,
                                        pte-no ,   CUR 1[

.b]i-qi-ja , / po-ni-ki-ja , a-ra-ro-mo-te-me-na , a-ra-ru-ja ,
                                                    a-ni-ja-pi

    .a Possibly small signs after pte-no , : po[-si]?

286

Sd 4406   (128)

.1   ]wi-ri-ni-jo , o-po-qo ,   [

.2a   ]ke-ra-ja-pi , o-pi-i-ja-pi   CUR[

.2b   ]-to , a-ra-ro-mo-te-me-na ,   [

        .2a CUR between lines.1 and .2a.
        .2b Perhaps traces of erasure.

Sd 4407 + 4414   (128)

.a   do-]we-jo , i-qo-e-qe , wi-ri-ni-jo , o-po-qo , ke-ra-ja-pi ,
                                         'o-pi-i-ja-pi'   CUR 2

.b   ]se-to-i-ja , mi-to-we-sa , a-ra-ro-mo-te-me-na

Sd 4408 + 4411 + 6055 + fr.   (128)

.a   ]a-ra-ru-wo-ja , a-ni-ja-pi , wi-ri-ne-o , o-po-qo ,
                                  ke-ra-ja-pi , o-pi-i[-ja-pi

.b   i-]qi-ja , / a-ja-me-na , e-re-pa-te[,]a-ra-ro-mo-te-me-na[,
                                          ]po-ni-ja-ja ,   CUR[

        .a Left tip now missing.
        .b i-]qi-ja : ja over erasure.

Sd 4409 + 4481 + fr.   (128)

.a   wi-ri-ne-o , o-po-qo , ka-ke-ja-pi , o-pi-i-ja-pi   CUR 1
.b   i-qi-ja , po-ni-ki-ja , a-ra-ro-mo-te-me-na , a-ja-me-na,

Sd 4412 + fr.   (128)

.a   ka-]ke-ja-pi , o-pi-i-ja-pi , o-u-qe , po-si , e-re-pa
.b   ]a-ja-me-na   CUR 1

Sd 4413   (128)

.a   a-ra-ru-]ja , a-ni-ja-pi , wi-ri-ni-jo , o-po-qo ,
                              ke-ra-ja-pi , o-pi-i-ja-pi   CUR[

.b   i-]qi-ja / pa-i-to , a-ra-ro-mo-te-me-na , do-we-jo ,
                              i-qo-e-qe , po-ni-ki[-ja

Sd 4415 + 4417 + 4469 + frr.   (128)

.a   wi-ri-ne-jo , o-po-qo , ke-ra-ja-pi , o-pi-i-ja-pi
                                                      CUR 2

.b   i-qi-jo , mi-to-we-sa , a-ra-ro-mo-te-me-na , a-ja-me

Sd 4416 + <u>fr</u>.   (128)

  .a]   o-u-qe , a-ni-ja , po-si ,   CUR [
  .b]i-qi-ja , / mi-to-we-sa , a-ra-ro-mo-to-me-na[a-ja-]me-na

Sd 4422   ASHM (128/?)

  .a] , o-pa //   o-u-qe , pe-qa-to , u-po,   CUR[
  .b]i-qi-ja , / a-ro-mo-te-me-na , o-u-qe , a-ni-ja , po-si ,
                                                        e-e-si[

        .a o-u-qe , pe-qa-to , u-po , over erasure:
          [[o   qe,   qe]] still visible.

Sd <4450> + 4483   (128)

  .a   ke-ra-i-ja-pi , o-pi[-i-]ja-pi
  .b   o-u-qe , pte-no , po-si , a-ra-ru-ja , a-ni-ja[-pi
                                   ]wi-ri-ne-o , o[-po-qo
  .c i-qi-ja / po-ni-ki-ja , a-ra-ro-mo-te-me-na , [[e-re-pa-te]] ,
                                    do-we-jo [i-qo-e-qe

      Sd 4450 missing; text from SM II, pl. 16.

Sd 4468   (128)

  .a]   wi-ri-ne-jo , o-po-qo , [
  .b i-]qi-ja , / a-ra-ro-mo-te[-me-na

Sd 5091 + 6066 + <u>fr</u>.   (128)

  .a]-jo , o-po-qo , ka-ke-ja-pi , o-pi-i-ja-pi , o-[
  .b   ]na , a-ra-ru-[

Sd 8544   (128?)

    sup. mut.
    ]ki-[
      Perhaps]ki-ja[and, in view of the scribe, po-ni]ki-ja[.

Se

Se 879   (127)

.a   a$_3$-ki-no-o

.b   pte-re-wa / pa-ra-ja , e-te-re-ta , po-ro-ti-ri   CUR[

      Cut at left.

    .b   <u>e-te-re-ta</u> : <u>re</u> over erased sign.

Se 880 + 1017   (127)

.1   ]   <u>vacat</u>

.2   ] , po-ni-ke-a , wo-ra-we-sa   CUR 1

      Cut at right.

    .2   Trace at left. <u>wo</u> over erasure, perhaps [[<u>wa</u>]] .
       CUR drawn across the line.

Se 881   (127)

    ]   CUR   1

Se 882   (127)

    po-]ni-ki-ja   CUR[

      <u>ki</u> over [[<u>ja</u>]] .

Se 883   ASHM (127)

.a   ]CUR 1

.b   ]pi

      Cut at right. <u>pi</u> possibly over erasure.

Se 890   (127)

    pte-re[-wa

Se 891 + 1006 + 1042   (127)

.A   e-re-pa-te-jo-pi , o-mo-pi [

.B   pte-re-wa / e-ka-te-re-ta , a$_3$-ki-no-o 2 e-re-pa-te-jo-pi , [

    .B   <u>ka</u> over [[<u>te</u>]] . Perhaps two dividers after
       <u>a$_3$-ki-no-o</u>? Trace at right.

Se 892   (127)

        pte-re-wa[
            Cut at left.

Se 893   (127)

        ]we-ja , / pte-re-wa , ka-ke[

Se 965 + 1008   (127)

  .A   e-wi-su-zo-ko , ka[
  .B   po-ni-ki-ja , /   [
            Cut at left.
            .A zo over erasure, perhaps [[s̥ṵ]] .

Se 1007   (127)

  .1   ]   e-wi-su-zo-ko ,   [
  .2   ] , e-re-pa-te-o , o-m̥ọ[
            .2 Trace at left, perhaps]z̥ạ.

Se 1048   (127??)

        ] , po-ni-ki-ja [
            Trace at left.

Se 5729   (127)

        ]p̥ṭẹ-re-wa / wi[

Se 7449   (127)

        ]CUR 1 [

Se 7920   (127)

        pte-re[
            Cut at left.

Se 8477   (-)

        ]CUR 1 [
        inf.mut.

290

Sf

Sf(2) 4418   (129?)

]i-qi-ja / e-ka-te-jo CAPS[

Sf(2) 4419 + 5119 + 5814   (129?)

]i-qi-ja / a-na-i-ta CAPS 80

a-na-i-ta : i over [[ta]] .

Sf(2) 4420   (129?)

.a   a-re-ki-si-to-jo , o-pa

.b i-qi-ja / a-na-ta , a-na-mo-to ,   CAPS 80

Sf(1) 4421   (128?)

i-qi-ja , a-na-mo-to , a-ja-me-na CAPS 27̣

7 perhaps over erasure (perhaps 24 with last three
units erased).

Sf(1) 4423 + 4471 + 5815   (128?)

]i-qi-ja , a-na-mo-to , a-na-to CAPS 56̣[

Sf(2) 4424 + 8321   (129)

i-qi-ja / a-ja-me-na CAPS 8

Sf(2) 4425   (129?)

i-qi-]ja / a-na-to CAPS[

Sf(2) 4426 + fr.   (129)

]i-qi-ja / a-ja-me-na CAPS 24[

Sf(1) 4427 + fr.   (128?)

]ị-qi-ja , / a-na-mo-to , a-ja-me-na CAPS 5̣[

Numerals very faint; possibly 1̣5̣[(but perhaps erased).

Sf(1) 4428   (128)

  .a   ] wi-ri-ne-o , o-po-qo , ke-ra-ja-pi , o-pi-i-ja-pi

  .b   i-]qi-ja , / po-ni-ki-ja , me-ta-ke-ku-me-na ,   CAPS 1

       .b Rudimentary form of CAPS ideogram.

Sf(2) 4465 + fr.   (129?)

    ] , a-na-mo-ta   *245 22   [

    Traces at left.

Sf(2) 4491   (129?)

    i-qi-ja[

Sf(2) 5106   (129?)

    i-]qi-ja / a-ja-me[

Sf 7450   (-)

     sup. mut.

    ] , a-na-mo-to[

Sf 7451   (-)

     sup. mut.

    ]a-na-i-ta[

Sf 7723   (-)

  .a ?a-]ja-me-na [

  .b ?a-]na-mo-ta [

Sg

Sg 884   (-)

    ]e-na-ri-po-to   CAPS[

Sg 885   (-)

    ] CAPS 1

    Cut at right. (Numbered 889 in SM II, pl. 66).

Sg 886   + fr.   (-)
    ]CAPS 1

        Cut at right. (Unnumbered in SM II, pl. 66; formerly
        published as 889).

Sg 887   (-)
    ]na   CAPS[

Sg 888 + 978   (-)
    po-ro-su-re / a-na-to , o CAPS[

Sg 889   ASHM (-)
    ] CAPS 1

        Cut at right. (Numbered 885 in SM II, pl. 66).

Sg 1811 + 7485 + 7870 + fr.   (1811 = 890 bis)   (-)
   .1   ]   CAPS   22[
   .2   ]   CAPS   224   [
   .3   ]-mi-we-te   ROTA ZE 21[
   .4   ]   ROTA ZE 8   [
   .5   o-da-]ke-we-ta   ROTA ZE 7 a-mo 1[
   .6   ]o-da-ke-we-ta   ROTA ZE 172
   .7   ]   vacat

   v.   176[
        .1 Perhaps only 12 corrected from 22.
        .2]te-mi-we-te possible.

Sg 8484   (-)
    ]CAPS[

Sk

Sk 789   (206)

.A   ]   qe-ro$_2$ 2 e-po-mi̤[-jo

.B   ]ra / e-pi-ko-ru-si-jo 2 pa-ra-wa-jo[

        .B <u>e-pi-ko-ru-si-jo</u> over erasure (perhaps [[p̤a̤-. . .]] .

Sk 5670   (206)

.1   ]q̤e̤-ro$_2$ 2 [

.2   ko-]ru GAL 1   o-pa-wo-ta[

Sk 7751   (-)

.1   ] qe-ro$_2$ 1 [

.2   <u>inf. mut</u>.

        .1 Perhaps]]̤.

Sk 8100   (206)

.A   qe-ro$_2$ 2 e-po-mi-jo 2 / o-pa-wo[-ta

.Ba   o-pa-wo-ta 2

.Bb pa-ra / ko-ru GAL 1 o-pi-ko-ru-si-ja 2 pa-ra-wa[-jo 2

        .B <u>o-pi-ko-ru-si-ja</u> 'o-pa-wo-ta' 4 perhaps intended.

Sk 8149   (206)

.A   qe-ro$_2$] 2 e-po-mi-jo 2̤[

.Ba   o-pa-wo-ta   2 [

.Bb ko-]r̤ṳ GAL 1   o-pi-ko-ru-si̤-ja̤[

Sk 8254   (206)

        <u>sup. mut</u>.

        ] ko-r̤ṳ   GAL 1[

294

So

So 894   ASHM (-)

.1   a-te-re-te-a ,/ pe-te-re-wa 'te-mi-dwe'   ROTA ZE [

.2   ka-ki-jo ROTA ZE 1 ka-ko-de-ta ROTA ZE [

.3   ki-da-pa , / te-mi-dwe-ta   ROTA ZE 41 MO[

.4   o-da-tu-we-ta / e-ri-ka ,   ROTA ZE 40[

        Cut at left.

So 1053 + 5171   (-)

.a   ]a , a-re-ki-si-to-jo   [

.b   te-mi-]dwe-ta   ROTA[

      .b Traces at right after ROTA, ZE[not excluded.

So(1) 4429 + 5790 + 6019 + frr. (4)   (130)

.a   ]   de-do-me-na

.b   ]a-mo-ta , / pte-re-wa , te-mi-dwe-ta ROTA ZE 23 ROTA 1

      .a de-do-me-na probably over erasure.

      .b pte-re-wa over erasure; [[pe-te[   ]]. Room for a
         small MO in a lacuna before ROTA.

So(1) 4430   (130)

.a   ko-ki-da , o-pa   ne-wa

.b   e-ri-ka , / o-da-twe-ta , a-ro$_2$-a ROTA ZE 22 MO ROTA 1

So(2) 4431 + 8378 + 8569   (131?)

    ]a-mo-ta / te-mi-dwe-ta , pte-re-wa ROTA ZE 22 ROTA 1[

    22 possibly corrected to 23.

So(1) 4432 + 5804 + frr.   (130)

    ]e-ri-ka o-da-twe-ta ROTA ZE 35 MO ROTA 1

So(2) 4433 + 4444   (131)

.a   ]   te-mi-dwe-te

.b   ] , a-re-ki-si-to , wo-zo-me-no ,   ROTA <u>ZE</u> 1

      .a Final -<u>te</u> over [[<u>ta</u>]] .

So(2) 4434 + <u>fr.</u>   (131)

      e-ri-ka , / te-mi-dwe-ta   ROTA <u>ZE</u> 2   / <u>MO</u> ROTA[1

      <u>e-ri-ka</u> over erasure; <u>te-mi-</u> probably over
      [[ẹ-ṛị]] . 2 perhaps corrected from 3.

So 4435   (128?)

.a   pte-re-wạ[

.b   a-mo-ta / o-da-ku-we-ta   ROTA <u>ZE</u> 40   e-ri[-ka

      .b 40 changed from deleted numeral, perhaps 6ʒ or 66.

So(1) 4436 + 8425 + <u>fr.</u>   (130)

.1   e-ri-ka , o-da-twe-ta   ROTA <u>ZE</u> 73   [

.2   <u>vacat</u>   [

      .1 Base of two signs at right, perhaps <u>MO</u> ṚOṬA[.
          73 changed from deleted numeral.

      .2 Traces of erasure.

So(1) 4437 + 5127   (130)

      a-mo-ta , / pte-re-wa , a-ro₂-jo , te-mi-dwe-te   ROTA <u>ZE</u> 5

So(2) 4438   (131)

      ]e-ri-ka , wo-zo-me-na   ROTA <u>ZE</u> 15 [

So(2) 4439 + 5415   (131)

      a-mo-ta / e-ri-ka , te-mi-dwe-ta   ROTA <u>ZE</u> 3   <u>MO</u> ROTA 1

So(1) 4440 + 8700 + 8702   (130)

.a   ]   de-do-me-na

.b   ] a-mo-ta , / pte-re-wa , o-da-twe-ta   ROTA <u>ZE</u> 6

296

So(1)   4441 + 5782 + 8541 + 8706 + <u>fr</u>.   (130)

      e-ri-ka , / o-da-twe-ta , de-do-me-na   ROTA   <u>ZE</u> 36[

v.   ]ka

          36[probably corrected from 56[.

          v. Perhaps ROTA. Perhaps trace of erased numerals.

So(2)   4442 + <u>fr</u>.   (131)

 .a   ]   o-pe-ro   [
 .b   ]-ja , / a-mo-te , pe-ru-si-nwa , / ta-ra-si-ja ROTA <u>ZE</u> 1 [

          Probably same tablet as X 4472 (if so, read:
          se-to[-]i-ja ...).

<u>So(2)</u>   4443   (131?)

 .a   ]   wa-ra-wi-ta   [
 .b   ]-ta   ROTA <u>ZE</u>[

So(2)   4445 + 8576 + <u>frr</u>.   (131)

      pte-re-wa / te-mi-dwe-ta   ROTA <u>ZE</u> 5 [

          Palimpsest with previous central rule.

So(2)   4446 + 5977   (131)

 .1   a-mo-ta[/ e-]ri-ka , o-da-ke-we-ta ROTA <u>ZE</u> 62[ ] <u>MO</u> ROTA[1
 .2   [[to[   ]   ]] o-pe-ro   ROTA <u>ZE</u> 16

v.   e-ko   ROTA [   ]<u>vacat</u>   [
<u>lat. inf.</u>   ROTA

          .1 <u>ZE</u> 62: traces of rewriting and surface badly cracked;
          perhaps 162, less probably 262. The dividing line
          ends after o-da-ke-we-ta, and <u>MO</u> ROTA[very probably
          goes with the first line.

So   4447   (129?)

      o-pe-te-we / e-ri-ka   ROTA <u>ZE</u> 3

So(1)   4448 + 5794   (130)

      pa-i-to , a-mo-ta , pte-re-wa , te-mi-dwe-ta ROTA <u>ZE</u> 3
      pte over [[<u>te</u>]] .

So(1) 4449 + 4432 bis   (130)

      pte-re-wa , / te-mi-dwe-ta , ne-wa   ROTA <u>ZE</u> 3

So 5789   (-)

     ]ROTA <u>ZE</u> 3 [

So 8251   (-)

  .a   ]-te   [

  .b   e-]ri-ko   ROTA [

       .a]<u>twe</u>-te possible.

Sp

Sp 4451 + 4476 + 8701 + <u>fr</u>.   (-)

      wo-ra-e / pa-ra[ ]-we-jo   *<u>253</u> 2 [

         Very little evidence for pa-ra-<u>ku</u>-we-<u>jo</u> (and join
         4451 + 4476 perhaps not entirely certain).

Sp 4452   (-)

      wo-]ra / ka-za   *<u>253</u> 1   [

298

Uc

Uc 160   ("124"d)

  .1   sup. mut.

  .2   ]   Z   3   [[   ]]

  .3   ]V   1   Z   1   VIN   S   1   V   3   Z   2

  .4   ]   V   5   Z   3   de-re-u-ko   VIN   S   4

  .5   ]V   5   Z   2   CYP   1[

                  inf. mut.

v.1   sup. mut.

  .2   a-pi-po-re-we $*209^{VAS}$ 6[

  .3   i-po-no $*\underline{213}^{VAS}$ 14 [

  .4   ]-ro $*\underline{212}^{VAS}$ 17   [

                  inf. mut.

    .3 S over erasure.

    .4 de-re-u-ko : three of these signs precede VIN, one follows it.

    .5 CYP[+?] possible.

    v.3 14 over erasure?

    .4 Trace before ro.

Uc 161   ("124")

  .1   ]OVIS 197   SUS 1   [

  .2   ] 3   OLIV 30   <u>NI</u> 10   VIN 60[

    .2 Trace before 3 possibly T.

    v.   Graffito.

Uf

Uf(1) 79   ("124")

    ]ka-wi-ja , <u>DA</u> 5

299

Uf(1) 120   ("124")

  .a   ti-ri-to <u>DA</u> 1 ri[
  .b   i-wa-ka , ra-mo , /   [

Uf(1) 121 + 6027 + 8140   ("124"n)

     ]ja / qe-da-do-ro , pa-na-so , <u>DA</u> 1

Uf(1) 198   ("124"o)

     pa-to-ro <u>DA</u> 1
       Cut at right.

<u>Uf(1)</u> <311>   ("124"?)

  .1   <u>sup. mut.</u>
  .2   ]ta-na-ti , <u>DA</u> 1[
  .3   <u>inf. mut.</u>
      Missing; text from SM II.

Uf 432   (-)

      <u>sup. mut.</u>
  .1   ]<u>DA</u> 1[
  .2   [.]-ro-[.]-pu   <u>DA</u> 1   <u>PA</u>[
  .3 pu_2-ru-da-ro   <u>DA</u> 1   <u>PA</u> 1
  .4   di-ra   <u>DA</u> 1   <u>PA</u> 2
  .5   <u>vacat</u>   [
  .6   e-te-do-mo , ki-te[
  .7   da-ru-*56   <u>DA</u>[
  .8   qa-ra-jo   [
      <u>inf. mut.</u>
     Probably cut at bottom.

<u>Uf(3)</u> 835   (123?)

  .a   ]   ke-ke-me-na
  .b   ]-do / e-ke , ti-ri-to , pu-te <u>DA</u> 1   <u>PA</u> 1
     Cut at right.

Uf(2) 836   (122)

.a   wo-we-u
.b   ku-ka-da-ro / qa-ra , pi-di-jo   DA 1   PA 3
         Cut at left.
         .a wo-we-u over erasure.
         .b pi-di-jo over erasure.

Uf(2) 837   (122)

.a   ]te-wa-te-u   [
.b   ]ta-ko-ro   DA 1   PA 1   [
         Possibly same tablet as Uf 980.

Uf(2) 838 + 5135   (122?)

      ]ta / a-ke-re-mo   DA 1
         Cut at right.

Uf(2) 839   (122)

.a   te-re-ta , ke-ma-qe-me , me-ra , [
.b   ko-do , / da-*22-to , ke-nu-wa-so   1[
         .b Traces of erasure before ke- .

Uf(3) 970   (123)

.a   ]   te-re-ta   [
.b   ]ra / ti-ri-to , wo-ne-[

Uf(2) 980   (122)

.a   ]   vest. [
.b   ]da-jo / qa-ra , te[
         Possibly same tablet as Uf 837.

Uf(3) 981   (123)

.a   ko-to-i-na   [
.b   e-ri-ke-re-we / e-ke-pu-te-ri-ja   [
         Cut at left.
         .a Trace at right.

Uf(3)   983   (123)

   .a   ]   o-pi , po-to-ri-ka-ta [
   .b   ]do-wo / e-ko-so , ke-ke-me-na [
            .b   ]<u>do-wo</u> over erasure.

Uf(3)   987   (123)

      a₃-ki-wa-to / ti-ri-to pu-te[
            Cut at left. Trace at right, but not necessarily from
            the same word as <u>pu-te</u>[.

Uf(2)   990   (122)

      a-ri-ja-wo / qa-ra , te-re-t̤a[
            Cut at left.

Uf(3)   991   (123)

      ]-si-jo / ti-ri-to , pu[-te(

Uf(3)   1011   (123)

      i-ra-ta / ti-ri-to , pu[-te(
            Cut at left.

Uf(3)   1022   (123)

   .a   ]   ko-to-i̤[-na
   .b   ]qo-ta / e-ke-pu-te[-ri-ja

<u>Uf(2)</u>   1023   (122?)

   .a   ]   wo[
   .b   ]nwa-jo / qa-ra , [

Uf(3)   1031 + 5738   (123)

   .a   k̤o̤-to-i̤-na
   .b   pe-ri-je-ja / e-ke , pu-te-ri-ja <u>DA</u> 1 ti-ri-to
            Cut at right (tablet complete).
            .b <u>ti-ri-to</u> written below <u>DA</u> 1.

302

Uf(3) 1038   (123?)

     te-wa-jo[
        Cut at left. Trace at right.

Uf   1522   (-)

  .1   te-ro-ri-jo   <u>DA</u> 1
  .2   pu$_2$-to   <u>DA</u> 1
  .3   me-ta-no-re   <u>DA</u> 1
  .4   mi-ni-so   <u>DA</u> 1
  .5   e-ke-da-mo   <u>DA</u> 1
  .6   ]1̣
  .7   ]<u>DA</u> 1
  .8-.16   <u>vacant</u>

        Cut at top. Tablet originally ruled lengthwise (4 lines)
        and erased. 3 horizontal lines drawn on the two side
        edges.

Uf(2) 5721   (122?)

     ]jo , / tu-qa-ni[

Uf   5726 + 5953 + 8539   (-)

       <u>sup. mut.</u>
    ka-da-i-to , / pu-te , [
        Trace at right.

Uf(2) 5973   (122?)

     ]1   <u>PA</u> 1 [

Uf(2) 7486   (122?)

     ]me-na   <u>DA</u> 1
        Cut at right.

Uf(2) 7487   (122?)

     ] <u>DA</u> 1

Uf(1)   7488   ("124")
        ]to-no   DA 7 [
               to probably over unerased wo. Perhaps cut at right.

Uf(1)   7489 + 8142   ("124"o)
        te-nu   DA 1

Uf(1)   7490   ("124"n)
        ] , DA 1

Uf(1)   7491   ("124")
   .a   ]2
   .b   ]ku-no   DA 1

Uf(1)   7492   ("124")
        ]no   DA 5

Uf(1)   7493   ("124")
        ]ri   DA 1
               Cut at right.

Uf(1)   7494   ("124"n)
        ]pa-na-so   DA 1

Uf(1)   7495   ("124")
   .1   ]   DA 1
   .2   ]ru-po   DA 1
               .1 Trace at left. Marks resembling dividers, but
                  probably traces of erased text.

Uf(1)   8141   ("124"n)
        ] , DA 1
               Trace at left, perhaps]so.

Uf   8485   (-)
        ]pu-te[

304

Uf(1) 8486   ("124"n)
    ]DA 1

U

U(1) 49   ("124")
    ri-*65-no / a-pe-re QO 1

U(1) 95   ("124")
    ] *178 3
        Probably cut at left.

U(1) 96   (-)
    ]ro   *179 2[
        Or]da.

U(1) 109 + 7499   ("124"p)
    a-ku-wo /   pa-ra-ja *256[
        pa- over [[de]] (cf. de-do-me-na *256 in U 7507).

U(1) 124   ("124"p)
    ]   pa-ra-ja *256 1
        Perhaps trace at left.

U(1) 172   ("124")
    ke-ti-ro   *180 1[

U 436   (-)
    ]10   *172+KE[
        Trace at left.

U 437   (-)
    ]ko-so-ni-ja   *246 6

U 736   (-)

   .1   ]na-u-do-mo
   .2   ]93 e-to-ro-qa-ta   *181 10

   v.   ]36
         .1 Perhaps divider before na-u-do-mo.
         .2 Perhaps not *181 10 but 110, but this is very doubtful.
         v. Trace of erasure. Perhaps tallying.

U 746   (-)

      ]20   *172+KE+RO₂   10
      Very likely half-formed RO₂ (not RO). Traces of
      erasure and of a previous division into two lines.

U 797   (-)

      ]so   *258 1
      Cut at right.

U 876   (-)

      ]   *182 8   a-pi-te[
      Trace at left.

U 1812   (= 1053 bis)   (-)

      ]wi-ja   *183 10 [

U 1813   (= 1539 bis)   (-)

      ]*184 2 [

U 4478 + 5645 + 5795 + <u>frr</u>.(6)   (202)

.1   si-ja-ma-to   e̲ *<u>177</u> 2
.2   me-wo-ni-jo   e̲ *<u>177</u> 2 ma·*<u>177</u> 2
.3   a₃-ki-si-jo   e̲ *<u>177</u> 2
.4   ta-u-po-no   ma̲ *<u>177</u> 1
.5   pu-re-wa   ma̲ *<u>177</u> 1
.6   pa-na-re-jo / ka-u-ja[   ] <u>vacat</u>
.7   de-u-ke-ro   [   ] <u>vacat</u>
.8   do-ri-ka-no   e̲ *<u>177</u>[   ] <u>vacat</u>
.9   a₃-ki-po   e̲ *<u>177</u>[   ] <u>vacat</u>
.10 ke-[   ] ma̲ *<u>177</u>[
.11 a-nu[
.12 e-ke-nu-wo   [
.13 e-da-[.]-ni-ja[
.14 ka-pa-ri-jo[
.15 we-ka-di-jo   [
.16 pi-ri-sa-ta   ma̲[
.17 ku-ro₂   ma̲[
.18 e-ke-me-de   ma̲ *<u>177</u>[
.19 pa-na-re-jo   e̲ *<u>177</u>[
.20 se-ri-na-ta   e̲ *<u>177</u>[
.21 pa-ke-ta   ma̲ *<u>177</u>[
.22 a-wi-to-do-to   ma̲ *<u>177</u>[
.23   ]   ma̲ [
.24   ]   <u>vestigia</u> ?   [

              <u>fragmentum separatum</u>

        .0 <u>sup. mut.</u>
        .1]   ma̲ *<u>177</u>[
        .2]wo   ma̲ *<u>177</u>[
        .3 <u>inf. mut.</u>
     .6 Possibly pa-na-i̲-jo.

U 5186   (-)

.1   ] *<u>246</u> 1   [
.2   ]1̲   [
.3   ]   <u>vacat</u>   [

307

21

U 5592   (-)

    ]3   *<u>134</u> 100[
    Possibly 2̣00[.

U 5653   (-)

    ]1̣ <u>KI</u> 5[
    inf. mut.
        Perhaps]2̣ <u>KI</u> 5[or]-<u>ki</u> 5[.

U 5717   (-)

    ] 90 <u>E</u> 40
    Cut at right. Trace at left.

U 7063   (-)

           <u>sup. mut.</u>
  .1   ] <u>vacat</u>
  .2]1̣ OVIS^m 2   OVIS^f 1 *<u>134</u> 6 VIN [
  .3]OVIS^f 1 <u>pa</u> OVIS^f 1   *<u>134</u> 4
  .4]OVIS^x 2[ ]ỌVỊṢ^{x}[
           <u>inf. mut.</u>
      .2 1 *<u>134</u> on right edge, 6 VIN on verso.
      .3 4 on right edge.

U 7501   (-)

    ] 22 [
    Trace of ideogram at left, possibly a kind of vessel.

U 7505   (-)

  .1] <u>vacat</u>   [
  .2a]ṃẹ-ṛị-te-o [
  .2b] *<u>168</u> 30[   ]<u>vest.</u>[
      .2a The word is partly written over the ruling.

U(1) 7507 + 8131   ("124"p)

    ]de-do-me-na   *2̣56[

U 8210   (-)

  .1]re-u-ka , si-ki-ro [
  .2] , <u>DI+PTE</u> 1   [
      .2 Trace at left.

Vc

Vc(1)   53   ("124")

    ko-ro-sa-no   1

Vc(1)   54   ("124")

    po-ro-tu-qo-no

Vc(1) 55   ("124")

    i-mo-ro-ne-u   1

Vc(1)   64   ("124"r)

    mi-ka-ta   1

        Cut at both ends.

Vc(1)   65   ("124"r)

    ka-ra-na-ta   1   [

Vc(1)   66   ("124"s)

    pe-ka-wo

        Cut at right.

Vc(1)   67   ("124"r)

    mi-ka-to

        Cut at right.

Vc(1)   68   ("124")

    a-ka-i-jo   1

        Cut at right. Trace of deletion between -jo and 1
        (perhaps [[1]]).

Vc(1)   72   ("124"s)

    ka-pa-ri-jo

        Cut at right.

Vc(1) 73   ("124")

    wa-na-ka , [

        Probably not cut at right, though there are traces of
        a vertical mark. Last sign possibly numeral 1.

Vc(1) 74   ("124"r)

    po-ru-ka-to

        Cut at right.

Vc(1) 81   ("124"r)

    a-ka-to-wa

        Cut at right.

Vc(1) 102   ("124"s)

    e-wi-ta-jo

        Cut at both ends.

Vc(1) 106   ("124"s)

    ] a-ki-re-u

        Cut at right.

Vc(1) 108   ("124"s)

    za-ki-ri-jo

        Cut at both ends.

Vc(1) 125   ("124"s)

    da-o-ta 1

        Cut at left.

Vc(1) 126   ("124"s)

    o-ko-te

        Cut at right.

Vc(1) 129   ("124")

    e-pi-da-o 1

        Cut at right. Possibly divider rather than numeral 1.

Vc(1)   171   ("124"r)

      ? pe-]ri-to-wo   1
            Cut at right.

Vc(1)   173   ("124")

      a-no-qo-ta , a₃[

  v.   je[
            Perhaps 1 rather than divider.

Vc(1)   174   ("124"s)

      pe-ri-to
            Cut at left.

Vc(1)   175   ("124"s)

      a-pi-da-ta   1
            Cut at both ends.

Vc(1)   176   ("124"s)

      po-ru-te-we   1
            Cut at right.

Vc(1)   181   ("124"s)

      pi-ra-qo
            Cut at both ends. Whole tablet perhaps over erasure
            (but no traces remain).

Vc(1)   183   ("124"s)

      pe-re-wa-ta
            Cut at right.

Vc(1)   184   ("124"s)

      a-ro-wo-ta   1
            Cut at left.

Vc(1)   185   ("124"s)

      a-ne-te-wa   1
            Cut at left.

                            311

Vc(1)   188   ("124")

        te-re-ja-wo   1

            Cut at both ends.   -ja- over erasure.

Vc(1)   195   ("124"r)

        ] pe-ri-to-wo

            Possibly cut at left.

Vc(1)   199   ("124"r)

        a-pi-re-jo   1

            Cut at left.

Vc(1)   201 + 7803   ("124")

        ta-ra-sa-ta 1   [

 v.   du[

Vc(1)   203   ("124"s)

        ra-wo-ti-jo 1[

            Cut at left.

Vc(1)   205   ("124"r)

        a-ke-ra-no 1

            Cut at right. Over erasure ?

Vc(1)   206   ("124"r)

        pa-pa-ro

            Cut at right.

Vc(1)   208   ("124"s)

        ]a-re-jo   1

Vc(1)   211   ("124"r)

        pa-sa-ko-me-no

            Cut at left.

Vc(1)   212   ("124"s)
        e-re-pa-i-ro
            Cut at right.

Vc(1)   215   ("124"r)
        a-ne-u-da   1 [

Vc(1)   285 + <u>fr</u>.   ("124"s)
        ]re-ka-se-ra-wo
            Perhaps trace on the broken edge of the verso.

Vc(1)   290   ("124")
        wo-ro-to-qo   1̣[
            <u>qo</u> perhaps over erasure.

Vc(1)   291   ("124"s)
        me-ta-ri-ko-wo
            Cut at right.

Vc(1)   293   ("124")
        di-wi-ja-wo 1
            Cut at right.

<u>Vc(1)</u>   <295>   ("124"?)
        ]ma-ti-ko 1
            Missing; text from SM II.

Vc(1)   303   ("124")
        ]ti̤-ri-jo-qa
   v.   ]wi
            Cut at right.

Vc(1)   312   ("124"s)
        e-we-de-u
            Cut at both ends.

313

Vc(1)   <316>   ("124"?)

     a-ke-ra-wo 1[

         Missing; text from SM II.

Vc(1)   <317>   ("124"?)

     ti-ma 1 [

   v.   a[

         Missing; text from SM II.

Vc(2)   569   (115)

     a-ta-no 1

         Cut at right.

Vc(2)   5510   (115?)

     ku-ru-ka 1

         Cut at right.

Vc(2)   5523   (115?)

     qe-ra-jo [

         Cut at left.

Vc(2)   7517   (115)

     da-*83-jo 1

         Cut at left.

Vc(2)   7518   (115)

     ka-na-a-po 1

         Cut at right. a small sized, inserted between na and po.

Vc(2)   7520   (115)

     ]ne-to 1

         Cut at right.

Vc(1)   7529   ("124"s)

     ]-wa-si-jo 1

       ]u-wa-si-jo possible.

Vc(1) 7531   ("124"r)

]-di-so 1 [

Vc(1) 7532   ("124"s)

]ra-wo 1
    Cut at right.

Vc(2) 7533   (115?)

]-to 1 [
inf. mut.

Vc(1) 7534   ("124"s)

]-ra 1
    Cut at right.

Vc(2) 7537 + 7652   (115)

ka-sa-to 1
    Cut at right.

Vc(1) 7540   ("124"r)

]pa-ta 1
    Cut at right.

Vc(1) 7575 + fr.   ("124")

ke-pu_2-je-u 1 [
    Cut at left.

Vc(1) 7612   ("124"s)

a_3-wa-ta
    Cut at right.

Vc(1) 7837   ("124"s)

]ra-ko 1 [

Vd

Vd 62   ("124"q)

    ]we̤-ro : a-ka-i-jo : [

Vd 136   ("124")

    ] : wa-na-ka[

Vd 137 [+] 137 bis   ("124")

    a-ta-ti-ṋu : si-wa-[- -]ko-to : pe-qe-u : o-ko-te : <u>vacat</u>[

Vd 138 + <u>fr</u>.   ("124"q)

    ]-me-no : da-te-[

V

V 52 + 52 bis + 8285   (-)

   .1   a-ta-na-po-ti-ni-ja 1 ṵ[   ]vest.[

   .2   e-nu-wa-ri-jo 1 pa-ja-wo-ne 1 po-se-da[-o-ne

<u>lat. inf.</u>   [[e-ri-nu-we   pe-rọ   ]] [

         .1]<u>vest</u>.[: perhaps]-wọ[.

        <u>lat. inf.</u> pe-ṛọ or <u>PE</u>] .

V(1) 56   ("124")

   .a   ko-no-si-jo   [

   .b   e-qe-a-o , a-to-mo   16 [

         Probably cut at right and nothing lost.

V(1) 57 + 8036 + <u>fr</u>.   ("124")

    e-u-da-mo , e-we-wa-ta

V(2) 60 [+] 151   (124)

.1   wo-di-jo / a-ni-o̱-ko 1 // qo-ta[   ] 1 [
.2   i-wa-ka 1 ka-pa-ri-jo[   ]ti-jo 1 ki-si-wi-jo̤[
.3   me-nu-wa 1 wi-da-jo 1̤[   ]1 di-we-so 1
.4   o-ku-na-wo 1 i-to-ma[   ]-ta 1 a-ke-u 1
.5   pe-ri-ta 1 a-ka[   ]   vacat
.6   vacat   [   ]   vacat

        Whole tablet deleted and reused, perhaps with more
        recent deletion under o-ku- (line 4).

        .1 a-ni-o̱-ko inserted in small signs spaced between the
           larger signs -di-jo 1 qo-. Perhaps]da̤ 1 [.

        .5 a-ka̤ 1[or a-ka-[.

V(1) 77   ("124")

.1   ]te-wa 1   ka-pa-ri-jo 1
.2   ]   vacat
        .2 Traces of erasure.

V(1) 114 + 158 + 7719   ("124")

.a   a-mi-ni-so
.b   pa-ze , / pe-da̤ , wa-tu ,

v.1   pa-ze , a-mi-ni-so , / pe-da , wa-tu
.2   vacat
        .b Over erasure.

V(2) 117 + 8573   ("124")

.1   ]ne-jo[
.2   ]-te 3 u-o[
.3   ]wo-ne , a-pe-o[
.4   inf. mut.

V(1) 118 + 7561   (124)

        po-ru-da-si-jo , / a_2-ke-te-re 2[
          a_2- over [[a̲]] .

317

sup. mut.

.1   ta-mo-[

.2   u-wo-qe-ne / u-du-ru-wo '4   o̱ 6'

.3   we-re-we / ku-pa-sa 4 o̱ 6

.4   we-re-we , / ka-ta-ra-pi̤ 4 o̱ 6

.5   a-ke-to-ro / to-ni 2̱ o̱ 10 [[   ]]

.6   [[40   o̱ 33]]

    .4 Numeral 6 running on to edge.

    .5 Perhaps to-ni 3̱. Something erased after o̱ and
        under 10; units erased after 10.

    .6 Perhaps majuscule sign (KE̤?) erased before 40.

V(2)   147   (124)

.1   we-we-ro   1

.2   e-u-ru-qo-ta   1

.3   na-e-si-jo   1

.4   da-te-wa   1

.5   te-ra-pe-te   1

.6   inf. mut.

    .1 Over erased ruling.

V(1)   150 + 7624   ("124")

    to-ko-so-ta , a-te-u-ke 1

      Cut at right.

V(2)   159 + fr.   ("124")

    sup. mut.

.1   ]te̤-[.]-ta 6̤[   ] vest.

.2   ]83 ru-ki-to 157̤

.3   ]55 ti-ri-to 45

.4   ]so 34   pu$_2$-te-re / wa-si-ro 18

.5   ] 10   ra-pte-re 20[

    .1 Possibly]te̤-re̤-ta.

    .2 Numerals after 100 badly damaged.

    .4 wa-si-ro in small signs between -te- and 8.

    .5 Traces of two signs at left.

    v.   Ruled (five lines) but not inscribed.

V(1) 210 + 8020   ("124")

      ]-su-pa-ta   1

v.   ]no

        ]ẹ-su-pa-ta or]pị-su-pa-ta.

V(2) 280   ("124")

  .1   wo-de-wi-jo

  .2-.4 <u>vacant</u>

  .5   to-pe-za , o-u-ki-te-mi X

  .6-.10 <u>vacant</u>

  .11   a-pe-ti-ra$_2$ / o-u-te-mi X

  .12   o-u-te-mi X

  .13   o-u-te-mi X

  .14   o-u-te-mi X

  .15   e-pi , i-ku-wo-i-pi

         <u>reliqua pars sine regulis</u>

         Many traces of erasure (probably palimpsest).

V(2) 337   ("124")

  .0   <u>sup. mut.</u>

  .1   a-pi-re-we 6[

  .2   da-mi-ni-jo[

  .3   ]pọ-mi-jo [

  .4   ]tọ-so 3[

       <u>inf. mut.</u>

v.0   <u>sup. mut.</u>

  .1   ]jo / mo-ni-kọ 3

  .2   ]   3   [

  .3   ]wi-to 10   o[

  .4   <u>inf. mut.</u>

       v.1 Perhaps <u>mo-ni</u> 5̣.

V(3) 429   (115)

.1   ]qa-ra-jo 1[

.2   ku-ka-so   1̣[

.3   ]ja-pa-ra-r̥o[

.4   ]vacat [

          .1.3 Probably nothing lost at left.

          .1   qa-ra-jo over erasure (qa- over [[q̠e]] or [[k̠a]]).

V(3) 431   (115)

.1   ] e-ra-jo , [

.2   ] pu-da-so[

.3.4 vacant [

          .1.2 Text certainly complete at left.

V(3) 466   (115)

.1   ]1̣ qa-ra-i-so 1 si-ra-no 1

.2   ]1̣ i-ra-ko-to 1 wa-na-ta-jo 1

.3   ] 1

.4   ]   vacat

V(3) 479   ASHM (115)

.1   du-pu₂-ra-zo 1 qe-ro 1 su-ko 1 di-zo 1

.2   pu-ri   1 wi-da-ma-r̥o 1 o-ro-qa 1 wa-je 1

.3   da-i-ra   1 e-[   ] 1   [

.4   vacat   [   ] vacat [

v.1 pe-ri-ro-qo   [

.2   da-*83-jo 1 e-r̥ị[   ]1 d̠ạ[

.3   o-du   1 te-ja-r̥o 1   [

.4   vacat   [

          Cut at left.

          v.2 e-w̠ẹ[possible. ụ[or s̠ẹ[possible.

320

V(3) 482 + 7868   (115)

```
.1      e-u-ko-ro 1   [
.2      qe-ra-jo 1  a-mi-nwa[
.3      nu-to 1  mi-ru-ro 1   [
.4         ]   vacat                    [
.5         ]me-to / ko̤-wo 2 // wo[
           .2 Probably a-mi-nwa 1̤[.
```

V(3) 488   (115)

```
.1    ]na-ko-to  1
.2    ]sa̤-de-so  1
```

V(3) 492   (115)

```
.1    ]dwo-jo 1  pa-ki[
.2    ]na-po 1   ru-ki[
.3.4 ]   vacant         [
```

V(3) 503   (115)

```
.1    a-nu-mo 1  ta-za-ro 1  wa-[
.2    *47-ti-jo 1  ja-ma-ra 1  pa-ja[
.3    po-mi-ni-jo 1  wa-du-na 1        [
.4       vacat                         [
         .1 Probably wa-jo̤[, less likely wa-na̤[.
```

V(4) 652 + 5915   (103)

```
.1    ]no-mo 1  tu-ti 1[
.2    ]ki-ti-jo 1         [
.3          ] ja-pa-ra-ro 1 [
              .3 Trace at left.
```

V(4) 653   (103)

```
.1    do-ti-jo , 'a-['
.2    *49-sa-ro 1  / po-ti[
.3    ra-ku 1  ku-ka-ro[
.4    ra-te-me 1    *56-[
              Cut at left.
              .1 -jo possibly over erasure.
```

321

V(3)   655 + 5606 + 5865 + 5988 + 8507   (115)

.1   e-re-dwo-e[ ] vac.[/]i-[//]sa-ma-ru[
.2   pe-ri-to-wo / da-wo 1 // ne-o[   ] 1 ja-ma-ta-ro[
.3   ta-de-so / ja-po 1   [   ]po 1 pe-to-me[
.4   ]-ko-to / pa-ro a-[   ]1[ ]   to-so[
.5   ]   vacat   [

        .1 Perhaps pa-]i-to[; traces of erasure and particularly
           of an earlier guide-line.1 .

        .3 Perhaps 1 // ta[.

V 684   (140)

.1   e-re-pa-to / ka-ra-ma-to   46
.2   ka-so , ke-ma-ta   8

        Palimpsest; previous text written other side up:

        .1 [[e-re-pa-to / ka-ra-ma...]] .

V(5)   756 + 7806   (125)

.A   '[po-ti-]ro', wa-wi 1 a-mu-ta-wo-qe[
.B   da-*22-ti-ja /   vacat   [
        Traces of erasure.

V(6)   831   (203)

.1   ]ra-to 1   e-ke-a 1   e-mi-ja-ta 1
.2   ]ka-mu-ko-to 1   ke-ra-ja 1
.3   ]-pu 1   we-ka-di-jo 1   ma-ke-ra 1
.4   ]de-ro 1   ma-ti-ko 1 a-ti-ka 1
.5   ]-we-u 1   qa-da-ro 1   ka-sa-no 1
.6   ]wo 1   to-ro-ki-no 1   [[to[ ]]
.7   ]no-re 1   wi-ri-ki-no 1   [
.8   ]ko-no-si-jo 1   do-ti-jo-no[
.9   ]   vacat   [
        Cut at bottom.

        .1 Or]ra-da?

        .2 ke of ke-ra-ja over erasure.

        .4 ma-ti- over erasure; -ti-ka over erasure.

322

V(6)   832 + fr.   (102)

.0   sup. mut.

.1   ru-ro   1[

.2   ta-u-ro   1 [

.3   u-ta-jo , 1   [

.4   ja-sa-ro   1

        reliqua pars sine regulis
        Cut at bottom.

V(6)   865 + 7526 + 8073   (-)

        sup. mut.

.1   ]1 X

.2   ru-ki-to , / a-ke-re-mo-no 1 X

.3   qa-ra / ko-re-te *258   1 X

.4   qa-ra / a-ke-re-mo-no   1 X

.5   qa-ra / po-ro-ko-re-te   1 X

.6   vacat

.7   vacat [

V(6)   958 + 962   (101?)

.1   ]ni-ja / wa[   ] //   ma-na-je-u[

.2a   ]   te-ra[ ]   e-da-e[-u?

.2b   ]1 te-te-u   1 do-ri-ka-o   [

.3a   ]a-ka   ka-ke-u   [

.3b   ]ka-ta 1   wi-pi-no-o   1 se-[

.4   ]pu-ra 1   [

        .1 After wa[   ], erased sign more likely than divider.

V(6)   960   (-)

.1   ]wo / wo-ka-re 4[

.2-.4]   vacant   [
        Cut at bottom.

V(6)   961 + 8666   (225)

   .1   <u>vestigia</u>
   .2   si-ra-pe-te-ṣọ 1 ka-pu-ro 1
   .3   ka-na-po-to   1 pi-ma[
   .4   ] 1 ạ[
           <u>inf. mut.</u>
         .2 Alternatively si-ra-pe-te-ṃẹ (certainly not -r̤i̤).

V(5)   1002 + 5766 + 7650   (125)
   .A   'po-ti-ro' , pi-ra-ki-jo 1 pe-ri-jo-ta-qe 1
   .B   da-*22-ti-ja /

V(5)   1003 + 5958   (125)
   .A   ]   'po-ti-ro' , [
   .B   ]ka-di-ti-ja /   [

V(5)   1004   (125)
   .A   ']po-ti-ro' , pa-na-re-jo 1 ku-da-jo-qe 1 [
   .B   ]<u>vest.</u>/   [
            .B Possibly]j̤a.

V(5)   1005 + 7530 + 7567   (125)
   .A   'po-ti-ro' , e-wa-ko-ro 1 pi-ra-k̤a-wo-qe 1
   .B   ki-ra-di-ja /   [   ] <u>vacat</u>

V(5)   1043 + 7709   (125)
   .A   ]   'po-ti-ro' **da-i-wo-wo** 1 to-no-qe 1
   .B   ]-p̤a-si-ja /
            .A Over erasure.
            .B Perhaps]k̤ụ-p̤a-si-ja.

324

                    sup. mut.
.1   ]vest.[
.2   ] , ta-ra-nu , a-nu[
.3   ]ta-ra-nu , a-nu[
.4   ta-]ra-nu qe-[
.5   ta-ra-]nu [
            inf. mut.
            .1]nu[possible.
            .4 Possibly qe-pi[.

                         sup. mut.
.1a   ]   i[-jo
.1b   ]ke , a[   ] wa-du-na , [. . . .]
.2   ]-to , e[   ] vacat
.3   ]sa-ka-ri-jo , [   ] vacat
.4a   i-jo   i-jo
.4b [o-]pi / di-zo , pi-ma-na-ro , zo-wi-jo 1 a-tu-qo-te-ra-to 1[
.5a   i-jo
.5b o-pi / ri-zo , pi-ma-na-ro   pi-ro-i-ta 1
.6   o-pi / pa-ka ,   di-wa-jo 1   [
.7   ]pi / o-na-se-u 1   ri-[
.8   ]-du 1 ke-[
.9   ]za[
                     inf. mut.
     .2 Perhaps]si-to.
     .4 a-tu-qo-te-ra-to and i-jo probably over erasure.
     .7]e possible. Strange circular mark below 1 after
         o-na-se-u.
     .8 Possibly]wi-du. Perhaps over erasure.

V(7) 1524   (105)

       sup. mut.

.1   ]qe   [

.2   ]ma-no-ne   [

.3   ] 1 po-da 1 se[

.4   ] po-da 1   do-ma[

.5   ]ki-si-wo po-da[

V(7) 1526   (105)

       sup. mut.

.1   a-mi-ni-si-ja[

.2   si-ja-ma 1 [

.3   pi-ro-i[

.4   vac.[

       inf. mut.

    Verso ruled (3 lines) but not inscribed. Probably
    same tablet as As 1520.

V(5) 1583 + 7747 + 7887   (125)

.A   ']po-ti-ro' , si-mi-te-u 1 a-ra-ko[

.B   ] vacat   [

V <1631>   (-)

.1   ]to-i-je[

.2   ]-ru-ko   1 [

.3   ]no-du   1 [

.4   ]da-na-jo   1   [

.5   ] vacat   [

    Missing; text from SM II. pl. 62.

V 5113   (-)

.1   ]me   300[

.2   ]zo , do-wa 10[

V(4) 5536   (103)
        sup. mut.
    .1   ]-ki̤-si[
    .2   ]ka-na-po 1 jo̤[
    .3   ]so̤ 1   te-[

V   5575   (-)
    .1   ]we-to-ro 35̤[
    .2   ]3   [
            .2 Trace of sign or of numeral at left of]3.

V(4) 5872   (103)
        sup. mut.
    .1   ]ja-ro 2[
    .2   ]ro-we 2[
    .3   ]se-me-ni[

V(4) 5946 + frr.   (103)
    .1   ]-ri-jo 1̤ qe-ro[
    .2   ]1̤ ku-ke-mo̤[
            .1 Perhaps]qe̤-ri̤-jo or]ka̤-ri̤-jo.

V(1) 7049 + 8639   ("124")
        ]ke-ti-ra-wo , wo-*79̤ 1   [

V(3) 7512 + 7714 + 7716   (115)
    .1   ] 3̤   u-su 4   a-mi-ni-si̤-jo [
    .2   ] ta-qa-ra-ti 1   ku-ma̤-to̤[
            Verso ruled (A.B) but not inscribed.

V(3) 7513   (115)
    .1   ]ma-ro 1   o-ru-[
    .2   ]1   qe-re-ma-o 1̤[
    .3   ]1̤   [
            .1 1 over erasure.

V(3) 7519   (115)

    .0   sup. mut.
    .1   ] 1   a[
    .2   ]-jo 1   [
    .3   ] vacat   [

V(2) 7523   ("124")

            sup. mut.
    .1   ] vacat [
    .2   ]me-ja 1
    .3   ]-ja   1
    .4   ] vacat
            inf. mut.

V(3) 7524   (115)

    .1   ]ṛo 1
    .2   ]ḷ ri-zo 1
    .3   ] vacat
        .2 Over erasure.

V 7527   (-)

    .1   ]ko 4
    .2   ] vacat

V(3) 7539   (115)

    .1   ]to 1
    .2.3] vacant

V(5) 7577 + 7734   (125)

    .A   po-tị[-ro
    .B   di-pi-ja / vac.[

V(3) 7620   (115)

    .1   a-qi-ta[
    .2   ]ki-ma-to   1[
    .3   ]ẹ-u-po-ro-wo   [
    .4   vacat   [
            .2 Uncertain whether or not a sign is lost at left.
            .3 Text probably complete at left.

V(5)   7670 + 7746   (125)

  .A   po[-ti-ro
  .B   a-pa-ta-wa-ja / vac.[

V(5)   7797   (125?)
  .1   ]ra-tu[
  .2   inf. mut.

V(1)   7839   ("124")
      ]ne 1 [
      Trace of sign, perhaps erased, at right.

V   7940   (-)
      ]te-we 1
      Cut at right.

V(5)   7964   (125)
      ]po-ti-ro[
      inf. mut.

V   8487   (-)
  .1   ]ko 2
  .2   ]1

Wb

Wb 1576   (-)

  .1]o-pe-re-ra[

  .2]me-na-qe[

     inf. mut.

Wb 1714   (-)

  .1 me-sa-to

  .2]*146 30

Wb 1816   (= 1714 b)   (-)

  .1 me-sa-to

  .2 *146[

     inf. mut.

Wb 1817   (= 1714 c)   ASHM (-)

     sup. mut.

  .1]vest.[

  .2 *146 30

Wb 2001   (-)

     ]i-to[

     Perhaps nothing lost at left.

Wb 2133   (-)

     sup. mut.

  .1 wa-[

  .2 me-no[

     inf. mut.

       .1 Probably wa-ri[.

Wb 5131   (-)

  .1]e-ke-pi[

  .2] a-ra[

       .1]e and pi[very doubtful.

Wb 5282   (-)

    da-wo[

Wb 5283   (-)

      sup. mut.
.1   ]-ti-[
.2   ] OVIS^m[

Wb 5527   (-)

      sup. mut.
.1   ]L LANA[
.2   inf. mut.

Wb 5662   (-)

    ku-ta-ti-jo[
     inf. mut.

Wb 5664   (-)

     sup. mut.
     ]OVIS^m
     inf. mut.

Wb 5665   (-)

    ?da-]*22-ti[

Wb 5697   (-)

     sup. mut.
    ? OVIS]^m [
      Possibly CAP^m, BOS^m etc.

Wb 5822   (-)

.1 me-sa-to
.2 inf. mut.

Wb 5824   (-)

.1]me-sa-to
.2 inf. mut.

331

Wb 5830   (-)
     da-mi[

Wb 5831   (-)
     ] OVIS^m [
        Perhaps] , OVIS^m [.

Wb 5835   (-)
     <u>sup. mut.</u>
     qa[

Wb 5836   (-)
     ]ja[

Wb 5837   (-)
     <u>sup. mut.</u>
     ]q̣ạ [

Wb 5857   (-)
     <u>sup. mut.</u>
     ]jo-jo[

Wb 5858   (-)
     ]ṛạ-to[

Wb 5860   (-)
  .1 <u>sup. mut.</u>
  .2   *<u>146</u>[

Wb 6058   (-)
  .1]ṛọ-we OVIS^m [
  .2]ra-ze[
        .2 OVIS^m over [[OVIS^f]] .

Wb 7139   (-)
     ]ka-do OVIS^m

332

Wb 7713 + 7738   (-)

   .1   ku-do-ni-ja , t̩a̩[
   .2   ]   <u>vacat</u>   [
   .3   <u>inf. mut.</u>

Wb 7907   (-)

        ]a̩-mo-ta[

Wb 8207   ASHM (-)

        <u>sup. mut.</u>
        [.]-m̩a̩-ja[.]

Wb 8488   (-)

        <u>sup. mut.</u>
        ] ra̩[
             Probably cut at right.

Wb 8489   (-)

   .1   ]k̩e̩ , n̩e̩-s̩o̩-p̩o̩[
   .2   ]   <u>vacat</u>   [
        .1 <u>ke</u> or <u>d̩e̩</u>; <u>n̩e̩</u> or <u>p̩o̩</u>; <u>s̩o̩</u> or <u>d̩i̩</u>; <u>p̩o̩</u> or <u>a</u>; text partly
             erased.

Wb 8490   (-)

        <u>sup. mut.</u>
        *<u>146</u>[

Wb 8491   (117?)

        <u>sup. mut.</u>
        ] , O̩V̩I̩S̩.^m[
             Possibly to be read the other way up (Bennett, in <u>KT</u>):
             ]p̩a̩ 1[.

Wb 8492 + <u>fr.</u>   (117?)

        <u>vestigia</u>

Wb 8711   (-)

           <u>sup. mut.</u>
   .1   ]o-a-pu-[
   .2   tu-na-no [
             <u>inf. mut.</u>
             Probably only two lines of text.]o-a-pu-d̩o̩[possible.

                          333

Ws

Ws 1701   (-)

.α   *185   supra sigillum

.β   ma-se-wi-ra₂-[.]

> .α Ideogram probably different from the one in Ws 8494.
> γ (= *257).
>
> .β Possibly two words : ma-se and wi-ra₂-[.].

Ws 1703   ASHM (-)

.α   *115   supra sigillum

.β   ta-to-mo

.γ   o-nu-ke

> .α On *115 standing for commodity, not weight, see
> M.A.V. Gill, Kadmos 5 (1966), p.4.

Ws 1704   (-)

.α   JAC   supra sigillum

.β   o-pa

.γ   pa-ta-ja

Ws 1705   (-)

.α   sigillum

.β   pa-ta-ja

.γ   vacat

> .β ta half-obliterated.

Ws 1707   (-)

.α.1]ke-wo-re-u-

 .2   -si

.β   do-ke

.γ   [.]-ja-wo-ne

> .α Perhaps]a₃-wo-re-u-si with no sign lost at left;
> otherwise probably one sign lost.
>
> .γ wi-ja-wo-ne is a likely reading.

Ws <1708>   (-)

    VIR   <u>supra sigillum</u>

       Missing; text from SM II, pl. 88.

Ws 8152   ASHM (-)

.α   LANA   <u>supra sigillum</u>

.β   ne-ki-

.γ   -ri-de

Ws 8153   ASHM (-)

.α   TELA^{3}+TE   <u>supra sigillum</u>

.β   te-pa

.γ   <u>vacat</u>

Ws 8493   (-)

.α   se-to-i-ja

.βa   ki-ri-ta-de

.b   <u>te</u>   LANA   do-ke

Ws 8494   (-)

.α   <u>sigillum</u>

.β   <u>vacat</u>

.γ   *<u>257</u>

       .γ Ideogram probably different from the one in Ws 1701.
         α (=*<u>185</u>).

Ws 8495   (-)

.α   JAC   <u>supra sigillum</u>

.β1   pa-ta-ja

.2   <u>vacat</u>

.γ   o-pa

Ws 8496   (-)

.α   *<u>134</u>   <u>supra sigillum</u>

.β.γ   <u>vacant</u>

Ws 8497   (-)

   .α   AES *246 <u>supra sigillum</u>
   .β   ke-ni-qa
   .γ   a-sa-mi-to
            .β -<u>qa</u> and remainder of face over erasure.

Ws 8498   (-)

   .α   <u>sigillum</u>
   .β   o-pa
   .γ   ko-we

Ws 8499   (-)

   .α   pi-mo-no
   .β   na-ki-zo
   .γ   pa-wo 1

Ws 8500   (-)

   .α   GRA <u>supra sigillum</u>
   .β.γ <u>vacant</u>

Ws 8712   (-)

   .α   e-po <u>supra sigillum</u>
   .β.γ <u>vacant</u>

Ws 8713   (-)

   .α   MUL <u>supra sigillum</u>
   .β.γ <u>vacant</u>

Ws 8752   (-)

   .α   MUL <u>supra sigillum</u>
   .β.γ <u>vacant</u>

Ws 8753   (-)

   .α   <u>sigillum</u>
   .β.γ <u>vestigia</u>

Ws <8754>   (-)

  .α <u>sigillum</u>

  .β ku-wa-ta

  .γ o-pi a-nu-wi-'ko'

       Plaster.

      .γ <u>ko</u> small sign above <u>a-nu</u>.

Xd

Xd 58   ("124")

    ra-to / pa-ta-re[

        Traces after <u>re</u>[(either a big sign (pa) or the

        beginning of signs in .a and .b).

Xd 70   ("124"r)

    ]o-ka[

Xd 75   ("124")

    di-ka[

Xd 78   ("124")

    ku-ka-ra-re[

Xd 80   ("124")

    ]pe-ka-wo , // ku-ta-to[

Xd 82 + 8136   ("124"r)

    a-ka-me-ne[

Xd 83   ("124")

    ]ka-no

        Cut at right.

Xd 84   ("124")

    ]a-ka-to[

Xd 86   ("124")

    ka-wi[

Xd 92   ("124")

    ]ru-po-to[

Xd 94 + 187   ("124")

    ki-je-u , / a-pi-ja-re[

  v.   tu   [

        Perhaps cut at right. a-pi-ja-re[written at a second
        stage, on drier clay and over erasure; two superimposed
        signs after -re : a large wo and a jo smaller than re;
        difficult to say whether wo was part of the erased word
        and whether jo was intended to be the end of a-pi-ja-re[.

Xd 97 + 284   ("124")

    di-wi-je-ja / di-wi-ja   [

        Perhaps cut at right. Erased sign after -ja, perhaps
        [[di]] or [[ta]] .

Xd 98 + 196   ("124")

    ki-si-wi-je-ja / pe-ra$_2$-wo[

Xd 99   ("124"r)

    ]-wi-jo

        Perhaps]ja-wi-jo.

Xd 100   ("124")

    ]*47-da , / mi-ko[

Xd 105 + 128   ("124")

    ]no , / i-ja[ ] // di / i-*65-ke-o , [

        Possibly cut at right. Whole tablet over erasure (but
        [[di-]] after]no,). Unerased but unidentifiable sign
        after i-ja[.

Xd 107   ("124")

  .a   o[

  .b   ma-ki / pa[

Xd 110   ("124")

    a-ku-di-ri-jo [

        Trace of sign at right end (ko[or ne[ ).

339

Xd 111 + 134   ("124")

.a]   a-pu₂-ka   [
.b]te-ja / za-mi-so , ku-ta-to , [
        Trace at right.

Xd 112   ("124")

    a-ku-di-ri[
        Traces of erasure.

Xd 116   ("124")

.a]o-ke-te , a-e[
.b] e-ro-e-o   [

Xd 119   ("124")

    ]-ne-ri-jo , e-[
        -jo over erasure, perhaps [[wo]] . Perhaps e-wo[or e-ta[.

Xd 122   ("124")

    ]ja / qe-re-wa ,   [
        Probably nothing lost at right.

Xd 123   ("124"s)

    ]qe-wa[

Xd 127   ("124"s)

    e-u-o-mo[
        Cut at left.

Xd 130   ("124")

    ]ru-o-wo[

Xd 131   ("124")

    da-*22-to , wo-no-da[
        Arcs of two circles visible at right.

340

Xd 133   ("124"s)

  ]i-ne-u[
         Over erasure.

Xd 140   ("124")

  .1   da-pu-ri-ṭo[
  .2a   pa-ze-qe , ke-wo[
  .2b   *47-ta-qo[
  .3   *47[
  .4   inf. mut.

Xd 141   ("124"r)

      pu-ra-ko[

Xd 142   ("124"r)

      pu-ko-ṛo[
           Perhaps over erasure.

Xd 143 + 7579   ("124")

      i-ke-se [

Xd 146 + 155   ("124")

  .0   sup. mut.
  .1   ] vacat   [
  .2   ku-[.]-i-to / a-pi-do-ro[
  .3   ma-u-do[
  .4   i-ja-wo-ne[
  .5   inf. mut.
            .1 Trace on left edge.
            .2 ku-ta-i-to not impossible.

Xd 148   ("124")

  .1   ro-a , ku[
  .2   qa-mo[
  .3   vacat[
            .1 ro- over [[qa]] .

341

Xd 149 + 8121   ("124")

 .0 sup. mut.

 .1 vac.[

 .2 e-ra [

 .3 tu-ni-ja [

 .4 ri-u-no [

 .5]to [

 .6 inf. mut.

v.   ]o 70 [

    inf. mut.

    Traces of previous ruling. Probably erasure in line 5.

    v.]o possibly to be read as ideographic.

Xd 154   ("124")

 .1 ra-wa-ke-si[

 .2 ma-ke-ra-mo[

 .3 qa-ra-su-ti-jo[

 .4 i-da-ra-ta [

 .5 [.]-to-ko-ro [

 .6]vest.[

   inf. mut.

v.1 sup. mut.

.2-.4] vacant

 .5]1

   inf. mut.

   v.5 Perhaps]21.

Xd 166   ("124")

 .1 [. .] , a-qi-ra[

 .2 e-u-ru-da-mo [

 .3]so-tu-wo-no [

 .4] vacat   [

   .1 Two signs only before a-qi-ra[, the first perhaps me.

   .3]mi-tu-wo-no also possible.

342

Xd 167   ("124")

      ] do-ri-wo [
         Probably cut at right.

Xd 168   ("124")

   .1 ko-no-si-jo [
   .2 ru-ki-ti-jo [

Xd 169   ("124")

     ]ku-do-ni-jo[
      ..

Xd 170   ("124"r)

    wo-ra-ke-re[
       Cut at left.

Xd 177   ("124"s)

    wa-ke-i-jo[

  v.   [[di]] [
      Perhaps <u>wa-ke-i-jo</u> 1[.

Xd 179   ("124"s)

    sa-u-ko
       Cut at right, but perhaps trace of sign at right, though it
       might be a nail-mark.

Xd 182   ("124")

    a-re-u-ke[
       Text on verso, recto blank.

Xd 186   ("124")

    ko-ma-ra[

Xd 189   ("124"r)

    a-re-se[

Xd 191   ("124"s)

    wa-ke-i-jo[
       Cut at left and right (curved cut at right).

Xd 197   ("124"r)

     wo-no-qi-[

Xd 200   ("124"r)

     pu-mo-ne[

         Cut at left.

Xd 202   ("124")

  .a]ja , u-ta-no , [

  .b] <u>vacat</u>   [

       .a Trace at right.

Xd 204   ("124")

     du-ni-jo[

Xd 207   ("124")

     pa-pa-ro / ra[

Xd 209   ("124"s)

     ma-ti-ri[

Xd 214   ("124")

     ]ja , / na-u-si-ke-re[

        Possibly]ja 1.

Xd 216   ("124"s)

  1 di-wo-a-ne[

        Cut at left. There is an undoubted stroke before di-,
        rather high for a divider (possibly the bar was divided
        at the wrong point, and the 1 belongs to the previous
        tablet). Traces of erasure.

Xd 282   ("124")

     ke-re-wa , wo-do [

Xd 287   ("124"s)

     ][[jo]] du-pi-jo

        Cut at right.

Xd 289   ("124")

        a-mi-ni-si-jo[
            Perhaps traces of erasure on the verso.

Xd <292>   ("124"?)

        te-u-to-ri-*65[
            Missing; text from SM II. Perhaps te-u-to ri-*65[-no.

Xd 294   ("124")

        ti-ri-jo-qa[

Xd <296>   ("124"?)

        qe-re-wa[
            Missing; text from SM II.

Xd 297   ("124")

        e-ru-ti-ri-jo[

Xd 298   ("124")

        ta-ra-i [
            Trace of sign at right, possibly BIG.

Xd <299>   ("124"?)

        e-ko-so-wo-ko[
            Missing; text from SM II.

Xd <300>   ("124"?)

        a-qi-ra[
            Missing; text from SM II.

Xd <301>   ("124"?)

        ma-se[
            Missing; text from SM II.

Xd <302>   ("124"?)

        e-na-i-jo[
            Missing; text from SM II.

345

Xd <304>   ("124"?)

   ]e-ri-ta-ri-jo[
       Missing; text from SM II.

Xd <305>   ("124"?)

   ]ra-ke-re-we[
       Missing; text from SM II.

Xd <306>   ("124"?)

   ]-ta , a-ke[
       Missing; text from SM II. Possibly]ke̯-ta or]de̯-ta.

Xd <307>   ("124"?)

   do-qi[
       Missing; text from SM II.

Xd <308>   ("124"?)

   po-ki[
       Missing; text from SM II.

Xd <309>   ("124"?)

   ]pa-no , qa[
       Missing; text from SM II.

Xd <310>   ("124"?)

   ]se̯-ke-ru-pa-ko-[
       Missing; text from SM II.]ȝ ke-ru-pa-ko-[KT³;
       possibly]se̯-ke-ru-pa-ko-a̯[.

Xd <313>   ("124"?)

   e-we-wa[

 v.   a[
       Missing; text from SM II.

Xd <314>   ("124"?)

   ru-ki-ti-ja[
       Missing; text from SM II.

                        346

Xd <318>   ("124"?)
        ]e-pi-ta
            Missing; text from SM II.

Xd <319>   ("124"?)
        te-me-u[
            Missing; text from SM II.

Xd <320>   ("124"?)
        ]a-pa-te[
            Missing; text from SM II.

Xd <322>   ("124"?)
        ]wo-ni-jo[
            Missing; text from SM II.

Xd <323>   ("124"?)
        ]a-ri-we-we[
            Missing; text from SM II.

Xd <324>   ("124"?)
        a-ta-wo-ne[
            Missing; text from SM II.

Xd <325>   ("124"?)
        we-wa[
            Missing; text from SM II.

Xd <326>   ("124"?)
        ]no-da-ma[
            Missing; text from SM II.

Xd <327>   ("124"?)
        e-ri-ra-i̧[
            Missing; text from SM II.

<u>Xd</u> <328>   ("124"?)

    ]pa-*34-so[

     Missing; text from SM II.

<u>Xd</u> <329>   ("124"?)

    ]re-mi-si-jo

     Missing; text from SM II.

<u>Xd</u> <330>   ("124"?)

    ra-wo-te[

     Missing; text from SM II.

<u>Xd</u> <331>   ("124"?)

    a-pu$_2$-ka[

     Missing; text from SM II.

<u>Xd</u> <332>   ("124"?)

    ]ja / i-da-wo[

     Missing; text from SM II.

<u>Xd</u> <333>   ("124"?)

    ze-pu[

     Missing; text from SM II.

<u>Xd</u> <334>   ("124"?)

    ]mo / ke-to-ri[

     Missing; text from SM II.

<u>Xd</u> <335>   ("124"?)

    ]ke-si-jo , ri[

     Missing; text from SM II.

<u>Xd</u> <336>   ("124"?)

    ]pe-ra-te-ro[

     Missing; text from SM II.

Xd 5074   ("124")

      ma-ti-[

          Perhaps cut at left. ma-ti-ko̤[not impossible.

Xd 5097 + 7928   ("124")

      a-ka-mu-[

          Perhaps a-ka-mu-kṳ[.

Xd 5838   ("124")

      di-[

Xd 5969   ("124")

      ]je-wa[

Xd 7510   ("124")

      ]*244[

          The sign is unparalleled; it could be an idiosyncratic
          form of qe.

Xd 7545   ("124"?)

      o-[   ]vest.[

Xd 7547   ("124"?)

         sup. mut.
  .1   ]vest.[
  .2a   [.]-wo-ta[
  .2b   ki-ni-[
  .3   o-ta-ke̤[
  .4.5 vestigia[

         .2a e̤-, o̤-, ke̤- possible.

Xd 7555   ("124")

      i-qa-ro [

          Over [[ni-wi̤[ ]] (and this perhaps itself over erasure).
          Trace at right.

Xd 7558   ("124")
        o-ko-te[

Xd 7568   ("124"?)
        a-pi-ja-re[
                ..

Xd 7570   ("124")
        a-na-pe-we[
            Possibly a-na-pe-we-[or a-na-pe-we 1[.

Xd 7586   ("124")
        mo-ro-qa[

Xd 7588   ("124")
        pi-ri-ja[
              ..

Xd 7590   ("124")
        ti-ri-to[
              ..

Xd 7595   ("124")
        ]ru-ko-si[

Xd 7596   ("124")
        e-na-i[

Xd 7597   ("124")
        ka-ta[

Xd 7598   ("124"?)
        ku-ru[

Xd 7604   ("124")
        qa-[

Xd 7606   ("124")
        e[

                            350

Xd 7607   ("124")
        pi-ri̤[

Xd 7609   ("124")
        ra-wi[

Xd 7610 + 7786   ("124")
        a-ko-to   [
            Trace at right.

Xd 7614   ("124")
        ru-wa[

Xd 7615   ("124"s)
        a-re-i̤[
            Cut at left.

Xd 7616   ("124"s)
        pa-ra̤[

Xd 7634   ("124")
        ]ka-ro-qo   [
            Possibly cut at left. Probably nothing lost at right.

Xd 7640   ("124")
        e-ko-[

Xd 7646   ("124"s)
        ]a-pi-[
            Perhaps cut at left.

Xd 7648   ("124")
        a-re[
    v.   a[

Xd 7649 + 7886   ("124")
        a-u-ta-na , [
            u over [[u]] .

Xd 7651   ("124")
        di-ki[

Xd 7654   ("124")
        ]e-u[

Xd 7656   ("124")
        ke-ku-ro[
              ..

Xd 7658   ("124")
        i-to-ma[
            ..

Xd 7662   ("124"r)
        ma-ra [
            Perhaps trace of sign at right.

Xd 7663   ("124")
        re-wo [
            Over erasure.

Xd 7664   ("124")
        wo-tu[

Xd 7665   ("124")
        ta-[
            Perhaps ta-ro[.
                       ..

Xd 7667   ("124")
        po-ta[

Xd 7674   ("124")
        a-ti[

352

Xd 7675   ("124")
     ]i-se-re̤[

Xd 7676   ("124")
     a-wa[

Xd 7680   ("124")
     ki-ri[

Xd 7701   ("124")
     a-[

Xd 7702 + 7957 + fr.   ("124")
     me̤-nu-wa[

Xd 7726   ("124")
  .a   ]   me[
  .b   ]pa-ro , / se[
          Perhaps beginning of .A.B.

Xd 7733   ("124")
        sup. mut.
  .1   ]-ri   [
  .2   ]   ja[
        inf. mut.
          .1 Perhaps]nṳ-ri. Trace at right, perhaps wo̤[.

Xd 7756   ("124")
        ] [[   ]][
  v.   ]ri-so-wa[

Xd 7757   ("124")
     ]o-pi , a-ne[

Xd 7761   ("124")
     ]wa / na-ni[

Xd 7766 + <u>fr.</u>   ("124")
      ]wi-pe-wa ḷ [

Xd 7780   ("124")
      ]du-wo-pe[

<u>Xd</u> 7783   ("124"?)
      ]ko-wo [

Xd 7790   ("124")
      ]ki-se[

Xd 7802   ("124")
  .a]6   qe[
  .b]   wa[
  v.   ]1   [
          v. Trace at right.

Xd 7807   ("124"s)
      ] [[   ]][
  v.   ]nu-a-[
          r. Perhaps [[g̲a̲]] .

Xd 7808   ("124")
      ]-*22-jo , [

Xd 7809   ("124")
      ]i-jo [

Xd 7811   ("124")
      ]me-re-ja[

Xd 7813 + 7953   ("124")
      ]ko , ke-ti-ro
  v.   ] qi
          Cut at right. ḷ less probable than divider.

354

Xd 7838   ("124"s)
        ]te-ta
            Cut at right.

Xd 7840   ("124"s)
        ]nwa-re
          ...
            Cut at right.

Xd 7841   ("124")
        ]u-te[

    v.   ]vest.[

Xd 7842   ("124"s)
        ]ne-u
            Cut at right.

Xd 7906   ("124")
        ]ka-ra-na-ta[

Xd 7913   ("124")
        ]ke-ke-me[

Xd 7914   ("124")
        ]-wa , pa[
            Perhaps]ke-wa.
                       ..

Xd 7933   ("124")
        ]we-wa-ta
            Cut at right.

Xd 7941   ("124")
        ]-re-wa
            Cut at right.

Xd 7943   ("124")
        i-ta[
            Cut at left.

355

Xd 7945   ("124"?)

        ]wo-no-da[

Xd 7948   ("124")

        ]ra-ko-ka[

Xd 7949   ("124")

        ]to , ti[

Xd 7954   ("124")

        a-me-ja[
            Smudged when wet.

Xd 7956   ("124")

        e-ke[

Xd 7961   ("124")

        ]ko-no [

Xd 7968   ("124")

        ]-ne-u[
            ]da-ne-u[or]ro-ne-u[.

Xd 7970   ("124")

        ]-na[

    v.]e-qe[
            ]da-na[or]ro-na[. Perhaps trace at right.

Xd 7974   ("124")

        ]no 1
            Cut at right. Perhaps]no , .

Xd 7975   ("124")

        ]ke-nu[

Xd 7978   ("124"?)

        ]e[

356

Xd 7982   ("124")

     ]-ro

        Cut at right.

Xd 7983   ("124")

     i-[

        Cut **at** left.

Xd 7986   ("124")

     ]mo[

<u>Xd</u> 8012   ("124"?)

       <u>sup. mut.</u>

  .1   ]1

  .2   ]34

  .3   ]62

       <u>inf. mut.</u>

        .3 Perhaps]72.

Xd 8021   ("124")

     ]ta

Xd 8030   ("124")

     ] 2

Xd 8032   ("124")

       <u>sup. mut.</u>

  .1   <u>vestigia</u>[

  .2   me-ri[

  .3   qi[

       <u>inf. mut.</u>

 v.1   <u>sup. mut.</u>

  .2   ]6

  .3   ] <u>vestigia</u>

       <u>inf. mut.</u>

        v.2]6 possibly over erasure.

Xd 8034   ("124")
        <u>sup. mut.</u>
 .1   ] <u>vacat</u>
 .2   ] <u>o</u> 8
 .3   ]ṭa-ra <u>o</u> 1
v.0   <u>sup. mut.</u>
 .1.2 <u>vacant</u> [

Xd 8037   ("124"s)
      ]wạ-jo 1
         Traces to right of 1 very faint and probably accidental.

Xd 8054   ("124"s)
      pa-pa-rọ[

Xd 8056   ("124")
      ] 1

v.   ]no-da 2
      r. Trace at left.
      v. Or]<u>no</u> <u>DA</u> 2 ? (but the two signs are very close
          together).

<u>Xd</u> 8060   ("124"?)
      ]7

<u>Xd</u> 8061   ("124"?)
      ]u-ke

Xd 8062   ("124")
      ]2

Xd 8082   (= 8026 bis)   ("124")
      ] 1
        Trace before 1 ( ]ṭa ?).

Xd 8127   ("124")
     qe-na-[
          Cut at left. Perhaps qe-na-mo[or (less likely) qe-na-te[.

Xd 8128   ("124")
     da-i-[

Xd 8129   ("124")
     qe[

Xd 8130   ("124")
     do-ri[

Xd 8132   ("124")
     ] , ri-mi[
          Trace at left. ri-*65[not impossible.

Xd 8134   ("124"?)
     sup. mut.
     ]ta   [

Xd 8135   ("124"?)
     sup. mut.
       ]ti[
          Trace of sign, perhaps majuscule, at left.

Xd 8137   ("124")
     ]no [

Xd 8138   ("124")
     ]-ke[

Xd 8139   ("124")
     ja-na-ti[
  v.   V 1[

Xd 8279   ("124")
        ]¹   KO 130[
            Trace at left and over]1.

Xd 8501   ("124")
        ]-a-jo 1[

Xd 8505   ("124")
        ]a[
        inf. mut.

Xd 8508   ("124")
        ] , di-[

Xd 8510   ("124")
        do[

Xd 8511   ("124")
        ]wo 1 [

Xd 8525   ("124")
        ]ja-me[

Xd 8553   ("124")
        ] , ku[

Xd 8566   ("124")
        sup. mut.
        ]me[

Xd 8583   ("124")
        qa[

Xd 8594   ("124")
        ]ro[

Xd 8596   ("124")

    ]ṣạ[
    inf. mut.

Xd 8597   ("124")

    si-ra-[

Xd 8605   ("124")

    ]ta-ta-ṛọ[
    inf. mut.

Xd 8635   ("124")

    zo-[

        Perhaps <u>zo-ạ</u>[.

Xd 8640   ("124")

    ] 1   [

        Sign at left possibly]1̣0̣0̣,]<u>kạ</u>,]<u> g̣ẹ</u> or]EQ̣Ụ.

Xd 8643   ("124")

    ] 1

        Cut at right. Trace at left (perhaps]<u>tị</u> 1).

Xd 8653   ("124")

    ]wa-jo [[1̣59]]

        Whole surface erased and]<u>wa-jo</u> written when the clay
        was dry.

<u>Xd</u> 8732   ("124"?)

    ]ṃạ[
    inf. mut.

        Probably first sign of tablet.

Xd 8734   ("124")

    ]g̣a-ṛạ[
    inf. mut.

<u>Xd</u> 8748   ("124"?)

     <u>sup. mut.</u>

.1   ] 3[

.2   ]<u>vac.</u>[

     <u>inf. mut.</u>

Xe

Xe 524   (103)

     <u>sup. mut.</u>

.1   ]o-pi po-po[

.2   ]o-pi ta-qa-ra-te[

       Text probably complete at left.

Xe 537   (103)

     <u>sup. mut.</u>

.1   ]25 me-ki-ta[

.2   ]2 o-pi i-ta-ja[

Xe 544   (103)

.a   pe-re-ko[

.b   da-*22-ti-ja / a-ze-ti-ri[-ja

<u>Xe</u> 657   (103?)

.1   a-ze-ti-ri-ja [

.2   o-no-we-wo-ro-[

<u>Xe</u> 664   (103?)

     ke-ke-me-na[

Xe 691   (103)

.1   o-pi , re-mo[

.2   o-pi qo-u[

       .1 <u>re</u>- over [[mo]] .

Xe 692   (103)

  .1a   o-nu[
  .1b o-pi , / pi-mo-no   ne-[
  .2   <u>vacat</u>   [
       .1b ne-wo̤[possible.
       .2   Trace at right.

Xe 5361   (103)

    ]-so[
    <u>inf. mut.</u>

Xe 5540 + 5871   (103)

  .A   ']e-ta-wo-ne'   re-po-so [
  .B   ]we-ke-s̤e̤   'e-ta-wo[']   [
       .B Trace after break following <u>e-ta-wo</u>[; probably only
          room for one sign in gap (<u>ne</u>?).

<u>Xe</u> 5546   (103?)

       <u>sup. mut.</u>
  .1   ]   do-ti[
  .2   ]   du-[
  .3   ]   m̤a[
       <u>inf. mut.</u>

Xe 5600   (103)

       <u>sup. mut.</u>
  .1   mi-ra[
  .2   i-[
       <u>inf. mut.</u>
       .2 Probably last line.

Xe 5630   (103)

  .1   <u>sup. mut.</u>
  .2   ]si-ja[
<u>lat. inf.</u>   ] zo[

363

Xe 5877 + 6031 + 8521   (103)

.1   ]-jo 'a-ka-to['   ]   do-e-ro [

.2   ]vest. / i-ta-no // do-e-ro [

.3   ] vestigia?   [

        .1.2 Traces at right, perhaps of erasures.

        .3 Vestigia or traces of erasure?

Xe 5887   (103)

.1   sup. mut.

.2a]e-to   [

.2b]jo   do-ti-ja[

        .2b Perhaps divider after]jo.

Xe 5891   (103)

        da-te-we-ja[

Xe 5899   (103)

.1   qi-ja-zo[

.2   vest.[

     inf. mut.

Xe 5900   (103)

        sup. mut.

.1   [.]-pi-pa-ro[

.2   e-zo-wo , [

Xe 5905   (103)

.1   ]pi-a-ze-ra[

.2   ]4 e-ra[

.3   ] vest.[

     inf. mut.

        .2 Perhaps]14.

364

Xe 5913 + 5921 + <u>frr</u>.   (103)

  .1   mi-ru-ṛo[

  .2   o-da-ra-o   [

  .3   nu-to   [

  .4   <u>vacat</u>   [

          .3 Perhaps <u>nu-to</u> 1̣. Perhaps [[ḳạ]] or [[g̣ẹ]] before the break.

Xe 6011 + 8599   (103)

  .1   ]ko-no-so[

  .2   ]e-ra[

      <u>inf. mut.</u>

<u>Xe</u> 6020   (103?)

      *56-ri-to[

<u>Xe</u> 6026   (103?)

      <u>sup. mut.</u>

      ] a-mo-te-re[

Xe 7437   (103)

  .1   ]ma-ta-ro[

  .2   ]te-i-ja   '<u>TA</u> 1' <u>E</u> 1   pạ[

  .3   ra-qa-ra   [

         .2 Text probably complete at left. Small <u>ta</u> above small <u>e</u>, both followed by units which were probably originally at least 6; only the last two were not erased or destroyed accidentally; uncertain if the numerals go with <u>ta</u> and <u>e</u> together or separately. Not]<u>te-i-ja</u>-'ta'?

         .3 Trace at right.

Xe 7711   (103)

  .a   ]pị-ri-jo do-ke [

  .b   ]   e-ta-wo-[

         .a Less probably]<u>tị-ri-jo</u>.

         .b Trace at left.

<u>Xe</u> 7805   (103?)

  no-da[
    ..

<u>Xe</u> 7826   (103?)

  ]ti[

<u>Xe</u> 7850   (103)

 .1 ri-jo-ni-jo[
       ..
 .2 e-ta-wo[-ne-?
     ..
   <u>inf. mut.</u>

<u>Xe</u> 7857   (103)

   <u>sup. mut.</u>
 .1] e-ta[
 .2]P   [

<u>Xe</u> 7988   (103?)

  ]ta [
  <u>inf. mut.</u>

<u>Xe</u> 8260   (103?)

 .1] ta[
 .2] <u>vac.</u> [
    .1 Over erasure.

<u>Xe</u> 8274   (103)

 .1]-si-ja[
 .2 <u>inf. mut.</u>
   ko-]<u>no</u>-si-ja more likely than ta-]<u>ra</u>-si-ja.
      ..   ..

<u>Xe</u> 8291   (103)

 .1]pa-<u>ro</u> , e-[
     ..
 .2]<u>vacat</u>[
    .1 e-<u>ta</u>[-wo-ne possible, cf. Ld 5615.
      ..

366

Xe 8516   (103??)

    sup. mut.
     e-[

Xe 8526   (103?)

    ]ja-wi[
    inf. mut.

Xe 8537 + 8565 + 8579   (103)

  .1   ]ka-re , 'po-me-no['
  .2   ]1   pe-ki-ṭi[
  .3   ] 1   [

Xe 8546   (103)

    ]ụ-ko-ro[
    inf. mut.

Xe 8563   (103?)

    sup. mut.
    ]-ma[
    inf. mut.
       Traces of two signs before ma, the first perhaps ụ.

Xe 8592   (103?)

  .a   ]   vest.[
  .b   ]ṛa / ṭo[
    inf. mut.

Xe 8593   (103?)

    sup. mut.
    [.]-ṛo[

Xe 8598   (103)

    sup. mut.
    ]-si[
      Perhaps]ma-ṇa-si[. Perhaps lat. inf.

Xe 8622   (103?)

  .1 <u>sup. mut.</u>

  .2]wa-ko[

     <u>inf. mut.</u>

Xe 8724   (103?)

  .a]   da[

  .b]ja /   [

     <u>inf. mut.</u>

       Probably same tablet as Ak 8334.

       .a Possibly DA[.

X

X 35   (-.)

     e-me-si-jo-jo [

       Trace at right.

X 37   (-)

     ru-ki-ti-jo[

X 38   (-)

     sa-me[

X 39   (-)

     ]ke-me-no[

X 44   (-)

  .A   wi-ri-[

  .B ku-ja-ro / qa-ra [

       .A Traces at right consistent with <u>za</u>.

X 408   (-)

  .1 a-]pu-do-ke , e-u-ro-wa-[

    .2   ] <u>vacat</u>   [

368

X 409   (-)
    .1   ku-ta-to , a-pu-do-si[
    .2   o-pe-ro   [

X 410   (-)
    .a   ]a-mi-ni-so-de[
    .b   ]mu-ki-ti ,   [

X 430   (-)
          ]mu-ti-ja[
              Trace at left. Perhaps divider after mu.

X 435   (-)
    .1.   sup. mut.
    .2   a-mi-ni-si[

X 443   (-)
          ]mu-ko[

X 444   (-)
          ]sa / po-ti-ni-ja[

X 450 + 5802   (-)
          ]to-sa / pu-si-ja , a[
              Traces of erasure.

X 451   (-)
    .1   si-ja-ma-to[
    .2   pa-sa-ja[

X 453   (138?)
    .1   ]zo , we-we-si-jo-jo , [
    .2   ]ri-si-ja   [

X 458   (-)
    .a   ]   a-pu-do[
    .b   ]to   [

369

```
X  459                                              ( - )
        ]ku-mi-so  [
              Perhaps trace of smaller sign at right ( e[ ?).


X  468                                              ( - )
    .1   ku-pi-ri-jo / ka-ra-[
    .2        vacat              [


X  <506>                                            ( - )
    .a               ti-ri[
    .b   tu-ri-so / pe-do[
              Missing; text from SM II.


X  522                                              ( - )
        pa-i-to , / e[


X  658                                              ( - )
        ne-wo , za-we[
    v.   ] a-ro-we a-nu-to
              v.  No separation marked between a-ro-we and a-nu-to.


X  660                                              ( - )
    .A               ka-[
    .B   se-to-i-ja / a[
              .B  -i- over erasure.  Perhaps da-[.


X  697                                              ( - )
    .1   ko-we-ja / pa-i-to[
    .2   a-nu-to-jo , [
              .2  Trace at right.


X  721                                              ( - )
        ]ke-do-ro[
```

X 722 + 725   (-)

  .a   di-wi-pa-ra   [

  .b   e-ra / te-wo , e-ra ri-ni-jo [

       .b Possibly <u>e-ra-ri-ni-jo</u>, but the gap between <u>ra</u> and <u>ri</u>
          is wide. Traces at right.

X 723   (-)

    da-da-re-jo-de[

X 728   (-)

  .A   ]   a-ro$_2$[

  .B   ]sa / a-pu-do-si , me[

<u>lat. inf</u>.] ka-a-na   [

       .B Accidental mark after]<u>sa</u>, not a divider.

X 737   (-)

    ko-a / ra-ja[

X 742   (-)

    to-so / e[

X 743   (-)

  .a   ]   a-[

  .b   a-]mi-ni-si-ja , /   [

X 744 + 7755   (-)

  .A   <u>vacat</u>   [

  .B   ma-sa-de / ti-ta-ma-i   [

X 745   (-)

  .1   a-ka-[

  .2   da-pu$_2$-[

       .2 Trace after <u>pu</u>$_2$ consistent with <u>ri</u>.

25

X <748>   (-)

        sup. mut.

.1   ]ra , [

.2   ]mi-ra , [

.3   ]a-sa-mi , [

.4   ]ka[
       . .

        inf. mut.

        Missing; text from SM II.

X 766   (-)

.1   ] , zo-wa , a-ze-to , e[

.2   inf. mut.

      .1 Trace at left.

X 768   (-)

.1 e-ka-te-jo , [

.2   ke-ni-qe-te-[

     .2 Trace at right edge possibly <u>we</u>.

X 770   (-)

.a   [. .] [

.b wi-tu-ri-jo , / a-mo-te-re [

X 793   (-)

    pa-ro , / a-da-ra-ko[

X 795   (-)

    ka-ta-no / wa-tu[

X 796   (-)

    pu-ko-to [

X 974 + 5742   (-)

.a]   si-ra-si-ja , ti-ta-ma[
         .

.b]pa-no / ku-pe-te-jo , ko-ro-ki-no-[

     .a <u>si</u> perhaps over erasure (presence of an extra
       horizontal stroke; but not <u>pi</u>).

     .b ko-ro-ki-no-ţọ[or ko-ro-ki-no-ŗọ[. Traces of erasure
       ([[jọ]] before <u>ko</u> and extra stroke after <u>ko</u>).

372

X 976 + 8263   (225)
    .1a   da-*83-ja po-pu-re-jo̦[
    .1b   to-so / wa-na-ka-te-ro   [
    .2   <u>vacat</u>   [

X 986   (-)
         tu-ru-pe-te[
            Over erasure.

X 993   (-)
         e-we-ki-ta [

X 998   (-)
         e-ru-sa-m̤o[
            <u>e-ru-sa</u> OLE[unlikely.

X 999 + 1001   (-)
         sa-pa-nu-wo-me-no , / pe-ra$_2$, w̤o[
            <u>sa</u> over erasure. Room for divider in small gap between
            <u>sa-pa-nu-wo</u> and <u>me-no</u>.

X 1010   (-)
         to-so   [

X 1013   (-)
         ko-ro-we-ja[
            Cut at left. Trace at right. This fragment (palimpsest) is
            an end of tablet, although cut at left.

X 1014   (-)
         ]ku-ru-so , po-ro-we[

X 1018   (-)
         ]ka-pu$_2$-s̤a-jo , / pa-na-so te-re-ta [
            ]ka-pu$_2$-n̤i̤-jo not entirely excluded, but less likely.

373

X   1019   (-)

    ]jo / da-mi-ni-jo , [
         Trace at right.

X   1024   (-)

    .1   ]ra-jo , ma-ti-jo[
    .2   ]e-ra-ja , qi-ni-te[

X   <1027>   (-)

    .a   te[
    .b   ko-no-si-ja , / ra-wa-ke[
              Missing; text from SM II.

X   <1033>   (-)

    ]ra-su-to[
         Missing; text from SM II.

X   1041   (-)

    ki-ri-ko , [
         Cut at left. Over erasure.

X   1045   (-)

    ]ru-wo , me-ri-du[-ma ?

X   1047   (-)

    .1   to-sa / ka-ro-qo[
    .2   to-sa , /ka-tu-re-wi[

X   1050   (-)

    ]no , / pu-sa-ra[
         Trace at right.

X   1051   (-)

    .a   ]   a-no-qo-ta[
    .b   ] , da-ma-o-te[
              .b Trace at left.

374

X 1052   (-)
        a-tu-ko / de-ra[

X 1385 + 1537   (-)
        ti-ri-ti-ja / ki-ta-no[

X 1432   (-)
        ]si-jo-jo , te-pa[

X 1463   (-)
        a-ra-si-jo / a[

X <1474>   (-)
        pa-i-to[
            Missing; text from SM II.

X 1525   (-)
    .1   ]ku-ru-ni-ta / to[
    .2   inf. mut.

    v.1   sup. mut.
    .2   ]sa-nu-we-si-jo[
            Probably nothing lost at left.

X 1538   (-)
             sup. mut.
    .1   ku-ta-ti[
    .2   da-wo , / ki[

X 1539   (-)
        pa-i-to[

X 1581   (-)
    .1   ma-ri-jo , si[
    .2   po-ka-[
            Both lines over erasure.
            .2 Probably po-ka-pi[or po-ka-e[, but po-ka-ro not
               entirely impossible.

                        375

X 1641   KAN (-)

  .1   a-mi-ni-si-jo , ka[

  .2]   <u>vacat</u>   [

     .1 Over [[a-mi-ni]] . ka[perhaps BIG[.

X ◁1642>   (-)

     qa-no-[

       Missing; text from SM II drawing (numbered 1642 bis);
       original drawing not yet found.

X 1801 + 37 bis + <u>frr</u>.(3)   (1801 = 36 bis)   (-)

  .0   <u>sup. mut</u>.

  .1   pi-za-ra [

  .2   ra-ni   [

  .3   sa-pi[

  .4   pi-ri-[

  .5.6 <u>vacant</u> [

       Perhaps cut at bottom.

X 1802   (= 41 bis)   (-)

     u-ta[

X <1901>   (-)

     sa-so[

       Missing; text from Evans' Notebook 1905, p. 9a.

X 2002   (-)

     ze-wa-so / pi-[

X 2003   (-)

  .1   ]ni-sa-[

  .2   ]te-u[

     .1 Perhaps]ni-sa-ro[.

376

X 2011   (-)

      ]   330[

         Possibly same tablet as Dp 5508 (cf. Dp 1061). Traces at
         left, possibly]LANA.

X 2128   (-)

  .1   o-pi[
  .2   we-a[

  v.   60[

X 2131 + <u>fr</u>.   (-)

      ]a[

X 2132   (-)

      ]te-wi-ja[

X 2134   (-)

      te[

X 4472   (-)

      se-to[

         Probably same tablet as So 4442.

X 4486   (-)

     *22-ja-ro [

        Possibly *22-ja-to.

X 4487   (-)

  .a   ]   e-ri-ko[
  .b   ]qa-ka-na-pi[

X 4492   (-)

     si-ja-pu$_2$[

X 4495   (-)

     pa-pu[

        Small bit now lost; good photograph by Evans.

X 5006   (-)
     .A   ] u-ta-no , / a[
     .B   ]   u-ta-no ,   [

X 5033   (-)
          ]-si-ja / <u>vest</u>.[
                    Possibly]<u>to</u>-si-ja. Perhaps <u>u</u>[.

X 5037   (-)
     .1   ]2
     .2   ]9
     .3   ] <u>vacat</u>

X 5040 + 7600   (-)
     .a   a-p<u>i</u>[
     .b   se-to-i-ja , / o-pi[
                    Perhaps traces of erasure.

X 5042   (-)
          ] 2000[

X 5044   (-)
          <u>sup. mut.</u>
          ]<u>i</u>-ta[

X <5051>   (-)
          ]ru-jo[
                    Missing; text from Bennett's 1950 drawing.

X 5055   (-)
          ]ja-[

X 5102   (-)
          ] pa-ra-ku[
                    Trace of a majuscule sign at left (perhaps]<u>ko</u>).

378

X 5104   (-)
        ]pa-i-to , e̅[
            Text complete at left.

X 5105   (-)
        i-se-we-ri-jo[

X 5111   (-)
        ka-ma[

X 5115   (-)
        o-pi[

X 5124   (-)
        ] 30 [
        inf. mut.
            Trace before 30.

X 5125   (-)
    .1   ] o-pe[
    .2   inf. mut.

X 5173   (-)
            sup. mut.
    .1   ] vest.[
    .2   ]-pi , ki-ri[
    .3   ] vacat [
            .2 Probably]o-pi.

X 5176   (-)
        pa-i[

X 5242   (-)
        ]-jo[

X 5309   (-)
        ]re-u[

379

X 5326   (-)

      sup. mut.

      ]2̣ Ṃ[

X 5334 + frr.   (-)

      sup. mut.

  .1   o-pị [

  .2   vacat [

      inf. mut.

X 5341   (-)

      sup. mut.

      ]-ke̤-[

X 5343   (-)

      a[

      inf. mut.

X 5422   (-)

      ]6   [

X 5509   (-)

      ri-*65[

  v.   tu-[

X 5513   (-)

      ]ra-to-po-ro̤[

        Text probably complete at left.

X 5514   (-)

      a-]mi-ni-si[

X 5516   (-)

      ]*64-jo , [

        Trace at right not m̤e̤, perhaps po̤[.

380

X 5521   (-)

    ]si-jo [

        jo over erasure.

X 5522   (-)

    ke-ne[

X 5525   (-)

  .1]te-ja-ro 1[

  .2] vacat [

X 5529   (-)

    ] 1 a-me[

        Trace at left:]pa or]te possible.

X 5531   (-)

    ]-te-re-wa[

X 5534   (-)

  .1 ku-ta[

  .2 vac.[

        .1 Second sign perhaps over erasure.

X 5537   (-)

    ]sa-ja [

        Perhaps beginning of .A.B.

X 5538   (115)

  .1 qa-na[

  .2 ka-sa-[

        .2 Possibly ka-sa-to[.

X 5554   (-)

    sup. mut.

      ]me[

X 5560   (-)

      ]ke / po-se-da-o-[
        Perhaps <u>po-se-da-o-no</u>[.

X 5570   (-)

      <u>sup. mut.</u>
 .A   ] <u>vestigia</u> [
 .B   ]ta / da-wo[

X 5573   (-)

 .1   ]-ra-i-ja [
 .2   <u>inf. mut.</u>

X 5577   (-)

      ]a-pi-da-[
        ]a- very doubtful.

X 5578   (-)

      ]si-jo GRA[
        Ideogram(?) very doubtful.

X 5583   (-)

 .1   ] 2   [
 .2   ]2   [

X 5586   (-)

 .1   ]3
 .2   ] <u>vacat</u>

X 5594   (-)

 .1   <u>sup. mut.</u>
 .2   wa-te[

X 5602   (-)

      mi[

X 5617   (-)

  ]ta-na-d̤ṳ[

  <u>inf. mut.</u>

X 5656   (-)

  ]-ru[

  <u>inf. mut.</u>

   Perhaps]<u>d̤ṳ-ru</u>[

X 5673   (-)

  ]23

X 5699   (-)

  ta-[

  <u>inf. mut.</u>

X 5716   (-)

  <u>sup. mut.</u>

  ]a-re[

  <u>inf. mut.</u>

X 5727   (-)

  ]-ja-me-na , a[

X 5730   (-)

 .A]   O̤V̤I̤S̤^{x}[

 .B]ja-we-jo / da-*22-to [

   .B Traces at right, perhaps O̤V̤I̤S̤^{f}.

X 5732 + 8673 + <u>fr</u>.   (-)

  po-ku-te-[

   po-ku-te-r̤o̤[not excluded.

X 5737   (-)

  ma-sa[

   Cut at left.

X 5743   (-)
    ]pu-do-si[

X 5750 + 8631   (-)
    wi-na-jo[
        Cut at left.

X 5751 + 5986   (-)
    ]di-du-mo[
        Perhaps] , di-du-mo[.

X 5756   (-)
    ]-re-wi[
        Perhaps]ku-re-wi[.

X 5759   (-)
.1   ]te-u , / e-se-[
.2   inf. mut.
    .1 e-se-ke[or e-se-de[possible.

X 5763   (-)
.a   ]te-wa-te[
.b   ] qa-ra , *83-re[
    .a Perhaps divider before]te-.

X 5774   (-)
    ]wo [

X 5784   (-)
    ]*22-ti[

X 5796 + fr.   (-)
    po-ko-me[

X 5825   (-)
    ]ri[

X   5832   (-)
        ]ra-so[

X   5881 + 8311   (-)
    .1   ]ti-ta-ma ; ma[
    .2   ]   vacat   [
            .1 Divider possibly 1. ma[possibly LANA[.

X   5889   (-)
        to-so[

X   5897   (-)
        ]te-wa-[
            ]te-wa-o[possible.

X   5898 + fr.   (-)
    .A   'vest.['
    .B   ]-ku / ke-[
lat. inf.   ] sa-mu[
            .A Probably 'ku['.
            .B Perhaps]ra-ku (probably only one sign lost before ku).

X   5904   (-)
    .1   da-ma[
    .2   vest.[
         inf. mut.

X   5936   (-)
        tu[

X   5952   (-)
    .a   ]po-ru-o[
    .b   ]vest.[
         inf. mut.

X   5960   (-)
        ra-[
           Cut at left.

385

X 5962 + 8602 + fr.   (-)
        ] su-ri-jo , mo[

X 5964   (-)
        sup. mut.
    .1   ]-ko-we[
         ˙˙
    .2   ]ko-so[
        inf. mut.
            .1 Traces consistent with]*56-ko-we.
                                         ˙ ˙˙ ˙˙

X 5968   (-)
    .a   ]   ru-ka[
    .b   ]do-ro   [

X 5979   (-)
        ] , me-[
            Trace at left (perhaps]ro /); perhaps me-wo[.
                                       ˙˙   ˙˙

X 5990   (-)
    .1   ]5   ke-ro[
                   ˙˙
    .2   ] vacat [
            .1]25 or]15 not impossible.
                  ˙   ˙

X 6004   (-)
        ]na-pu[
        inf. mut.
        Text probably complete at left.

X 6006   (-)
        sup. mut.
    .1   vacat [
    .2   ko-no[
        inf. mut.
            .1.2 Traces of erasure.

386

X 6008   (-)

    <u>sup. mut</u>.

    ]au[

       Text probably complete at left.

X 6029   (-)

    ]pa-[

    <u>inf. mut</u>.

       Beginning of tablet. Perhaps]pa-no[.

X 6030 + <u>fr</u>.   (-)

    ]ka-po [

       Traces of erasure. Trace at right.

X 6032   (-)

    to-so , ne[

       Perhaps qa[.

X 6034   (-)

    e-[

       Trace of two signs after <u>e</u>, (perhaps <u>e</u>-[.]-pa[ ).

X 6039   (-)

    <u>sup. mut</u>.

    ]u-jo / ke[

    <u>inf. mut</u>.

X 7073   (-)

  .A]100[   ]590

  .B] <u>vacat</u>

  v.]300

       .B Trace at left and possibly [[5]] after it.

X 7094   (-)

  .A   ]   <u>vac</u>.[

  .B se-]to-i-ja / ra$_3$[

       .B OLIV perhaps better, but would not be expected at this place.

X 7218 (120?)

]-so [

Traces at right probably accidental.

X 7259 (-)

] 4 [

Trace at left.   Trace of erasure below 4.

X 7351 (-)

sup. mut.

] 6

Traces of an earlier ruling, erased. Traces before 6
of lower part of ideogram, preceded by a small sized
sign ( ]ro ?).

X 7375 (-)

.a   ]pi , e-sa-pa-ke-me[
.b   ]nu-ka   [

X 7386 (-)

]-ro / u-ka   OVIS^m[

X 7502 (-)

to-so / i-ka[

i- over [[ka]] .

X 7511 (-)

]du[

inf. mut.

X 7522 (-)

sup. mut.

.1   ]-wo 7[
.2   inf. mut.

.1   ]ko-wo possible.

388

X 7528   (-)
   .1   ]71
   .2   ] <u>vacat</u>

X 7546   (-)
   .A   o-pi[
   .B   pa-i-to , / pa[
               Cut at left.

X 7548   (-)
   .1   ru-ki-t̩o̩[
   .2   pi-po-to[

X 7550   (-)
   .1   [.]-ka-to , [
   .2   <u>vacat</u>   [

X 7551   (-)
         <u>sup. mut.</u>
         [.]-pa̩-jo[

X 7552   (-)
         ku-do-ni[

X 7553   (-)
         da-*22-to , / *65[
               Cut at left.

X 7554   (-)
         pa̩-i-ti-ja̩[

X 7556 + 8654   (-)
   .A   a[   ]6̩0̩[
   .B   a-re-ta$_2$ /   <u>vestigia</u>   [

389

X 7557   (-)

        ki-do-ro [

X 7559   (-)

        ka-ne-u-ta[

X 7560   (-)

        u-ta-ni-jo [

X 7562   (-)

        ]su-ki-ri[-ta
            Text possibly complete at left.

X 7564   (-)

        ko-no-so , / t̤a[
            Possibly s̤o[or a̤[.

X 7565   (-)

        ma-[.]-t̤o[
            Possibly ma-p̤e , t̤w̤e̤-[. Over erasure, first sign
            erased na.

X 7566 + 8110   (-)

        to-ro-wa-ko ,   [
            Traces at right (BOS or CROC ?).

X 7569   (-)

        ]e-ki-si-j̤o̤[

X 7572   (-)

        o-ki[
        inf. mut.

X 7573   (-)

        e-wa-[

X 7574   (-)

     su-ko[

  v.   to-sa[

X 7576   (-)

     de-[

       Cut at left. Second sign (over erasure) possibly a̲.

X 7580   (-)

     ke-me̤[

X 7581   (-)

     to-sa̤[

X 7582   (-)

     o-pe[

X 7583   (-)

     ]ka-ni-to̤[

X 7584   (-)

     da-wo , [

       Trace at right.

X 7585   (-)

     te-ra$_2$[

X 7589   (-)

     a-mo[

       Over erasure.

X 7592   (-)

     da-*83[

       Cut at left.

X   7599   (-)

      me-wo̤[

X   7603   (-)

      to-[

         Perhaps to-ro̤[.

X   7608   (-)

      qa[

X   7611   (-)

      su[

X   7621   (-)

      sup. mut.

  .1   vestigia[
  .2   wo-no[

      inf. mut.

        .1 Possibly rṳ-ki̤-[.

X   7622   (-)

  .1   te-[
  .2   inf. mut.

X   7623   (115?)

  .1   sup. mut.
  .2   ke-[

X   7627   (-)

      di-ki-mo[

         Cut at left.

X   7628 + 7893   (-)

      to-so / a-po-[

X   7629   (-)

      pa-i-to[

392

X   7631   (-)
        o-ka-ra[

X   7632   (-)
        ru-ki-to[

X   7633   (-)
        tu-ni-ja , [
             Cut at left.

X   7635 + 7977   (-)
   .A   ]   qa[
   .B   ]a-wi-je-mo , [

X   7642   (-)
        ku-do[
             Cut at left.

X   7643 + 7960   (-)
        me-ti-[.]-ta[
             me-ti-ro-ta[possible.

X   7644 + fr.   (-)
   .1   ku-ko-wi-ra , [
   .2   vacat   [
             .1 Over erasure.

X   7655   (-)
        da-*22[

X   7659   (-)
        tu-ni[

X   7668   (110?)
        ku-re[

393

X 7669   (-)
    a-pa-[

X 7672   (-)
    ku-do[
        Cut at left.

X 7673   (110?)
    tu-ma-[
        tu-ma-i̥[or tu-ma-r̥e̥[.

X 7677 + 7973   (120?)
    ru-da-to [

X 7682   (137?)
    ]r̥i-si-[
        Perhaps]r̥i-si-jo̥[.

X 7692   (-)
    sa[

X 7693 + fr.   (-)
    ka-da-i[

X 7695   (-)
    ku-[

X 7696   (-)
    na-[
        Perhaps na-e̥[or na-pi̥[.

X 7699   (-)
    e-[

X   7706   (-)
    .A   ]   e-me[
    .B   ]-jo , / da-wo ,   [

X   7707 + 8014 + fr.   (-)
    .1   ] 120 [ ] 2
    .2   ] 120[   ]7   [
    .3   ]   vacat
             .1 Trace at left. Trace before 2.
             .2 Trace at left.

X   7708   (-)
        ]to-wo / ti-ri-to[

X   7710   (-)
    .A   ]   vac.[
    .B   ]we-ja / ko[

X   7712   (-)
    .a   ]   [[p̣o-]][
    .b   ]re-ki-si , / a[

X   7715   (-)
    .1   ]62
    .2   ]2
             Cut at right.

X   7717 + fr.   (-)
    .1   ]8
    .2   ] vacat

X   7720   (-)
        ]ko-wa 3̣[

X   7722   (-)
        to-]sa / ne-wa[

395

X 7725   (-)

       sup. mut.
.1   ]me-te 1[
.2   inf. mut.

X 7728   (-)

.1   sup. mut.
.2   ]ko-ro   [
          .2 Trace of sign at right.

X 7730   (-)

       sup. mut.
.1   ] vestigia [
.2   ]to-so-p$\d{a}$[
       inf. mut.

X 7732   (-)

        sup. mut.
   ] , ke-ke-me[
     Trace of sign at left.

X 7735   (-)

.1   ]-to , [
.2   ]qo-i-n$\d{a}$[
        .1 Perhaps]s$\d{a}$-to.
        .2]-qo-i-n$\d{a}$[?

X 7737   (-)

       sup. mut.
   ]$\d{a}$-ze-ti-ri-ja[

X 7739   (-)

.A   ]   [[ti-]][
.B   ]di-ra$_3$ [
        .B Trace at right.

X 7741   (-)
   .a   ]de , da-*22-to-qe [
   .b   ?te-]re̥-ta   ri-no   [
              .b Trace at right (a̰₃[?).

X 7743   (-)
   .1   ]-ka-to ฺ si̥[
   .2   pu̥-ta-ta   [

X 7744   (-)
        ]-no-no si-ṟa̤[
          inf. mut.
             Perhaps]ki̤-no-no si-ṟa̤-ko̤[.

X 7749   (-)
   .1   ]-to-[
   .2   inf. mut.

X 7750   (-)
   .1   tu-ri[-so ?
   .2   ? tu-]ni-ja [
           inf. mut.

X 7752   (115?)
   .a   ]   ko[
   .b   ] ta-qa-ra[

X 7753   (-)
        ]ki-ti-me̤[
           ]ki-ti-ṣa̤[and]ki-ti-je̤[possible.

X 7754   (-)
   .A   ]   [
   .B   ]ra-ti-jo , [
           Division into .A .B not absolutely certain.

                           397

X 7758   (-)

    <u>sup. mut.</u>
    ]ta-de-s̤o̤[

X 7759   (-)

    ]r̤o̤ , / da-ra-ko , we-we-si[-jo

X 7760   (-)

    ]da-ra-ko[

X 7762   (-)

    <u>sup. mut.</u>
    ]ra-je-we[

X 7763   (-)

    ]ki-ti-se-[
        Possibly]ki-ti-se-w̤e̤[. [[<u>ti</u>]] between <u>ki</u> and <u>ti</u>;
        <u>se</u> over erasure.

X 7765   (-)

.a   ]‖s̤a‖   [
.b   ]pa-ta-re[

X 7768   (-)

    ]e-sa-re[
        Perhaps]e-sa-re-w̤i̤[.

X 7770   (-)

    ]de / ku-pa[

X 7773   (-)

    ]-ta-ra-pi , OVIS̤^{m}[
        Possibly]<u>ka</u>-ta-ra-pi.

X 7774   (-)

    ]s̤i̤-ta-ro [
        Text probably complete at left.

X 7775   (-)
      ]re-u [

X 7776   (-)
      ] ma-sa [

X 7778   (-)
      sup. mut.
      ]me-no [

X 7784 + fr.   (-)
      su-ri-mo[
            ..

X 7789   (-)
      me-wi[
         ..
      inf. mut.

X 7791   (-)
      ]ki-si[

X 7792   (-)
      ]ko-ke[
          ..
         Trace at left, perhaps]to/.
                                  ..

X 7793   (-)
      ]ko-ro [
         Trace at right (SUS[?).
                          ...

X 7794   (-)
      ] , u-a[
         Trace at left.

X 7795 + fr.   (-)
      ]ta-pa-no[
         Trace at right.

                        399

X 7796   (-)

       sup. mut.
       ]ki̤-si̤[

X 7799   (-)

       to̤-ro-[
            Cut at left.

X 7801   (-)

       ]-ra[

X 7804   (-)

       ]je-mo[

X 7810   (-)

       ]te-jo [

X 7812   (-)

    .1   sup. mut.
    .2   ]-ta / me[

X 7814   (-)

    .1   sup. mut.
    .2   ?e-re-]pa-te-jo-pi̤[

X 7816   (-)

       ] ra̤[

X 7817   (-)

       ]-ru , [

X 7819   (-)

       ]q̤i-ja [

X 7820   (-)

       sup. mut.
       ]do-si [

X 7822   (-)

    ]-si-jo[

X 7823   (-)

 .a   ] vest.[
 .b   ] , po[
      .a Perhaps pu[.

X 7824   (-)

    ] te-[
      Possibly te-ra[.

X 7827   (-)

    ]50[

    inf. mut.

X 7828   (-)

    ]ma-ri[

X 7829   (-)

    ]ti-[
      Probably complete at left. Possibly]ti-ri[.

X 7830   (-)

    ]23 [

X 7832   (-)

    ]qa[
    Probable trace of a previous central ruling.

X 7836   (-)

    ]23 [

X 7845   (115)

 .1   qa-[
 .2   sa-ma[
 .3   vacat [
      .1 qa-sa[or qa-ni[.

X 7846   (-)

  .a]ẉo-a   [
  .b]*<u>161</u> , to-te-[

        .b Trace at right, perhaps ẹ, before *<u>161</u>:]ẹ-*<u>161</u>?
        Or does *<u>161</u> stand alone⁻(cf. Ld 787)?

X 7848 + 7854   (-)

  .1]si-ni-ja , me-[
  .2]6   [

     inf. mut.

       .1 Perhaps me-dụ[or me-ḳị[.
       .2 Possibly]ₔ; perhaps ḳọ[.

X 7860   (-)

  .1]pi-ra$_2$-mọ[
  .2]ra-su-to[

      .1 Over erasure.

X 7861   (-)

  .A]re[
  .B]<u>vac.</u>[

X 7862   (-)

  .1 <u>sup. mut.</u>
  .2]no-[

X 7865   (-)

  .1]5
  .2] 30

      Cut at right.
      .2 Trace at left; possibly]ḳị OVỊS^{m}.

X 7872   (-)

  .0 <u>sup. mut.</u>
  .1] <u>vacat</u> [
  .2]ke   [
  .3 <u>inf. mut.</u>

X 7873   (-)
       sup. mut.
 .1   ] vest.[
 .2] qa-ra$_2$[
 .3   ] vest.[
       inf. mut.

v.1   sup. mut.
 .2]-na[
 .3] vac. [
       inf. mut.
         v. Text from photograph (surface of tablet now damaged).

X 7875   (-)
       ]-ku[

X 7876   (-)
 .a]32 [
 .b   ]vest.[
       inf. mut.
         .b Perhaps]ko̤[.

X 7878   (-)
 .1]1
 .2] vacat

X 7880   (-)
       ]ta-ra-jo[

X 7884   (-)
       ]za̤ / o-pe-ro[

X 7888 + fr.   (-)
 .1]70 [
 .2 inf. mut.
      .1 Traces at left, probably not 1̤0̤0̤ (and thus reading
      ]1̤70): perhaps]ma̤ or]LA̤N̤A̤.

403

27

X 7891 + 7990   (118?)

    ku-ta-i-si-[
        ku-ta-i-si-j<u>o</u>[possible.

X 7894   (-)
    ⸍]<u>ta</u>-ti-jo[
        ⠒⠒

X 7895   (-)
    ]jo / e-[

X 7897   (-)
    .a]   <u>vest</u>.[
    .b]ku-ta-ti-jo   [

X 7900   (-)
    ] re-si-jo[

X 7909   (-)
    .a]   po[
    .b]pa /   [
        <u>inf. mut</u>.

X 7910   (-)
    ]ko   [
        Trace at right.

X 7916   (-)
    ]-ke-ta[
        Perhaps]<u>na</u>-ke-ta[.
                  ⠒⠒

X 7918 + 7931   (-)
    ka-ri-pi-jo , [
        Cut at left.

X 7921   (-)
    ]we-si-[

404

X 7924   (-)
     ]ta-wo[

X 7926   (-)
     ]po[

X 7929   (-)
     ]za-jo[
       ..

X 7930   (-)
     e[

X 7932   (_)
  .1]12[
  .2]2

          .2 Trace at left; perhaps numeral, but more likely
              ideogram.

X 7935   (-)
  .1]te-we[
  .2 inf. mut.

X 7936   (-)

     sup. mut.
     ]-ja-no-ri[
              ..
          Perhaps]pi-ja-no-ri[.
                    .   ..

X 7939   (-)
     ]na-to[

X 7944   (-)
     ]e-[
          Text perhaps complete at left.

X 7947   (-)
     ]ma-ro , [

                        405

X   7955   (-)
     di-ka[

X   7965   (-)
     ja-[

X   7966   (-)
     ]si-pe-[
        Perhaps]si-pe-we̤[.

X   7972   (-)
     sup. mut.
     ]wo̤-ko-ro̤[
     inf. mut.

X   7976   (-)
     ]de-sa-[
        Probably]de-sa-to̤[.

X   7979   (-)
     sup. mut.
      ]me[
     inf. mut.

X   7981   (107?)
     ]wo[

X   7985   (-)
     sup. mut.
     ]-se[

X   7989   (-)
     ja̤[
     inf. mut.
        Cut at left.

X 7991   (-)

    ]-ja[

X 7994   (-)

    ]re-wa [

X 7995   (-)

    <u>sup. mut.</u>
    pte[
       Cut at left.

X 7996   (-)

    ] 2
       Cut at right. Trace at left ( ]OVIS^{m} ?).

X 7999   (-)

    ] 5 [

X 8000   (-)

    <u>sup. mut.</u>
    ] 8̣ [ ] 5̣ [
      Traces of ideograms before both numerals.

X 8001   (-)

    ]176[

X 8007   (-)

    ] 6[
    <u>inf. mut.</u>

X 8009   (-)

    ]6̣2̣[
    <u>inf. mut.</u>
      Trace to left:]OVIS^{x} ?

X 8010   (-)

    ]120 [

X 8011   (-)
        ]1 [

X 8013 + 8027   (-)
    .1   ]63   [
    .2   ]68   [
            Palimpsest (previously ruled in the other direction).

X 8017   (-)
        sup. mut.
    .1   ]vest.[
    .2   ]-ja , da-mo-ko[
        inf. mut.
            .2   ]ri-ja or]we-ja.

X 8019   (-)
    .1   ]2
    .2   ]11
    .3   ]15
            .3 Fifth unit possibly accidentally erased.

X 8024   (-)
    .1   ]60
    .2   ] vacat

X 8025   (-)
        ]30

X 8026   (-)
    .1   ]8
    .2   ] vacat

X 8029   (-)
        ] 9
            Trace at left possibly]TELA^x.

X   8031 + 8033   (-)
     ] 95
          Trace at left ?

X   8035   (-)
     ] 15
          Trace at left ( ]TELA^x ?).

X   8039   (-)
     ]60

X   8042   (-)
  .1   ]5
  .2   ]3

X   8043   (-)
  .1   ] 100
  .2   ] vacat
          .1 Trace at left suggests TELA^x.

X   8044   (-)
  .1   ] 2
  .2   ] vacat
          .1 Perhaps]LANA.

X   8050   (-)
     ] 1
          Trace of erasure at left ?

X   8051   (-)
  .1   ]6
  .2   ]2

X   8052   (-)
  .1   ]2
  .2   ]1
          Cut at right.

X 8055   (-)
    ]3

X 8063   (-)
    ] 1
        Just possible: .a]1̣
                    .b]TEL̤Ạ^{x} 1.

X 8064   (-)
    ]52

X 8066 + fr.   (-)
    ]7̣

X 8068   (-)
    ]8̣

X 8070   (-)
    ]3
    inf. mut.
        Perhaps]1̣3, or trace of sign at left.

X 8071   (-)
    sup. mut.
    ]o 12̣[

X 8072   (-)
  .1] vacat
  .2]ja-mi-[.]
    inf. mut.
        .2 Perhaps]ja-mi-ṣạ or]ja-mi 1̣.

X 8074   (-)
    ]3 [
    inf. mut.

X 8101   (-)
   .1   ]su-ra , ka-ta-ro , ku-ri-sa-to , ra-wi[
   .2   ]ṛọ   [
   .3   ]   vacat   [
           .2 Or]da.

X 8104   (-)
       ]kụ-we-jo   [
           Traces of erasure at right.

X 8107   (-)
       ] e-re-pa-te-[
           Possibly e-re-pa-te-jạ[,   -te-ọ[or -te-mẹ[.

X 8108   (-)
       ]ru-wa-ni[
           Perhaps cut at left.

X 8109   (-)
       ]ụ / pa-sa   [

X 8111   (-)
   .1   ]200
   .2   ] vacat

X 8112   (-)
       sup. mut.
   .a   ]ke-[
   .b   ]e-we-o-sị[

X 8113   (-)
       ]-no[
           Perhaps]ṭạ-no[.

X 8114   (-)
       ]9

X 8126   (-)

        sup. mut.
     ]re , / dwo-jo 1
       Perhaps dwo-jo-[.].

X 8133   (-)
     ]ma[

X 8143   (-)
     ] 5
       Cut at right.

X 8147   (-)
  .1   ]de
  .2   ] vacat

X 8148   (-)
     ka[
       Cut at left.

X 8154 + fr.   (-)
       sup. mut.
  .1   ]-na 1 i[
  .2   inf. mut.

X 8155   (-)
     sup. mut.
     ]du 1[
     inf. mut.

X 8156   (-)
  .0   sup. mut.
  .1   ]so-i[
     inf. mut.

X 8158   (-)

   .0 <u>sup. mut.</u>

   .1]k̞u-mi[

   .2] <u>vac.</u>[

   .3 <u>inf. mut.</u>

X 8164   (-)

   .1]-se-wi-jo[

   .2]-r̞i-ku̞[

   <u>inf. mut.</u>

X 8166   (-)

   <u>sup. mut.</u>

   .1]d̞i[

   .2]*56-z̞a[

   <u>inf. mut.</u>

X 8167 + <u>fr.</u>   (-)

   .1]se-te-jo , m̞e̞[

   .2]   <u>vacat</u>   [

X 8168   (-)

   <u>sup. mut.</u>

   .1 ko-wa [

   .2.3 <u>vacant</u> [

X 8171   (-)

   .1]M̞ 5

   .2] <u>vest.</u>

   <u>inf. mut.</u>

      Possibly same tablet as M 8170.

X 8182   (-)

   e-ri-[

      Traces favour <u>e-ri-k̞a̞</u>[or <u>e-ri-g̞e̞</u>[.

413

X 8190   (-)

    ]ḍo / *56-kọ[-we

X 8191   (-)

    ] 'ạ['

inf. mut.

      Trace of two signs at left.

X 8195   (-)

    sup. mut.
.1   ]Ṃ[
.2] po-[
.3] X [
      .2 Perhaps po-sọ[.

X 8196 + fr.   (-)

    we-we-si-jo-jo   [

lat. inf.   o-[

      Whole tablet (of .A.B type) erased and re-used.

X 8198   (-)

    sup. mut.
    ]kọ-no-[
    inf. mut.

X <8204>   (-)

.1]ku-ku-mo[
.2] vacat [
    inf. mut.

      Missing (cf. BSA 57, p.65); text from Evans' photograph.

X <8205>   (-)

    sup. mut.
    kị[
      Missing (cf. BSA 57, p.65); text from J. Raison's drawing.

X 8211   (-)
.1   ]si-ja , [
.2   ]ta-ra-si-ja[

X 8212   (-)
     ra-qa-ra-to[

X 8213   (-)
     sup. mut.
     ]-mi-[

X 8214   (-)
       sup. mut.
.a   ]te-re-u 1 [
.b   ]ru-si   [
       inf. mut.

X 8215   (-)
       sup. mut.
     ]pa-te-o [

X 8255   (-)
.a   ]a-di-je[
.b   ]tu-ni[
       .a je clear on
          Bennett's
          photograph
          of 1950.

X 8261 + 8551   (-)
.1   ]ku-do-ni-ja[
.2   ]5
lat. inf.   ]ja , e-te[
       .1 Over erasure.

X 8265   (-)
.a   ]te-u   [
.b   ]te   [

X 8266   (-)
       sup. mut.
.A   ] vacat [
.B   ]   re[
       .B Trace of two
          majuscule signs
          at left.

X 8267 + fr.   (-)
.1   ]   ko-pu[
.2   ] X   po-[
.3   ] vacat [
.4   ]   X [

X 8270   (-)
       sup. mut.
     ] , e-te-wa-o [
          Trace at left.

X 8272   (-)
     i-[

X 8273   (-)
       sup. mut.
     ]ri-ja[
          ja especially doubtful.

X 8275   (-)
       sup. mut.
     ]-ta / e[
          Possibly]nu-ta.

X 8277   (-)
       sup. mut.
     ]ka-mo[

X 8282   (-)
      ]-ma[
      inf. mut.
          Perhaps]tu̯-ma[.

X 8283   (-)
      ]ma[

X 8284   (-)
      sup. mut.
      ]mi̤[
          Trace at left.

X 8286   (-)
      ]no-[
      inf. mut.
          Perhaps]no-ro̤[.

X 8292   (-)
      ]pi-ri-ja[
      inf. mut.

X 8293   (-)
      sup. mut.
   .a]vest.[
   .b]pi̤-ra₂[

X 8295   (-)
      ]-pu₂-no[.

X 8296   (-)
      ]qa-ra[
          Over erasure.

X 8298   (-)
      ]qe[
      inf. mut.

X 8301   (-)
      ]qa-ta-[
      inf. mut.

X 8312   (-)
      ]-ja[
          Possibly]we̤-ja[.

X 8314   (-)
          sup. mut.
   .a]ke̤   [
   .b]   wa[

X 8319   (-)
      ]5

X 8320   (-)
   .1 sup. mut.
   .2]5[
          .2 Trace at left.

X 8322   (-)
      ]4
      inf. mut.

X 8323   (-)
      ]9   [

X 8324   (-)
      ]11
          Cut at right.

X 8325   (-)
      ]12

X 8326 + fr.   (-)
      ] 17 [

X 8327   (-)
     ]18 [
     inf. mut.

X 8328   (-)
     ] vestigia[
 v.a]20   20 [
 .b   ]2   4 [
     v. Tallying.

X 8329   (-)
 .1ʹ]35   [
 .2   ] vacat [

X 8330   (-)
     ] 43[
     Trace at left
     (possibly MUL).

X 8353   (-)
     ]3[

X 8502   (-)
 .a   ]a-ke-o-jo[
 .b   ] vest. [
     inf. mut.

X 8506   (-)
     a[

X 8509   (-)
 .1   ]do-ro [
 .2   inf. mut.
     .1 Or]je-ro ?

X 8514   (-)
 .1   ] e-u-ko[
 .2   ] vacat ?[

X 8515   (-)
     ] e-u[

X 8518   (-)
     sup. mut.
     e[
     inf. mut.

X 8519   (-)
     i[

X 8520   (-)
     i[

X 8523   (-)
     sup. mut.
 .1   ]-i   [
 .2   ] vest. [
     inf. mut.
     .1 Trace of two signs
     before i (perhaps
     ]-ja-i).

X 8524   (-)
     ]i[
     inf. mut.
     Rather doubtful;
     perhaps]OLIV[.

X 8527   (-)
     sup. mut.
     ]ja[

X 8528   (-)
     sup. mut.
 .1   ]-ja[
 .2   ]vest. [
     inf. mut.

X 8530   (-)

       ]-jo / pu-so pi-ru[

          pi with two vertical
          strokes in the
          middle.

X 8531   (-)

       ]-jo-e[

       inf. mut.

          Perhaps]-jo-pi[.

X 8532   (-)

         sup. mut.

  .1   ]-jo / a-ja-me-no [
  .2   ]-u[   ] P 30[

         inf. mut.

X 8533   (-)

  .A   ] vac.[
  .B   ]-jo ,   [

X 8535   (-)

       ]jo [

       inf. mut.

X 8536   (-)

         sup. mut.

       ]jo[

       inf. mut.

X 8538   (-)

         sup. mut.

       ]ka-[

         Perhaps to be read
         the other way up.

X 8540   (-)

       ka[

X 8542   (-)

         sup. mut.

       ] ka[

       inf. mut.

X 8543   (-)

       ]ke-[

         Perhaps]ke-ra[.

X 8545   (-)

         sup. mut.

  .1   ]-ki[
  .2   inf. mut.

X 8549   (-)

       ko[

       inf. mut.

X 8550   (-)

         sup. mut.

       ]ko[

       inf. mut.

X 8552   (-)

         sup. mut.

       ]ku-ta[

X 8555   (-)

       ku[

X 8557   (-)

       ]ku[

       inf. mut.

         Rather doubtful; perhaps
         ko badly drawn.

X 8560   (-)

    ma[

      Cut at left.

X 8561   (-)

    sup. mut.

    ]da-ma[

    inf. mut.

X 8562   (-)

  .1 sup. mut.

  .2]ma-[

        .2 Perhaps LANA and
            traces of numerals.

X 8564   (-)

  .a]   a[

  .b]ma / [

    inf. mut.

  v.]vest.[

X 8567   (-)

  .1 sup. mut.

  .2]mi[

  .3 inf. mut.

X 8570   (-)

    ]mo[

    inf. mut.

X 8571   (-)

    ]na , wo[

X 8575   (-)

    ]-nu-[

    inf. mut.

      Perhaps]te-nu-[.

X 8577   (-)

    sup. mut.

    ]o[

      Traces at left and
      right.

X 8580   (-)

    sup. mut.

    ]ku / po[

X 8581   (112?)

    ] po[

X 8584   (-)

    ]qa[

X 8590   (-)

    ]ro / a-e-da[

X 8591   (-)

    ]u[

    inf. mut.

X 8595   (-)

    ]sa-nu[

    inf. mut.

X 8603   (-)

    sup. mut.

    su[

X 8604   (-)

  .1 sup. mut.

  .2] vestigia [

  .3]   ta-jo[

  .4 inf. mut.

X 8607   (-)
  ]-ta[

X 8609   (-)
  ]te-ru[
  inf. mut.

X 8610   (-)
  te[
  inf. mut.

X 8611   (-)
  sup. mut.
  ]ti[
  inf. mut.

X 8612   (-)
  sup. mut.
  ]ti[

X 8614   (-)
  to-sa[

X 8615   (-)
  ]to-so[
  inf. mut.

X 8616   (-)
  sup. mut.
  ]-to[
   Perhaps]mu-to[.

X 8617   (-)
  tu[
  inf. mut.

X 8621   (-)
  ]-wa-ja [
   Beginning of division
   into .A .B .

X 8624 + fr.   (-)
 .1 e[
 .2 wa[
  inf. mut.

X 8625   (-)
 .1]we-si-jo [
 .2]-ri-jo [

X 8626   (-)
  ]ko-we[
  inf. mut.

X 8627   (-)
  ]we-i-[
  inf. mut.

X 8628   (-)
  ]-we[
  inf. mut.
   Perhaps]i-we[or
   ]ma-we[.

X 8630   (-)
  sup. mut.
  ]we[
   Perhaps bottom of M.

X 8632   (-)
  sup. mut.
  wo-pi[

X 8634   (118?)
    ]-za-ra-ro [
        Perhaps division into
        .A.B with OVIS^x[in .A.

X 8638   (-)
    ]2

X 8641   (-)
    ]10

X 8645   (-)
    ]2
        Perhaps]4.

X 8647   (-)
    ]1 [

X 8648   (-)
    ]1
        Cut at right.

X 8649   (-)
    ]2 [

X 8650   (-)
    ]6 [

X 8651   (-)
    .1   ]3
    .2   ] vacat
            .1   ]a possible but
                 rather doubtful.

X 8652   (-)
    .1   ]179 [
    .2   ] vestigia

X 8655   (-)
    .1   ]1[
    .2   ]vest.[

X 8656   (-)
    .1   ]32   [
    .2   ]3   [

X 8657   (-)
    ]21[

X 8658 + frr.   (-)
    .1   ]18   [
    .2   ]8[
            Tablet much damaged;
            originally two or three
            lines.

X 8659   (-)
    ]66 [

X 8660   (-)
    ]30
        Bennett read]pa or]te
        in .a in 1950, on a piece
        now damaged.

X 8663   (-)
    .1   sup. mut.
    .2   ]2   [
         inf. mut.

X 8664   (-)
    sup. mut.
    ]20[
    inf. mut.

X 8665   (-)

      sup. mut.

      ] 20[

         Trace of 2 or 3
         signs at left.

X 8668   (-)

      su[

      inf. mut.

X 8669   (-)

      sup. mut.

.1   ]9 [

.2   inf. mut.

      .1 Perhaps]19.

X 8670   (-)

      sup. mut.

.1   ] 6 [

.2   inf. mut.

X 8672   (-)

      sup. mut.

.1   ]3[

.2   inf. mut.

        .1 Or]te[.

X 8674 + 8697   (-)

.1   ]8[

.2   inf. mut.

X 8675   (-)

      sup. mut.

.1   ]12[

.2   inf. mut.

X 8676   (-)

      sup. mut.

.1   ]2[

.2   ]20[

X 8677   (-)

      sup. mut.

.1   ]2[

.2   ]4 [

X 8678   (-)

      sup. mut.

      ]80 [

         Hastily written; over
         erasure?

X 8679   (-)

      ]92 [

      inf. mut.

         Probably over erasure.

X 8680   (-)

      sup. mut.

      ]6   [

X 8682   (-)

.1   ]3   [

.2   inf. mut.

X 8685   (-)

      ]20[

      inf. mut.

X 8686   (-)

      ] 1 [

      inf. mut.

X 8688   (-)
        ]22[
        inf. mut.
            Perhaps]32[.

X 8689   (-)
        ]10[
        inf. mut.

X 8690   (-)
        ]16 [
        inf. mut.

X 8692   (-)
        ]13[
        inf. mut.

X 8693   (-)
        ]31[
        inf. mut.

X 8694   (-)
        sup. mut.
    .1] 20[
    .2 inf. mut.

X 8695   (-)
        sup. mut.
        ]2 [
        inf. mut.
            To be read other
            way up?

X 8696   (-)
    .1 sup. mut.
    .2]   11[
    .3 inf. mut.

X 8698   (-)
        sup. mut.
    .1]3   [
    .2 inf. mut.

X 8699   (-)
        ]100[
        inf. mut.

X 8709   (-)
        se-to[

X 8714   (-)
        sup. mut.
        ]-e[

X 8718   (-)
        i[

X 8719   (-)
        sup. mut.
        ]ka[
        inf. mut.

X 8720   (-)
        ]4   [
        inf. mut.

X 8721   (-)
    .1 sup. mut.
    .2] 1
    .3] vacat
        inf. mut.
        .2 Trace at left.

X 8725　　　　　　(-)
　　　sup. mut.
　　　]di̤ [

X 8726　　　　　　(-)
　.1　sup. mut.
　.2　]dṳ[
　　　inf. mut.
　　　　.2 Or]me̤[?

X 8727　　　　　　(-)
　　　]i̤[
　　　inf. mut.
　　　　Or]re̤[?

X 8731　　　　　　(-)
　　　sup. mut.
　　　ki̤-[

X 8733　　　　　　(-)
　　　o[
　　　inf. mut.

X 8735　　　　　　(-)
　　　sup. mut.
　　　qa̤[

X 8736　　　　　　(-)
　　　sup. mut.
　　　]ra̤-no̤[

X 8737　　　　　　(-)
　　　]re̤[
　　　inf. mut.

X 8738　　　　　　(-)
　.1　]ro̤ [
　.2　inf. mut.
　　　　.1 Or]ro̤ , [.

X 8739　　　　　　(-)
　　　sup. mut.
　　　]sa[
　　　　Perhaps Wb.

X 8740　　　　　　(-)
　　　] OLE̤[
　　　inf. mut.
　　　　Less likely] so̤[.

X 8741　　　　　　(-)
　　　sup. mut.
　　　o[
　　　　Perhaps sṳ[or ta̤[.

X 8743　　　　　　(-)
　　　sup. mut.
　　　]ṳ-[
　　　inf. mut.

X 8744　　　　　　(-)
　　　sup. mut.
　　　]we̤-ko̤ , [
　　　　Or]we̤-ki̤ ?

X 8745　　　　　　(-)
　　　]1
　　　　Cut at right.

X 8746　　　　　　(-)
　　　]1

424

X 8747   (-)
   .1   <u>sup. mut.</u>
   .2   ]2[

        <u>inf. mut.</u>

X 8750   (-)
        <u>sup. mut.</u>
        ]10   [
        · Trace at right?

X 8751   (-)
   .1   <u>sup. mut.</u>
   .2   ]40   [
           .2 Perhaps]80.
               Trace at right.

CONCORDANCE TO TABLET NUMBERS

One asterisk (*) opposite a number means that the
corresponding tablet contains no legible signs;
two (**) mark numbers left blank; three (***) indicate
documents not in Linear B. < ˋ indicates a tablet
now missing, ( ) a tablet not known under this number
but identified with another existing tablet.

1	Fp	27	Fp 14	49	U
2	Fs	28	Fp 14	50	Ce
3	Fs	29	Fs	51	F
4	Fs	30	Fp	52	V
5	Fp	31	Fp 1	52 bis	V 52
6	Fp	<32>	Fs	53	Vc
7	Fp	33	C	54	Vc
8	Fs	<34>	Ga	55	Vc
9	Fs	35	X	56	V
10	Gg	36	E	57	V
11	Fs	(36 bis)	X 1801	58	Xd
12	Fs	37	X	(58 bis)	Og 1804
13	Fp	37 bis	X 1801	59	Ce
14	Fp	38	X	60	V
15	Fp	39	X	61	Ce
16	Fp	40	As	62	Vd
17	Fs	41	B	63	Ai
18	Fp	(41 bis)	X 1802	64	Vc
19	Fs	42	Dq	65	Vc
20	Fs	43	Dp	66	Vc
21	Fs	44	X	67	Vc
22	Fs	45	Dq	68	Vc
23	Fs	46	Dq	(69)	X 745
24	Fs	47	Dl	70	Xd
25	Fs	(47 bis)	Dq 1803	71	E
26	Fs	48	Fp	72	Vc

73	Vc	109	U	145	V
74	Vc	110	Xd	146	Xd
75	Xd	111	Xd	147	V
76	Ce	112	Xd	148	Xd
77	V	113	Ce	149	Xd
78	Xd	114	V	150	V
79	Uf	115	Ai	151	V60
80	Xd	116	Xd	152	Ce
81	Vc	117	V	153	F
82	Xd	118	V	154	Xd
83	Xd	119	Xd	155	Xd 146
84	Xd	120	Uf	156	Ce
(84 bis)	Ai 1805	121	Uf	157	F
85	Np	122	Xd	158	V114
86	Xd	123	Xd	159	V
87	Ag	124	U	160	Uc
88	Ag	125	Vc	161	Uc
89	Ag	126	Vc	162	Ce
90	Ag	127	Xd	163	Ce
91	Ag	128	Xd 105	164	B
92	Xd	129	Vc	165	E
93	K	130	Xd	166	Xd
94	Xd	131	Xd	167	Xd
95	U	132	E	168	Xd
96	U	133	Xd	169	Xd
97	Xd	134	Xd 111	170	Xd
98	Xd	135	Sc	171	Vc
99	Xd	136	Vd	172	U
100	Xd	137	Vd	173	Vc
101	B	137 bis	Vd 137	174	Vc
102	Vc	138	Vd	175	Vc
103	Sc	139	Ce	176	Vc
104	L	140	Xd	177	Xd
105	Xd	141	Xd	178	L
106	Vc	142	Xd	179	Xd
107	Xd	143	Xd	180	Og
108	Vc	144	Ce	181	Vc

182	Xd	218	Sc	254	Sc	
183	Vc	219	Sc	255	Sc	
184	Vc	220	Sc	256	Sc	
185	Vc	221	Sc	257	Sc	
186	Xd	222	Sc	258	Sc	
187	Xd 94	223	Sc	259	Sc	
188	Vc	224	Sc	260	Sc	
189	Xd	225	Sc	261	Sc	
190	Ai	226	Sc	262	Sc	
191	Xd	227	Sc	263	Sc	
192	L	228	Sc 224	264	Sc	
193	F	229	Sc	265	Sc 249	
194	Ai	230	Sc	266	Sc	
195	Vc	231	Sc	267	Np	
196	Xd 98	232	Sc	268	Np	
197	Xd	233	Sc	269	Np	
198	Uf	234	Sc	270	Np	
199	Vc	235	Sc	271	Np	
200	Xd	236	Sc	272	Np	
201	Vc	237	Sc	273	Np	
202	Xd	238	Sc	274	Np	
203	Vc	239	Sc	275	**	
204	Xd	240	Sc	276	Np	
205	Vc	241	Sc	277	Np	
206	Vc	242	Sc	278	Np	
207	Xd	243	Sc	(279)	Np 278	
208	Vc	244	Sc	280	V	
209	Xd	245	Sc	281	L 178	
210	V	<246>	Sc	282	Xd	
211	Vc	247	Sc	283	Ce	
212	Vc	248	Sc	284	Xd 97	
213	B	249	Sc	285	Vc	
214	Xd	250	Sc	286	Np	
215	Vc	251	Sc	287	Xd	
216	Xd	252	Sc	288	E	
217	Sc	253	Sc	289	Xd	

290	Vc	<326>	Xd	361	Fh
291	Vc	<327>	Xd	362	Fh
<292>	Xd	<328>	Xd	363	Fp
293	Vc	<329>	Xd	364	Fh
294	Xd	<330>	Xd	365	Fh
<295>	Vc	<331>	Xd	366	Fh
<296>	Xd	<332>	Xd	367	Fh
297	Xd	<333>	Xd	368	Fh
298	Xd	<334>	Xd	369	Fh
<299>	Xd	<335>	Xd	370	Fh
<300>	Xd	<336>	Xd	371	Fh
<301>	Xd	337	V	372	Fh
<302>	Xd	338	Ai	373	Fh
303	Vc	339	Fh	<374>	Fh
<304>	Xd	340	Fh	375	Fh
<305>	Xd	341	Fh	<376>	Fh
<306>	Xd	342	Fh	377	Fh
<307>	Xd	343	Fh	<378>	Fh
<308>	Xd	344	Fh	<379>	Fh
<309>	Xd	345	Fh	380	Fh
<310>	Xd	346	Fh	<381>	Fh
<311>	Uf	347	Fh	<382>	Fh
312	Vc	348	Fh	<383>	Fh
<313>	Xd	349	Fh	<384>	Fh
<314>	Xd	350	Fh	<385>	Fh
(315)	Xd 7568	350 bis	Fh 381	386	Fh
<316>	Vc	351	Fh	<387>	Fh
<317>	Vc	352	Fh	<388>	Fh
<318>	Xd	353	Fh	<389>	Fh
<319>	Xd	354	Fp	<390>	Fh
<320>	Xd	355	Fh	<391>	Fh
<321>	Ai	356	Fh	<392>	Fh
<322>	Xd	357	Fh	393	Fh
<323>	Xd	358	Fh	394	C
<324>	Xd	359	Fh	(395)	X 7900
<325>	Xd	360	Fh	(396)	Ga 7426

(397)	Ga 7425	433	L	469	L	
(398)	Ga 7431	434	K	470	L	
<399>	*	435	X	471	L	
<400>	*	436	U	472	L	
<401>	*	437	U	473	L	
<402>	*	438	Dq	474	L	
<403>	*	439	Dq	475	L	
<404>	*	440	Dq	<476>	X 7633	
<405>	*	441	Dq	(476 bis)	X 7776	
<406>	*	442	Dq	(477)	X 7559	
<407>	*	443	X	(478)	X 7632	
408	X	444	X	479	V	
409	X	445	Dq	480	L	
410	X	446	Lc	481	Lc	
411	D	447	Dq	482	V	
412	D1	448	Dq	483	Lc	
413	D1	449	Dq	484	L	
414	D1	450	X	485	Od	
415	Ga	451	X	486	Od	
416	Ga	452	F	487	Od	
417	Ga	453	X	488	V	
418	Ga	454	Ga	489	L	
419	Ga	455	L	(490)	X 5037	
420	Ga	456	Ga	491	L	
421	Ga	(457)	Ga 5088	492	V	
422	Ga	458	X	493	Pp	
423	Ga	459	X	494	Pp	
424	Ga	460	L	495	Pp	
425	Ga	461	Ga	496	Pp	
426	Ga	462	Fh	497	Pp	
427	Gs	463	D1	498	Pp	
428	Ga	464	Ga	499	Pp	
429	V	465	Ga	500	Pp 493	
430	X	466	V	501	L	
431	V	467	M	502	Od	
432	Uf	468	X	503	V	

504	Lc	538	Lc 535	574	Ld
(505)	L 7514	539	Od	575	Ld
<506>	X	540	Lc	576	Ld
(507)	Lc 7377	541	Lc	577	Ld
(508)	X 7546	542	Lc 531	578	L
(508 bis)	Od 7375	543	Lc	579	Ld
(509)	V 7513	544	Xe	580	Ld 575
(509 bis)	Ak 1807	545	Lc 529	581	Lc
(510)	V 7620	546	Lc	582	Lc
511	D 411	547	Lc	583	Ld
512	Lc	548	Lc	584	Ld
513	L	549	Lc	585	Ld
514	L	550	Lc	586	L
515	L	551	Lc	587	Ld
516	L	552	Lc	588	L
517	Ga	553	Lc	589	Ld 587
518	Ga	554	Lc 532	590	L
519	Ga	555	Lc	591	Ld
520	L	(556)	Lc 557	592	L
521	Gg	557	Lc	593	L
522	X	558	Lc	594	L
523	L	559	M	595	Ld
524	Xe	560	Lc	596	Ld 587
525	Lc	561	Lc	597	Am
526	Lc	562	Od	598	Ld
527	Lc	563	Od	599	Ld
528	Lc	564	L	600	Am
529	Lc	565	L	601	Am
530	Lc	566	As	602	As
531	Lc	567	L	603	As
532	Lc	568	Am	604	As
533	Lc	569	Vc	605	As
534	Lc	570	Od	606	As 604
535	Lc	571	Ld	607	As
536	Lc	572	Ld	608	As
537	Xe	573	Ld	609	As

610	Ak	646	Lc	682	Od
611	Ak	647	L	683	M
612	Ak	648	L	684	V
613	Ak	649	Ld	685	Ga
614	Ak	650	As 602	686	Dq
615	Ak	651	L	687	Od
616	Ak	652	V	688	Od
617	Ak	653	V	689	Od
618	Ap	654	Le	690	Od
619	Ak	655	V	691	Xe
620	Ak	656	Ld	692	Xe
621	Ak	657	Xe	693	L
622	Ak	658	X	694	Ap
623	Ap 618	659	Dd	695	L
624	Ak	660	X	696	Od
625	As	661	Ld 598	697	X
626	Ak	662	Lc 646	698	L
627	Ak	663	L 592	699	Dp
628	Ap	664	Xe	700	K
629	Ap	665	Am 600	701	Gg
230	Ak	666	Od	702	Gg
<631>	Ak	667	Od	703	Gg
632	Ai	668	E	704	Gg
633	Ap 618	669	E	705	Gg
634	Ak	670	E	<706>	Gg
(635)	Ak 7022	671	Dk	707	Gg
636	Ak	672	Dq	708	Gg
637	Ap	673	Ga	709	Gg
638	Ak	674	Ga	710	Gg
639	Ap	675	Ga	711	Gg
640	Ak	<676>	Ga	712	Gg 521
641	Le	677	Ga	713	Gg
642	Le	678	Ga	714	Od
643	Ak	679	Ga	715	Od
644	L 588	680	Ga	716	Od
645	As	681	Od	717	Gg

718	Od	753	Ai 752	787	Ld
719	M	754	Ai	788	Ld
720	M	755	B	789	Sk
721	X	756	V	790	Dl
722	X	757	M	791	Dl
723	X	758	L	792	Dl
724	M	759	L	793	X
725	X 722	760	G	794	Dl
726	F	761	L	795	X
727	Dk	762	Ai	796	X
728	X	(763)	X 5040	797	U
729	M	764	L	798	B
730	Oa	765	Od	799	B
731	Oa	766	X	800	B
732	Oa	767	C	801	B
733	Oa	768	X	802	B
734	Oa	769	Ap	803	B
(734 bis)	Oa 1808	770	X	804	B
735	L	771	L	805	B
736	U	772	B	806	B
737	X	773	K	807	B
738	Ga	774	K	808	B
739	Ai	775	K	809	B
740	K	776	K	810	B
741	F	(776 bis/a)	K 773	811	B
742	X	(776 bis/b)	K 1810	812	B
743	X	777	E	813	B
744	X	778	K	814	B
745	X	779	B	815	B
746	U	780	Ak	816	B
747	D	781	Ak	817	B
<748>	X	782	Ak	818	B
749	E	783	Ak	819	Am
750	Ai	784	Ak	820	G
751	Ai	785	Ld	821	Am
752	Ai	786	Ld	822	B

823	B	859	Np	894	So
824	Ai	860	Np	895	Ca
825	Ai	861	Np	896	Ch
826	Am	862	Gv	897	Ch
827	Am	863	Gv	898	Ch
828	Ak	864	Gv	899	Ch
829	K	865	V	900	Ch
830	Ak	866	F	901	C
831	V	867	F 841	902	C
832	V	868	L	903	Co
833	Og	869	L	904	Co
834	Ga	870	L	905	C
835	Uf	871	L	906	Co
836	Uf	872	K	907	Co
837	Uf	873	K	908	C
838	Uf	874	K 829	909	Co
839	Uf	875	K	910	Co
840	Gm	876	U	911	C
841	F	877	K	912	C
842	E	878	Oa	913	C
843	E	879	Se	914	C
844	F	880	Se	915	C
845	E	881	Se	916	D1
846	E	882	Se	917	C
847	E	883	Se	918	[+] C 917
848	E	884	Sg	919	Do
849	E	885	Sg	920	Dk
850	E	886	Sg	921	Do 919
851	F	887	Sg	922	C
852	F	888	Sg	923	Do
853	F	889	Sg	924	Do
854	F	890	Se	925	Dk
855	Np	(890 bis)	Sg 1811	926	Dc
856	Np	891	Se	927	Do
857	Np	892	Se	928	D1
858	Np	893	Se	929	Do

930	D1
931	Dk
932	D1
933	D1
934	D1
935	D1
936	Dk
937	Dp
938	D1
939	D1
940	D1
941	C
942	D1 935
943	D1
944	D1
945	Dk
946	D1
947	D1
948	D1
949	D1
950	D1
951	Dk
952	D1
953	Ga
954	C
955	[+] Ga 953
(956)	Ak 643
(957)	L 588
958	V
959	Og 833
960	V
961	V
962	V 958
963	D1 932
964	Dk
965	Se

966	Ai
967	C
968	D1 933
969	Dk
970	Uf
971	E
972	Ch
973	C
974	X
975	D1 933
976	X
977	D1 948
978	Sg 888
979	C
980	Uf
981	Uf
982	Ai
983	Uf
984	Ra
985	B
986	X
987	Uf
988	B
989	C
990	Uf
991	Uf
992	Ga
993	X
994	Gg 713
995	Gg
996	Do
997	Dp
998	X
999	X
1000	Np
1001	X 999

1002	V
1003	V
1004	V
1005	V
1006	Se 891
1007	Se
1008	Se 965
1009	Ld 787
1010	X
1011	Uf
1012	Ai
1013	X
1014	X
1015	Ch
1016	C 941
1017	Se 880
1018	X
1019	X
1020	Ga
1021	Ga
1022	Üf
1023	Uf
1024	X
1025	B
1026	Dq
<1027>	X
1028	Ra
1029	Ch
1030	C
1031	Uf
1032	C 979
<1033>	X
1034	Ch
1035	E
1036	Ai
1037	Ai

1038	U f	1073	Dk	1109	De	
1039	C	1074	Dk	1110	Db	
1040	Ga	1075	Dk	1111	Dv	
1041	X	1076	Dk	1112	De	
1042	Se 891	1077	Dk	1113	Dv	
1043	V	1078	Da	1114	Da	
1044	C	1079	Da	1115	Db	
1045	X	1080	Da	1116	Da	
1046	Dl	1081	Da	1117	Dc	
1047	X	1082	Da	1118	Dc	
1048	Se	1083	Da	1119	Df	
1049	Dk	1084	De	1120	Df	
1050	X	1085	Dv	1121	Df	
1051	X	1086	Dv	1122	Dc	
1052	X	1087	Da	1123	Da	
1053	So	1088	Dn	1124	Dv	
1053 bis U 1812		1089	Dn	1125	Dv	
1054	Do	1090	Dn	1126	Db	
1055	B	1091	Da	1127	Da	
1056	Fh	1092	Dn	1128	Dv	
1057	Fh	1093	Dn	1129	Dc	
1058	Ga	1094	Dn	1130	Dc	
1059	Fh	1095	Dn	(1131)	Dc 1129	
1060	Dl	1096	Dn	1132	Da	
1061	Dp	1097	Db	1133	Dv	
1062	Od	1098	Da	1134	Da	
1063	Od	1099	Db	1135	Da	
1064	Dk	1100	Dv	1136	De	
1065	Dk	1101	Dg	1137	Da	
1066	Dk	1102	Dg	1138	De	
1067	Dk	1103	Dv	1139	Dv	
1068	Dk	1104	Dv	1140	Db	
1069	Dk	1105	Db	1141	De	
1070	Dk	1106	Dd	1142	Dv	
1071	Dk	1107	Dg	1143	Da	
1072	Dk	1108	Da	1144	Dd	

1145	Dv	1181	Dm	1217	Dv
1146	Dv	1182	Dm	1218	Dd
1147	Da	1183	Dm	1219	Df
1148	Dc	1184	Dm	1220	Dc
1149	Dd	1185	Db	1221	Da
1150	Dd	1186	Db	1222	Df
1151	De	1187	Df	1223	Df
1152	De	1188	Dv	1224	Da 1221
1153	De	1189	Da	1225	Db
1154	Dc	1190	Dv	1226	Dv
1155	Db	1191	Dv	1227	Db
1156	Da	1192	Dv	1228	Dc
1157	Dd	1193	Dd	1229	Df
1158	Dg	1194	Da	1230	Df
1159	Db	1195	Da	1231	De
1160	Db	1196	Db	1232	Db
1161	Da	1197	Da	1233	Df
1162	Da	1198	Db	1234	Dq
1163	Da	1199	Dv	1235	Dg
1164	Da	1200	Dn	1236	Db
1165	Db	1201	Dd	1237	Dv
1166	Db	1202	Da	1238	Da
1167	Dc	1203	Dc	1239	Dv
1168	Db	1204	Db	1240	Dh
1169	Dv	1205	Dv	1241	Db
1170	Da	1206	Dv	1242	Db
1171	Dd	1207	Dd	1243	Dh
1172	Da	1208	Db	1244	Dd
1173	Da	1209	Dn	1245	Db
1174	Dm	1210	Df	1246	Db
1175	Dm	1211	Db	1247	Db
1176	Dm	1212	Db	1248	Dv
1177	Dm	1213	Dv	1249	Dv
1178	Dm	1214	Dv	1250	Db
1179	Dm	1215	Dv	(1251)	Dv 1511
1180	Dm	1216	Dv	1252	Dd 659

1253	Da	1289	Da	1325	Df	
1254	De	1290	Df	(1326)	Db	1327
1255	Dv	1291	Dd	1327	Db	
1256	**	1292	Dv	1328	Dv	
1257	**	1293	Da	1329	Db	
1258	**	1294	De	1330	Dv	
1259	**	1295	Db	1331	Dv	
1260	De	1296	Dd	1332	Dv	
1261	Db	1297	Db	1333	Da	
1262	Db	1298	Dc	1334	Dv	
1263	Db	1299	Da	1335	Ga	
1264	De	1300	Dd	1336	Dn	1096
1265	Db	1301	De	1337	Dc	
1266	Dv	1302	Db	1338	Da	
1267	Dv	1303	Dc	1339	Da	
1268	Da	1304	Db	1340	Db	
1269	De	1305	Db	1341	Da	
1270	Dc	1306	Dd	1342	Dd	
1271	Dd	1307	De	1343	Da	
1272	Dv	1308	Dv	1344	Db	
1273	Da	1309	Dv	1345	Db	1327
1274	Db	1310	Dv	1346	**	
1275	Da	1311	Dn 1094	1347	**	
1276	Da	1312	Dv	1348	**	
1277	Da	1313	Da	1349	**	
1278	Dg	1314	Da	1350	Da	
1279	Db	1315	Da	1351	Da	
1280	Dg	1316	Dg	1352	Da	
1281	Dd	1317	Da	1353	Da	
1282	Db	1318	Dg	(1354)	De	1136
1283	Dd	1319	Dn	1355	Da	
1284	Dd	1320	Dk	1356	Dd	1271
1285	Df	1321	Da	1357	Dv	1226
1286	Dd	1322	De	1358	De	1136
1287	De	1323	Da	1359	Dc	
1288	Da	1324	Db	1360	Df	

1361	De	1397	Dc 1364	(1433)	De 1138
1362	De	1398	De	1434	Dv
1363	Da	1399	Dk	1435	Da
1364	Dc	1400	Da 1163	1436	Dv
1365	Da	1401	Da	1437	Da 1137
1366	Dd	1402	Dd	1438	Dg
1367	Db	1403	Dv	1439	Dv
1368	Db	1404	Dv 1330	1440	Da 1273
1369	Dc	1405	Da 1378	1441	Dv
1370	Dv	1406	Dh	1442	Dv
1371	De	(1407)	Da 1343	1443	Dv
1372	Db	1408	De 1269	1444	Dv 1190
1373	Db	1409	De	1445	Da
1374	Dd	1410	Dv	1446	Db 1105
1375	Db 1212	1411	Dv	1447	Dv
1376	Dd	1412	Dv	1448	Da 1338
1377	Dq	1413	Da 1091	1449	Dv
1378	Da	1414	Dn 1089	1450	Dv
1379	Da	1415	Da	1451	Dv
1380	Dd	<1416>	Dv	1452	Da 1350
1381	De	1417	Dv	1453	Df 1230
1382	Da	1418	Dv	1454	Dv
1383	De	1419	Dc	1455	Dc 1228
1384	Da	1420	Dv	1456	Dm 1175
1385	X	1421	Da 1164	1457	Dv
1386	Dv	1422	Dv	1458	Da 1315
1387	Dc 1359	1423	Db	1459	Dv
1388	Dv	1424	De	1460	Dv
1389	Db	1425	Dd	1461	Da
1390	Da	1426	Db	1462	Dv
1391	Db 1367	1427	Dv	1463	X
1392	Da	1428	Dv	1464	Db
1393	Dc 1337	1429	Dd	1465	Dv
1394	Dv	1430	Dv	1466	Dv
1395	Da 1313	1431	Dm 1181	1467	Da 1353
1396	Da	1432	X	1468	Dd

1469	Df	1505	Dv	1540	Ra
1470	Dv	1506	Dv	1541	Ra
1471	Dv	1507	Db	1542	Ra
1472	Dv	1508	Mc	1543	Ra
1473	De 1362	1509	Da	1544	Ra
<1474>	X	1510	De	1545	Ra
1475	Db 1373	1511	Dv	1546	Ra
1476	Dc 1203	(1512)	Dv 8289	1547	Ra
1477	Db 1265	1513	Db 1367	(1547 bis)	Ra 1814
1478	Dv	1514	Dv 1410	1548	Ra
1479	Dv	1515	Dc	1549	Ra
1480	De 1371	1516	As	1550	Ra
(1481)	X 6032	1517	As	1551	Ra
1482	Da 1382	1518	As	1552	Ra
(1483)	Dv 5054	1519	As	1553	Ra
1484	Dv 1188	1520	As	1554	Ra
1485	Da	1521	V	1555	Ra
1486	Db 1262	1522	Uf	1556	Ra
1487	Dv	1523	V	1557	Ra
1488	Dv 1370	1524	V	1558	Ra
1489	Dd 1106	1525	X	1559	Ra
1490	Dv	1526	V	1560	Ra 1543
1491	Dk	1527	Og	1561	C
1492	Dv	(1528)	Mc 1508	1562	R
1493	Dv	1529	As 1518	1563	R 1562
1494	Df 1325	1530	Ga	1564	Mc 1508
1495	Da	1531	Ga 1530	1565	Dk
1496	Dv	1532	Ga	1566	Ra 1543
1497	De 1381	1533	Ga	1567	Dk
1498	Dv 1146	1534	Ga	1568	Ln
1499	Db 1140	1535	Ga	1569	E
1500	Dv	1536	Ga	1570	**
1501	Dv	1537	X 1385	1571	Dg 672
1502	Dv	1538	X	1572	**
1503	Dv	1539	X	(1573)	X 8204
1504	Dv	(1539 bis)	U 1813	1574	E

440

(1575) Xd 314	(1611) Db 1344	1646 Dh
1576 Wb	(1612) Db 5041	1647 L
(1577) Do 996	1613 Dk	1648 De
<1578> **	(1614) Da 1343	1649 L
1579 Dd	1615 D	1650 D
1580 Lc	1616 L	1651 Sc
1581 X	1617 De 1409	(1652) Dg 8208
1582 C	1618 De	(1653) Wb 1817
1583 V	1619 Da 1392	1654 Ag
1584 Df 1469	1620 ***	
1585 De	1621 Dv	1701 Ws
1586 Dd 1579	1622 **	(1702) Ws 8494
(1587) Dc 5030	1623 **	1703 Ws
1588 Da	1624 **	1704 Ws
1589 Df	1625 **	1705 Ws
1590 Db 1389	1626 **	(1706) Ws 8152
<1591> Df	1627 **	1707 Ws
1592 Dd	1628 **	<1708> Ws
1593 Dd 1402	1629 **	1709 *
(1594) Ak 2126	(1630) E 5000	1710 *
(1595) L 2127	<1631> V	1711 *
(1596) X 2128	<1632> C 954	1712 *
(1597) D 2130	(1633) Ga 7496	1713 *
(1598) Dv 1370	(1634) B 7035	1714 Wb
<1599> L	(1635) Dl 932	(1714 b) Wb 1816
(1600) Dd 2010	(1636) Ws 1708	(1714 c) Wb 1817
1601 Dv	1637 ***	1715 (vase)
1602 Df	(1638) Dp 1061	
1603 Dq	1639 As 602	1801 X
1604 Dv 1438	1640 ***	1802 X
(1605) Dk 2129	(1640 bis) Sc 242.v	1803 Dq
1606 Db 1250	1641 X	1804 Og
1607 Dv	<1642> X	1805 Ai
(1608) Dm 1180	(1643) Dl 8103	(1806) X 7776
(1609) Da 1379	1644 Sc	1807 Ak
1610 Db	1645 M	1808 Oa

1809	K 773	2024	Dd 1207	4418	Sf
1810	K	2025	**	4419	Sf
1811	Sg	2026	Od	4420	Sf
1812	U	2027	Da	4421	Sf
1813	U			4422	Sd
1814	Ra	2126	Ak	4423	Sf
1815	R	2127	L	4424	Sf
1816	Wb	2128	X	4425	Sf
1817	Wb	2129	Dk	4426	Sf
		2130	D	4427	Sf
<1901>	X	2131	X	4428	Sf
<1902>	C	2132	X	4429	So
		2133	Wb	4430	So
2001	Wb	2134	X	4431	So
2002	X	2135	*	4432	So
2003	X	2136	*	4432 bis So 4449	
2004	Dp	2137	*	4433	So
2005	Da	2138	Np	4434	So
2006	Fh 380			4435	So
2007	Dd 1402	4401	Sd	4436	So
2008	Fh 462	4402	Sd	4437	So
2009	Am	4403	Sd	4438	So
2010	Dd	4404	Sd	4439	So
2011	X	4405	Sd	4440	So
2012	L 647	4406	Sd	4441	So
2013	Fh	4407	Sd	4442	So
2014	Fh	4408	Sd	4443	So
2015	Da 1333	4409	Sd	4444	So 4433
2016	Dn	4410	Sd 4405	4445	So
2017	Dv 1502	4411	Sd 4408	4446	So
2018	Da 1276	4412	Sd	4447	So
2019	Dv	4413	Sd	4448	So
2020	Db	4414	Sd 4407	4449	So
2021	Dl	4415	Sd	<4450>	Sd
2022	Da 1485	4416	Sd	4451	Sp
2023	Da 1435	4417	Sd 4415	4452	Sp

4453	Mc	4488	Nc	5027	C 912
4454	Mc	4489	Nc	5028	B
4455	Mc	4490	Nc	5029	B
4456	Mc	4491	Sf	5030	Dc
4457	Mc	4492	X	(5031)	X 8632
4458	Mc 4454	<4493>	As	5032	De
4459	Mc	(4494)	X 8101	5033	X
4460	Mc	4495	X	5034	*
4461	Mc			5035	**
4462	Mc	5000	E	(5036)	Ga 1534
4463	Mc	5001	F	5037	X
4464	Mc	5002	Np	5038	Da
4465	Sf	5003	Od	5039	Da 5038
4466	E	5004	Np 1000	5040	X
<4467>	Og	5005	F	5041	Db
4468	Sd	5006	X	5042	X
4469	Sd 4415	5007	Gg	5043	F
4470	Nc	5008	Np	5044	X
4471	Sf 4423	5009	Ak	(5045)	U 1813
4472	X	5010	Do	5046	Sc
4473	Nc	5011	**	5047	Np 85
4474	Nc	5012	Dd	5048	Dm 1180
4475	Nc	5013	Np	5049	Dv
4476	Sp 4451	5014	Dn	(5050)	Dh 1406
4477	Mc 4456	5015	Dn	5051	X
4478	U	5016	C 954	5052	Dv
4479	Nc	(5017)	L 771	5053	Lc
4480	Nc	5018	De	5054	Dv
4481	Sd 4409	5019	Og	5055	X
4481 bis	R 1815	5020	Ga	5056	**
4482	R	5021	Ga	5057	Sc
4483	Sd 4450	5022	Gg 707	5058	Sc
4484	Nc	5023	De 1424	5059	Sc
4485	Nc	(5024)	Db 1372	5060	Sc
4486	X	5025	B	5061	Sc
4487	X	5026	B	5062	Sc

5063	**	5099	Nc 4490	5135	Uf 838
5064	**	5100	Nc	5136	Sc
5065	Sc	5101	Da 1321	5137	Sc
5066	Sc	5102	X	5138	Sc
5067	Sc 5061	5103	Nc	5139	Sc
5068	Sc	5104	X	5140	Sc 5060
5069	Sc 103	5105	X	5141	Sc
5070	Sc	5106	Sf	5142	Sc
5071	Sc	5107	Mc	5143	Sc 5062
5072	Sc	5108	L	5144	Sc
5073	Sc	5109	Nc	5145	Sc 103
5074	Xd	5110	Nc	5146	Sc
5075	Dv	5111	X	5147	Sc 221
(5076)	Dv 1607	5112	Nc	5148	Sc
5077	Ap	5113	V	5149	Sc 135
5078	Dc 1419	5114	Sd 4403	5150	Sc
5079	F	5115	X	5151	Sc
5080	Dv 5054	5116	Dv 1621	5152	Sc 5144
(5081)	X 8536	5117	Nc	5153	Sc
5082	Od	5118	Mc	5154	Sc
5083	Sc	5119	Sf 4419	5155	Sc
5084	Sc	5120	Nc	5156	Sc
5085	Sc	5121	Nc	5157	Sc
5086	Sc	5122	Nc	5158	Sc
5087	Sc	5123	Mc 5107	5159	Sc
5088	Ga	5124	X	5160	Sc
5089	C	5125	X	5161	Sc
5090	L	5126	Nc	5162	Sc
5091	Sd	5127	So 4437	5163	Sc
5092	L	5128	Nc	5164	Sc
5093	As 40	5129	Nc	5165	Sc
5094	D	5130	Nc	5166	Sc
5095	Og	5131	Wb	5167	Sc
(5096)	Ak 643	5132	B	5168	Sc
5097	Xd	5133	B	5169	Sc
5098	Mc 4457	5134	B	5170	Sc

5171	So 1053	5207	Da 1379	5243	Da 1323
5172	B	5208	Da 5205	5244	Da
5173	X	5209	Dv	5245	Da
5174	Dd	5210	Dd 1468	5246	Fh
5175	Da 1495	5211	Df	5247	Da 1277
5176	X	5212	Db	5248	Dv
5177	Db 1225	5213	Dv	5249	Da 1396
5178	Dv	5214	Da	5250	Dc
5179	Da	5215	Dd 5174	5251	Da
5180	Dd 2010	5216	Da 1114	5252	Dv
5181	Dm	5217	Da	5253	Dv
5182	Df	5218	Da	(5254)	Dn 2016
5183	Dk	5219	Dv	5255	Da 1351
5184	Gg	5220	Da	5256	Dv
5185	Gg	5221	Dv 1113	5257	Db 5212
5186	U	5222	Df 1229	5258	Dv
5187	Mc	5223	Da	5259	Dv
5188	**	5224	Dv	5260	Df
5189	Dk 1067	5225	Da	5261	Dc 5228
5190	Dc	5226	Dm	5262	Dd
5191	Df 1325	5227	Dm 1183	5263	Db 1340
5192	Da	5228	Dc	5264	Dd 1429
5193	Dv	5229	Df 1602	5265	Dm 1174
5194	Dn 5015	5230	Da 5217	5266	Dd 2010
5195	Da	5231	Db	5267	Df 1325
5196	Df 1602	5232	Dv	5268	Dd
5197	Dv	5233	Dk	5269	Df 5238
5198	Dv	5234	Da	5270	Da
5199	Dd 1592	5235	Dv	5271	Dv
5200	Dv	5236	Dv	5272	Db
5201	Dk	5237	Dm	5273	Dv 1214
5202	De 1136	5238	Df	5274	Db
5203	Dv	(5239)	Da 5195	5275	Df
5204	Da	(5240)	Da 1189	5276	**
5205	Da	5241	Dv	5277	Dm 5237
5206	Dv 1205	5242	X	5278	Dv

5279	Dv	5315	Dv	5351	Da 1390
5280	Dg	5316	Da 1317	5352	Db
5281	Dk 5201	5317	Da	5353	De
5282	Wb	5318	Dn	5354	Da
5283	Wb	(5319)	X 8680	5355	Da 5220
5284	L	5320	*	5356	Da
5285	Dv	5321	Dv 1125	5357	Dv
5286	Dn	5322	Dv	5358	Dc 1203
5287	Dv	5323	Dm	5359	Db
5288	Dd 1376	5324	Dv 1334	5360	Dd 1366
5289	Da 1339	5325	Da 1323	5361	Xe
5290	Dm 5226	5326	X	5362	Dn 5286
5291	Dv	5327	Dd 1429	5363	**
5292	Dk 1077	5328	Dv	5364	Dm 1179
5293	Dv 5241	5329	Dv 5236	5365	Dv 5296
5294	Dv	5330	Da 5220	5366	Da 2005
5295	Da	5331	Dv 1217	5367	Db
5296	Dv	5332	Da 5308	5368	Dv
5297	Dv	(5333)	Dn 5318	5369	Da 5356
5298	Dv 1214	5334	X	5370	Dd 1193
5299	Da 5245	5335	Dv	5371	Dv 5368
5300	Dv 5256	5336	De	5372	Dv
5301	Dv	5337	Fh	5373	Dn 1089
5302	Dv	5338	Dv 5278	5374	Dm 5323
5303	Db 1126	5339	Da 1396	5375	Dm 1176
5304	Df 1360	5340	**	5376	Dv 5328
5305	Da 1379	5341	X	5377	Dv 5322
5306	Db 1204	5342	Df 1229	(5378)	Db 1155
5307	Dn 1319	5343	X	5379	Dn 1092
5308	Da	5344	Dd	5380	De 5353
5309	X	5345	Da 5204	5381	Df 5211
5310	Db	5346	Dv	5382	Da 1390
5311	Da 1315	5347	Dv 5256	5383	Dd
5312	Dv	5348	Df 5260	5384	Da 5295
5313	Df 5211	5349	Dv	5385	Db
5314	Db 2020	5350	Dv	5386	Dn 5014

5387	Dg 1438	5423	Db 2020	5459	Fh
5388	Dd 1425	5424	De 1264	5460	Fh 367
5389	Db 1211	(5425)	X 8693	5461	Fh 5432
5390	Db	5426	De 5032	5462	Fh 386
5391	Df	5427	Da	5463	Fh
5392	Dc	5428	Fh	5464	Dk
5393	Df 1222	5429	Fh	5465	Fh
5394	Db 5231	5430	Fh	5466	Fh
5395	Df 5391	5431	Fh	5467	Fh
5396	Dc 5250	5432	Fh	5468	Fh
5397	Da 1317	(5433)	Fh 8297	5469	Dq 439
5398	Dv	5434	Fh	5470	Fh 462
5399	Db	5435	Fh	5471	Fh
5400	Dg 1235	5436	Fh	5472	Fp
5401	Dg 5280	5437	Fh	5473	Fh
(5402)	Dv 8395	5438	Fh 5434	5474	Fh 372
5403	Dk	5439	Fh 2014	5475	Fh
5404	Dv 1471	5440	Fh	5476	Fh
5405	De	5441	Fh 5436	5477	Fh
5406	Df	5442	Fh	(5478)	Fh 8504
5407	Dv	5443	Fh	5479	Fh
5408	Dd 5344	5444	Fh	(5480)	Fh 8299
5409	Db 1295	5445	Fh 380	5481	Fh
5410	Dc 5392	5446	Fh	5482	Fh 5459
5411	Dv 1272	5447	Fh	5483	Fh
5412	Dv	5448	Fh 371	5484	Fh 5465
5413	Dv	5449	Fh	5485	**
5414	Dv	5450	Fh	5486	Fh
5415	So 4439	5451	Fh	5487	Fh
5416	Dv	5452	Fh	5488	Db 1208
5417	Da 1390	5453	Fh	5489	Fh 373
(5418)	X 8688	5454	Fh 5443	5490	Fh
5419	Dc 5228	5455	Fh	5491	Fh 5465
5420	De 5353	5456	Fh	(5492)	Fh 8646
(5421)	X 8665	5457	Fh	5493	Fh
5422	X	5458	Fh	5494	Fh

5495	Fh 386	5531	X	5567	Dv 1128
5496	Fh 5451	5532	E 749	5568	Dn 1319
5497	Fh	5533	Ap 618	5569	L
5498	Fh	5534	X	5570	X
5499	Fh 368	5535	Dl	5571	Dc 5228
5500	Fh 5428	5536	V	5572	Da 5192
5501	Fh	5537	X	5573	X
5502	Fh	5538	X	5574	Dv 5219
5503	Fh	5539	Og 5515	5575	V
5504	Fp	5540	Xe	5576	Da
5505	Fh	(5541)	Df 5406	5577	X
5506	Fh	5542	As	5578	X
5507	Lc 551	5543	Ai	5579	Dv
5508	Dp	5544	C	5580	Dv
5509	X	5545	D	5581	Df 5275
5510	Vc	5546	Xe	5582	L
5511	Od	5547	Ap	5583	X
5512	Dv	5548	Gg	5584	B
5513	X	5549	As	5585	Dv 5279
5514	X	(5550)	X 8650	5586	X
5515	Og	5551	Og	5587	Dc
5516	X	5552	Gg	5588	Dv 5291
5517	Dv	5553	Ak	5589	Db 5352
5518	Og 5515	5554	X	5590	Da 1313
5519	D	(5555)	X 8255	5591	Dd 1106
5520	D	5556	E	5592	U
5521	X	5557	As	5593	Dv
5522	X	5558	Od	5594	X
5523	Vc	5559	Dn	5595	Dq
5524	As 607	5560	X	5596	Da 5195
5525	X	5561	L	5597	Dk 1613
5526	K	5562	Dk 5403	5598	Dd 1592
5527	Wb	5563	Da 1495	5599	L
5528	G	5564	De 5032	5600	Xe
5529	X	5565	Db 5359	5601	Ld
5530	Dl	5566	Dk	5602	X

5603	Dv	(5639)	X 8634	5675	Dv
5604	Ak	5640	Dv	5676	Dc 5392
5605	As	(5641)	Ak 8334	5677	Dc
5606	V 655	(5642)	X 8696	5678	Dh 1406
5607	L	(5643)	X 8690	5679	De 1383
(5608)	Xe 5877	(5644)	X 8682	5680	Db
5609	As	5645	U 4478	5681	Dv 2019
(5610)	Xe 8546	5646	Le	5682	Dc 1515
5611	Ak	5647	Ld	5783	Dv 1428
5612	Lc	5648	Ak	5684	Da 1384
(5613)	Dv 8308	(5649)	X 8676	5685	De 1307
5614	Fh	(5650)	Ak 8341	5686	Dv 5232
5615	Ld	(5651)	X 8531	5687	Dc
(5616)	Da 1392	5652	**	5688	Db 1155
5617	X	5653	U	5689	Dv
5618	Dv	(5654)	V 655	5690	Dv
(5619)	L 8503	5655	Ak	5691	Dv1434
5620	Od	5656	X	5692	Dd
(5621)	Xe 8622	(5657)	Ak 5648	5693	Mc 5107
(5622)	Dv 7176	5658	Df 5391	5694	Dv
(5623)	Uf 5726	(5659)	Le 5629	(5695)	Da 1392
5624	**	5660	L	5696	Dv
(5625)	X 8292	(5661)	Le 5629	5697	Wb
(5626)	Xe 6011	5662	Wb	5698	Db 1329
(5627)	Ak 8218	5663	Dv	5699	X
(5628)	Xe 8598	5664	Wb	5700	Db 1140
5629	Le	5665	Wb	5701	Dv 1292
5630	Xe	5666	B 164	5702	Da 1384
(5631)	X 8737	5667	Dv	5703	Db 1225
(5632)	Le 5629	5668	Dn	5704	Dv
5633	Ak 619	5669	C	5705	Da 1588
5634	Da 1352	5670	Sk	5706	Dc 5677
(5635)	Ak 5648	5671	Ga 1058	5707	Da 1143
(5636)	X 8320	5672	Ga	5708	**
5637	Gg	5673	X	5709	Da
5638	Dq 5595	5674	Da 5179	5710	Db 1198

5711	Od	5747	E 1035	5783	Df 5182
5712	L 868	5748	Ap	5784	X
5713	Dc 1515	5749	B	(5785)	X 8270
5714	Db	5750	X	5786	Mc 4459
5715	Db	5751	X	5787	Nc
5716	X	5752	B	5788	Gm
5717	U	5753	C	5789	So
5718	B 1025	5754	Ch	5790	So 4429
5719	As	5755	Am	5791	De 1409
5720	Do	5756	X	5792	Mc 4462
5721	Uf	5757	L	(5793)	X 8624
5722	Fh	5758	Od	5794	So 4448
5723	Fh	5759	X	5795	U 4478
5724	Ch	5760	Ch 1029	5796	X
5725	Np	5761	B 988	(5797)	Fp 1
5726	Uf	5762	Dq 439	5798	Mc 4453
5727	X	5763	X	5799	B
5728	Ch	5764	C 922	5800	***
5729	Se	5765	C	(5801)	X 435
5730	X	5766	V 1002	5802	X 450
5731	Dk	5767	Ak 634	(5803)	Sd 4408
5732	X	5768	Dk	5804	So 4432
5733	Dk	(5769)	X 8319	5805	L
5734	C	5770	Do	5806	Ga 419
5735	Dv	5771	Dc	5807	Da 1445
5736	Ga	5772	Nc	5808	Mc 4462
5737	X	5773	Da 1321	5809	Mc
5738	Uf 1031	5774	X	5810	D
5739	E 487	5775	Dv	5811	Dc 1220
5740	Do	5776	Ga 1536	5812	Dv
5741	Ak	5777	L 588	5813	Pp 493
5742	X 974	5778	Og	5814	Sf 4419
5743	X	5779	Nc 4473	5815	Sf 4423
5744	C 989	5780	Ga	5816	Mc 4462
5745	L	5781	Mc 4461	(5817)	X 8275
5746	Lc	5782	So 4441	5818	Mc

5819	**	5855	**	5891	Xe
5820	Mc	5856	**	5892	Ak 619
(5821)	Wb 1816	5857	Wb	5893	Ak
5822	Wb	5858	Wb	5894	Ld
(5823)	Mc 4454	(5859)	Wb 8488	5895	Ak 5741
5824	Wb	5860	Wb	5896	Ak
5825	X	(5861)	Wb 8491	5897	X
5826	Dv	(5862)	Wb 8492	5898	X
5827	**	5863	As 604	5899	Xe
5828	**	5864	Ap	5900	Xe
5829	**	5865	V 655	5901	Ap 5748
5830	Wb	5866	As 609	5902	Am 5882
5831	Wb	5867	Le 5629	5903	Le
5832	X	5868	Ap	5904	X
5833	Dm 1176	5869	As 605	5905	Xe
(5834)	Dm 5323	5870	As 625	5906	Db 1368
5835	Wb	5871	Xe 5540	5907	Ak
5836	Wb	5872	V	5908	As
5837	Wb	5873	Ld 5615	5909	L
5838	Xd	5874	**	5910	L
5839	Dv	5875	Lc 646	5911	As 605
(5840)	Nc 8276	5876	Ak	5912	Le 5646
5841	Dv	5877	Xe	5913	Xe
(5842)	Dv 8637	5878	**	5914	L
5843	Dv	5879	Ak	5915	V 652
(5844)	Da 8355	5880	As	5916	Ld
5845	Ld	5881	X	5917	L
5846	Od	5882	Am	5918	Ak
5847	Db 1426	(5883)	C 8578	5919	D
(5848)	X 8660	5884	Ak	5920	L 5910
5849	Ai	5885	Lc 5612	5921	Xe 5913
(5850)	Dv 8429	5886	Np 5725	5922	Ap 618
5851	**	5887	Xe	5923	Ap 5748
5852	**	5888	As	5924	L
5853	**	5889	X	(5925)	B 799
5854	**	(5890)	Am 600	5926	Ak

451

5927	L	5963	Ak 619	5999	As 5605
5928	Ak 5876	5964	X	6000	L 5924
(5929)	C 7698	(5965)	X 8261	6001	Fh
5930	Le	5966	Od	6002	L
5931	As 605	5967	Ak 5648	6003	Le 5930
5932	As	5968	X	6004	X
5933	Ak 5926	5969	Xd	6005	Ch 5724
5934	Dv	5970	Fh	6006	X
5935	Ap 628	5971	Ak 5876	6007	L 5909
5936	X	(5972)	X 8324	6008	X
5937	Le 5903	5973	Uf	6009	Ch 5754
5938	Ch	5974	L 647	6010	Ak 619
5939	L 5909	5975	Ch 5754	6011	Xe
5940	Ak	5976	Ai	6012	Le 5646
5941	As	5977	So 4446	6013	As 5944
5942	As 625	5978	Dv 1607	6014	Le
5943	L 647	5979	X	6015	Lc 646
5944	As	5980	Np	6016	Dl 414
5945	Np	5981	As	6017	Db 1344
5946	V	5982	Np	6018	Dv
5947	F 853	5983	As 5880	6019	So 4429
5948	Ak	5984	B	6020	Xe
5949	L	5985	C	6021	C
5950	Le 642	5986	X 5751	6022	Dv
5951	**	5987	L	6023	Da 1132
5952	X	5988	V 655	6024	Ld 583
5953	Uf 5726	5989	Dv	6025	Dv
5954	D	5990	X	6026	Xe
5955	Ld	5991	Dq 442	6027	Uf 121
5956	As	5992	L 593	6028	Ak 620
(5957)	L 8246	5993	Le 5646	6029	X
5958	V 1003	(5994)	Xe 8260	6030	X
(5959)	Dv 8290	5995	**	6031	Xe 5877
5960	X	5996	As 607	6032	X
5961	L	(5997)	Ak 8218	(6033)	Ap 5868
5962	X	5998	L	6034	X

6035	F 853	7001	Ak	7037	B
6036	**	7002	Ak	7038	B 1025
6037	Ak 5009	7003	Ak	7039	B 5752
6038	As	7004	Ak 780	(7040)	B 988
6039	X	7005	Ak	7041	B
(6040)	Ai 5976	7006	Ak	7042	B
(6041)	X 8515	7007	Ak	7043	B
6042	B	7008	Ak	7044	B
(6043)	C 5734	7009	Ak	7045	Ak 780
(6044)	Dv 8382	7010	Ak	7046	C 5753
6045	Dv	7011	Ak 783	7047	Ch
(6046)	Np 8457	7012	Ak	7048	C
(6047)	Db 8352	7013	Ak	7049	V
<6048>	Ak	7014	Ai	7050	F
6049	**	7015	Ak	7051	C 979
6050	**	7016	Ak	7052	C 979
(6051)	Wb 8207	7017	Ai	7053	C 1044
6052	**	7018	Ak	7054	C
6053	B 806	7019	Ak	7055	C 1030
6054	Dv	7020	Ak	7056	Co
6055	Sd 4408	7021	Ak	7057	C
6056	Dv	7022	Ak	7058	C
6057	Dv	7023	Ai	7059	C
6058	Wb	7024	Ak	7060	C
6059	Dv	7025	Ak 627	7061	Ce
6060	De	7026	Ai	7062	C
6061	Da	7027	Ai	7063	U
6062	Db 5310	7028	Ak	7064	C
6063	Db 5367	7029	Ai	7065	Ch
6064	Da 5218	7030	Ak	7066	Ch
6065	Da 1189	7031	Ak	7067	C
6066	Sd 5091	7032	Am 827	(7067 bis)	Dc 8080
6067	As 5609	7033	Ag 88	7068	De 1510
6068	Ak 5876	7034	B	7069	Dl 794
		7035	B	7070	Db 1464
7000	Ag	7036	B	7071	Dl

7072	D1	7108	Db	7144	Dk
7073	X	7109	Da	7145	D1 949
7074	Da 1415	7110	Db 1165	7146	D
7075	D1	7111	Dv 7098	7147	D1
7076	D1	7112	Da 1392	7148	De 1398
7077	Da 1509	7113	Dq	7149	Dv
7078	Df 5275	7114	D1	7150	Dv 1460
7079	Do	7115	De 1371	7151	Dd 1380
7080	Da	7116	D1	7152	Dv
7081	Da	7117	Dk	7153	Da 1253
7082	D1 934	7118	Db	7154	Dc 5687
7083	Dq 1603	7119	Dq	7155	De 1398
7084	Do 5010	7120	Do	7156	Dc 1369
7085	D1	7121	Da 1173	7157	Dc 5190
7086	D1	7122	D	7158	Dd 1296
7087	Do	7123	Dd 1468	7159	Dd 7105
7088	C	7124	Dv	7160	Da 5576
7089	Dv 5301	7125	D1	7161	Dc
7090	Da	7126	Dq	7162	Db 1262
7091	Da 1461	7127	D	7163	Dc
7092	D1	7128	Dh	7164	Db
7093	Do	7129	D1 7114	7165	Da
7094	X	7130	D	7166	Da 7109
7095	Db 5352	7131	*	7167	Dv
7096	De	7132	D1	7168	Db 1168
7097	Dv 1417	7133	Co 909	7169	Da 1164
7098	Dv	7134	D	7170	Dd
7099	Dv 1492	7135	Dp	7171	De 1618
7100	Ch	7136	B 164	7172	Db
7101	D	7137	Dq	7173	Df
7102	D	7138	D1	7174	De 1618
7103	D	7139	Wb	7175	Dv 1267
7104	Lc 541	7140	Dv	7176	Dv
7105	Dd	7141	D1	7177	Dq
7106	Dd	7142	Dv	7178	Da 1123
7107	Db	7143	Lc 527	7179	Dc 7161

7180	Dv 5704	7216	Db 1245	7252	D		
7181	Dv	7217	Dc 5587	7253	Do 7093		
7182	Da 1135	7218	X	7254	D		
7183	Dv 1503	7219	*	7255	Dv 5054		
7184	Da 5223	7220	Da 1435	7256	Da 1365		
7185	Da	7221	De 1294	7257	Da 5179		
7186	Da	7222	Da 1143	7258	Dv 1447		
7187	Da 1161	7223	Dv	7259	X		
7188	Df	7224	Dv 5989	7260	Dq		
7189	Dv 1370	7225	Db 1426	7261	Dq 1234		
7190	Dv	7226	Db 1165	7262	Dv		
7191	Df 1187	7227	Dv 7181	7263	De 5336		
7192	Da 1079	7228	Dv 1496	7264	D1 7141		
7193	Dv 1511	7229	Db 7118	7265	De 1510		
7194	Dc 1167	7230	Dv 5372	7266	Dq 1234		
7195	Dv	7231	Dh	7267	Dv		
7196	Dv 5235	7232	Gg	7268	Db 1344		
7197	Db 1389	7233	Da 1588	7269	Dv		
7198	Dv 1511	7234	Dc 5587	7270	Dv		
7199	De 1398	7235	Do 996	7271	Da 7165		
7200	Dv	7236	Da 1156	7272	Dv		
7201	De 5336	7237	Db 5212	7273	Dq 1026		
7202	Dv	7238	D1	7274	Db 5715		
7203	De	7239	Do	7275	Db 5352		
7204	Dk	7240	Dv	7276	Dv 1607		
7205	Dv 5193	7241	Dv 1420	7277	Dc 1220		
7206	Dp 997	7242	D	7278	Dd 659		
7207	Dv 5398	7243	D	7279	D1 7132		
7208	Db 1126	7244	Dv 1496	7280	Dp		
7209	Dc 5687	7245	Dv	7281	D1 1046		
7210	Dc 7163	7246	Dv	7282	D1 7249		
7211	Db	7247	Da 1384	7283	D1		
7212	De 1153	7248	Dv	7284	D1 930		
7213	Da	7249	D1	7285	Lc		
7214	Db 5359	7250	Ce 283	7286	Ga		
7215	Dv 1267	7251	D	7287	D1		

7288	D1	7324	Od	7360	F
7289	Lc	7325	Dk	7361	F 193
7290	D1 930	7326	Od	7362	F
7291	D1 932	7327	Dk	7363	K
7292	D1 794	7328	Dk	7364	G
7293	Dk 931	7329	Dk	7365	Ga
7294	Dk 920	7330	Dk 920	7366	Ga 423
7295	Dk	7331	Lc 527	7367	Ga
7296	Od 539	7332	D1 7085	7368	Ga 7367
7297	Dk	7333	D1 930	7369	Gg
7298	Od	7334	D	7370	Gg 995
7299	Dk	7335	Fh 5436	7371	Gg
7300	Dk	7336	Fh	7372	Gg
7301	Dk	7337	F	7373	M
7302	Od	7338	E	7374	Oa
7303	Dk	7339	E	7375	X
7304	Dk	7340	E	7376	Lc
7305	Od	7341	E 847	7377	Lc
7306	Dk	7342	F 7050	7378	Ld 787
7307	Od	7343	F	7379	Lc 553
7308	Dk	7344	Ga	7380	L
7309	Od	7345	F	7381	Lc 550
7310	Od	7346	F	7382	L
7311	Dk	7347	Ga	7383	Lc 536
7312	Od	7348	F 153	7384	Lc 530
7313	Dk	7349	E 1569	7385	Lc 7377
7314	Dk	7350	E	7386	X
7315	Dk	7351	X	7387	L
7316	Dk	7352	G	7388	Od
7317	Od	7353	K	7389	L
7318	Lc	7354	E	7390	L
7319	Lc	7355	G	7391	L
7320	Od 765	7356	F	7392	Lc
7321	Lc	7357	F	7393	L
7322	Dk	7358	Ga	7394	Lc
7323	Dk	7359	F	7395	Lc 7289

7396	L	7432	Og	7468	Sc	
7397	Lc 551	7433	Lc	7469	Sc	
7398	Lc 7392	7434	Np 855	7470	Sc	
7399	L	7435	Og	7471	Sc	
7400	L	7436	Np 278	7472	Sc 7469	
7401	L	7437	Xe	7473	Sc	
7402	L 7400	7438	Lc	7474	Sc	
7403	L	7439	Np	7475	Sc	
7404	L	7440	Og	(7475 bis)	Sc 8081	
7405	L	7441	Np	7476	Sc	
7406	L	7442	Np	7477	Sc 5169	
7407	L	7443	Og	7478	Sc	
7408	L	7444	Sc	7479	Sc	
7409	L	7445	Np	7480	Sc	
7410	L	7446	Ga	7481	Sc	
7411	L	7447	Np	7482	Sc 5144	
7412	L 515	7448	Pp 494	7483	Sc	
7413	L	7449	Se	7484	Sc 248	
7414	L	7450	Sf	7485	Sg 1811	
7415	L	7451	Sf	7486	Uf	
7416	L	7452	Sc	7487	Uf	
7417	Np	7453	Sc	7488	Uf	
7418	Np	7454	Sc	7489	Uf	
7419	Np 272	7455	Sc	7490	Uf	
7420	Np	7456	Sc	7491	Uf	
7421	Np	7457	Sc	7492	Uf	
7422	Np	7458	Sc 7455	7493	Uf	
7423	Np	7459	Sc	7494	Uf	
7424	Np	7460	Sc	7495	Uf	
7425	Ga	7461	Sc	7496	Ga	
7426	Ga	7462	Sc	7497	L	
7427	B 5584	7463	Sc	7498	Ra	
7428	Ga 1021	7464	Sc	7499	U 109	
7429	Ga	7465	Sc 254	7500	L 7380	
7430	Og	7466	Sc	7501	U	
7431	Ga	7467	Sc	7502	X	

7503	D1	7539	V	7575	Vc
7504	Og	7540	Vc	7576	X
7505	U	7541	D	7577	V
7506	*	7542	F	7578	L
7507	U	7543	C 7064	7579	Xd 143
7508	Np	7544	B 164	7580	X
7509	G	7545	Xd	7581	X
7510	Xd	7546	X	7582	X
7511	X	7547	Xd	7583	X
7512	V	7548	X	7584	X
7513	V	7549	Lc	7585	X
7514	L	7550	X	7586	Xd
7515	C	7551	X	7587	Lc 560
7516	C	7552	X	7588	Xd
7517	Vc	7553	X	7589	X
7518	Vc	7554	X	7590	Xd
7519	V	7555	Xd	7591	Gg 995
7520	Vc	7556	X	7592	X
7521	Dv 5193	7557	X	7593	B 801
7522	X	7558	Xd	7594	Ga
7523	V	7559	X	7595	Xd
7524	V	7560	X	7596	Xd
7525	G	7561	V 118	7597	Xd
7526	V 865	7562	X	7598	Xd
7527	V	7563	Do 924	7599	X
7528	X	7564	X	7600	X 5040
7529	Vc	7565	X	7601	B 988
7530	V 1005	7566	X	7602	Od 539
7531	Vc	7567	V 1005	7603	X
7532	Vc	7568	Xd	7604	Xd
7533	Vc	7569	X	7605	Ai 7023
7534	Vc	7570	Xd	7606	Xd
7535	Ak 783	7571	Fh	7607	Xd
7536	Sc 5169	7572	X	7608	X
7537	Vc	7573	X	7609	Xd
7538	**	7574	X	7610	Xd

7611	X	7647	Lc 534	7683	Dc 1154
7612	Vc	7648	Xd	7684	Da 1143
7613	Do	7649	Xd	7685	Dc 1122
7614	Xd	7650	V 1002	7686	Dv 1308
7615	Xd	7651	Xd	7687	Da 1275
7616	Xd	7652	Vc 7537	7688	Dv 7240
7617	Dv	7653	De 7096	7689	Df 1121
7618	Am 827	7654	Xd	7690	Dv
7619	Dl 792	7655	X	7691	Sc 250
7620	V	7656	Xd	7692	X
7621	X	7657	C 979	7693	X
7622	X	7658	Xd	7694	Dv
7623	X	7659	X	7695	X
7624	V 150	7660	Dl 949	7696	X
7625	Ch 1029	7661	C 901	7697	Dv
7626	Dl 947	7662	Xd	7698	C
7627	X	7663	Xd	7699	X
7628	X	7664	Xd	7700	*
7629	X	7665	Xd	7701	Xd
7630	C 5753	7666	Dc 1167	7702	Xd
7631	X	7667	Xd	7703	Ch 7100
7632	X	7668	X	7704	B 7035
7633	X	7669	X	7705	B 7034
7634	Xd	7670	V	7706	X
7635	X	7671	Dl 7138	7707	X
7636	B 816	7672	X	7708	X
7637	Da 1343	7673	X	7709	V 1043
7638	Dl 7503	7674	Xd	7710	X
7639	Ch 897	7675	Xd	7711	Xe
7640	Xd	7676	Xd	7712	X
7641	Np 7423	7677	X	7713	Wb
7642	X	7678	Dv	7714	V 7512
7643	X	7679	Df 1360	7715	X
7644	X	7680	Xd	7716	V 7512
7645	De 1138	7681	Db 1327	7717	X
7646	Xd	7682	X	7718	Gg 708

7719	V 114	7755	X 744	7791	X
7720	X	7756	Xd	7792	X
7721	Dl	7757	Xd	7793	X
7722	X	7758	X	7794	X
7723	Sf	7759	X	7795	X
7724	D 7134	7760	X	7796	X
7725	X	7761	Xd	7797	V
7726	Xd	7762	X	7798	Sc
7727	D	7763	X	7799	X
7728	X	7764	Gg 995	7800	Sc 5058
7729	C 917	7765	X	7801	X
7730	X	7766	Xd	7802	Xd
(7731)	Lc 536	7767	Ak 780	7803	Vc 201
7732	X	7768	X	7804	X
7733	Xd	7769	Ga 677	7805	Xe
7734	V 7577	7770	X	7806	V 756
7735	X	7771	Dl	7807	Xd
7736	Dv	7772	Sc	7808	Xd
7737	X	7773	X	7809	Xd
7738	Wb 7713	7774	X	7810	X
7739	X	7775	X	7811	Xd
7740	Do	7776	X	7812	X
7741	X	7777	Dv	7813	Xd
7742	Dp	7778	X	7814	X
7743	X	7779	Od	7815	Lc 560
7744	X	7780	Xd	7816	X
7745	Ai	7781	Dk	7817	X
7746	V 7670	7782	Sc	7818	Lc 534
7747	V 1583	7783	Xd	7819	X
7748	F	7784	X	7820	X
7749	X	7785	Dv	7821	Sc
7750	X	7786	Xd 7610	7822	X
7751	Sk	7787	Fh 5447	7823	X .
7752	X	7788	Ca	7824	X
7753	X	7789	X	7825	Sc 5058
7754	X	7790	Xd	7826	Xe

7827	X	7863	Dv	7899	Dk
7828	X	7864	Dl 7138	7900	X
7829	X	7865	X	7901	Lc
7830	X	7866	L	7902	Dk
7831	Dk 7306	7867	Ai	7903	De 7096
7832	X	7868	V 482	7904	Dv
7833	L	7869	Do 924	7905	Dl
7834	L	7870	Sg 1811	7906	Xd
7835	Co 909	7871	Dl 932	7907	Wb
7836	X	7872	X	7908	Dv
7837	Vc	7873	X	7909	X
7838	Xd	7874	Ga 7367	7910	X
7839	V	7875	X	7911	Dv
7840	Xd	7876	X	7912	Ch 898
7841	Xd	7877	C 7059	7913	Xd
7842	Xd	7878	X	7914	Xd
7843	E 1569	7879	G 7509	7915	Np 856
7844	Og 7504	7880	X	7916	X
7845	X	7881	Db 7118	7917	Np 856
7846	X	7882	Sc	7918	X
7847	Dl 7503	7883	Ai	7919	Dh 1646
7848	X	7884	X	7920	Se
7849	Sc	7885	Dv 7248	7921	X
7850	Xe	7886	Xd 7649	7922	C 7058
7851	Dl 7147	7887	V 1583	7923	Np
7852	Dq	7888	X	7924	X
7853	E 5000	7889	Sc	7925	B 7043
7854	X 7848	7890	Ai	7926	X
7855	Ai 966	7891	X	7927	Od
7856	Ai 966	7892	C 7698	7928	Xd 5097
7857	Xe	7893	X 7628	7929	X
7858	Ak	7894	X	7930	X
7859	B	7895	X	7931	X 7918
7860	X	7896	Fh 5449	7932	X
7861	X	7897	X	7933	Xd
7862	X	7898	Da 5223	7934	Dv

7935	X	7971	D1 7141	8007	X
7936	X	7972	X	8008	Co 904
7937	Ch	7973	X 7677	8009	X
7938	Np 85	7974	Xd	8010	X
7939	X	7975	Xd	8011	X
7940	V	7976	X	8012	Xd
7941	Xd	7977	X 7635	8013	X
7942	Db 5715	7978	Xd	8014	X 7707
7943	Xd	7979	X	8015	L 764
7944	X	7980	De 5018	8016	Lc 7377
7945	Xd	7981	X	8017	X
7946	Dv 7240	7982	Xd	8018	Dk
7947	X	7983	Xd	8019	X
7948	Xd	7984	D1 7141	8020	V 210
7949	Xd	7985	X	8021	Xd
7950	Db 1344	7986	Xd	8022	L 192
7951	Dv 5841	7987	Fh 5435	8023	L 759
7952	Ai	7988	Xe	8024	X
7953	Xd 7813	7989	X	8025	X
7954	Xd	7990	X 7891	8026	X
7955	X	7991	X	(8026 bis) Xd 8082	
7956	Xd	7992	Db 1327	8027	X 8013
7957	Xd 7702	7993	Dv 5812	8028	F 7360
7958	Dv 5301	7994	X	8029	X
7959	D1	7995	X	8030	Xd
7960	X 7643	7996	X	8031	X
7961	Xd	7997	C 989	8032	Xd
7962	Ai	7998	Da 1401	8033	X 8031
7963	De 1381	7999	X	8034	Xd
7964	V	8000	X	8035	X
7965	X	8001	X	8036	V 57
7966	X	8002	D1 930	8037	Xd
7967	Np	8003	Np	8038	Og .
7968	Xd	8004	E 1569	8039	X
7969	Ai 7962	8005	Ga	8040	E
7970	Xd	8006	B	8041	E 5000

462

8042	X	8078	**	8130	Xd
8043	X	8079	**	8131	U 7507
8044	X	8080	Dc	8132	Xd
8045	Lc 541	8081	Sc	8133	X
8046	Dh 1406	8082	Xd	8134	Xd
8047	Dp 937			8135	Xd
8048	Sc 5154	8100	Sk	8136	Xd 82
8049	C 901	8101	X	8137	Xd
8050	X	8102	Ga 427	8138	Xd
8051	X	8103	Dl	8139	Xd
8052	X	8104	X	8140	Uf 121
8053	Gg	8105	L	8141	Uf
8054	Xd	8106	Nc	8142	Uf 7489
8055	X	8107	X	8143	X
8056	Xd	8108	X	8144	Nc
8057	Np 85	8109	X	8145	Nc
8058	L	8110	X 7566	8146	Nc
8059	Np	8111	X	8147	X
8060	Xd	8112	X	8148	X
8061	Xd	8113	X	8149	Sk
8062	Xd	8114	X	8150	Og
8063	X	8115	*	8151	Dv
8064	X	8116	**	8152	Ws
8065	B 1025	8117	**	8153	Ws
8066	X	8118	**	8154	X
8067	B 814	8119	**	8155	X
8068	X	8120	B 164	8156	X
8069	Ch 898	8121	Xd 149	8157	As 603
8070	X	8122	E	8158	X
8071	X	8123	Np	8159	L
8072	X	8124	Sc	8160	L
8073	V 865	8125	Sc	8161	As
8074	X	8126	X	8162	Ap 5547
8075	Lc 540	8127	Xd	8163	L
8076	**	8128	Xd	8164	X
8077	**	8129	Xd	8165	L 8159

8166	X	8202	Od	8238	Db 5274
8167	X	8203	Dv	8239	Dv
8168	X	<8204>	X	8240	De 1361
8169	Ld 649	<8205>	X	8241	Dv
8170	M	8206	B	8242	F
8171	X	8207	Wb	8243	Gg 5637
8172	Nc	8208	Dq	8244	K
8173	Nc	8209	Dk	8245	Ld
8174	D	8210	U	8246	L
8175	Nc	8211	X	8247	L 5607
8176	Nc	8212	X	8248	Ld 5615
8177	D1	8213	X	8249	Np
8178	Nc 5787	8214	X	8250	L 7400
8179	Nc 5130	8215	X	8251	So
8180	Nc 5103	8216	D1	8252	Nc 4480
8181	Nc	8217	D1	8253	Sc
8182	X	8218	Ak	8254	Sk
8183	Nc	8219	Ak 5926	8255	X
8184	Nc 5100	8220	Ap 5868	8256	Ce 152
8185	Nc 4489	8221	As 5880	8257	As 607
8186	Nc	8222	Ch	8258	Ak 619
8187	Nc	8223	C 7698	8259	F 5079
8188	Nc	8224	C 5734	8260	Xe
8189	Dm 5226	8225	C	8261	X
8190	X	8226	C 7064	8262	Ld 587
8191	X	8227	Da 5195	8263	X 976
8192	Ld	8228	Da	8264	Mc 4457
8193	Dv	8229	D1	8265	X
8194	Dc 5190	8230	De 7203	8266	X
8195	X	8231	Dv 7202	8267	X
8196	X	8232	Dv	8268	Ai 5976
8197	Dv	8233	Db 1196	8269	Da 5223
8198	X	8234	De 1264	8270	X
8199	L 7403	8235	Db 1344	8271	Sc
8200	Da 1221	8236	Dv	8272	X
8201	Da	8237	Dc 1515	8273	X

8274	Xe	8310	L 592	8346	Ce
8275	X	8311	X 5881	8347	Co
8276	Nc	8312	X	8348	C 7062
8277	X	8313	Nc	8349	D
8278	Dv	8314	X	8350	D
8279	Xd	8315	Nc	8351	Dq
8280	Dv	8316	Dv 1500	8352	Db
8281	Dv 7176	8317	Nc	8353	X
8282	X	8318	Nc	8354	Dc
8283	X	8319	X	8355	Da
8284	X	8320	X	8356	Dv
8285	V 52	8321	Sf 4424	8357	Dv
8286	X	8322	X	8358	Dv 6018
8287	Dv	8323	X	8359	Dv 5407
8288	Dv	8324	X	8360	Db
8289	Dv	8325	X	8361	Dv
8290	Dv	8326	X	8362	Dv
8291	Xe	8327	X	8363	Dv
8292	X	8328	X	8364	Db 7172
8293	X	8329	X	8365	Dc 7161
8294	Dv	8330	X	8366	Dv
8295	X	8331	Dv 5696	8367	Dv
8296	X	8332	Dv	8368	Dv
8297	Fh	8333	D	8369	Dv
8298	X	8334	Ak	8370	Dv
8299	Fh	8335	Ak 8334	8371	Df 5406
8300	Nc	8336	Ak 8218	8372	Df 1210
8301	X	8337	Ak	8373	Dv 7863
8302	Dv	8338	Ak	8374	Db 5715
(8303)	Gg 5637	8339	Ak 781	8375	Db 5310
8304	L 7409	8340	Ak	8376	Db 1274
8305	Mc 4464	8341	Ak	8377	Da
8306	B 799	8342	As	8378	So 4431
8307	Am 600	8343	As 5941	8379	Dv 1447
8308	Dv	8344	Ch 1015	8380	Db 7107
8309	Nc	8345	Ce	8381	Dv

8382	Dv	8418	De 7203	8454	Nc	
8383	Dv	8419	Dv	8455	Nc	
8384	Dv	8420	Dv	8456	Nc	
8385	Dv	8421	Dv	8457	Np	
8386	Dv 5232	8422	Dv	8458	Np	
8387	Dv	8423	Dv	8459	Np	
8388	Dn 5318	8424	De 1307	8460	Np 8123	
8389	Dv 1100	8425	So 4436	8461	Np 7923	
8390	*	8426	Dv 8383	8462	Np	
8391	Dv	8427	Db 7107	8463	Dk	
8392	Dv	8428	Db 1160	8464	Dk	
8393	Dv 1334	8429	Dv	8465	Od	
8394	Dv	8430	Dv 1100	8466	Og	
8395	Dv	8431	Dv 5412	8467	Sc	
8396	Dv	8432	Dv	8468	Sc	
8397	Dv 6054	8433	Dv	8469	Sc	
8398	Dv	8434	Dv	8470	Sc	
8399	Da 8377	8435	E	8471	Sc	
8400	Da	8436	Fh	8472	Sc	
8401	Dv	8437	F	8473	Sc 7470	
8402	Dv 7863	8438	Ga	8474	Sc	
8403	Dk	8439	Ga	8475	Sc	
8404	Dv	8440	K	8476	Sc	
8405	Dv	8441	L	8477	Se	
8406	Dv	8442	L 7578	8478	Sc	
8407	Dn 2016	8443	L	8479	Sc	
8408	Dm 1184	8444	Ak	8480	Sc	
8409	Dv	8445	L 8443	8481	Sc	
8410	Dv	8446	Le 5629	8482	Sc	
8411	Dd 5383	8447	Mc	8483	Sc	
8412	Dv 8332	8448	Mc	8484	Sg	
8413	Dv	8449	Mc 4455	8485	Uf	
8414	Dc 5687	8450	Mc 4462	8486	Uf	
8415	Dv 8383	(8451)	Mc 4454	8487	V	
8416	Dd 1144	8452	Mc	8488	Wb	
8417	Db 7108	8453	Nc	8489	Wb	

8490	Wb	8526	Xe	8562	X
8491	Wb	8527	X	8563	Xe
8492	Wb	8528	X	8564	X
8493	Ws	8529	F 7748	8565	Xe 8537
8494	Ws	8530	X	8566	Xd
8495	Ws	8531	X	8567	X
8496	Ws	8532	X	8568	Sc 7782
8497	Ws	8533	X	8569	So 4431
8498	Ws	8534	Dk 7204	8570	X
8499	Ws	8535	X	8571	X
8500	Ws	8536	X	8572	Lc
8501	Xd	8537	Xe	8573	V 117
8502	X	8538	X	8574	As 5549
8503	L	8539	Uf 5726	8575	X
8504	Fh	8540	X	8576	So 4445
8505	Xd	8541	So 4441	8577	X
8506	X	8542	X	8578	C
8507	V 655	8543	X	8579	Xe 8537
8508	Xd	8544	Sd	8580	X
8509	X	8545	X	8581	X
8510	Xd	8546	Xe	8582	Ga 992
8511	Xd	8547	Dv 8383	8583	Xd
8512	Le 5629	8548	Da 1384	8584	X
8513	Dd 1144	8549	X	8585	Dv
8514	X	8550	X	8586	Nc
8515	X	8551	X 8261	8587	L 593
8516	Xe	8552	X	8588	Ak 5009
8517	Lc 646	8553	Xd	8589	As 609
8518	X	8554	Mc 4455	8590	X
8519	X	8555	X	8591	X
8520	X	8556	Da 5179	8592	Xe
8521	Xe 5877	8557	X	8593	Xe
8522	Le 5629	8558	Ap 5748	8594	Xd
8523	X	8559	Le 5629	8595	X
8524	X	8560	X	8596	Xd
8525	Xd	8561	X	8597	Xd

8598	Xe	8634	X	8670	X
8599	Xe 6011	8635	Xd	8671	Db 1160
8600	Dv 5258	8636	Dv	8672	X
8601	Dv 5200	8637	Dv	8673	X 5732
8602	X 5962	8638	X	8674	X
8603	X	8639	V 7049	8675	X
8604	X	8640	Xd	8676	X
8605	Xd	8641	X	8677	X
8606	Ak 5648	8642	Sc 5166	8678	X
8607	X	8643	Xd	8679	X
8608	Dd 1380	8644	Ce 8346	8680	X
8609	X	8645	X	8681	Db 5274
8610	X	8646	Fh	8682	X
8611	X	8647	X	8683	Dc 5687
8612	X	8648	X	8684	Lc 7394
8613	Mc 4464	8649	X	8685	X
8614	X	8650	X	8686	X
8615	X	8651	X	8687	Ak 619
8616	X	8652	X	8688	X
8617	X	8653	Xd	8689	X
8618	Dh 7128	8654	X 7556	8690	X
8619	*	8655	X	8691	Ld 8245
8620	Sc 7471	8656	X	8692	X
8621	X	8657	X	8693	X
8622	Xe	8658	X	8694	X
8623	Ak 5893	8659	X	8695	X
8624	X	8660	X	8696	X
8625	X	8661	*	8697	X 8674
8626	X	8662	Ai 7026	8698	X
8627	X	8663	X	8699	X
8628	X	8664	X	8700	So 4440
8629	Dm 5323	8665	X	8701	Sp 4451
8630	X	8666	V 961	8702	So 4440
8631	X 5750	8667	Ak 5940	8703	Mc 5809
8632	X	8668	X	8704	Dv 7190
8633	Sc 7471	8669	X	8705	Mc

8706	So 4441	8742	Dv
(8707)	Mc 4454	8743	X
8708	Mc	8744	X
8709	X	8745	X
8710	Dv 8280	8746	X
8711	Wb	8747	X
8712	Ws	8748	Xd
8713	Ws	8749	Dv 5398
8714	X	8750	X
8715	Dv	8751	X
8716	Dv	8752	Ws
8717	Dv	8753	Ws
8718	X	8754	Ws
8719	X		
8720	X		
8721	X		
8722	Od		
8723	Sc		
8724	Xe		
8725	X		
8726	X		
8727	X		
8728	Nc		
8729	Ld 8245		
8730	Da 1365		
8731	X		
8732	Xd		
8733	X		
8734	Xd		
8735	X		
8736	X		
8737	X		
8738	X		
8739	X		
8740	X		
8741	X		

a	jo	nu	ra₂	ti	22
a₂	ka	nwa	ra₃	to	34
a₃	ke	o	re	tu	35
au	ki	pa	ri	twe	47
da	ko	pe	ro	two	49
de	ku	pi	ro₂	u	56
di	ma	po	ru	wa	63
do	me	pte	sa	we	64
du	mi	pu	se	wi	65
dwe	mo	pu₂	si	wo	79
dwo	mu	qa	so	za	82
e	na	qe	su	ze	83
i	ne	qi	ta	zo	84
ja	ni	qo	ta₂	18	86
je	no	ra	te	19	89

IDEOGRAPHIC SIGNS

AES	HAS(ta)	TUN(ica)
ARB(or)	HORD(eum)	VAS See *202-*229
ARC(us)	JAC(ulum)	VIN(um)
AROM(aticum) s	LANA	VIR
BIG(ae)	LUNA	WEIGHTS AND MEASURES
BOS	MUL(ier)	L
CAP(er)	OLE(um)	M
CAPS(us)	OLIV(a)	N
CORN(u)	OVIS	P
CROC(us)	PUG(io)	Q
CUR(rus)	PYC	S
CYP(erus)	ROTA	T
EQU(us)	SAG(itta)	V
FAR	SUS	Z
GAL(ea)	TELA[1]	

*134	*177	*211^{VAS}
*146	*178	*212^{VAS}
*150	*179	*213^{VAS}
*155	*180	*214^{VAS}
*158	*181	*217^{VAS}
*161	*182	*218^{VAS}
*164	*183	*227^{VAS}
*165	*184	*229^{VAS}
*166	*185	*244
*167	*202^{VAS}	*245
*168	*205^{VAS}	*246
*170	*207^{VAS}	*253
*171	*208^{VAS}	*255
*172	*209^{VAS}	*257
*174	*210^{VAS}	*258